donated by
carol s. kitz, Psy. D.
(GSAPP) 1977

Early Childhood Assessment

Early Childhood Assessment

———— ◆ ————

Carol S. Lidz

John Wiley & Sons, Inc.

Library of Congress Cataloging-in-Publication Data:
Lidz, Carol Schneider.
    Early childhood assessment / Carol S. Lidz.
      p. cm
    Includes bibliographical references and index.
    ISBN 0-471-41984-2 (alk. paper)
    1. Behavioral assessment of children.   2. Psychological tests for children.   3. Observation (Psychology)—
Methodology.   I. Title.

BF722.3 .L53 2002
155.42'3'0287—dc21   2002028827

Printed in the United States of America
10 9 8 7 6 5 4 3 2 1

*This book is dedicated to the individuals who have played a direct role
in providing me with the opportunities to work with preschool children
and to gain whatever level of expertise I can now claim
that gave me the courage (OK, chutzpah) to write this book.*

◆ *Acknowledgments*

After many years of working in school systems with school-age children, my first opportunity to work intensively with preschool children was at Moss Rehabilitation Hospital, when the psychology department was under the direction of Phillip Spergel. Phil assigned me to the pediatric unit, where I had the good fortune to work with the large number of children brought to Moss through a contract with the Get Set day care program of the Philadelphia Board of Education. It was through this work that I discovered I really enjoyed working with this age group and that I also discovered the limited information that was available at the time. Thanks, Phil.

For the following five years, I worked at Hall-Mercer Community Mental Health/Mental Retardation Center of Pennsylvania Hospital, where I was assigned to consult with the therapeutic nursery program. This was under the clinical directorship of Carl Gasta, who, sadly, died a number of years ago.

I was next hired by Bill Dibble, the associate director of United Cerebral Palsy Association of Philadelphia and Vicinity to create and direct the (then) Head Start Clinic Team. For over eight years I was the administrator and senior psychologist for this team, which provided a model for services to children with special needs throughout the Philadelphia area. This was also my first opportunity to carry out research as an applied psychologist. Thanks, Bill.

Following my work with the Clinic Team (though continuing there on a part-time basis—not being able to let the baby go!), I was introduced to academia by Sylvia Rosenfield, who invited me to be the coordinator of her grant for an early childhood specialization with Temple University's School Psychology Program. This was my first opportunity to teach the preschool assessment course, where I consistently overwhelmed students with the large number of handouts because there was no satisfactory text at that time. Thanks, Sylvia (and my apologies to my students; you can buy this book now!).

My final thanks go to H. Carl Haywood, who by inviting me to design and direct the School Psychology Program within the newly created Graduate School of Education and Psychology at Touro College, provided me with continued opportunities to teach and develop the preschool assessment course, as well as to conduct research related to my work with dynamic assessment and parent-child interactions with young children. (The students there also complained about the workload. My apologies also to you. This is one response to the yet unasked question of what the Temple and Touro programs have in common. You, too, may buy this book!) Thanks (again), Carl.

Of course I must express gratitude to the wonderful children and families, as well as the teachers and supervisors, with whom I have had the privilege of working over these many years. My special thanks to the darling children of the Head Start programs throughout Philadelphia. We will never really know how we touched each other's lives.

♦ *Preface*

This is a book for practitioners by a practitioner. This is a book for academics by an academic. No, I am not having an identity crisis. I stand with my feet firmly planted in both worlds. Primarily, this is a book I need for teaching my graduate students in school psychology, and it is the book I wish I had had when I began my work as a school psychologist.

There are other books that tackle the topic of assessment of preschool children, but while I have used them as references and greatly value their content, I never selected any of them as a text for my course in early childhood assessment. The books that are available focus on specific tests, are organized according to disability, or commit to one specific model. To my amazement, some of these omit in-depth discussions of play, parent-child interaction, and dynamic assessment. Because most of them are edited volumes, there is inevitable redundancy across chapters. The greatest limitation is that it is difficult for practitioners to walk away from these books feeling as if they were put on the road to application of the content. Although any book is limited in its ability to prepare practitioners for practice, there remains a gap in the availability of a book that focuses primarily on such applications.

The purpose of this book is to provide general guidelines for designing and conducting assessments of young children between the ages of 3 through 5 years: the preschool years. Although details are provided regarding some informal procedures (e.g., interviews, observations), specific standardized procedures are mentioned only briefly, with more space dedicated to issues regarding their administration and application. Similarly, this book does not cover specific disorders. However, to say that this book offers general guidelines is not to imply that it avoids specifics. Some areas neglected by other books are described in detail, such as parent-child interaction and dynamic assessment, and other areas, such as interviews and observations, are detailed with forms and formats unique to this text. Another important aspect of this book is that it offers an integrated discussion and format for assessment of young children. Each chapter offers discussion of a specialized topic, but always with awareness of content in other chapters, and always with a sense of moving toward an integrated application of procedures to the whole child.

This book is appropriate as a graduate school text in school or clinical psychology and for practitioners who either have never received formal training in the assessment of young children or wish to review and update their thinking and practices in this area. To facilitate the use of this book with graduate students, suggested activities are listed at the end of each chapter under the headings of scholarship and application. Course instructors can use these suggestions as they wish, for example, by asking students to select one or more scholarship and application activity from among the chapters to fulfill course requirements.

This book also expresses an attitude and a commitment to the idea that best assessment practices should reflect what is good for families and for children and not just what is fast and cheap to implement. Of course, there are economic realities that must be faced, but we have an ethical obligation to resist and to protest against practices that threaten to cheat our clients of effective and meaningful services and interventions.

This book walks the reader through a comprehensive assessment, touching each of the major data sources necessary for a full understanding of children and their environments. It is organized primarily in terms of these data sources, rather than in terms of diagnostic category, functional domain, or specific procedure. Assessment is a complex process, and any procedure generates information that crosses domains. There is no such thing as a purely cognitive or purely social-emotional measure. Although it may be helpful to divide the discussion into functional domains when assembling a final report, during the course of the assessment the psychologist must first parse out the information from each procedure to decide what that procedure is measuring at that time for that child, and ask the question: What did I learn about this child from what I just did? Only in this way can we put Humpty-Dumpty back together again and give meaning to our statements about the whole child.

Assessment is a journey. We begin with an idea of where we want to go and carry a map to guide the way, but we can never predict what we meet along the way or exactly how that will affect the point at which we arrive. This text attempts to provide a map that reflects the richness and complexity of children's development and the lives they live within their communities and families. The journey never fails to be interesting and challenging for those whose eyes and minds are open. Welcome to the world of early childhood assessment.

◆ *Contents*

◆ *Supplementary Materials*

Tests Reviewed

Forms

Tables

Figures

Reports

Early Childhood Assessment

Chapter One

♦

In the Beginning . . .

♦

Prior to the 1960s, few psychologists conducted assessments of preschool children. Before this time, early childhood assessment was largely an activity for researchers and, particularly, for those engaged in longitudinal studies. With the 1960s the government established federally funded compensatory education programs such as Head Start and acknowledged the need to determine their effectiveness (Kelly & Surbeck, 2000). Programs for young children with and without special needs now abound, and psychologists are expected to be skilled in their assessment. It is increasingly clear that special skills and a knowledge base are necessary for the proper assessment of young children and that psychologists are not adequately prepared by merely including tests for young children within the general cognitive education course or through continuing education courses. This text provides guidelines for the challenging and interesting journey into early childhood assessment.

A good journey begins with an itinerary, and a good itinerary balances careful preplanning with opportunities for exploration and spontaneous adventure. This is the goal of this introductory chapter and, ultimately, the book. In this chapter I discuss issues and practices related to setting up an assessment. The emphasis is on assessment of individual children of preschool age (between the ages of 3 and 5 years) for diagnostic exploration of referral concerns, usually initiated by parents, teachers or program personnel, or physicians. These concerns most frequently involve language development or other developmental delays, as well as specific conditions or syndromes that may have consequences for development of learning and social competence.

The early stages of the assessment process are arguably the most important; to a significant extent, what is revealed at the beginning influences what follows, and what follows should flow in an integrated way from the purposes of the assessment. Therefore, it is important for assessors to think about and plan for what needs to happen at the beginning so that what follows can develop logically from this foundation and so that a meaningful relationship among assessment, intervention, and follow-up can result.

However, we must first have an idea of what is meant by the term *assessment,* primarily to distinguish it from any specific activity such as testing (Bagnato, Neisworth, & Munson,

1997). Assessment is a broad, comprehensive process, not any specific activity or technique (Batsche & Knoff, 1995; Danielson, Lynch, Moyano, Johnson, & Bettenburg, 1989; Lidz, 1981; McConnell, 2000). Primarily, assessment is a mental activity of the assessor, and the assessment tasks are chosen to facilitate this process; it does not take place on a sheet of paper, but within the brain of the individual who integrates and interprets the information. I define *assessment* as the process of data gathering that informs decision making. If this is the case, then the first step of assessment is to be explicit regarding the nature of the decisions to be made, followed by determining the most likely sources of data that will inform these decisions. Such an approach to assessment requires flexibility, which is now increasingly advocated by lawmakers (Lidz, Eisenstat, Evangelista, Rubinson, Stokes, Thies, & Trachtman, 2000). Flexibility in assessment involves tailoring the procedures to fit the referral questions and issues rather than reflexively administering the same battery of tests to all children. Contrary to some practices, flexible assessment does not mean doing less; it may even mean doing more. It certainly means doing assessment differently—different from the past and from still existing practices, and different for each child. If we expect teachers to individualize their classroom practices to meet the needs of their pupils, then assessors should be capable of this as well.

The three major purposes of assessment are entitlement-classification (also referred to as eligibility for special education services), planning of interventions, and evaluation of outcomes (Rosenfield & Nelson, 1995). Alternatively, the kinds of decisions to be made concern diagnosis, description of current states, and generation of prescriptive interventions (Simeonsson & Bailey, 1988), as well as evaluation.

This book focuses on procedures and methods for conducting an assessment with any preschool-age child, rather than on specific kinds of disorders. Disorders and disabilities are well reviewed in other texts, but other texts generally fail to provide in-depth coverage of the wide array of assessment approaches now available for application to young children, with the intent of facilitating the utilization of these procedures. There was a time when taking a course on preschool assessment meant learning the Bayley, the Wechsler scales, and the Stanford-Binet. In my many years of teaching a course on preschool assessment, such standardized instruments were delegated about 3 to 4 of the total 15 weeks available, with the other weeks providing hardly sufficient time to squeeze in the many other viable and frequently more useful sources of data for this population. Thus, our journey is not limited to a review of tests, and is certainly not restricted to standardized tests; these are discussed when appropriate to the context. Our journey is through the many choices of approaches to data gathering available to the thinking assessor. The assessor who uses these approaches will never be functioning on automatic. This assessor will not become bored or burnt out. This assessor will don the cap of Sherlock Holmes and become a detective, generating hypotheses, searching for the pieces to construct a situation and solve a problem, and, most of all, finding ways to improve the competence of the children referred for services and their families who provide contexts for their development.

The general model of assessment advocated in this text is best conceptualized as ecological or context-based (Bronfenbrenner, 1979; Paget & Nagle, 1986; Tharinger & Lambert, 1989). Our referrals may be child driven, but our assessments must be ecologically valid and look at the child in the contexts of home, community, and program. Using this model, we will never assume that a problem exists solely within the referred child, although the child's predispositions and "hardware" may indeed be a significant issue. We will always consider history, meaning, and opportunity in any approach to problem solving. We will work with families and other referral sources as collaborative consultants, and we will invite and expect them to become part of the problem-solving process. We will not blame parents or teachers, but we will certainly consider their roles in the referral issues and work with them to ameliorate any problems that become apparent. We will not describe children solely in terms of deficits but will consider their many positive characteristics and current methods of coping. We will write reports that link assessment with intervention and that describe children in a way that is recognizable and helpful to their caregivers. All of these resolutions are complex and challenging and require preparation, supervision, and application. Good practitioners need good models and mentors, not just words in a book. This book offers as much as is possible on the printed page. Recommended activities appear at the end of each chapter, and a myriad of forms and formats for each assessment approach are illustrated throughout the book. Each chapter also features recommendations for additional readings. The rest is in the hands of the reader, who should take advantage of the opportunities for additional study and practice that become available. Some of these are found, and some of these made. Readers must be active learners.

One word that will guide our assessment is *multiple* (Barnett, Bell, Gilkey, et al., 1999; Lidz, 1986, 1990; Meisels & Provence, 1989; Wachs & Sheehan, 1988a). Particularly with young children, but with other clients as well, we will need multiple samples of data from multiple sources in multiple contexts. We need to observe in multiple settings and work with the child on multiple occasions using multiple measures that sample multiple domains (Bagnato et al., 1997). Will this take time? Yes. Good work takes time, and young children cannot be rushed. We can increase our efficiency with the use of interviews and well-selected rating scales and of procedures that address the referral issues, but good, comprehensive assessment will probably require several hours over a number of days (some estimates average about 7 to 10; my team averaged at least that, with a range of 5 to 15). Fischetti (2000) surveyed psychologists in suburban Connecticut school districts and found that their assessments required a mean of 16.81 hrs per pupil for those determined to be eligible for special services, with a mean of 13.95 for those not eligible. In this study students with social-emotional issues required the most time. Fischetti also cited a study of psychologists in San Diego that reported an average of 8.4 hrs per assessment. Without adequate allotment of time, our role becomes reduced to that of screeners, and one of the messages of this chapter is that the activity that should follow screening is comprehensive assessment, not placement or programming. Fund providers who challenge these assertions need to be asked what they would want for their own children—would any less be acceptable? Good diagnostic assessment followed by good programming, guided by good assessment, should in the long run represent good economics and good ethics.

Practitioners who are forced to provide services under considerably less than optimal circumstances have the options of trying to work with their colleagues to pressure the system to become more aware of the existing service delivery problems, to join organizations that advocate for improved practice conditions, and to try to find opportunities to improve practices within existing conditions. Although we need to acknowledge the fact that poor conditions for practice indeed exist, we must be aware of what good practice can be and try to advocate for these more ideal circumstances. Without this, there is no hope for improvement.

Assessment of young children who are found to have special needs should never be a one-time event. Children who are eligible for services based on the assessment need to be monitored and reevaluated to follow their progress and to determine their ongoing needs. Certainly, any child who is found to be at risk, even if not actually eligible, should be reevaluated regularly.

Many children do not show their full array of needs until they become older and exposed to the challenges of school and social expectations in other settings.

INTERVIEWING

There are at least five purposes for interviews with caregivers, some of which occur prior to direct contact with the child and some afterward (Meisels & Provence, 1989). These include developing rapport, which also involves beginning to establish a collaborative relationship, with the assessor primarily in a consultative role while providing expertise as appropriate. There is also the need to exchange information. Caregivers are the primary sources of historical information, and the assessor needs to offer information to prepare them regarding what to expect from the assessment and what the mutual roles will be. Following data collection, the assessor will meet with the caregivers to provide feedback and to begin the planning that will ultimately involve the full team.

Being a good interviewer requires good clinical skill that is part common sense and part professional training and experience. Interviewers need to be sensitive to the underlying messages and concerns of their clients and would do well to function according to the golden rule of trying to walk in the other person's moccasins. Some aspects of interviewing that are the most difficult to master are how to ask questions in an open-ended and nonleading way, how to express empathy and understanding while maintaining professional objectivity, how to keep focused on the purposes of the interaction, and how to avoid getting sucked into providing specific advice when this is not appropriate. The new interviewer needs to make the important transition from interacting as a concerned friend to acting as a trained professional. Often it is necessary to suspend one's value and belief systems in order to be helpful to clients, who need to be helped within their own values and beliefs unless these clearly conflict with reality and the prospects for helping the child. Active listening, with attention paid to clarifying communication and promoting the client's ability to problem solve and cope, is a foundation skill. Clients need to leave the interaction feeling that they have been heard and understood and that they have a clear idea of the events and issues that will follow. They should not feel judged and evaluated or pressured.

Sattler (2002) provided a helpful outline for the parent interview:

- Greet parents.
- Give your name and professional title.
- Make an introductory statement and invite the parents to give their reasons for coming.
- Review background questions (see questionnaire provided in Form 1.1).
- Describe assessment procedure (and expectations regarding parents' roles).
- Arrange for future contacts and feedback.
- Summarize and close the interview.

Form 1.1 provides a format for the initial interview to help assessors gather the necessary background information to allow them to make decisions about how to proceed with the assessment. Despite the structure of the interview, it must be communicated within a clinical style and not administered rigidly as if read directly from the page. Responses from the assessor should open communication, not close it down. However, assessors do need to record the responses while at the same time maintain focus on the speaker. Recording should be carried out

Intake Interview

I need to ask you some questions that will give me information to help plan this assessment.

Date of Interview: _____   Interviewer: _____

What is your child's full name? _____ Your full name? _____

What is your relationship to the child? _____

What is your child's birth date? _____ Age now? _____

What is your address? _____

What program does your child attend? _____

What is the address and phone number of the program? _____

_____

What is the teacher's name? _____

Who are the child's primary caregivers? _____

What are the ages and occupations of primary caregivers? _____

_____

What was the final school grade completed by primary caregivers? _____

Marital status of parents? _____

If divorced or separated, what are the living arrangements regarding the child? _____

_____

Who are the legal guardians? _____

Who lives in the home? _____

Names and ages of siblings? _____

In what country/state/city was child born? _____

In what country/state were caregivers born? _____

What language(s) is spoken in the home? _____

If English is not dominant, who speaks which language to whom?_____

_____

If parents are not U.S. born, what were the circumstances of immigration? _____

_____

What is child's dominant language? _____

Who is primary medical care provider? _____

Please tell me what brings you here._____

_____

Who referred you?_____

Form 1.1

Have there been any previous evaluations? Please give me the approximate dates, and if you have not already provided copies of reports, please sign a release so that these can be obtained. _____

_____

What specific questions do you have for the assessment? What information would you like to find out?_____

_____

I need to ask you for some additional background information to help answer your questions. How would you describe your child? _____

_____

_____

_____

What do you enjoy the most about your child? _____

_____

_____

What do you find the most challenging about raising your child? _____

_____

_____

Tell me about your child's early development. What do you remember about the pregnancy and delivery? _____

_____

[Note: If child was adopted, be careful regarding confidentiality in front of child. Note circumstances of adoption and anything known about early history. Does child know about adoption?]

Complications regarding pregnancy?

Medications while pregnant?

Bleeding?

Any substances (smoking, alcohol, drugs)?

Emotional climate during pregnancy?

Gestation period?

Length/difficulty regarding labor?

Birth weight?

Delivery complications?

Medications?

Condition of baby?

Do you remember the Apgar scores?

Form 1.1 (*continued*)

How was the baby when first brought home? Any concerns? _____

_____

What is child's current health status?

Any illnesses?

Accidents?

Hospitalizations?

Lead ingestion?

Seizures?

Allergies?

Sleeping?

Eating?

High fevers?

Ear infections?

I will ask you some questions about the child's early development.

At what age did the child first:

Sit?

Walk?

Say first words? (What were they?)

Say full sentence? (What was it?)

Toilet train?

What is the child able to do independently now? Bathing?

Dressing? Playing? Out in neighborhood?

Who is involved in taking care of the child when not in a program or when caregivers are away? _____

_____

What are the child's experiences regarding separation other than day care or preschool?

_____

_____

Status of child's hearing and vision? When checked? _____

_____

Is the child taking any medication? What? How much? For how long? With what results?

_____

_____

Form 1.1 (*continued*)

Has anyone in the family needed any special help in school or have history of special education? _____

Is there any family history of mental illness? Please explain. _____

Tell me about a typical day for you and your child; start when you get up. _____

Now tell me about a typical week; start with Monday._____

Tell me about your neighborhood. What is it like? _____

Tell me about your home. What is it like? _____

Where and with whom does your child play? _____

Describe your child's play. _____

What opportunities does your child have to play with other children? _____

Does your child participate in any organized recreation? _____

Let's review the sequence of program experiences for your child from the very earliest to the present. Also, tell me how well your child did in each. What did the teachers tell you?

How do you handle discipline? Who does what regarding discipline? How often is it necessary to discipline your child, and for what? _____

Form 1.1 (*continued*)

What are the primary sources of stress in your family? _____

_____

_____

_____

What are the primary sources of support in your family? _____

_____

_____

Are there any experiences that you think might have had an important impact on your child?

_____

_____

_____

_____

You have already thought a lot about the reasons you brought your child here. What have you told yourself; what do you think is going on that accounts for your concerns?

Also, what have others, perhaps in your family or from your friends, told you?

_____

_____

_____

Is there anything else you think I should know that would be important for understanding you and your child? _____

_____

_____

_____

_____

Is there anyone who should get a copy of my report? _____

_____

_____

To summarize:

You are mainly concerned about:

You are asking for information about:

What I'll be doing will be:

You will be involved in the assessment, but . . .

I won't be able to answer your questions about how your child did until we are finished. Then I will meet with you and we will review your questions and look at what the assessment offers to address these. We will work together to make the best possible plan for your child.

Form 1.1 (*continued*)

as nonintrusively as possible, using abbreviations and shortened sentences for efficiency. It is advisable to apologize for the need to write but state that it is a necessary aid to memory and accuracy. Avoid burying your nose in the form, and maintain a conversational, clinically sensitive, and open style of communicating. The interviewees should never feel that the primary agenda is to complete the form; the form is a means to facilitate the interaction, and what they have to say is of utmost importance. Nevertheless, there is an agenda to secure this important information, and the assessor needs to exert subtle control over the interaction to reach this goal.

In addition to determining this information, the interview also provides an opportunity for the caregivers to get a feeling for the assessor and for the assessor to get a feeling for the personalities and interaction styles of the caregivers. If the child is present, this serves to introduce the assessor to the child as well, and it is useful for the child to hear the assessor interact with the caregivers without being pressured to respond. Of course, if the child is present, it is necessary to use good judgment regarding the content of the conversation, and the assessor may need to suggest an opportunity for a private conversation for sensitive material.

Sattler (2002, p. 20) also listed a number of types of statements that are helpful for further probing without leading the interviewees in any particular direction. These include the following:

- *Tell me more about that.*
- *Is there anything else?*
- *Please go on.*
- *What happened then?*
- *Please expand on that.*
- *What happened before?*
- *What happened after?*
- *How did you feel? (Please do not overuse that one!)*
- *What were you thinking?*
- *Any other reasons?*

These of course need to be used appropriately. Sattler (p. 23) further offered a number of reflective statements that would contribute to a sense of active listening that is so important in interview situations:

- *You felt that . . .*
- *As you see it . . .*
- *It seems to you that . . .*
- *In other words . . .*
- *What you seem to be saying is . . .*
- *You believe . . .*
- *It seems as if . . .*
- *I hear you saying . . .*

Such statements help convey a feeling of being heard and understood and avoid implications of evaluation or judgment by the assessor.

Lentz and Wehmann (1995) also provided a number of helpful suggestions to facilitate active listening (p. 642):

- Decide to listen closely.
- Be alert, lean forward, maintain eye contact, use appropriate facial expressions.
- Keep in mind that the goal is to understand, not to evaluate.
- Be reactive, with nods and vocalizations.
- Allow the speaker to finish speaking.
- Show empathy with actions and words, try to see the situation from their point of view.
- Ask clarifying questions.
- Notice nonverbal behavior.
- Avoid thinking about yourself.
- Avoid hasty conclusions.
- Correct environmental distractions.

Assessors need to learn about themselves as well, particularly in terms of how they come across to others and of the types of reactions that they tend to elicit in others. However, it is not advisable to bring this self-consciousness into the interview unless the assessor can quickly process how he or she may have provoked or elicited a particular response from the interviewee. As a general rule, I try to process what I am hearing in terms of how it will help me understand the situation, make decisions about how to proceed with the assessment, and communicate how I can (or cannot) be helpful. Assessors need to clarify the caregiver's expectations and be explicit about how these will be addressed in ensuing sessions.

DEVELOPMENTAL HISTORY

One of the most important components of any assessment is to gather a comprehensive history of the child's development, including family information, cultural background, and educational experiences. This information relies considerably on the accuracy of recall and reliability of the informants, although assessors are also strongly encouraged to gather information that is available from hospital reports, as well as previous assessments. The accuracy of parent recall has mixed reviews, although it is documented to be generally reliable for parents of higher socioeconomic levels; however, some of these studies involve parents who are participants in longitudinal studies, which would be expected to involve parents who not only have more stable life experiences (i.e., do not move to a significant extent) but also are more aware of their child's development because of anticipation of the periodic checkups from the study staff. The Wenar and Coulter (1962) study of mothers' recall of their children's early development 3 to 6 years following their child's enrollment in a therapeutic nursery showed agreement for 57% of the statements reviewed; that is, there were differences for 43% of the items, with 40% of these considered to be "marked" differences. Although there were no definitive patterns regarding information recalled accurately or inaccurately, there was a tendency for information with affective content to be more distorted on later recollection. There was good reliability regarding information concerning whether the baby was wanted, the parents' gender preference, whether the baby was breast-fed or bottle-fed, sleep patterns, illnesses, and motor development. Distortions concerned the mother's health during pregnancy, discipline practices, and relationships between the child and parents. Robbins (1963) found that parent recall was more accurate in terms of whether an event occurred than in terms of the specific times of onset. This study also found that in this highly educated sample, inaccuracies, particularly by the mothers, were biased in the direction of the prevailing child development literature (Dr. Spock, for those of us with longer histories).

Simons, Ritchie, Mullett, and Liechty (1986) reported high concordance of recall between mothers and fathers regarding the medical complications of their infants, but both parents tended to underreport the extent of the medical complications that their infants experienced following delivery. Treharne's (1992) study reported highly reliable recall for toilet training and weaning and a pattern of better recall when milestones coincided with other meaningful events such as a birthday or holiday; there was generally poor recall of speech milestones.

The impression from these studies, which tend to be limited by low numbers of participants, is that there is general accuracy for most parents regarding whether an event has occurred but less reliability regarding the details of onset. Better recall is more likely for parents of higher socioeconomic status (and those involved in longitudinal studies). The implication for the assessor is the need to make a judgment regarding the accuracy of the informants, with an attempt for further documentation of important information. It is probably more effective to ask parents whether they recall developmental milestones to have been generally on time or late rather than to seek specific times of onset. Some parents keep records of these events, however, and these should be accessed if available. In addition, information can be sought independently from more than one family member, although mothers tend to recall some information more accurately than do fathers (at least if the mothers were more involved during very early years). Information regarding delivery and birth complications should be available from the hospital. No assumptions can be made regarding the direction of inaccuracies; the assessor should look for inconsistencies in all of the information reported.

SCREENING

Brooks-Gunn and Lewis (1981) made a good case for the value of screening with measures that identify risk rather than relying on identification of children in need through observing their accomplishments of developmental milestones. The researchers pointed out that reliance on milestones means that the potential problem will not be noticed until the milestone has not been accomplished, and the ranges for these accomplishments can be very wide. Furthermore, with such an approach, social-emotional needs are often ignored. Therefore, it is considered better practice to try to identify early signs of risk that are precursors to later development of dysfunctions (although milestones will nevertheless play a role in this identification and are usually the alerting factors for parents and physicians).

According to Kenny and Culbertson (1993) screening is the process of "sorting out from among a presumably normal population those individuals at risk for a certain disorder. The purpose of screening is not to diagnose a disorder or to plan a treatment approach, but rather to suggest to the professional *when* and *to whom* to refer for further diagnostic evaluation" (p. 73). Despite all-too-frequent practice, virtually all authors agree that screening is an activity that should precede comprehensive assessment (e.g., Gredler, 1997; Lichtenstein & Ireton, 1984; Meisels & Provence, 1989; Satz & Fletcher, 1988; Telzrow, Fox, Sanders, Barnett & Cryan, 1989); that is, the next step following screening and determination of risk should be diagnostic assessment, not placement—and certainly not exclusion. The purpose of screening is to categorize children into risk, caution, and no-risk groups. Children in the caution group would need to be rescreened at a later time. When screening is carried out with large groups, the procedures need to be brief, cheap, and accurate (Gridley, Mucha, & Hatfield, 1995). This means that the procedures used for screening need to be selected carefully to meet standards of reliability, validity, and criteria of sensitivity and specificity and need to have a good hit rate (these terms are explained shortly). The screening program also needs to be designed with awareness of federal, state, and local regulations and policies and to be submitted to the district's board of education prior to implementation (Telzrow et al., 1989).

Authors generally agree that screening should be conducted only when there is treatment available for those individuals identified as being at risk (e.g., Frankenburg, 1985; Meisels, 1985; Telzrow et al., 1989). This is an ethical issue. Once need is determined, these needs should be addressed. Therefore, any screening program must be well thought-out, carefully planned, and adequately funded. The purpose of the screening needs to be determined, and the procedures should fit the purpose. Because a screening program involves significant investment of funds and personnel, it is also critical that the staff be well trained and monitored and that the effects of the program be evaluated: Did it accomplish its purpose? (Note therefore that it is necessary to have a clear purpose!)

Although the psychologist is not necessarily directly involved in administering the screening procedures, it is appropriate for the psychologist to be involved in the planning and administrative aspects of the screening (Harrington, 1984). Because of economic considerations, paraprofessionals (e.g., teacher aids or parent volunteers) are often used for large-scale screening, and they need to be trained and monitored. These tasks are appropriate for the psychologist. Critical steps in the screening process include designating a coordinator, establishing a planning team, carrying out the planning process, collecting and interpreting the data (including selecting procedures), monitoring the process, and evaluating the results (Gridley et al., 1995). These are likewise tasks in which the psychologist can be appropriately involved.

Sometimes the psychologist may decide to engage directly in screening for an individual child, as in the case of triennial reevaluations, when a comprehensive assessment may or may not be necessary. In this case, it is useful to screen the child's primary functional domains such as cognition, language, motor, and preacademic to determine the need for further exploration.

It is not always clear when a procedure is best described as intended for screening or diagnosis. The purpose of the assessment instrument should be described in its manual, and if it is used for screening, it must be evaluated in relation to its success with identifying children in need of further evaluation, particularly by weighing overreferrals against underreferrals. Screening instruments are usually brief and more superficial in coverage than are diagnostic instruments, but the threshold for these qualities is not so clear. One person's screener may be another person's diagnostic procedure. There is often so much pressure on meeting timelines that what passes for diagnostic assessment all too often can best be described as screening.

The outcome of assessment should be determination of the child's needs for service with implications for programming. The outcome of screening should be determination of the child's need for diagnostic assessment. Thus, intention and outcome play major roles, and procedures need to be selected with these in mind.

As indicated previously, in addition to the usual psychometric standards of reliability and validity, screening procedures must also meet standards of sensitivity and specificity. These relate to issues of over- and underreferral (referred to as *hit rate*). There will always be errors in identifying children. These need to be minimized as well as understood. Overreferral results in an economic penalty in which children who do not necessarily need special education services nevertheless receive costly diagnostic assessment and, possibly, costly intervention services.

Large expenditures of these funds can reduce the availability of funds for those truly in need. There are also consequences for the caregivers, who may become anxious or upset when they are told erroneously that their child is in a risk category. The primary consequence of underreferral is that children who need services are deprived of service. Many researchers have concluded that it is better to overrefer than to underrefer because the consequences appear to be more benign; that is, the child would be involved in services that may be helpful and are certainly unlikely to cause harm (Kenny & Culbertson, 1993).

Sensitivity refers to "the ability of a test to classify abnormal results as abnormal," and *specificity* "refers to a test's ability to identify normal performance as being normal" (Kenny & Culbertson, 1993, p. 87). That is, sensitivity detects need, whereas specificity detects normality. The methods for determining these derive from the following chart based on Frankenburg (1985) and Lichtenstein and Ireton (1984):

Screening Test Findings	Diagnostic Findings	
	Child needs services	Child does not need services
Refer: High risk (+)	A Accurate referral (valid positive)	C Overreferral (false positive)
Do not refer: Low risk (–)	B Underreferral (false negative)	D Accurate nonreferral (valid negative)

$$\text{Sensitivity} = \frac{A}{A + B} \times 100$$

$$\text{Specificity} = \frac{D}{C + D} \times 100$$

$$\text{Overreferral rate} = \frac{C}{A + C} \times 100$$

$$\text{Underreferral rate} = \frac{B}{B + D} \times 100$$

According to Glascoe (1991), a desirable level for sensitivity is a minimum of 80%; for specificity, a minimum of 90%; and for overreferrals, a rate of no more than 1.5 to 2 times the number of truly delayed, as determined by the follow-up assessment. He also suggested that interrater agreement (reliability) should be at least 80%, with test-retest stability of at least .90 and concurrent validity at least .60.

It is also possible to determine base rates, which would vary between 5% and 10% of the total population; these would be the proportion, or *prevalence,* of children who are actually determined to have a problem. The referral rate would be the children who are referred for diagnostic assessment based on their screening results; and according to Lichtenstein and Ireton

(1984), these would range between 1.5 to 2.5 times the base rate; that is, more children would be referred for further assessment than would be determined eligible for treatment. Of course, if referrals are generated from a population already defined as being at risk, such as would typify a population of very low socioeconomic status, these rates will be greatly magnified.

Test Reviews 1.1 through 1.6 present a number of frequently used screening procedures available for working with preschool children.

Tests used for screening are sometimes referred to as readiness tests, and these tests are at times inappropriately used to determine eligibility of children for inclusion in regular education (National Association for the Education of Young Children [NAEYC], no date). Screening in this case does not concern eligibility for intervention, but for school entry itself. Readiness tests address skills that the child has acquired that relate to what will be learned in the regular school curriculum (Gredler, 1997; Gridley et al., 1995; Meisels, 1985, 1987). These are assumed to differ from developmental procedures, which are said to describe the child's ability to learn or profit from instruction, although this claim is disputable. According to Meisels (1987), readiness tests are appropriately used for curriculum planning, not for school entry decisions. They describe current characteristics and are not intended for (or very good at) predicting long-range outcomes. Meisels specifically criticized the Gesell (Ilg & Ames, 1965) tests (with their norms based solely on White Connecticut residents), for which there is very little reliability or validity information, and I pointed out that the information that is available provides very mixed reviews (Lidz, 1991a). Furthermore, there is very little documentation of any positive effects of delayed school entrance over the long term (Guilford Press, 1997). Although this remains an option for individual children, it is not a viable general solution for those who show low levels of readiness and may in fact be denied access to experiences that they so badly need. Even in the Pianta and McCoy (1997) study, which documented fine motor and cognitive skills of the child and mother's educational level as significant predictors regarding which child would not have problems in school, these authors concluded that the predictions were not a sufficient basis for high-stakes decisions such as determination of school entry. Finally, it is no small point that there is no general agreement regarding preschool curriculum (Boehm & Sandberg, 1982); therefore, to use an existing preschool curriculum as a criterion for readiness is highly inappropriate, as the child may be ready in relation to one curriculum but not ready in relation to another.

The increasing consensus is that schools should be ready for children rather than requiring children to be ready for school (NAEYC, 1995), and I suggested that the more important concern is to determine the basis for development of a good foundation for learning once children have entered school (Lidz, 1999), thus avoiding the circularity of the idea that children need to be ready to get ready to learn.

Many of the procedures used for screening involve parent completion of questionnaires and rating scales. It is therefore relevant to determine the degree of concordance of the results from these two sources, and this has been the purpose of several investigations. For example, Gradel, Thompson, and Sheehan (1981) found moderate to high levels of agreement between the ratings of the mothers in their study and those of professional diagnosticians, and higher levels of agreement were found for children of preschool age than for infants. Meltzer et al. (1983) found general consistency among the ratings of parents, teachers, pediatricians, and psychologists on a 34-item checklist reporting developmental skills for preschool children; there was greater consistency regarding language, memory, and academic skills than regarding the motor domain. Sexton, Miller, and Rotatori (1985) compared completion of a developmental profile for

Test Review 1.1

Test Name
Ages and Stages Questionnaires (ASQ): A Parent-Completed Child-Monitoring System–Second Edition (1999)

Authors
Diane Bricker and Jane Squires

What the Test Measures
There are 19 questionnaires for age intervals from infancy through preschool years, to be completed by caregivers, based on 30 items/activities for the five domains of communication, gross motor, fine motor, problem solving, and personal-social. The questionnaires may be photocopied. Each item is scored in terms of yes, sometimes, or not yet, with cutoff points empirically determined to detect need for further assessment and referral. The items are written at a sixth-grade reading level, designed for cultural sensitivity. The forms are available in Spanish, French, and Korean, with plans to develop forms in Mandarin, Russian, and Arabic.

Age Range
4 months through 60 months

Administration Time
10 to 15 min

Publisher
Brookes Publishing
PO Box 10624
Baltimore, MD 21285-0624
800-638-3775
www.brookespublishing.com

Norms
This is not a normed procedure.

Reliability
Internal consistency correlations ranged from .73 to .83 for 36 months, from .66 to .82 for 48 months, and from .44 to .58 for 60 months. Test-retest stability with a 2-week interval resulted in percentage of agreement of 94%. Interobserver reliability comparing scores of parents and professional examiners was 94%, although many protocols had to be eliminated because the professional examiner had no opportunity to observe some behaviors.

Validity
Items were based on reviews of other tests, as well as texts and literature concerning developmental milestones; items were written to reflect behaviors that could be easily observed or elicited by parents, as well as those that would be likely to occur within the home.

Information is presented to support concurrent validity. There was 92% agreement with other standardized tests at 36 months and 86% overall agreement. The questionnaires showed good ability to detect children with typical development but had a 72% hit rate for children with delayed development (separate analysis is reported at 96% hit rate for developmental delay).

Test Review 1.2

Test Name

Denver Developmental Screening Test-II (1990)

Authors

W. K. Frankenburg, J. B. Dodds, P. Archer, B. Bresnick, P. Maschka, N. Edelman, and H. Shapiro

What the Test Measures

There are 125 tasks in four areas, including personal-social, fine motor–adaptive, language, and gross motor; all items are administered; examiners begin near the child's chronological age level. Items are scored by direct administration, parent report, or observation. There is a training tape available. The test includes a behavior rating scale that rates the child's test-taking behavior on dimensions of compliance, interest in surroundings, fearfulness, and attention span, as well as speech intelligibility. Scoring is bilevel, with one level indicating pass/fail/refused and another level indicating normal/advanced/caution/delay or no opportunity. These yield an overall classification of normal, abnormal, questionable, or untestable.

Age Range

Birth to 6 years

Administration Time

20 min

Publisher

Denver Developmental Materials
10200 E Girard Ave No. A111
Denver, CO 80231-5547
303-695-1462

Norms

There were 2,096 in the norm group, all from the state of Colorado in an attempt to represent the Colorado population. Norms are stratified by age, race, region, and mother's educational level, all within the state of Colorado. New, revised, and retained items were assigned to domains based on clinical judgment.

Reliability

Interrater agreement and test-retest reliability with 5- to 10-min interval and 7- to 10-day interval were determined. The authors report high levels of agreement between raters as well as between scores for pretest and posttest interval administrations.

Validity

The authors assigned ages at which each of the items was passed by 25%, 50%, 75%, and 90% of the population, and items were also examined for bias in relation to demographic variables. The final items were selected from a much larger item pool based on criteria such as frequency of refusals or indications of no opportunity, reliability, amenability to observation or report, and minimal need for elaborate materials.

The authors claim face validity in terms of representation of the growth curves of the items selected for the test. Other validity evidence remains to be determined.

Neither the reliability nor the validity of the behavior rating scale was examined.

Test Review 1.3

Test Name

Developmental Indicators for the Assessment of Learning–Third Edition (DIAL-3) (1998)

Authors

Carol Mardell-Czudnowski and Dorothea S. Goldenberg

What the Test Measures

DIAL-3 assesses the child's functioning in the five domains of physical, cognitive, communication, social or emotional, and adaptive. There is also a 9-item rating scale of social-emotional behaviors and of intelligibility. The Speed DIAL uses 10 items from the Motor, Concepts, and Language domains. Forms are available in both English and Spanish. Parents complete a questionnaire with background information and their concerns. Scores yield conclusions regarding potential delay (requires further assessment), or OK (development appears satisfactory). There are also percentile ranks and standard scores with a mean of 100 and *SD* of 15. A training tape is available.

Age Range

3 years to 6 years 11 months

Administration Time

30 min; Speed DIAL: about 15 min

Publisher

American Guidance Service, Inc.
4201 Woodland Road
Circle Pines, MN 55014-1796
800-328-2560
www.agsnet.com

Norms

The test was normed on 1,560 English-speaking children and 605 Spanish-speaking children. The norm group was stratified to reflect the 1994 U.S. Census on parameters of age, gender, race, region, and parent education, and included some children who were involved with special services.

Reliability

Internal consistency ranged from .66 (motor) to .85 (social), with the total for Speed DIAL .80 and for DIAL-3 .87. Test-retest total for DIAL-3 was .88 for children 3-6 to 4-5 and .84 for children 4-6 to 5-10 for Dial-3; and for Speed DIAL, .84 for children 3-6 to 4-5 and .82 for children 4-6 to 5-10. Subtest coefficients were higher (above .80) for the younger children, with the exception of Motor (.69).

Validity

Information is presented to support concurrent, and content validity.

Test Review 1.4

Test Name
Early Screening Inventory–Revised (1997)

Authors
Samuel Meisels, Dorothea B. Marsden, Martha Stone Wiske, and Laura W. Henderson

What the Test Measures
Designed to identify children who may be appropriate for referral for special education; to be used along with the Parent Questionnaire (included) and a general physical exam. This is only to determine risk and should be followed by more comprehensive assessment. Functioning in the areas of speech, language, cognition, perception, and fine and gross motor coordination are sampled as developmental tasks, not intelligence. Scores include "refer" and "rescreen" or no need for assessment. The tasks were selected to represent broad areas of development, as well as with regard to ease of administration and scoring, along with reliability. The content is grouped into the more general areas of Visual-Motor/Adaptive, Language and Cognition, and Gross Motor. The final recommendation regarding referral reflects the total score. Memory is embedded within the Visual-Motor/Adaptive and Language and Cognition domains. The Parent Questionnaire provides family, developmental, and medical information.

Age Range
3 to 6 years; Preschool Version for children ages 3 through 4 1/2 years

Administration Time
15 to 20 min

Publisher
Rebus, Inc.
715 North University Avenue, Suite 6
PO Box 4479
Ann Arbor, MI 48106-4479
800-435-3085

Norms
For Preschool Version: The total group $N = 977$, divided into three 6-month groups. The sample includes an equal number of boys and girls, but a high proportion of children from African American and "other" background (Asian, American Indian . . .), which does not seem to include Hispanics. Most of the children attended Head Start programs.

Reliability
There is strong positive evidence of interrater reliability, test-retest stability, and low standard error of measurement. For example, test-retest results yielded a correlation of .98 and a mean standard error of .20.

Validity
The authors present evidence of discriminant validity of the items in terms of their ability to differentiate children who were referred from those who were not. Predictive validity in relation to the McCarthy Scales administered 6 months later yielded a .73 correlation. Analysis of specificity and sensitivity showed some tendency to overrefer (false positives), but generally supportive results, with a Sensitivity score of .92 and Specificity score of .80.

Test Review 1.5

Test Name

AGS Early Screening Profiles (ESP) (1990)

Author

Patti L. Harrison (with A. S. Kaufman, N. L. Kaufman, R. H. Bruininks, J. Rynders, S. Ilmer, S. S. Sparrow, and D. V. Ciccetti)

What the Test Measures

The ESP is intended for ecologically valid screening of children in order to identify those at risk for learning or developmental problems, who require more comprehensive assessment. There are seven components: a Cognitive/Language Profile, Motor Profile, and Self-Help/Social Profile. There is an articulation survey, home survey, health history survey, and behavior survey. The first three profiles are administered directly to each child, and the remaining components are in questionnaire form to be completed by teachers, caregivers, and assessors as appropriate. The cognitive/language profile includes four subtests: visual discrimination, logical relations, verbal concepts, and basic school skills. The Motor Profile assesses fine and gross motor skills. The Self-Help/Social Profile includes communication, daily living skills, socialization, and motor skills domains. The entire battery or selected portions of it may be used.

Age Range

2 years through 6 years 11 months

Administration Time

15 to 30 min for direct testing and 10 to 15 min for parent and teacher questionnaires

Publisher

American Guidance Service, Inc.
4201 Woodland Road
Circle Pines, MN 55014-1796
800-328-2560
www.agsnet.com

Norms

The national sample included 1,149 children representative of the data from the 1990 Census on variables of geographic region, parent education level, and race and ethnicity. The numbers included in the sample for each component vary, with the profiles completed for the larger sample numbers and the surveys for considerably lower numbers of children. Scores are determined in 3-month intervals.

  Subtest scores are standardized with a mean of 10 and SD of 3, and profile scores, as well as cognitive and language subscales, have a mean of 100 and SD of 15.

Reliability

Internal consistency alpha coefficients for all profiles except Motor are reported to range from the high .80s to mid .90s. The alphas for the Motor Profile range from .60 to .78, with a median of .68. For the surveys, alpha coefficients for Articulation are mostly in the high .80s to low .90s; for the Home Survey, they range from .37 to .52 (median .41); and for the Behavior Survey, they are mostly in the .70s.

Test-retest stability with an interval of 5 to 21 days were all above .80 except for the Motor Profile at .70; coefficients for the indexes were all above .70, with the exception of the indexes at .56. Stability with an interval of 22 to 75 days were all above .70, with the exception of the Motor Profile at .55; coefficients for the index scores ranged from the .60s to the .80s, with the exception of the Motor Profile at .31.

Interrater reliability was carried out only for the Motor Profile, which is more subjective than the other subtests. All coefficients were above .80, with many well above .90. Standard errors of measurement are generally low, with a slight tendency to increase at age 6, and with generally high standard errors of measurement for the Motor Profile.

Validity
Evidence is presented in the manual to support content, construct, concurrent, predictive, and discriminant validity.

Test Review 1.6

Test Name
FirstSTEP: Screening Test for Evaluating Preschoolers (1993)

Author
Lucy J. Miller

What the Test Measures
The purpose is to screen children who are at risk for developmental delay for further comprehensive assessment. The 12 subtests tap the areas of cognition, communication, motor, social-emotional (optional), and adaptive (optional) functioning. Only the scores from the first three subtests make up the composite. There is also an optional parent-teacher scale that provides further information. Each of the three core domains has four subtests as follows: cognition (quantitative reasoning, picture comparison, visual position in space, and problem solving), language (auditory discrimination, word retrieval, association, and sentence-digit repetition), and motor (visual-motor integration, fine motor planning, balance, and gross motor planning). The social-emotional scale includes ratings by the assessor of the child's behaviors during the test session; these include task confidence, cooperative mood, temperament and emotionality, uncooperative antisocial behavior, and attention-communication difficulties. The adaptive behavior scale asks for the caregivers' ratings regarding degree of the child's independence in the areas of daily living, self-management and social interaction, and functioning within the community; there are three levels, administered according to age of the child. The adaptive behavior scale is completed by the assessor as a result of interviewing the caregiver, whereas the parent-teacher scale is completed by these individuals.

The first item of each subtest can be taught to the child if the child does not understand. The domains have a mean of 10 with SD of 3, and the composites are T scores with a mean of 50 and SD of 10. Zero scores are assigned a scaled score. The optional scales have cutoff scores to signal risk.

(continued)

Age Range
2.9 years to 6.2 years

Administration Time
15 min

Publisher
The Psychological Corporation
555 Academic Court
San Antonio, TX 78204
800-211-8378
http://www.PsychCorp.com

Norms
The total sample consisted of 1,433 children, selected to reflect the 1988 U.S. Census on variables of gender, geographic region, community size, race and ethnicity, and parent education level. Scores are provided for 6-month age groups.

Reliability
Information is provided for internal consistency, decision consistency, interscorer agreement, test-retest stability, and standard error of measurement. The standard errors of measurement are generally low. The average coefficients for internal consistency exceed .80 for all domains except cognitive (.75) and motor (.71). The test-retest interval for children randomly selected from the standardization sample was 1 to 2 weeks. These coefficients all exceeded .80, with the composite of .93. For the same group, the consistencies of decision cutoff scores all exceeded .85. The interscorer agreement coefficients also exceeded .80 except for the social-emotional ratings (.77).

Validity
Information regarding content, construct, concurrent, and criterion validity is presented in the manual. The domains were reviewed by experts for each area. Factor analysis supported a three-factor solution (language, motor, and cognition), except that two of the four of the cognitive subtests loaded at a higher level on the language rather than the cognitive factor. A second factor analysis appeared also to support a three-factor solution, but this time only the language factor was clearly supported, with the other two mixed. Classification accuracy was 89% with more false positives than negatives, which is a more acceptable direction because the error would mean that somewhat more children would be referred for further evaluation than necessary (preferable to missing children with special needs). Correlations with other measures are at a high moderate level, supporting concurrent validity. Discriminant validity received strong support as well.

children with a variety of disabilities resulting in developmental delays by their parents (mothers and fathers) and by professional evaluators and found high levels of agreement; they also reviewed studies that documented generally high levels of agreement but that had a tendency for mothers to rate their children at a higher level than professionals rated them. In the Sexton et al. study, family income level positively related to congruence of results, and these authors also found that both parents rated their child as having passed more items than did professionals. Finally, Dinnebeil and Rule (1994) reported the results of their review of 23 studies using 37 measures. These authors found a mean correlation of .73 ($R = .36–.97$) between the ratings of parents and professionals and a mean percentage of agreement of 82.4 ($R = 75\%–92\%$). The parents in these studies generally estimated the developmental level of their children (chronological ages between 14 and 51 months) an average of 3.6 months higher than did the professionals.

Most authors point out that despite the trend for higher ratings by parents compared with professionals, there is no assumption that these higher ratings are incorrect because parents have considerably more extensive opportunities to observe their children than do professionals. Therefore, information about the child's developmental competence as observed by parents is an important source of information when guided by the structure and specificity of a good rating scale or questionnaire. In fact, some screening measures, such as the Denver II (Frankenburg, Dodds, Archer, Shapiro, & Bresnick, 1992), allow for alternative sources of information for item completion (although the effects of these alternatives on scale outcomes are rarely if ever compared).

RISK AND RESILIENCE

Because the purpose of screening is to find children who are at risk, we need to consider the issue of what they are at risk for. In the educational setting the primary concern would be to determine risk for learning problems, which of course must consider the sensory, motor, and health status of the children as well as the cognitive-language-emotional-behavioral functions related to school success. The measures need to be related to the functions assessed, and both the screening and the assessment need to include the contributions of the many sources of variance contributing to the child's current functioning. Along with issues of determining risk are issues of prediction.

Risk implies projection into the future. We need to know which factors matter to future projection; therefore, predictive validity becomes particularly important to early childhood assessment. Screening measures need to predict diagnostic procedures, and diagnostic procedures need to predict future functioning.

Prediction under any circumstances is a risky business. Not only is there a lack of one-to-one correspondence or lack of linearity regarding any specific condition, but also there are issues of variables of resilience among the individuals experiencing these conditions (Meisels & Anastasiow, 1982). What makes the most sense is to restrict predictions to the near future and to use multiple sources of information that reflect currently available evidence regarding predisposing factors for negative outcomes. Any prediction can be made only in terms of probability and not with certainty, and predictions about complexly interacting variables are best reflected in a transactional model in which each of the variables affects the others and outcomes result from these mutual and ongoing interactions (Meisels & Anastasiow, 1982). Dunst and Rheingrover (1981), for example, found little stability in the development of preschool children except with regard to sequence, and they noted the difficulty of predicting the causes of development except for children who are functioning at a very low level. As Clarke and Clarke (1984) concluded from their highly influential longitudinal study, "Neither genetic programs nor social influences necessarily unfold in a constant way, and their interactions are complex" (p. 50). We may seek and wish for simplicity, but we are not going to find it.

When assessing children to determine risk and evidence of special needs, it is helpful to have an idea of what the competent, well-developed child is like. White (1975) identified many years ago characteristics that distinguished competent 6-year-olds and that were in evidence as early as age 3. These include the following (pp. 245–247):

Social Abilities

- Securing and maintaining adult attention in socially acceptable ways
- Using adults as resources for difficult tasks
- Expressing both affection and hostility with adults
- Expressing both affection and hostility with peers
- Taking roles of both leader and follower with peers
- Competing with peers
- Praising oneself and showing pride in one's accomplishments
- Expressing a desire to grow up, such as by role-playing adults

Nonsocial Abilities

- Linguistic competence regarding vocabulary, grammar, articulation, and expression
- Intellectual competence
  —Noting sensory discrepancies
  —Anticipating consequences
  —Dealing with abstractions (numbers, letters, rules)
  —Making interesting associations
- Executive abilities
  —Planning and carrying out multistep activities
  —Using resources effectively
  —Maintenance of attention and dual focus

White noted that evidence of these abilities was associated with competence in first grade.

It is often the case that retrospective studies identify factors associated with dysfunction that are not borne out by prospective studies. That is, large proportions of individuals with problems later in life may have similar aspects of their developmental histories, but not everyone with these factors in their development will develop problems. This is the issue of mediating factors, and family circumstances are primary among these. We also need to remember that risk factors are those that are associated with—not necessarily directly causative of—negative outcomes (Dunst, 1993). Cause is extremely difficult to demonstrate with human subjects because of the impossibility of experimentally manipulating variables with potentially negative outcomes. However, some positive decisions can be made on the basis of accumulating a preponderance of correlational evidence, particularly if there is the possibility of improving human conditions.

Meisels and Provence (1989) specified three areas that are usually considered for determination of risk: biological (e.g., prematurity, low birth weight), environmental (e.g., poverty, poor nutrition, abuse and neglect), and established conditions (e.g., syndromes, cerebral palsy, myelomeningocele). These are not mutually exclusive; however, although some single factors may be particularly potent in predisposing individuals to developmental risk, there is evidence that the number of factors may be even more powerful (Sameroff & Chandler, 1975; Sameroff & Fiese, 2000). This is referred to as cumulative risk, with the probability of risk mounting with the accumulating numbers of risk conditions somewhat independently of the specific conditions themselves. However, the study by Hooper, Burchinal, Roberts, Zeisel, and Neebe (1998) provided only weak support for this model, showing how difficult it is to generate predictions even with a more complex approach. One complicating issue is that both risk and resilience appear to function differently for boys versus girls (Zimmerman & Arunkumar, 1994), and it is further doubtful that there is complete homogeneity even within these gender groups regarding response to circumstances. There are also developmental influences for interpretations of risk and resilience in that different factors seem to offer protection or risk at different developmental stages (Zimmerman & Arunkumar, 1994).

Feuerstein et al. (e.g., Feuerstein, Rand, & Hoffman, 1979) have suggested that most so-called risk factors such as poverty or even neurological predispositions can be considered distal causes of behavior, whereas the more proximal determination of outcome would be the impact that these variables have on the interactions between and among individuals, with these interactions causing many of the behaviors that we consider handicapping. Others, such as Meisels and Anatasiouw (1982), would agree from their review of the literature that "the quality of the transactions that take place between a caregiver . . . and an infant can either facilitate or retard development" (p. 270) and therefore influence the causal trajectory affecting developmental outcome.

Doll and Lyon (1998) summarized studies of resilience or protective factors as follows:

Children who show resilience in the face of adversity typically have good intellectual functioning, positive/easygoing temperament, positive social orientation (friendships, internal locus of control), strong self-efficacy, achievement orientation with high expectations, positive self-concept, faith, high rate of involvement in productive activities, and close, affective relationship with at least one caregiver, effective parenting, access to positive extrafamilial models, and strong connections with prosocial institutions. (p. 355)

Sameroff and Fiese (2000) listed 10 factors that show evidence of negatively affecting children's development in and of themselves, but even more so in combination (4-year-olds with more than five of these risks were over 12 times more likely to develop mental health problems than were low-risk children): history of maternal mental illness, high maternal anxiety, rigid parental attitudes and beliefs about child development, limited positive maternal interactions during infancy, head of household in an unskilled occupation, low level of maternal education, disadvantaged minority status, reduced family support, stressful life events, and large family size. It is easy to see how Feuerstein and his associates (e.g., Feuerstein et al., 1979) would view many of these as distal—for example, family size and mother's education, which would impinge on the quantity and quality of adult-child interactions.

Despite the lack of certainties regarding future projections and the caveat regarding the necessity of considering multiple circumstances and contexts, some issues deserve particular attention and early screening. One is the area of hearing and related auditory functioning. It is critical that issues of hearing be ruled in or out for children who are referred with concerns regarding language development. Postnatal factors that can affect auditory functioning include middle ear infections (otitis media), meningitis (infection of the lining of the cerebrum), viral infections, ototoxic drugs (those that specifically affect hearing), and noise (Shah & Bliss, 2000). Auditory functions are basic not only for development of language but for cognitive and social functions as well. Most children with auditory problems are not deaf but are either hearing impaired or experience inconsistent (i.e., fluctuating) hearing related to ear infections. For example, they may appear to hear normally because they respond to sound, but they may not hear adequately if there is background noise or if the speaker is not close. Alternatively, they may be hearing many sounds, but the range may be restricted so that they are missing word endings or small modifying words that are not emphasized in speech. Hearing can be tested even in behaviorally uncooperative children with techniques such as play audiometry, reinforcement approaches, and computerized brain stem response technology (Bergman, 1985; Kramer & Williams, 1993; Madell, 1988). The assessor should refer any suspicions of possible hearing deficits, and if these results are not satisfactory, the child should be rereferred. I have frequently cited a case that I experienced of a child with severely delayed language at age 4, as well as significant behavior problems. He could easily have been diagnosed as being mentally retarded or having a pervasive developmental disorder. He had passed a hearing assessment at a major university clinic, and his mother insisted that he was able to hear. I persisted in my attempts to refer him for auditory evoked potential (computerized brain stem) testing, and his father, who was more open to the idea, followed through; we discovered that the child had profound hearing loss in both ears, requiring bilateral amplification (hearing aids). It is difficult to test very young children reliably; therefore, impressions of normality from approaches such as play audiometry may not be sufficient for a firm diagnosis. It cannot be overemphasized that there is no substitute for clinical observation, and it is better to overrefer a child such as the one in this example than to miss identifying a very serious obstruction to a child's functioning. Assessors should be on the alert for all major sensory functions, with vision also being of obvious importance (Atkinson, 1985; Fewell, 2000).

The importance of language development and the effects of experience on language development have been documented by many researchers, including White and his associates. White, Kaban, Shapiro, and Attanucci (1977) found that the infants they studied spent much time listening to live language, and those who did so showed better development than did those who spent more of their time procuring objects. Rescorla (2000) presented evidence to support the relationship between early language development and language-related skills in early adolescence.

There is evidence regarding at least three additional conditions that warrant automatic screening prior to preschool, if possible, but certainly during the preschool years. These include maternal exposure to alcohol and cocaine during pregnancy and the infant or child's ingestion of lead at any age. The seminal work of Streissguth and her associates in Seattle has documented the association of maternal ingestion of alcohol during pregnancy and its long-term negative consequences for development (Connor, Sampson, Bookstein, Barr, & Streissguth, 2001; Kelly, Day, & Streissguth, 2000; Streissguth et al., 1984; Streissguth, Barr, Bookstein, Sampson, & Olson, 1999), as well as the (at least) short-term effects of cocaine abuse during pregnancy (J. C. Martin, Barr, Martin, & Streissguth, 1996; Swanson, Streissguth, Sampson, & Olson, 1999). Streissguth et al. (1984) also showed negative consequences for the fetus of smoking during pregnancy. Similarly, the work of Needleman and his associates has been seminal in documenting the association of exposure to lead with the development of learning and behavior problems (Bellinger & Needleman, 1985; Campbell, Needleman, Riess, & Tobin, 2001; Needleman, 1982, 1985; Needleman, Riess, Tobin, Biesecker, & Greenhouse, 1996; Needleman, Shell, Bellinger, Leviton, & Allred, 1999).

ASSESSMENT

Assessors of young children should have materials and a room arrangement appropriate for this age group. There should be child-sized furniture and a minimum of attractive objects within reach or purview aside from those intended for use during the assessment. In communicating with children, Kamphaus, Dresden, and Kaufman (1993) warned that assessors should "never give a child a choice unless they do in fact have one" (p. 60). In other words, do not begin a sentence with "Do you want to . . . ?" Instead, begin with "Let's . . ." or "We are going to . . ."

If the model for the school psychologist is that of a data-oriented problem solver, then the model for good assessment is the problem-solving process. This includes the following steps (Surber, 1995):

- Collecting all available data, including reports from outside agencies
- Meeting with the referral source to develop
  —A problem statement
  —Behavioral descriptions of the problem
  —Desired outcomes for the referred child
  —A description of the child's strengths and current functioning
  —Development of referral questions in measurable terms in a way that is relevant to the child's educational functioning

A general outline of the assessment process appears in Table 1.1, which moves the assessor from the point of referral through the assessment to feedback, follow-up, and monitoring. Beside each step is a sample of the thought processing or decision making that may accompany a move to the next step.

When the assessment is triggered by a referral within a program, a referral process must be in place. Each program will have its own forms and procedures, but Form 1.2 provides one

Table 1.1   ASSESSMENT SEQUENCE

Referral	What is the nature of the needs? How urgent? What are initial data needs?
Review File	What has already been done? What do we know to date?
Interview Key Figures	What are the assessment questions? What are the history and resources of the program and home?
Observe Child	What aspects of the assessment issues are observable? What are the situational variables that relate? How does the child look in relation to the group and in relation to the situational demands?
Determine Further Assessment Needs	What further data are needed to respond to the assessment questions? What further questions are there?
Gather Data to Respond to Questions	What will be the responses to the referral questions? What do we know now?
Feedback with Referral Sources	Has the information addressed the referral questions? Do referrers have ideas about how to proceed? Do they know more now than before?
Develop Intervention Plan	Does everyone agree to the plan? Is everyone clear regarding what will be done, by whom, how, and when? What is needed to implement the plan?
Provide Consultation/Training as Needed	Are the plan implementers ready and able to proceed?
Monitor Implementation	Is the plan being done?
Evaluate Response to Intervention	How well did the plan work?
Reassess as Needed	What are the remaining questions? What else do we need to know?

Referral for Services

Child's Name: Referrer's Name:

Date of Birth: Child's Age:

Address: Program:

Phone: Program Address:

Caregivers' Names: Program Phone:

Relationship: Referral Date:

Legal Guardians? Yes / No

What are your concerns?

What previous assessment(s) have been done? By whom?

What services is this child receiving at this time?

What interventions have been tried up to this point, and with what results?

What do you know about the child's background, including medical, health, and family history?

What information would you like from this assessment?

Have you discussed this with the child's caregivers?

Have you attached a signed permission form for this assessment?

When are you available to meet to discuss this referral?

Form 1.2

possible format. This format reflects the need to elicit relevant information that will help to inform the assessment while minimizing the time required for paperwork to initiate the assessment process. This is a delicate balance. Referrers should not take referral lightly, as it is costly and time-consuming, yet they should not be obstructed in their desire to refer by the amount of paperwork involved. Form 1.3 is useful to complete along with the referral form to provide a profile of areas of concern, as well as indications of intensity of concern. The combination of forms such as Forms 1.2 and 1.3 should provide the basis for communicating the basic concerns and degree of urgency to the assessor to begin the assessment planning process.

Completion of these forms, along with the signed permission of the legal guardians, is then followed by an interview of the referrer for clarifying the problem further and for soliciting the referrer's collaboration in the assessment. Too many teachers assume that the act of referral forfeits their involvement with the special needs of the referred child or view assessment as intervention rather than as the route to intervention. Once this information has been gathered, decision making regarding procedures can begin. These decisions continue throughout the assessment process as questions and hypotheses develop in response to the results of the data gathered.

Bagnato et al. (1997) outlined six standards to guide selection of assessment methods for use with young children:

1. *Authenticity:* real behaviors in real settings
2. *Convergence:* multiple sources of information
3. *Collaboration:* working and sharing particularly with caregivers
4. *Equity:* accommodations to the child's special needs
5. *Sensitivity:* inclusion of sufficient items for planning decisions and for detecting change
6. *Congruence:* developed and field tested with children similar to those to whom the procedure will apply

Hubert and Wallander (1988) noted three primary issues in instrument selection: practical considerations, psychometric considerations, and assessment objectives. An example of a practical consideration would be the use of a play scale with a child with severe motor disability (not practical). Psychometric considerations involve the usual suspects of reliability and validity, as well as sensitivity and selectivity in the case of screening, with the addition of utility. Consideration of assessment objectives concerns the match between the data needed and the data collected in relation to the decisions to be made. Hubert and Wallander therefore suggested that assessors needed to know the objectives of the assessment, the decisions to be made, the characteristics of the child, and an appropriate repertory of procedures. No training program can prepare its students to be aware of or to develop competence with all of the available procedures. The most that any program can accomplish is to introduce students to a sample of the approaches that are available and to develop a beginner's level of mastery with a sample of these. It is up to each individual to gain further expertise in response to their professional needs, as well as in response to the developments in the field. Even the most familiar tests will change. (For example, I was trained to use the Stanford-Binet Intelligence Scale L-M, but most readers won't even know what that is!)

Assessment of young (I think all) children needs to be conducted with the view of optimizing their performance (Lidz, 1990). Particularly in the case of young children, the state of the organism can play a major role in the determination of manifest functions (e.g., whether the child is alert or sleepy). Although both the range and the typicality of behaviors

Referral Profile

Referral Profile for _____ Completed by _____ Date _____

[This form is intended as a support for making the decision to refer this child for assessment. It is not to be used for screening. Each of the items represents a possible reason for referral. Please attach a completed profile to the referral form. This will help to increase the appropriateness of the assessment process. Thank you.]

Key: NP   (No problem)
      NO   (No opportunity to observe)
      MI   (Observable to mild degree)
      MO   (Observable to moderate degree)
      S   (Observable to severe degree)

Behaviors	NP	NO	MI	MO	S	Comments
1. COGNITIVE AREA • Requires more time/practice than others to learn something new • Lacks concepts necessary for understanding lessons • Lacks curiosity • Uses materials inappropriately • Poor attention • Poor memory • Does not know how to use materials • Impulsive with materials • Hard time finishing work						
2. SPEECH/LANGUAGE • Drools, breathes with mouth open • Repeats speech of others • Responds inappropriately • Uses single-word or short-phrase sentences • Stutters • Struggles to get words out • Difficult to understand • Difficulty following directions • Delays before responding • Voice volume unusually loud or soft • Voice sounds hoarse or nasal						

Form 1.3

Behaviors	NP	NO	MI	MO	S	Comments
3. EMOTIONAL • Reactions not appropriate • Easily upset • Excessively anxious • Frequent changes in emotion • Excessively withdrawn • Excessively aggressive • Excessively angry • Excessively shy • Flat; nonreactive • Does not follow routines • Easily frustrated						
4. SOCIAL INTERACTION • Plays alone • Does not initiate play • Refuses invitations by others to play • Problem maintaining interaction • Does not comply with teacher's requests • Disturbs play of others • Seems to lack social skills • Does not use teacher as resource for learning or solving problems • Argues with peers						
5. MOTOR • Unable to use crayons or pencil for scribbling • Unable to approximate drawing of circle • Hands tremble/shake • Sloppy eater • Unable to button or zip clothing • Unable to catch a large ball • Awkward movements • Falls frequently • Bumps into things • Unable to ride tricycle • Hard time stopping once gets going • Moves constantly • Seems weak • Tires quickly						

Lidz, Carol S. *Early Childhood Assessment.* Copyright 2003, John Wiley & Sons.

Form 1.3 (*continued*)

are of relevance and interest, if we are to draw inferences about the child's capacities, we need to base these observations on optimal circumstances. This means that children need to be seen at times when they are alert and willing to interact. They need exposure to age-appropriate materials and directions, a pleasant and comfortable environment, and an assessor who is accessible, flexible, and comfortable with young children. Optimizing the assessment also reduces measurement error by reducing the variance, as the child is pushed to respond as close to the child's ceiling level as possible. Another way to optimize performance is to ensure that the child experiences sufficient competence during testing with minimal frustration. This may mean starting standardized tests below the baseline, interspersing easier with more challenging tasks, or providing for breaks or snacks. It may mean terminating a session if the child is too distressed, changing the assessment procedure, or even modifying the administration (see Chapter 6 and 7 for further discussion of dynamic and standardized assessment).

In the "olden" days, when I was trained, it was automatic to see children of all ages without their parents. Part of the description of the child in the report addressed the ease or difficulty of this separation. Somewhere along the line of my professional practice, I asked myself why and decided that there was not sufficient justification to sustain this practice, particularly if we keep in mind the issue of optimizing the child's performance. Once we have determined that the child will scream uncontrollably when separated from his parents, what do we accomplish by spending the next hour trying to calm him or her down? And what can we conclude from this reaction in any case? I now most often see very young children in the company of their caregivers and use the caregiver as a collaborator-informant to help me understand the child. This is not a rigid alternative. Children seen within programs do not always have parents who are available or willing to accompany them. In this case, I ensure that the child is familiar with me by visiting and interacting within the classroom, and consider asking an aid to accompany us if the child is too stressed to leave. Apparently, I am not alone in this practice. According to Greenspan and Meisels (1994), "young children should never be challenged during assessment by separation from their parents or familiar caregivers" (p. 7).

Although psychologists make a very important contribution to the assessment and planning for young children and their families, they also need to function as members of a team. Psychologists need to become familiar with their team members and their various areas of expertise. The individuals who are most likely to participate in a team would be a speech and language pathologist, occupational therapist (who usually focuses on fine motor functions, daily living skills, and sensorimotor integration), physical therapist (who usually focuses on gross motor functions, particularly lower extremities), and nurse. Teachers (regular and special education) are also team members, as are parents.

Nagle (2000) described the three basic types of team organizations: multidisciplinary, interdisciplinary, and transdisciplinary. In the case of multidisciplinary teams, each member functions independently, completes the assessment, sends it in, and hopes that someone coordinates the input and service delivery. In most cases the assessment is usually solicited by someone who is coordinating the service delivery and who solicits the assessment to inform this process. In the case of an interdisciplinary team, each member conducts an assessment within her or his area of expertise, but the team members also interact to formulate a coordinated plan and participate as a group in the various team meetings, and they are often available for further follow-up. Transdisciplinary teams delegate the primary assessment function to one or two of its members, and the others accomplish their assessment goals through these direct assessors. Transdisciplinary teams are characterized by *role release,* in which the designated individuals carry out the functions of other team members. Needless to say, these teams are complex entities, and a significant aspect of professional functioning involves development of working relations among the team members. There are often significant turf issues. As a rule, psychologists are trained to consider and address the *whole* child. Therefore, it can become difficult to function within this role when a social worker does the developmental history, an educational diagnostician does the academic piece, and an occupational therapist includes cognitive testing among the fine motor scales. I assume that assessment is carried out as an integrated, holistic process. How this plays out within any particular team will vary, and each professional will have to negotiate a role and find a way to function effectively. In my view, the role of the psychologist and the psychological assessment is to solve a problem; humans function in an integrated way. To do the job properly, we have to consider all the many contributing pieces and how they are or are not integrated and how they reflect the many possible contributing factors.

Assessment of young children is not an easy task—certainly not one for the weak of mind or heart, as acknowledged by Goodman and Field (1991): "Preschool children in trouble mean trouble for diagnostic evaluators. The psychologist is apt to face reluctant subjects, extremely serious differential diagnostic questions, and an inadequate array of testing instruments" (p. 219). On the other hand, most of the children are also appealing, fun, and interesting. Work with children in this age range provides opportunities to help both children and their families find their way onto a productive developmental path. Although methods of assessment always need improvement, there is now a sufficient array of data sources to provide meaningful documentation of needs and guidelines to build a foundation for promising interventions. Despite the continuing need for more and better, we have come a long way.

As recently as 2000, Alfonso, Oakland, LaRocca, and Spanakos found that only 32% of their survey respondents from U.S. school psychology programs offered separate courses in preschool assessment. After reviewing the chapters in this book, readers should become convinced of the need for a special course in the area of early childhood assessment; in fact, some may well wonder if just one course is sufficient.

SUMMARY

This chapter provides an introduction to assessment of young children. Assessment is defined as a broad data-gathering process that informs decision making, rather than being aligned with any specific procedures such as testing. The model advocated in this book is ecological and context based and considers the many complexly interacting variables that contribute to the functioning of the child who is referred for assessment. The chapter provides formats and suggestions for interviewing and carrying out the full assessment process from referral through feedback and follow-up. Screening is differentiated from assessment with regard to intent and depth. The point is emphasized that screening should be followed not by placement but by further assessment for children who are determined to be at risk for later developmental problems. The chapter reviews a sample of screening tests along with criteria for evaluating screening procedures and issues of determining risk. The chapter also discusses parents as raters, as well as agreement between the ratings of parents and professionals.

SUGGESTED ACTIVITIES

SCHOLARSHIP

Select a risk factor and review and critique the relevant literature documenting this as a risk factor.

APPLICATION

Conduct and audio- or videotape at least two practice intake interviews (these can be with friends or family members who have children). Review these tapes and take note of the sequence of your questions and the responses that follow. Evaluate these in terms of the extent to which your questions and comments facilitate or obstruct the communication and in terms of the degree to which your communication reflects the recommendations in this chapter. How could you improve? (Develop these thoughts in a self-reflective paper and provide examples.)

Chapter Two

---◆---

Observing Children, Programs, and Teachers

---◆---

Imagine a scenario in which a very precise tornado descends on psychologists and magically lifts away all their test kits. Could we survive? I would like to think that the answer would be yes. If we truly believe that assessment is not synonymous with testing and that assessment is an internal mental activity of the assessor, then even if we were stranded on that perennial desert island, we should be able to carry out what would pass for a meaningful psychological assessment (assuming that we were not alone!).

The cornerstones of assessment have always been good interviews and observations. Testing without these remains dry and reflexive, with little depth or meaning. Testing is, after all, a structured, quantifiable opportunity for interview and observation. Within the model of an ecological approach to assessment and an interactive view of behavior, it is necessary to view the child in as natural a context as possible (Pelligrini, 1996). This not only allows us to derive a deeper understanding of the child's behavior but also promotes linkage of the assessment with intervention because we are able to understand the relevant variables more fully and process the observations in terms of what can be done to improve the child's functioning. Observation is particularly relevant for use with young children, as many who are difficult to test with more direct approaches can nevertheless be observed and are minimally affected by the presence of an observer (Barton & Ascione, 1984; Goodwin & Driscoll, 1980; Pelligrini, 1996). But the primary advantage of observation is that it is not necessary to generalize to the real situation; it *is* the real situation. Hintze and Shapiro (1995) went so far as to call observation "the most direct and desired approach to data collection" (p. 651).

This chapter discusses issues of observing children in their natural contexts of home, school, or program. The chapter also discusses observation of contextual variables—in this case, the instructional environment, including both physical and human contributors (home and family variables are the focus of a separate chapter). It is difficult to draw clear lines for each chapter, especially regarding the interactions of all the variables; thus, functional behavioral assessment is reserved for the chapter on assessment of social-emotional functioning (Chapter 8) because this approach is used primarily with children with significant social-emotional issues, whereas the general topic of behavioral observation is introduced in this chapter. However, this chapter places greater emphasis on contextual variables, whereas Chapter 8 highlights individual, child-related variables. Observation as an assessment activity is appropriate for all referrals, not just for children experiencing social-emotional difficulties.

Zeitgeists come and zeitgeists go, and it is difficult to imagine a time when psychologists needed to be reminded that behavior is not determined simply by internal traits but is a function of interaction with environments. The pendulum has moved to the opposite extreme as well, to the point where any consideration of events in the black box of the brain was considered unscientific and of ill repute, with only environmental, observable, noninferred events granted scientific plausibility. Bronfenbrenner's work (e.g., 1976a, 1976b, 1989a, 1989b) has been perhaps the most influential in promoting a context-based approach to viewing development and, as a consequence, assessment.

ISSUES OF OBSERVATION

Observation as an assessment approach is far from new. The heyday of promoting observation as an alternative method occurred in the 1970s and 1980s (Greenwood, Schulte, Kohler, Dinwiddie, & Carta, 1986). This more ecologically valid assessment approach was advocated as an antidote to those more embedded in the medical model, which emphasized intrapsychic factors (e.g., Dickinson, 1978; Sitko, Fink, & Gillespie, 1977).

Observation can be both systematic and tailor-made for the situation. Although observation has the advantage of tapping behavior within natural contexts, all approaches must be selective, as it is not possible to perceive or record all of the simultaneously occurring variables. Good observation systems specify the target behaviors to be observed in a way that is both precise and noninferential in order to maximize objectivity and reliability. Although issues of validity that relate primarily to the degree to which the behaviors observed are representative and free of observer effect exist, the primary issues concern reliability (Sattler, 2002). Challenges to reliability reflect issues of both the observer and the individual being observed—the observer with regard to inter- and intraobserver agreement, and the observee with regard to stability of behavior over time and situations. Assessors need to train themselves or be trained to be reliable, and they should check themselves either against other observers or against an expert criterion of prescored observations. Reliability of behavior over time and situation can be addressed through definitions of behavior that balance breadth with specificity, that is, that are neither too broad nor too narrow.

The easiest and perhaps most frequently used measure of inter- and intraobserver agreement is the following formula:

$$\frac{\text{Number of agreements}}{\text{Number of agreements} + \text{disagreements}} \times 100$$

This yields the percentage of agreement but does not account for chance agreements (Lipinski & Nelson, 1974; Pelligrini, 1996). An acceptable level of agreement would be 80% or higher (Allessi & Kaye, 1983; Boehm & Weinberg, 1997), and Alessi and Kaye even suggested 90% or higher for placement decisions.

Determination of percentage of agreement is best calculated in relation to the assessor's agreement with a criterion observation completed by an expert, rather than with another peer observer, because both may agree yet be wrong (Frick & Semmel, 1978). The reliability statistic of choice seems to be Cohen's kappa (Cohen, 1960), which avoids the issue of chance agreements and can be tested for significance. Although possibly too complex for the purpose of informal diagnostic assessment, this would be recommended for purposes of research or formal system development.

The four most frequently discussed approaches to observation include running record, time sampling, event sampling, and rating scale or checklist (Alessi & Kaye, 1983; Lidz, 1981). In this chapter the rating scale approach will be applied to observations of both programs and teachers, and a combination of the running record and event sampling approach will be applied to observations of individuals. *Time sampling* tends to be applied more for research than for diagnostic purposes. Any observation approach is best for frequently occurring behaviors, but useful data can be derived for almost any observable behavior. The key word in this is *observable*.

Any behavior has a number of parameters that can be useful to observe and record, and the assessor needs to make a decision about which are the most appropriate. These parameters include frequency, duration, latency, intensity, and rate (Bailey & Wolery, 1989, mentioned even endurance and accuracy). *Frequency* is the number of times the behavior occurs during the time of observation. *Duration* refers to how long a specific behavioral episode lasts. *Latency* concerns the time between a trigger and the occurrence of the target behavior (e.g., how long does it take for the child to comply with the teacher's request to perform an act?). *Intensity* is a judgment and may be best rated on a scale, although in some cases it may be behaviorally described (e.g., noise level in terms of decibels). *Rate* relates to the number of occurrences within a specified time period. In many cases, frequency would be a parameter of choice, particularly for frequently occurring behaviors. However, for a behavior such as a temper tantrum, which may occur only once or twice a day, parameters such as duration and intensity may be more appropriate, and the assessor would then need to find a way to measure these objectively, such as duration in seconds plus a scaled judgment for intensity.

Once the target behaviors and their parameters have been specified, the assessor can decide how to record them. The most frequently used method is *event sampling,* in which each occurrence of the target behaviors is recorded. To make this approach more informative, it is often embedded in what is called the *ABC method,* or antecedent-behavior-consequence. That is, not only the target behavior, but also what occurred just prior to this behavior (as well as just subsequent to it), is noted. Such a strictly behavioral approach assumes that the cause (or at least control) somehow lies in these antecedent (trigger) and consequent (reinforcer) events, which may or may not be the case, as there are a number of mediating factors such as the individual's prior history and beliefs, values, and interpretations that affect behavioral outcomes. Nevertheless, it can be useful to look for patterns, which, if they are found, can inform intervention. For example, if it becomes obvious from the observation that the teacher is ignoring most instances of the child's prosocial behavior while reacting and attending to almost every instance of antisocial behavior, then the assessor can suggest reversing the emphasis of this cycle.

The greatest challenge for beginning assessors tends to be the specification of target behaviors, as well as the objective recording of events. For example, if a teacher refers a child for disruptive behavior, this must be described in a way that is sufficiently precise to reduce inference and yet sufficiently comprehensive to generalize across situations. For example, disruptive behavior could be destroying constructions of other children during play, running around the room during periods of sit-down or table activities, or throwing materials on the floor during setup time for new activities. Is calling out during circle time disruptive? This would have to be included or not in the definition.

When there are a number of behaviors to be observed, it promotes efficiency of recording to devise a code for each. It is easiest if the code reflects the specific behavior, such as RR for running around the room or TM for throwing materials. However, I will use the terms target (TG) and terminal (TM) as codes, with numerals to indicate the specific behaviors observed within each category.

It is very useful when conducting observations to record instances of positive behaviors that are the flip side of the negative, referral-oriented behaviors (Keller, 1980) as well as to record or make informal notes of the behaviors of nonreferred children. For example, while the referred child is engaged in a target behavior, what are the other children doing?

Other important points include the need to schedule the observation at a time when the target behaviors are likely to occur; to observe the child for a length of time that is sufficient to capture the full situation, but not too long to lose observer vigilance; and to take more than a single sample of the behaviors (i.e., observe more than one activity or on more than one day). Observers are usually advised to be as nonintrusive and neutral as possible, which is a real challenge in a preschool environment. It is important to be as little of a novelty as possible, so there should be an effort to desensitize the children to the observer's presence and to get the children accustomed to the idea of a friendly but noninvolved adult. Actually, I usually begin as a neutral, uninvolved observer, taking all the notes I need during that period of time, and then move in to interact with the referred child in the context of other children and to participate in the program's activities.

In a *running record* the assessor records all events as they occur naturally during the period of observation. When there are target behaviors related to the referral, the assessor can make special note of these as they occur by underlining, circling, or otherwise highlighting their occurrences (we will use codes). My preferred approach to observation is to embed notation of these target behaviors within a running record, also making side notes that indicate my processing with regard to precipitating and other contextual events, as well as brainstorming possible approaches to intervention. I maintain this side column as my way of talking to myself as I process the events of the observation, and I find that I rely on these notes when I make my final recommendations for intervention. This approach combines the complexity and depth of the full interactional context while allowing for some quantification of the target behaviors; it is easy to go back to count frequencies and to utilize notations regarding parameters of intensity, duration, or latency if these were appropriate to record. This format appears in the section on observing children later in this chapter.

The length of observation time is a point of discussion in some of the literature. This depends to some degree on the circumstances of the observation. Boehm and Weinberg (1997) recommended three visits of 30 min each as adequate, although one of the studies they reviewed specified five visits as optimal, and Shapiro and Skinner (1990) concurred that three visits are optimal. However, the working circumstances of most school psychologists do not allow for this amount of time, so it would be especially necessary to consult with the teacher or parent following the observation to derive a sense of how typical the situation is (W. W. Lynch, 1977). If not typical, then the observation should be rescheduled.

OBSERVING CHILDREN

Assessors must first determine the purpose of their observations. I have found that if the purpose is to gather context-based information to promote in-depth understanding of the child's functioning, a combination of running record and event sampling is the most useful approach. If the purpose is to develop a baseline from which the child's response to intervention will be monitored, then a stricter, quantifiable, behavioral approach is necessary. In the latter case, it would be necessary to gather baseline data over a period of at least four visits of 20 min each, scheduled during the same time and same activity period each visit. Recordings of specific relevant parameters such as frequency or duration would be averaged and plotted on a graph for the purpose of determining the effects of intervention.

Good observations depend greatly on conducting good teacher or parent interviews (Alessi & Kaye, 1983). It is very important to gather specific information about the behaviors of concern, the most likely time of their occurrence, and the typical circumstances so that the observation's usefulness can be maximized. An interview such as that in Form 2.1, adapted from the information offered by Allessi and Kaye, should be helpful to pinpoint the focus as well as the schedule of observation.

Based on the information in Form 2.1, the assessor should be able to determine both target and terminal behaviors in a way that closely matches the referral concerns. This match is important if the feedback and recommendations for intervention are to be useful to those working with the children. In addition to the behavior-based questions of this form, the assessor should gather information and make inferences about the teacher's or parent's beliefs and values regarding the teaching and learning processes and the behaviors of concern. For example, is there a priority for behaviors to change? How important is it that the child change? Is the parent or teacher hoping for total reversal or extinction of these behaviors, or just amelioration? What will be most affected by such changes? For example, is the issue primarily compliance or the effects on the child's learning? Are these behavioral expectations developmentally appropriate for the age and level of functioning of the child? These are judgmental issues that can be gleaned either from direct questioning or from inferences made from the information provided, but they are of importance for informing the final recommendations.

For diagnostic purposes, this chapter follows the observation format outlined in Form 2.2. This approach is an adaptation of the work of Bersoff and Ericson (1972), Bersoff and Grieger (1971), and Ellett and Bersoff (1976), called *psychosituational assessment.* I agree with Barnett, Bell, and Carey's (1999) recommendation to use real-time recording, although they predetermine the time intervals and make a behavioral notation for each interval (e.g., every 1 or 2 min). I think that making occasional time notations that suggest the flow and duration of critical behaviors is sufficient to capture the nature of the situation. However, the Barnett and Bell approach remains a viable alternative.

The adapted format maximizes flexibility and combines both qualitative and quantitative information, as well as promoting linkages between assessment and intervention. The first step of this approach is to identify TG and TM behaviors as specifically and precisely as possible, based on the teacher-parent interview information. *Target behaviors* are those of concern that precipitated the referral and presumably need to be changed. *Terminal behaviors* are those that are desired and are usually the flip side of target. In a semihypothetical example, consider a 4-year-old boy who has been referred by his program teacher for aggressive behavior. Following an interview with the teacher, we determine that the target behaviors are as follows:

TG1: grabs materials from other children
TG2: hits other children
TG3: destroys products or constructions of peers
TG4: trips children who pass near him

Preobservation Teacher-Parent Questionnaire

Child: _____   Teacher: _____   Date: _____

Please describe your concerns:

Would you give me specific examples?

When do these typically occur?

About how often?

How long do they last?

What would be preferred or desired behaviors?

About how often do these more desired behaviors occur? Any ideas about when?

What have you tried so far? With what results?

Do you have any ideas about what might be causing or setting off the problem?

What would be the best times for me to observe? Schedule time.

Form 2.1

Observation Recording Sheet (page 1)

Child Name: _____ Date: _____ Place: _____ Observer: _____

Target Behaviors (TG): _____

Terminal Behaviors (TM): _____

Time/task notations	Running record: Note target behaviors (TG), terminal behaviors (TM), antecedent (A), and consequent (C) conditions	Inferences, hypotheses derived from behavioral observations	Ideas for possible interventions

Form 2.2

Observation Recording Sheet (page 2)

Child Name: _____

Time/task notations	Running record	Inferences, hypotheses	Interventions

Form 2.2 (*continued*)

Based on these targets and further discussion with the teacher, we determine that the terminal behaviors are

TM1: plays and works parallel to peers without incidence
TM2: initiates play with peers without incidence
TM3: maintains play with peers without incidence
TM4: spontaneously offers to help another child

The next step is to schedule the observation at a time when the target behaviors are most likely to occur. Ideally, there would be more than a single observation, but the reality is that more than one opportunity is not always possible. In this case, it is important to observe for a sufficiently long period of time to provide a good sample of the child's behavior. It is advisable to observe children over the course of several activities to look at their behavior and activity interactions (does the nature of the activity make a difference?), as well as their transition from one activity to the other. So, in the sample case we have determined that the best observation time is during free play, and we will remain in the room through transition to circle time and small-group structured activities.

The psychosituational assessment approach is a variation of the ABC format, in which the observer notes antecedent (A) and consequent (C) conditions, that is, those situations that immediately precede and follow the TG and TM behaviors. This information allows us to look for patterns of triggers that may precipitate the TG and TM behaviors, as well as those that may serve as reinforcers. When and if these patterns occur, it then becomes possible to modify and thereby control the behaviors; however, these patterns are not always so clear, and the antecedents or reinforcers are not always so immediate or observable.

During the time of observation, the assessor should be positioned in as inconspicuous a location as possible, showing a general interest in the classroom activities but without giving clear cues regarding the specific child who is being observed. The observer needs to be close enough to the action to enable accurate and meaningful recording and to take language samples when possible. It is optimal for observers to have desensitized the group to their presence, but if this is not the case and the children ask what is going on, the observer should just provide some neutral comments such as, "I'm just visiting and want to see what you do in your class."

Using Form 2.2, the observer records the time and nature of the activities as they occur naturally in the extreme left column. If duration or latency are parameters of interest for the behaviors, these can be recorded in this column when the relevant behaviors occur. If the observer is not taking a precise behavioral baseline, it is sufficient to self-count seconds to estimate time. The observer then makes a running record in the next column of the events as they occur in the classroom. When a target or terminal behavior occurs, this is noted (TG1, TM3, TG4, etc.), along with notation of the antecedent and consequent events.

In our case example, the running record may look something like the following:

M. enters the class, puts his coat into his cubby, and goes immediately to the block area. A peer approaches and takes a block from the shelf (A), and M. hits him (TG2) and grabs the block from his hand (TG1). The child screams and calls to his teacher, and the teacher puts M. on time-out (C). As children pass by M. on time-out (A), he tries to trip them (TG4) and goes unnoticed (C). The teacher tells him he can go back to the block area but needs to play "nicely" (A). M. returns and asks a boy if he can play with the blocks (TM2). The boy agrees, and M. joins him to build a castle. This lasts about 5 min (TM3). M. then runs to the other end of the block area and knocks over the block castle built by one of the boys (TG3). The boy screams for the teacher, who puts M. on time-out (C). . . .

During this recording time, the assessor is also processing the events and gets ideas about what seems to be occurring, as well as brainstorming possibilities for intervention. In this case, the assessor may begin to think that M.'s negative behaviors are attracting teacher attention and reinforcement, while his prosocial behaviors tend to be ignored. Regarding intervention possibilities, the assessor notes that M. responded well to the direct instruction to "play nicely." Although he did not sustain this for long, he may profit from more of such direct instruction, and the assessor remains on the alert to verify or negate this hypothesis. The assessor also makes notes to question whether M.'s interactions relate to issues of impulse control or to socialization experiences, and the assessor forms a mental plan to carry out a more in-depth family interview, as well as parent-child interaction observation and direct assessment.

Following the observation, the assessor counts up the number of occurrences of target and terminal behaviors and looks for patterns regarding antecedent and consequent events. For M., it is indeed the case that although TG behaviors do outnumber TM behaviors, there are nevertheless a good number of TMs, and these almost always go unnoticed. Furthermore, in looking at the nature of the TG behaviors, it seems that most of these reflect M.'s intent to become involved with other children, but he seems to lack the skills to do this in a consistently positive way. These observations lead to the eventual recommendation to counsel the staff to make a special effort to notice M.'s "good" behaviors and to give him attention for these while coaching him into more successful play interactions with peers. The assessor also resolves to include M. in a social skills training program and to pair him with a play buddy from within the class: a child who is successful with social interaction and is coached to play for several minutes per day with M. The assessor also notes that time-outs are often of unspecified duration and that the teacher sometimes forgets to release M. from these; M. often gets into tripping episodes during these times. Through program administration, the assessor therefore provides the teacher with a timer and encourages restricting these episodes to no more than 5 min, with the child released at the sound of the timer bell. In fact, it might be a good idea to teach him to set the timer bell as a way to facilitate his self-regulation.

Thus, with this approach it is possible to combine the benefits of both quantitative and qualitative parameters and to embed the benefits of a behavioral model while extending this information into useful inferences and hypotheses that link with recommendations for intervention. Because of the availability of the quantitative information, it is possible to return to the classroom for follow up once the interventions have been put in place and to rerecord the occurrences of both TM and TG behaviors to assess their response to intervention.

OBSERVING PROGRAMS

The premier tool for evaluating programs for young children is the Early Childhood Environment Rating Scale–Revised Edition (ECERS; Harms, Clifford, & Cryer, 1998), designed to reflect the standards for high-quality programs set by the National Association for the Education of Young Children (NAEYC). This is a relatively inexpensive instrument, and there are training videotapes available. The ECERS contains 43 items, each rated on a 7-point scale ranging from excellent to inadequate, covering the seven parameters of space/furnishings, personal care routines, language/reasoning, activities, interaction, program structure, and parents/staff. The scale can be obtained from its publisher, Teachers College Press (http://store.tcpress.com).

Bagnato et al. (1997) noted that the ECERS had been used primarily in relation to regular education settings but was being applied increasingly to special education programs, and the revision added items to increase its relevance for inclusive preschool settings. These authors concluded that the "ECERS fulfills a pressing need in a relatively uncharted early intervention area" (p. 170).

In the Peisner-Feinberg et al. (2001) longitudinal study of the relationships between preschool variables and children's development in second grade, there was a positive relationship between preschool scores on the ECERS and the children's second-grade cognitive skills.

OBSERVING TEACHERS

The importance of considering teaching and its impact on children's learning and development seems hardly in need of defense. However, there are data to document these relationships (e.g., Good & Brophy, 1991; Kontos & Wilcox-Herzog, 1997), even though this area remains understudied. Some of the variables include teachers' beliefs and attitudes, as well as management of time and class organization, whereas other variables address more proximal interactions with students. Kontos and Wilcox-Herzog (1997), in their review of studies, noted the importance of teachers' interactions for child developmental outcomes—for example, the positive relationship between teachers' verbal elaboration and divergent questions in high-quality preschool settings, compared to the relative lack of these behaviors among teachers in more mediocre settings. These authors cited evidence of a positive relationship between teacher responsiveness and the quality of children's object play, as well between the quantity of teachers' verbal interactions and the children's task orientation and intellectual development. Peisner-Feinberg et al. (2001) documented a positive relationship between teacher-child relationship variables (e.g., regarding sensitivity and responsivity) during preschool and the children's social and cognitive development in second grade.

Parameters for observations of teaching are usually embedded within instruments designed for other purposes or are very complex coding systems designed for research and requiring significant training and monitoring of observers. Most are not comprehensive in their coverage of the complex array of interactive teaching behaviors that characterize a typical instructional situation. The Guidelines for Observing Teaching Interactions shown in Form 2.3 reflect the components of Feuerstein's (e.g., Feuerstein, Rand, & Hoffman, 1979) conceptualization of mediated learning experience (MLE), which is described in greater detail in Chapter 3 (and is also discussed in Chapter 6).

Briefly, MLE describes 12 components of adult-child interactions that promote the development of higher mental functioning in children. Children who experience optimal mediation are hypothesized to develop self-regulation, strategic problem solving, and representational thinking. These components consist of intent, meaning, transcendence, joint regard, shared experience, task regulation, praise/encouragement, challenge, change, differentiation, contingent responsivity, and affective involvement. The specific definitions for each of these appear in Chapter 3 and are operationalized by the items of the scale. For example, the component of intent describes communication of a clear message to involve the child in the interaction, as well as interactions that maintain the child's involvement. Intent is operationalized by the first three items of the scale, which rate the degree to which the teacher provides a clear message to engage in the lesson, successfully maintains the students' attention, and does these in a way that promotes the students' self-regulation rather than dependence on the teacher.

Guidelines for Observing Teaching Interactions

These guidelines describe interactions of teachers with students that can be described as mediated learning experiences. *Mediated learning experience* is a term used by Feuerstein and his colleagues to summarize interactions that optimize learning and cognitive development; these interactions help children to become self-regulating, strategic problem solvers and competent symbolic thinkers. These guidelines are primarily for use by school psychologists in the role of either teacher consultant or student assessor. The information is to be shared collaboratively with teachers who request such feedback or to enable consultants to develop hypotheses regarding the effects of the instructional environment on a referred pupil's performance; it is not intended as a report card for teachers.

TEACHER'S NAME:_____ DATE OF OBSERVATION: _____

LOCATION:_____ LESSON:_____

OBSERVER:_____ PUPIL'S NAME (if appropriate):_____

Observe teacher throughout the course of an entire lesson. (write NA if item does not apply)
Use the following rating scale and record additional descriptive comments below:

4	3	2	1
evident at high level	evident at moderate level	evident at emergent level	not evident

1. Teacher provides clear message to students of intention to engage them in a lesson — 4   3   2   1
2. Teacher successfully maintains the attention of the students throughout the course of the lesson — 4   3   2   1
3. When students lose attention, teacher at times goes beyond stating the need to pay attention and provides a reason or basic principle (e.g., so you'll know what to do). — 4   3   2   1
4. Teacher provides appropriate tangible/visible props to support the lesson — 4   3   2   1
5. Teacher uses voice, gesture, and movement to liven the presentation of the lesson — 4   3   2   1
6. Teacher specifically points out features and elements of materials and content that are important to note — 4   3   2   1
7. Teacher goes beyond labeling what is presented to students to provide elaborations that enhance perceptions (e.g., do you hear rhythm of this poem?) — 4   3   2   1

Form 2.3

8. Teacher promotes thinking that connects the lesson to previous experiences	4	3	2	1
9. Teacher promotes thinking that connects the lesson to future experiences	4	3	2	1
10. Teacher promotes cause-effect thinking (looking backward from present observation)	4	3	2	1
11. Teacher promotes hypothetical and if . . . then thinking (looking forward from present observation or thought)	4	3	2	1
12. Teacher expresses awareness of pupil's experiences or perspectives (what student might be thinking or feeling)	4	3	2	1
13. Teacher shares own thoughts or experiences relevant to the lesson	4	3	2	1
14. Teacher joins pupil's learning experience as a learner, self-talking through a problem-solving situation	4	3	2	1
15. Teacher clearly communicates the purpose of the lesson in terms of what the pupil is expected to learn; this outcome includes processes	4	3	2	1
16. Teacher's organization or plan of the lesson is clear	4	3	2	1
17. Teacher promotes strategic thinking in the students (e.g., asking "how" questions, suggesting strategies)	4	3	2	1
18. When giving instructions about how to perform a task, teacher includes information about basic principles of the task	4	3	2	1
19. Teacher helps students who don't know how to proceed to develop competence in ways that help students arrive at improved performance	4	3	2	1
20 Teacher offers positive comments and encouraging remarks	4	3	2	1
21. Teacher's remarks about student performance include feedback about what worked(and what did not), i.e., informed feedback	4	3	2	1
22. Teacher elicits thinking and responses from students and does not disproportionately "talk at" them	4	3	2	1
23. Teacher succeeds in creating and maintaining a "challenge zone," of being slightly ahead without overly frustrating students	4	3	2	1
24. Teacher reads students' behavioral cues and is responsive to student behaviors and needs, responding in a timely and appropriate way (this includes providing adequate "wait time")	4	3	2	1

Form 2.3 (*continued*)

	4	3	2	1
25. Teacher is able to balance needs of higher performers with those of students with greater need	4	3	2	1
26. Teacher relates with warmth and a sense of caring	4	3	2	1
27. Teacher provides opportunity for students to observe that they have learned successfully and how they have changed as learners (e.g., using examples of their work to note growth)	4	3	2	1
28. Teacher provides opportunities for students to reflect on how they arrived at an answer or solution and not just what the right answer is; this includes requests to justify answers or responses	4	3	2	1
29. Teacher's requests or questions promote integration of information from more than one source	4	3	2	1
30. Teacher provides opportunity for students to summarize their learning experiences	4	3	2	1
31. Teacher evaluates student learning of lesson objectives before moving on (includes checking that students have necessary prerequisite knowledge and skills to engage in new learning)	4	3	2	1
32. Teacher's interactions promote self-regulation and promotion of personal responsibility for actions	4	3	2	1
33. Nature of lesson and selection of materials promotes active involvement of students	4	3	2	1
34. Content of lesson allows for alternative responses and solutions	4	3	2	1

Summary of TEACHER INTERACTIONS:

Summary of CLASSROOM ENVIRONMENT:

Describe STUDENT PARTICIPATION and RESPONSIVENESS:

RECOMMENDATIONS:

Form 2.3 (*continued*)

PROFILE OF CLASSROOM MEDIATED LEARNING EXPERIENCES

[average the items from the guidelines, record observations with different color for each, and create a key to associate color with time]

Time 1: Date: _____ Color: _____

Time 2: Date: _____ Color: _____

Time 3: Date: _____ Color: _____

Time 4: Date: _____ Color: _____

Intent	4	3	2	1
Items: 1, 2, 3				
Meaning	4	3	2	1
Items: 4, 5, 6, 7				
Transcendence	4	3	2	1
Items: 8, 9, 10, 11				
Joint Regard	4	3	2	1
Items: 12, 14				
Shared Experience	4	3	2	1
Items: 13				
Task Regulation	4	3	2	1
Items: 15, 16, 17, 18, 28, 29, 30, 34				
Praise and Feedback	4	3	2	1
Items: 20, 21				
Challenge	4	3	2	1
Items: 23				
Change	4	3	2	1
Items: 27				
Differentiation	4	3	2	1
Items: 19, 22, 31, 32, 33				
Contingent Responsivity	4	3	2	1
Items: 24, 25				
Affective Involvement	4	3	2	1
Items: 26				

Form 2.3 (*continued*)

My first attempt to operationalize MLE into a rating scale is reflected in the parent-child interaction scale described in Chapter 3. Because teachers are also primary mediators of children's development, I designed the format in Form 2.3 to capture the same MLE components within the more formal, more group-oriented interactions within educational settings. The components of the two scales are identical. Examples of six of the less inferential, more verbally dependent components appear in Table 2.1.

The examples in Table 2.1 are restricted to these components because it is difficult to provide an explicit example of others such as the warmth of affective involvement or the nonverbal dance of contingent responsivity.

To apply the guidelines from Form 2.3 to teaching situations, the assessor should observe an entire natural teaching lesson and rate the occurrence of the items as they apply to that entire lesson. As is good practice for any observation, assessors should observe more than a single instance to make generalizations regarding the instructional environment. The primary purpose of the scale is to generate a description of the teacher as mediator for at least two purposes: to understand the contribution of the instructional situation to the functioning of the referred child, and to serve as a basis for making recommendations to improve instruction. As with any tool, the assessor should not be restricted by the items but should make ongoing notes to describe how each of the MLE components is (or is not) represented in the behavior of the individual observed, as well as make any additional descriptive notes to enhance understanding of the instructional context. Assessors should be careful to avoid using this tool as an explicit evaluation of the teacher and should use it only to guide processing with regard to the referred child, as well as for generation of recommendations. Teachers should not be judged to be "good" or "bad" as a result of these observations, and the results of this scale should not be shared with teachers' supervisors. Assessors who are perceived by teachers as entering their classrooms to evaluate them will lose their welcome and, in fact, may be considered to be out of line in their professional function.

After all of the items are rated following the observed lesson, these are moved onto the Profile of Classroom Mediated Learning Experiences of Form 2.3. Observations across time or contexts can be represented by use of different colors on the same profile. When used to generate recommendations, the assessor would make note of how well the teacher is realizing some of the components while also selecting one or two that warrant attention and improvement. Any suggestions for improvement should be positively stated and, if possible, framed in terms of the needs of the student rather than stated as "shoulds" for the teacher. For example, if the observer finds that the teacher offers very few instances of transcendence (or bridging; see Chapter 3 for explicit definitions of these terms) and, in fact, misses many opportunities for this, the assessor could state that the child has difficulty understanding how things are connected and that the child would profit from special efforts to make connections between what is being taught and events in that child's life (with an example provided from the lesson). For teachers who are weak on several points, it is better to set some priorities and select one or two to highlight rather than mentioning each and every item that could be improved.

LIMITATIONS

Although observation can be the most fruitful of all the approaches to assessment, it is not without its limitations. Boehm and Weinberg (1997) noted that the main challenges to the reliability of observations are observer bias, drift, and inadequate training. Observer drift, the ten-

Table 2.1 ELABORATIONS AND EXAMPLES OF COMPONENTS OF MEDIATED LEARNING EXPERIENCES

---

1. Intent

Elaboration: Communication should contain the elements of soliciting and maintaining attention, stating clearly that the mediator wishes to involve the child in an activity, and promoting self-regulation of attention in the child.

Examples:
Teacher-Child

"I'd like you to sit here now and do this activity with me."

"Now be sure to listen so you'll know what to do."

"I think you pay attention better when we put the toys we don't need out of sight. Then you won't be noticing them."

2. Meaning

Elaboration: This involves use of tangible props, as well as use of voice and gesture to enliven the communication; it also involves highlighting either perceptually or through conversation what is important and what should be noticed.

Examples:
Teacher-Child

"Wow! Wasn't that a funny story! Didn't they dress up really funny with those big hats and shoes with blue and yellow stripes?!"

"You know, if you look straight into the eyes of that picture, he looks just like he's looking back at you!"

"Did you notice that the snowman has a small circle for a head, then a bigger circle for the chest, and then a really big circle for the bottom? Do you see how it gets bigger and bigger each time?"

3. Transcendence

Elaboration: This involves building bridges of thinking between experiences and events, suggesting and asking how they are related. It also involves encouraging the child to consider implications and to make inferences, as well as to speculate about possible causes of events.

Examples:
Teacher-Child

"Do you remember when we read the story last week about the girl on the swing? Is this story anything like that one?"

"Can you think of how this will help us when we visit the zoo tomorrow?"

"What if we didn't have any parks to go to? Then what would it be like?"

4. Joint Regard

Elaboration: This involves trying to see and state the situation from the point of view of the child, as well as trying to experience the situation as a learner-collaborator.

Examples:
Teacher-Child
Child looks and points: *"Yes, that's a bus. What a big bus!"*

"That sure was a funny story. It made you laugh. You didn't know what the clown would do next! You like surprises, don't you?"

"You didn't think you could do that, and now look how well you did."

"Wow. That was a hard one. I had to think hard about that one too."

(continued)

Table 2.1 Continued

---

5. **Task Regulation**

Elaboration: The most important aspect here is to help the child consider if a plan is needed and to make that plan, as well as to consider what the best strategy might be. All plans and strategies should be evaluated. This also involves giving a basic principle of task solution when appropriate.

Examples:
Teacher-Child

"Well, there sure is a lot to do here. I think we need a plan. Shall we do the easy things first, and then take our time with the hard ones?"

"You know, if you make the bottom really wide, then you can make a really tall tower, and it won't fall down."

6. **Praise and Encouragement**

Elaboration: In addition to offering praise and making encouraging remarks, the mediator needs to offer specific information about what seemed to work or not work about the child's approach to the activity.

Examples:
Teacher-Child

"Oh, yes. I really like that. And I especially liked the way you held your crayon when you did that. Your lines are so straight now."

"Did you see how you made a mistake when you tried to talk and work at the same time? You do much better when you wait to talk."

Note: These are merely examples and should not be considered scripts to follow. Mediators are encouraged to come up with their own examples based on the basic ideas conveyed here.

dency to change the way behaviors are scored over time, is a threat also to validity because validity depends on the adequacy of the behavior sampled. Goodwin and Driscoll (1980) noted disadvantages of observation in terms of high cost of time and training, noting that a great deal of the value depends on the adequacy of the system employed for observation. Others cited the potential for observer effects on the behavior of those observed, although the direction and nature of these effects are not always clear (Lipinski & Nelson, 1974); and in the case of young children, it is generally agreed that these effects are minimized.

Observation is obviously a strong approach for detecting what is observable. It is obviously not the best for recording intraindividual or historical events that may impact the behaviors observed, although hypotheses may be generated. Any observation requires interpretation, as the meaning of any context may not be apparent to the observer. Observation is only as good as the observer and the system for recording events. If important information is missed, conclusions and interpretations will be obstructed.

To overcome these limitations, it is necessary for assessors to receive adequate training and to become aware of and address their biases. When conducting an observation, intrusiveness needs to be minimized, and observees should be debriefed regarding the validity of the situation observed.

Despite these limitations, observation remains the backbone of a good assessment and offers the most contact with reality, requiring the least amount of inferential generalization. So if interview and observation are so great, why don't we stop here? Why do we need all the chapters that follow? I agree with Bronfenbrenner (1989a), who, taking perspective on his own writings and research and on the works of others inspired by his work, concluded, "It would be a mistake to assume . . . that the environment does the job [of development] all by itself, independent of the organism" (p. 198). And so we go on to consider the full, complex palette of all the complex contributions to children's functioning and their assessment.

SUMMARY

This chapter discusses observation as one of the major cornerstones of any assessment. Observation addresses the need to understand the functioning of children within their natural contexts. Issues of observation include the need to reduce inference and maximize interobserver agreement. The four most frequently used approaches for observing the behavior of children—running record, time sampling, event sampling, and rating scales—are discussed. The chapter provides specific guidelines for utilizing an approach that combines running record with time sampling, and this approach is viewed as being the most sensitive to referral issues, along with providing some quantification of the behavioral data. Observation is also a tool for program evaluation, and the ECERS is reviewed as the most frequently used approach for observation of preschool classrooms. Teaching behaviors can be observed and described by using the MLE guidelines for observing teaching interactions. Finally, the chapter discusses the limitations of observation procedures, including issues of observer bias, drift, training costs, observer effects, and restrictions to observable behavior.

SUGGESTED ACTIVITIES

SCHOLARSHIP

Trace and discuss contrasting models of observation and implications regarding their outcomes and applications for children, families, and programs.

APPLICATION

1. Write a description of the classroom environment in which the course is being taught and share the descriptions. This is an exercise to practice descriptive narrative writing, with the goal of capturing the salient elements in an objective, noninferential way.
2. With a partner from the class, observe a young child in an interactive situation and complete Form 2.1. Compare notes and determine interrater agreement.
3. With a partner from the class, observe an instructional situation in a preschool setting and rate the teacher on Form 2.3. Compare the ratings and notes to justify the ratings with your partner. Determine interrater agreement.
4. Using the ECERS, with a partner from the class, complete the ratings of a preschool setting and compare the ratings and conclusions with your partner. Justify your ratings with your notes from your observations and try to come to an agreement. Determine interrater agreement.

Chapter Three

———— ◆ ————

Families, Homes, and Cultural Contexts

———— ◆ ————

Early childhood services are by necessity a collaborative and contextual process (Powell, 1989). The younger the child, the more important it is to view the child within the contexts of the family, culture, and community because the characteristics of these agents of socialization have not yet been internalized (Wilson, 1986). Because students and new professionals are often younger than the parents of their clients and because the emphasis of services to older clients has at times overly highlighted assessment, full collaboration with families can at first appear threatening, particularly if the service provider is not a parent (Mowder, 1994; Widerstrom, Mowder, & Willis, 1989). However, one of the important contributions to models of service delivery by those who have worked in the area of early childhood is development of truly collaborative relationships with the parents of the children who are referred and the recognition of the importance of this relationship. Families have come to expect this, and treatment outcomes depend on it.

In order to work effectively with families, we need to be aware of their beliefs and attitudes, which reflect their cultural and experiential backgrounds, and we need tools for accessing information about family systems and their interactions with the children who are referred for our services. We need to be aware of the impact that a child with special needs can have on the family and how the culturally influenced attitudes and beliefs of family members can affect the family's interactions. These important issues form the topics of this chapter.

THE FAMILY AS A SYSTEM

The first question we must address when a child is referred is, Who is the family? As in any clinical work, we must carefully avoid preconceptions, withhold our own attitudes and beliefs, and merely ask the question without reacting to the response. We need to know both who the legal guardians of the child are and who the primary caregivers are. We need to know other potential sources of influence on the child's development. In other words, we need a map of the child's family system. This map may be verbal and conceptual, or it may be an actual diagram of relationships. Bailey and Simeonsson (1988) described two approaches to visual portrayal of family relationships that can provide a clear picture of the family constellation, as well as of the roles and relationships within this constellation. These include an *eco map,* originally described by Hartman (1978), and Bailey and Simeonsson's detailing of a *genogram.* Another approach to developing an eco map is described by Telzrow et al. (1989), and this approach has been adapted in Figure 3.1.

This figure provides a very succinct summary of the family relationships, as well as the family's networks of support. In this approach, anyone in the family could be placed in the center,

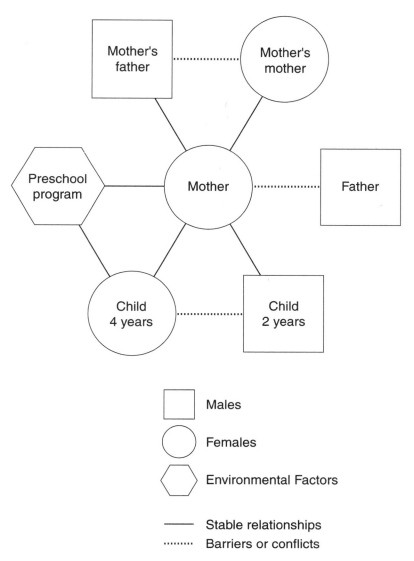

Figure 3.1   Eco Map.
Adapted from Telzrow et al. (1989).

with relationships drawn to indicate supports, barriers, and tenuous relationships. Supports within the immediate, as well as the extended, family can be portrayed, as well as those within the community, as the arms branch outward.

Barnett and Hall (1990) found eco maps useful for identifying figures in the child's life who should be included in assessment and program planning. Using figures such as these also emphasizes the fact that families are systems and that an impact on one impacts all. These figures portray to some degree the structure of the family, but families also have functions and development. The functions are reflected in the genogram, which indicates the roles of the various members. Family development is captured in the stages of the family life model developed by Duval in 1957 (in Robinson, Rosenberg, & Beckman, 1988), including the following:

1. Establishment
2. First parenthood
3. Family of preschoolers
4. Family of school-age children
5. Family of adolescents
6. Family as launching center
7. Family in middle years
8. Family in retirement

Although contemporary families rarely follow so neat a path, such a listing at least represents the idea that families develop, just as the individuals within the family develop, and that each of the stages of development has its themes and challenges.

PARENTING A CHILD WITH SPECIAL NEEDS

Children may not come with instructions, but most parents have experiences with their own parents or caregivers to provide some model for how to raise their children. Few parents who have a child with a disability have such models. Parents certainly did not plan for such a child (with the exception of those who knowingly adopt a child with special needs), and they most likely did not include the challenges of raising such a child in their fantasies of parenting. Therefore, when parents are informed or discover that their child has a disability, they need to process this information and adjust their perceptions, expectations, and attitudes. How this is done is very much related to cultural background, the nature and extent of the disabling condition, and the personality characteristics of the parents (Davis, Stroud, & Green, 1988; Seligman & Darling, 1989), but each individual must find her or his own way to deal with this situation. Seligman and Darling pointed out the controversy regarding the existence of stages in parents' adjustment to the discovery that their child has a disability, suggesting that the reactions may not be sequential, may be ongoing, or may reoccur. Typical reactions would include shock, denial, sadness, anger, anxiety, and, in the best scenario, eventual adaptation and reorganization. There may be feelings of guilt as well, related to the appearance and degree of disability of the child; this guilt may reflect the parents' experience of negative feelings; parents are "supposed" to love their children. As the children move to different levels of development, the array of emotions in the parents may be rekindled in relation to the expectations that the parents may have for their children and the increasing realization of what the future may hold for them.

For young children, the consequences of the parents' reactions to the disability are likely to have an effect on the process of attachment, particularly if the primary caregiver experiences depression and other negative reactions that result in emotional distancing of the parent from the child. If the disability affects the child's ability to respond to the parent, then the consequences for attachment place the relationship at an even higher level of risk.

Reactions to having a child with a disability not only are influenced by the cultural contexts of the family but also serve to influence the families' interactions within these contexts. These are now parents with a "special" child, and this will elicit reactions from various encounters of the family with others in their community and certainly within their family, not the least of which are the other children in the family. The family is launched on a journey that it could never have anticipated. Family members will deal with agencies and professional services that they may never have known existed, and they will need to become knowledgeable about procedures and laws of which they were previously unaware.

Access to parents with similar experience can be a very effective intervention for these parents, but each parent has to know when he or she is ready to acknowledge the child's disability and discuss it with others. Being in touch with other parents is helpful not only for providing a sympathetic and empathic forum for sharing concerns but also—and perhaps even more important—for obtaining information about resources. Caregivers who have good support systems tend to do better (Hauser-Cram, Warfield, Shonkoff, & Krauss, 2001), and involvement in intervention programs can be helpful both in relieving the parents of some of the burden of educating their child and in putting them in touch with people and community resources to help them create a network of support.

Having a child with a disability can affect the quality and quantity of interactions between caregivers and their children (Hodapp, 1988; Marfo & Kysela, 1988). Mothers have been the focus of most studies, and there is a pattern for mothers of children with disabilities to be more directive. Marfo and Kysela documented more visual contact and more directive instruction between these dyads. While early interpretations of findings such as this were initially negative, researchers now recognize that the differences in interactions between caregivers of children with and without disabilities can be a positive adaptation, responsive to the needs of the child. When there is a systematic pattern across different types of parents, it is likely that the behaviors represent some adaptive responsiveness to the cues of the situation, and caregivers who spend prolonged and intensive time with their children have no doubt learned how to adjust their behavior to elicit and maximize the responsiveness of the child to their efforts. Responsiveness of the partner in any dyad is extremely powerful, and caregivers can teach program personnel important lessons about how they have maximized the responsiveness of their children.

However, it is also useful to consider the potential effects of caregiver interactions on the development of the child so that interventions can be devised to enhance the child's development. For example, in the M. A. Fischer (1988) study of mothers' linguistic interactions with their children with Down syndrome, the mothers tended to be less responsive to the bids for social communication of their nonhandicapped child, which forced the child to make revisions; by being more responsive to the bids of the child with Down syndrome, the child was not required to adjust his behavior to improve the effectiveness of these communications. When the mothers were trained to reduce their responsiveness, the children improved their initiations of social signals. This represents an instance when an adaptation to the child's needs can be counterproductive and may be increasing the handicapping consequences of the disability.

CULTURAL ISSUES

The family may be the most important context for the child, but the culture and community provide the contexts for the family. Families are cultural mediators, and if we are to understand the child, we need to understand these sources of influence (Meller, Ohr, & Marcus, 2001; Mosley-Howard, 1995; Roopnarine & Carter, 1992). If we are to offer services to the child and family, we need to be sensitive to these factors (Okagaki & Diamond, 2000).

Geertz (in Mosley-Howard, 1995) offered a particularly cogent definition of culture as a "historically transmitted pattern of meaning" (p. 337). This definition appropriately connects meaning and perception, as the meanings conveyed by culture determine how we perceive and interpret our experiences. Nevertheless, despite the depth of these experiences and influences, individuals are adaptable and can make changes to fit comfortably within new cultures, or even develop ways of living their lives biculturally. E. W. Lynch (1998) enumerated three important generalizations about culture:

1. *Culture is not static.* . . .
2. *Culture, language, ethnicity and race are not the only determinants of one's values, beliefs and behaviors.* . . .
3. *In describing any culture or cultural practice, within-group differences are as great as across-group differences. (p. 27)*

We sometimes need these reminders because it is easy to lapse into stereotypes when we discuss cultural issues and because it is necessary to be aware of cultural contexts. The position paper of the National Association for the Education of Young Children regarding how to respond to issues of cultural and linguistic diversity (Appendix D) and the guidelines developed by the Task Force on the Delivery of Services to Ethnic Minority Populations of the American Psychological Association (1993) provide detailed suggestions about how to address cultural issues while providing professional services.

Ogbu (1988) discussed the differences between voluntary and involuntary minority groups, between those who came to the United States to seek economic improvement or religious freedom and those who were either brought into the country by force or whose cultures were conquered. In the case of voluntary minorities, there may a greater willingness to adopt to the culture and to develop the prerequisite competencies for success in the culture, whereas individuals from involuntary minority groups may adopt styles of coping that are in opposition to the mainstream, such as dress or language codes that alienate them from the majority.

Culture may induce gaps between people, but it is possible to communicate across these gaps and to develop cross-cultural competence. E. W. Lynch (1998) defined cross-cultural competence as "the ability to think, feel, and act, in ways that acknowledge, respect, and build upon ethnic, [socio-]cultural, and linguistic diversity" (p. 49). Lynch went on to suggest that development of cross-cultural competence begins with self-awareness, including awareness of our own roots, values, beliefs, and attitudes. Cross-cultural competence does not mean dressing or speaking in a way that imitates another culture. There is no way to do so without appearing caricatural, and such superficial imitation does not convey respect; however, it is important to learn as much as possible about the cultural backgrounds of the clients with whom we work; to learn as much of the language as possible; and, most of all, to access cultural mediators for information, interpretation, and guidance regarding behaviors that will help to cross boundaries as well as avoid unintentional insults. We need information about how to address the adults, about whom to include in our consultations, and about how to behave during moments of greeting and communication. For example, when I worked in a community of very orthodox Jews, I had to learn to refrain from offering to shake the hands of the men because I did not know which men would shake my hand and which would find this offensive; therefore, I just waited until a hand was offered to me (or not). When the assessor has not had the opportunity to become informed about the cultural practices of the family, the best approach is to state this openly and invite the family to educate the assessor regarding the relevant issues.

CONDUCTING A FAMILY INTERVIEW

It is particularly important during the initial phases of assessment not only to gather information about the child but to consider the family as well. Bailey and Simeonsson's (1988) book is particularly helpful, and it contains forms and formats to facilitate the process. They list five domains of importance for this process:

1. The child's needs and characteristics that are likely to affect the family's functioning (e.g., developmental delays, communication barriers)
2. Parent-child interactions (e.g., methods of discipline, opportunities for interaction)
3. Family needs (e.g., information regarding services available, learning to read or master English)
4. Critical events (e.g., circumstances of immigration, losses and stresses within the family)
5. Family strengths (e.g., resources and supports within the immediate and extended family)

We also need to know the family's goals and priorities, and E. W. Lynch (1998) adds the need to gather information about the family's structure and arrangements for caregiving; knowledge of the family's child-rearing practices, including family sleeping patterns; and the family's perceptions about disability, health and healing, and help seeking and intervention. This type of information helps with the development of appropriate planning for services to the child and family.

The sources of data for these domains come from tests, observations, interviews, and rating forms. The Bailey and Simeonsson (1988) book has a useful form for eliciting family needs. Their child observation form covers developmentally referenced assessment and has a section for family supports and needs, and this chapter offers my own procedure for assessment of caregiver-child interactions. Readers may also find the Parenting Stress Index (Abidin, 1995) a useful instrument, and Trivette, Dunst, Deal, Hamer, and Propst (1990) described several family strength scales. For children between the ages of birth to 3 years, the information from these sources facilitates the development of the Individualized Family Service Plan (IFSP; Johnson, McGonigel, & Kaufmann, 1989), which is required for provision of early intervention services. For service provision to preschool children (ages 3 to 5), there is no formal IFSP (although there is an Individual Education Plan for the child), but the idea of a family service plan is very useful for continuity with early intervention and for reminding service providers of the need to address family issues.

There are very few choices of procedures that guide assessment of home variables. The Home Observation for Measurement of the Environment (HOME; Caldwell & Bradley, 1978) is widely used and has a considerable research history. It can be helpful for guiding observa-

tions during home visits and has the advantage of being norm based, with demonstrated reliability and validity. Administration of the HOME requires training. The Home Screening Questionnaire (Coons, Gay, Fandal, Ker, & Frankenburg, 1981) taps variables similar to those in the
HOME, with which it has a high correlation, and does not require a home visit. However, the
information from these measures may not have equal predictive validity across racial and ethnic groups (Mariner, Zaslow, & Sugland, 1998); therefore, assessors must be careful about interpretations when using these measures with families other than those for whom research information is available. Assessors should interpret the resulting information in the context of the
individuals from the specific group to which it will be applied.

When working with individuals from non-English-speaking backgrounds, assessors often
rely on interpreters. At times, a family member may serve as an interpreter, but this can present problems because that person is unlikely to have been trained in the techniques of interpretation. For example, I had an experience in which the interpreter clearly omitted some information and added her own interpretations to what the family member communicated. In
addition to issues of confidentiality, there are issues of familiarity with the vocabulary, as well
as tendencies to filter information and to editorialize on the content being discussed. It is important for assessors to work with a professional interpreter to discuss the necessity for confidentiality, to familiarize the interpreter with the ideas and vocabulary for the ideas that will be
discussed (particularly if it involves test interpretation), and to caution against nonliteral interpretation. Although it is helpful for interpreters to give explanations as an elaboration on
their interpretations to enhance the assessor's understanding of the cultural context of the remarks, it is not helpful if they edit or change in any way what was said by any of the parties. In
general, it is preferred to work with a professional, but when this is not possible, an alternative
less formal arrangement will need to be accepted, along with the assessor's attempts to prepare
the individual who will interpret.

E. W. Lynch (1998) noted that when working through interpreters, it is important to speak
and look directly at the family members and not at the interpreter. Although it is ideal to have
the involvement of bilingual staff members, as well as to be bilingual oneself, this, too, is not
free of issues. Within each culture there are perceptions of caste so that the professional, even
if speaking the same language, is not necessarily perceived as existing within the same cultural
frame of reference as the family members. In addition, there is great diversity within any sub-
group, so that to be viewed as Latino, for example, can mean so many different things, not the
least of which is the family's country of origin, ranging from Europe, to Central America, to
South America, to the United States. The implication is that although it is helpful to be able
to communicate in the same language as the family members, there are still a number of other
issues of cultural boundaries that may not have been crossed or even understood. For example,
when I worked as a director of a regional team providing services to a number of widely diverse preschool centers, I assigned a Spanish-speaking psychologist to work with the centers
that had the highest proportion of Spanish-speaking children and families. He informed me
that he was having some difficulty being accepted by the families because he was from a country with a background very different from theirs. He also told me that in order to build rapport with the families, he would have to spend some time socializing and schmoozing with
them before working with their children in an assessment mode. Well, perhaps he just wanted
to spend some time "hanging out," but it is true that in many cultures it is necessary to engage
in a period of informal conversation and socialization to build trust before getting down to
business.

CAREGIVER-CHILD INTERACTIONS

Although all of the factors we have discussed so far are important to the child's development, they are distal influences. These factors impact the child's development through the interactions that take place within these environments; these are the proximal influences. We now know a great deal about the outcomes of a variety of interactions at least within our own culture. We are relatively ignorant about these interactions and their effects within other cultures, so the approach described here to assessment of caregiver-child interactions must be viewed within the constraints of the culture within which it was developed, and we must be very careful about generalizations.

Early childhood is a time of particular sensitivity to the effects of caregiver-child interactions (Pianta, 1997). As I discuss in Chapter 9, early childhood is a time of rapid development of executive functions, and caregiver-child interactions impact the development of these functions, with important consequences for the child's development of self-regulation. Hauser-Cram et al. (2001), in their longitudinal study of 183 children with a variety of disabilities, found that the child's self-regulatory processes and mother-child interactions when the child was 3 years old were the key predictors of both child outcome and parent well-being when the child reached 10 years. These interactions are in turn mediated by the cultural contexts of the family as they influence the caregiver's values, attitudes, and beliefs. However, within our culture there is a tendency for a positive association between educational level and the attitudes, values, and beliefs of caregivers that in turn influence their interactive behaviors with their children, so that as educational level increases, these beliefs, attitudes, and values become more homogeneous across individuals and groups (e.g., Zambrana-Ortiz & Lidz, 1995).

Even though assessment of caregiver-child interactions has been recommended by major sources of influence regarding early childhood practices, there remains sufficient controversy about this source of assessment information to warrant some caveats (Mahoney, Spiker, & Boyce, 1996). Caregivers are usually more comfortable with submitting their children to assessment procedures than with submitting themselves. Direct exploration of the contribution of caregivers to the functioning of their children may elicit defensive reactions, and it is especially important, when using these procedures, to do so on a foundation of trust and with positive intentions. Engaging in observation of caregiver-child interactions is justified within the context of attempts to understand the nature of the child's experiences within the home, to contribute to determination of the repertory of caregiver strengths and needs, to elicit child behaviors that are not otherwise accessible to the evaluator, and to provide an opportunity for the caregivers to teach the service providers about their child. Assessment of caregiver-child interaction in my experience is one of the most valuable and informative sources of information that can be derived from the assessment process. Once I began including it in my repertory, I wondered how I ever managed without it.

Although interview and completion of self-report measures offer interesting and valuable information, there is nothing like direct observation for tapping the full complexity of human behavior (Miller & Hauser, in Grotevant & Carlson, 1989). However, because of this complexity, guidelines are needed to filter and organize the information, and the rating scale described by Miller and Hauser offers such a map. This map represents a point of view and theory that selects behaviors to observe as well as speculation regarding the potential outcomes of these behaviors.

As is the case with any observation, the caregiver must make efforts to reduce self-consciousness and anxiety and to induce trust and spontaneity of the individuals who will be observed. Interactions should be videotaped, if possible, to allow for more reliable scoring, as well as availability for feedback review with the caregivers and for documentation of change in response to program interventions (Farran, Clark, & Ray, 1990). In my experience, caregivers can quickly adapt to the presence of a camera if the assessor is clearly comfortable with its use and convinced of its importance. (Be aware that caregivers should sign a form granting permission to be videotaped if the tape is to be used for training and professional purposes.) I usually joke with the caregiver to try to "interact as normally as you can with your child with the camera staring at you and me sitting here writing notes." The importance of rapport and trust with this assessment approach cannot be overstated. An important contributor to this trust is the assessor's conviction that this observation is critical information that will be useful to the caregiver and to the development of an appropriate program for the child. However, videotaping is more important for training and research than for practice.

The good news about observing caregiver-child interactions with young children is that the children cannot help but be spontaneous, and this almost inevitably draws out spontaneous and representative behaviors from the adults. Nevertheless, it is always advisable to debrief the caregiver following the interaction to discuss how it felt and how typical the interaction was.

Although there are a number of approaches that have been developed to guide observation of caregiver-child interactions, most of these are appropriate for children under the age of 3, involve complex coding systems, and are not easily accessible because none of them has been published by a mainstream test distributor (Farran et al., 1990; Munson & Odom, 1996). The approach discussed in this chapter first appeared in Lidz (1991b) and is called the Mediated Learning Experience Rating Scale (MLERS). It primarily reflects the work of Feuerstein and his colleagues (e.g., Feuerstein et al., 1979), who have developed an elaborate theory that includes the issue of identifying the potent variables within adult-child interactions that promote the development of higher mental processing in the child. In the previous chapter I referred to the components of MLE and looked at teacher-child interactions, and these ideas are revisited in the discussion of dynamic assessment in Chapter 6, where the components of MLE will describe the assessor's interactions with the child. In the present chapter the full and original scale is offered (see Form 3.1), as well as the research that has been accomplished with it to date. There is also a form that can be given directly to parents that reframes the same components in a more accessible format; the parent edition (see Form 3.2) can be used for education and training programs focusing on teaching mediational approaches to caregivers.

Prior to designing the scale, I reviewed the research literature to confirm the most important characteristics of adult interactions with children that related to their cognitive, as well as social-affective, development (Lidz, 1991b). This search confirmed the importance of most of the components discussed by Feuerstein (others were not refuted, but not as well documented) and led to the addition of two (affective involvement and contingent responsivity, defined later) and to some minor changes and reframing of Feuerstein's original concepts.

The MLERS represents a description of the mediational repertoire of the adult in interaction with a young child. It is a modified operationalization of Feuerstein's conceptualization of MLE. MLEs are those behaviors that promote four outcomes in the child: active learning, self-regulation, strategic problem solving, and representational thinking. These outcomes reflect the values and attitudes of so-called Western cultures. The underlying assumption of applying this scale is that there will be a positive relationship between MLE and the development of the four outcomes in the child. Therefore, to a significant extent, as with other assessment tools,

Mediated Learning Experience Rating Scale

(for use with parent/child, teacher/child/examiner/child interactions with preschool children)
(based on Feuerstein et al., 1979, 1980)

Child: _____ Mediator: _____ Task: _____
Rater: _____ Date: _____ Location: _____

1. INTENTIONALITY: a conscious attempt by the mediator to influence the behavior of the child. This includes communication to the child of the purpose for the interaction, as well as attempts by the mediator to maintain the child's involvement in the interaction. For children who are already self-regulating and do not require interventions by the mediator to engage them in the activity, rating of intentionality includes the readiness of the mediator to become involved as necessary; therefore, the mediator shows ongoing interest in the active involvement of the child (Assign 2 in this case).

   0 = no evidence
   1 = inconsistently present; loses involvement
   2 = consistently in evidence
   3 = in evidence with statement or encouragement of a principle to induce self-regulation in the child; this principle would apply to the child's ability to maintain attention and inhibit impulsivity.

   NOTES:

2. MEANING: moving the content from neutral to a position of value and importance; this may be done by affective emphasis, gesture, movement of the materials, or by stating that the object or aspect of focus is important and should be noticed (or vice versa, that it is negative and to be ignored or avoided).

   0 = not in evidence
   1 = calling up labels or concepts already within the child's repertoire; saying that it is important and should be noticed (e.g., "look at this"), but without elaboration.
   2 = adding animation or affect to make the activity come alive and provoke interest.
   3 = elaboration that expands the information about the activity or object or that provides information about the cultural meaning or relevance.

   NOTES:

Form 3.1

3. TRANSCENDENCE: promotion of cognitive bridges between the task or activity and related but not currently present experiences of the child; these may refer to the past or may anticipate the future. This must promote visual images and help to move the child from the perceptual to the conceptual, that is, to what the child can not now see.

   0 = not in evidence
   1 = simple, non elaborated reference to past or future experience
   2 = elaborated reference
   3 = elaborated reference includes hypothetical, inferential, or cause/effect thinking

   NOTES:

4. JOINT REGARD: looking and/or commenting on an object of focus initiated by the child; this also includes trying (figuratively or literally) to "see" the activity from the child's point of view, for example, changing posture or making a comment to express empathy and state a feeling or thought that the child might be experiencing. Finally, this also includes statements expressing the "we-ness" of the experience, as in using the term "let's . . .", for example: "wow; that was really hard; we had to work a long time to figure that one out!"

   0 = not in evidence
   1 = clear occurrence, but unelaborated reference
   2 = simple elaboration
   3 = helping the child express a thought that the child was otherwise unable to elaborate; the expression of the thought should appear to be an accurate reflection of the child's thinking or feeling.

   NOTES:

5. SHARING OF EXPERIENCE/THOUGHT: communication to the child of an experience or thought the mediator had that the child had not previously shared or experienced with the mediator. For example, comments including "when I was a little girl . . .", or "this makes me think of. . . ." This should relate to the activity being shared.

   0 = not in evidence
   1 = clear, but non elaborated reference
   2 = elaborated reference
   3 = elaborated reference includes hypothetical, cause/effect, or inferential thinking

   NOTES:

Form 3.1 (*continued*)

6. TASK REGULATION: promoting competence through manipulation of the task to facilitate mastery by the child.

    0 = not in evidence

    1 = simple directions or passive manipulation of the task, e.g., holding it, moving pieces toward the child.

    2 = elaborated directions or nonverbal organization into a kind of conceptual grouping.

    3 = induction/statement/encouragement of strategic thinking and a planful attitude, e.g., "where shall we start?" "what should we do first?" The mediator can be rated a (3) also if there is statement of a principle that the child can use to solve similar problems.

NOTES:

7. PRAISE/ENCOURAGEMENT: promoting competence through verbal or nonverbal communication to the child that s/he did a good job. (Deduct one point for negative, put-down remarks, i.e., one total point for each remark.)

    0 = not in evidence

    1 = occasional display of nonverbal touch/hug; occasional statement of good, fine, right . . .

    2 = frequent displays of nonverbal touch/hug or frequent statements of good, fine, right . . . (frequent = three or more) (two points are also given if the mediator provides encouraging remarks in an attempt to help preserve the child's self-esteem, even if these are not clear praise).

    3 = occasional or frequent praise includes information about the child's performance that seemed to help the child, e.g., "you really looked at all the choices; that was great!"

NOTES:

8. CREATING A CHALLENGE ZONE: (for application to teachers and assessors; may be omitted for parents for short interactions). Promoting competence through creating a challenge zone involves maintenance of the activity or task within the child's "zone of proximal [or next] development," i.e., neither too high nor too low for the child's ability to deal with the task demands; the child should be challenged to reach beyond the current level of functioning, but not so overwhelmed as to be discouraged from attempts to engage in the task.

    0 = not in evidence or activity is overly frustrating or much too below the level of challenge

    1 = some success in accurate maintenance within the child's range; inconsistently maintained.

Form 3.1 (*continued*)

2 = generally successful; more in evidence than not.

3 = general success includes articulation to the child the principle that was involved, e.g., stating that "you really had to think and work hard on this, but you were able to do it with only a little help!" or "I want to make this a little hard for you so you have to think; but I'll give you some help so you will know what to do."

NOTES:

9. PSYCHOLOGICAL DIFFERENTIATION: maintenance of the idea that the role of the mediator is to facilitate the learning of the child, not to have a learning experience for oneself (at this time). Thus, there would be no indications of competitiveness with the child or of rejection of the child's efforts to engage in the task. The focus of the mediator is on provision of a good learning experience rather than on creation of a good product; if something has to be sacrificed, it is the end product, not the child's experience. (1 point is deducted if the mediator rejects the child's efforts to become involved).

    0 = not in evidence; mediator poorly differentiated
    1 = activity is mostly mediator's; only occasionally the child's
    2 = activity is mostly child's, with only occasional lapses by the mediator
    3 = activity is clearly and consistently child's, with mediator maintaining an objective facilitating role.

NOTES:

10. CONTINGENT RESPONSIVITY: ability to read the child's cues and signals related to learning, affective, and motivational needs, and then respond in a timely and appropriate way.

    0 = not in evidence
    1 = infrequent, inconsistent (ill-timed or not appropriate)
    2 = present, but occasionally misses the mark either in timing or in appropriateness
    3 = consistently well timed and appropriate to child's cues and signals

NOTES:

11. AFFECTIVE INVOLVEMENT: communication of a sense of caring about and enjoyment of the child; this may be overt or more quietly covert, but it should be clear that there is a feeling of joy in the child's presence with signs of emotional attachment. This would appear more strongly in a parent compared to teacher or examiner, but should be in evidence in any of the mediators.

Form 3.1 (*continued*)

0 = not in evidence; indifferent; may be negative
1 = minimal evidence; neutral but not negative or indifferent
2 = clear evidence; may have lapses
3 = clear and consistent enjoyment

NOTES:

12. CHANGE (for application to teachers and assessors): communication to the child that s/he has profited in a positive direction from the experience, that s/he has improved and changed in some way compared to the starting point. This includes providing the child with actual pre/post product comparisons, as well as pre/post behavioral descriptions.

0 = not in evidence
1 = weak evidence
2 = strong, but unelaborated evidence
3 = strong indications include elaborated feedback regarding what the child did and what the changes were; these might include elicitations from the child regarding what s/he notices has changed.

NOTES:

SCORE SEPARATELY AND DO NOT INCLUDE IN MLE TOTAL, BUT INCLUDE FOR ALL ACTIVITIES:

RECIPROCITY OF CHILD:* the level of receptivity of the child to the mediational interactions with the adult; how open is the child to input from the mediator? how able or willing to "receive" or cooperate?

0 = highly resistant; cannot effectively proceed
1 = minimally receptive; frequent resistance
2 = moderately receptive; occasional lapses
3 = consistently receptive and cooperative

NOTES:

* A separate Reciprocity Scale is available in "research" format and included in this text. Researchers who are interested in contributing to the development of this scale may contact the author at zdilsc@aol.com

Form 3.1 (*continued*)

PROFILE OF MEDIATOR FUNCTIONING ON THE
MEDIATED LEARNING EXPERIENCE RATING SCALE

	3	2	1	0
1. Intentionality				
2. Meaning				
3. Transcendence				
4. Joint Regard				
5. Sharing of Experiences				
6. Task Regulation				
7. Praise/Encouragement				
8. Challenge				
9. Psychological Differentiation				
10. Contingent Responsivity				
11. Affective Involvement				
12. Change				

Child's Responsivity:

Summary:

Form 3.1 (*continued*)

Mediated Learning Experience Rating Scale–Parent (Self-Rating) Edition

(recommended for use with Parent Training Program for videotaped interactions in collaboration with program leader)
(based on Feuerstein et al., 1979, 1980)

Parents do many things to help children learn. Here is a list of many of these things that most parents do that help children develop good thinking and self-control. After viewing your interaction with your child, how do you think you did? (Please keep in mind that just as every meal doesn't have to include all of the vitamins in existence, every interaction need not include each of these behaviors!)

Name: _____ Child: _____ Date: _____
Task: _____ Scale: _____

4	3	2	1
yes, definitely	yes, but needs work	well, a little	no, not yet

1. **INTENT:**
   MESSAGE: This is what I want you to do; let me help you pay attention so you can do this.
   DID YOU
   a. give a clear message of what you want?   4 3 2 1
   b. help your child develop SELF-control?   4 3 2 1
   NOTES:

2. **MEANING:**
   MESSAGE: Let me help you notice and learn what is important and valuable to know.
   DID YOU
   a. let your child know by your tone of voice or what you said what is important to notice about what you were doing together?   4 3 2 1
   b. give your child some new information (beyond name or label) about what you were doing?   4 3 2 1
   NOTES:

Form 3.2

3. **BRIDGING:**

   MESSAGE: This experience is not only meaningful now, but it relates to other things you have done before or that you will do in the future. This is not an isolated event.

   DID YOU

   a. relate what the child is doing to something the child did before?   4 3 2 1

   b. relate what the child is doing now to something that will happen in the future?   4 3 2 1

   c. help the child think in cause/effect or what-if, if/then ideas?   4 3 2 1

   NOTES:

4. **JOINT REGARD:**

   MESSAGE: we are having a learning experience together and I understand you as a learner.

   DID YOU

   a. look at and comment on what your child showed you s/he is interested in?   4 3 2 1

   b. make a statement to show you understand how your child is feeling or what your child is thinking?   4 3 2 1

   NOTES:

5. **TASK REGULATION:**

   MESSAGE: You are competent and able to learn this. I will find a way to help you learn it.

   DID YOU

   a. give a clear, simple direction?   4 3 2 1

   b. make adjustments in the materials to help your child succeed?   4 3 2 1

   c. tell or show some general problem-solving principle that can be applied to other situations also?   4 3 2 1

   d. give the idea of proceeding according to a plan, or using some strategy?   4 3 2 1

   NOTES:

6. **PRAISE/ENCOURAGEMENT:**

   MESSAGE: I appreciate you and am aware that you can learn.

   DID YOU

   a. praise your child by word or gesture?   4 3 2 1

   b. tell your child what it was that was so good?   4 3 2 1

   NOTES:

Form 3.2 (*continued*)

7. **CHALLENGE:**
MESSAGE: I want you to reach beyond what you already know; stretch yourself. I will help you do this by keeping the task just ahead, but not too far beyond you.
DID YOU
a. keep the task and your requests within the "challenge range" of your child?   4   3   2   1
NOTES:

8. **PSYCHOLOGICAL DIFFERENTIATION:**
MESSAGE: I am here to help you, not for me.
DID YOU
a. keep yourself in the role of helper/teacher?   4   3   2   1
NOTES:

9. **CONTINGENT RESPONSIVITY:**
MESSAGE: I will notice and respond promptly to your cues and signals to help you have a good learning experience.
DID YOU
a. accurately read your child's cues and signals?   4   3   2   1
b. promptly respond to your child's cues?   4   3   2   1
NOTES:

10. **AFFECTIVE INVOLVEMENT:**
MESSAGE: I love you and enjoy being with you and care about your having a good experience.
DID YOU
a. communicate feelings of joy and affection?   4   3   2   1
b. have fun?   4   3   2   1
NOTES:

SUMMARY

I am doing just fine with:

I need just a little attention to:

I REALLY need to work on:

Some ideas:

Lidz, Carol S. *Early Childhood Assessment.* Copyright 2003, John Wiley & Sons.

Form 3.2 (*continued*)

this scale is also a measure of acculturation when applied with caregivers from non-Western or nonmainstream backgrounds.

The rating scale format was chosen because of the several advantages of this approach. Rating scales are generally easy to use, quick to administer, and easy to score, and they show better predictive validity and are at least as stable as coding systems (Munson & Odom, 1996). The disadvantages of rating scales include their subjectivity and susceptibility to the *halo effect* (the tendency to apply a general impression of goodness to all of the items) and, conversely, the *negative halo effect* (applying a generally negative impression to all of the items), both of which can be addressed in the design but need to be kept in mind during both training and application. The types of behaviors being observed through the MLERS lenses are considered molar or categorical rather than micro or specific, with the intent of trying to capture generalizable interactions.

THE COMPONENTS OF MEDIATED LEARNING EXPERIENCES

Following are the 12 components of the MLERS, defined in terms of their optimal occurrence, as represented within the context of optimal MLE:

1. *Intent:* This component involves the mediator's ability to engage the child in the interaction, as well as to maintain the child's involvement in the interaction. This includes giving the child a clear message of the mediator's intent to interact. The process that is addressed in the child is primarily attention, and the communication to the child should concern the child's ability to self-regulate. Therefore, if the child loses attention, the mediator should communicate in a way to promote self-regulation—for example, "I think we need to move you a little closer to the table" or "I think you pay attention better when there are fewer things to look at; let's take some of these away." Telling the child just to "pay attention" or "look at this" warrants a rating of 2, not 3, as it does not give the child the tools for future self-regulation.

2. *Meaning:* This involves reference to the aspects of the task and situation that are perceptible and tangible and the mediator's ability to highlight and move these from neutral to awareness. The process addressed within the child is primarily perception. The mediator communicates what is important to notice, gives it meaning (good or bad), and uses voice, gesture, and affective expression for this highlighting. For example, the mediator may say, "This is important" or "Look at this—how blue, how round, how jagged, and so on," may dance a piece around the table, or may point a finger or use voice modulation, all in the service of enhancing the meaning of the object and making the child more aware of what to notice about it. At an optimal level, the mediator goes beyond labeling or simple enhancement to more elaborated information about what to notice, for example, "See how this part of the Lego sticks out; that helps the pieces stick together so they won't fall over."

3. *Transcendence:* This component moves the child's thinking from perception into conceptualization; it is the mediator's ability to provide a bridge from what can be seen, felt, and heard in the situation to what can only be mentally conceived. This involves references to the past and to the future, as well as to higher levels of thought involving cause-effect and if-then hypothetical thinking. The mediator may remind the child of something or someone in the child's experience that relates to what the child is doing ("Isn't this like the one you have at home?" or "Doesn't this make you think of Daddy?"). At the highest level, the

mediator would promote hypothetical or cause-effect thinking, for example, "If we made the roof like this instead of this, how would that be good?"

4. *Task Regulation:* This concerns the actual way the task is presented to the child and involves the instructions that are offered, the way materials are provided, and the manner in which the task is adjusted to promote the child's competence. However, at the highest, optimal level, it would be necessary for the mediator to address the strategies that would be helpful for doing the task (or to suggest proceeding in a planful, strategic manner) or to offer a basic principle of task solution. For example, for block building, the mediator may suggest, "It helps to make the bottom wider if you want to keep the blocks from falling down" or, "Well, how shall we go about this. What should we do first?"

5. *Psychological Differentiation:* This is the "intrusion" factor, and it describes the extent to which the task remains the child's rather than the caregiver's. The focus should be on helping the child to have a good experience or to learn something rather than the product to be made. The question to be asked is, Whose task was this (the mediators or the child's)?

6. *Praise/Encouragement:* There is some controversy regarding the importance or effectiveness of the use of praise while teaching children, but this component refers primarily to the offering of informative feedback to the child about what worked or did not work, and there is strong research support for the importance of this. The mediator would receive a score of 1 or 2 for expressions of praise and encouragement; the mediator would have to provide information feedback to receive a 3—for example, "Wow! You see how well it worked when you made the bottom big like that?!"

7. *Change:* This is a component that may be omitted when the scale is used for caregiver interactions because there often are no opportunities to elicit this; however, inclusion or exclusion is up to the assessor's judgment. It is to be included, however, for dynamic assessment and for teacher-child interactions because there are opportunities within these situations to provide this mediation for the child. Change involves communicating to the child that she or he has successfully learned as a result of this interaction. In the case of teachers or assessors conducting a dynamic assessment, actual before-after products can be reviewed with the child to demonstrate growth and change, or it may involve a statement of what changed and how well the child learned. This provides evidence of the child's increasing competence and helps children develop the feeling that they can learn.

8. *Challenge:* This component refers to the mediator's ability to keep the demands of the interaction within the child's zone of proximal development. This involves keeping language, instructions, and task selection just beyond what the child is able to do independently—not too easy and not too hard. Here, it is important that some challenge be built into the interaction, with invitations for the child to stretch beyond current functioning but adjusted back when the content becomes too frustrating. Challenging children helps them stretch to a higher level of functioning.

9. *Joint Regard:* This involves communication that the interaction is a shared experience and also involves the mediator's ability to see the situation from the child's point of view. Joint regard goes beyond simple use of the word "we" to working with the child to make it a shared experience and offering empathic statements to give voice to what the child may not be able to articulate regarding thoughts or feelings—for example, "You really thought this was going to be too hard, and you were afraid to try it, and now look at how well you did!" or "I'll help you with this; we'll do it together and be partners."

10. *Sharing:* This involves the mediator's sharing his or her thoughts or experiences that relate to what is occurring in the interaction with the child. Sharing should serve the purpose of enhancing the child's knowledge or experience base. Examples include "You know, when I was little, I had one sort of like this, but I had to crank it up and couldn't just push a button" and "That reminds me of a story about a little train engine that kept trying and never gave up. I'll tell it to you one day."

11. *Contingent Responsivity:* This component refers to the nonverbal dance between two participants, specifically, the mediator's ability to respond in a timely and appropriate way to the child. Timing is a very culture-relevant variable, and assessors need to be informed about cultural expectations for the individuals involved. The important thing is to notice the child's response, particularly with regard to degree of responsiveness versus frustration: Does the child have to start whining to get the parent's attention? Does the child withdraw because of lack of responsiveness? Does the parent respond but keep misreading the child's signals? Is the child a poor signal sender and hard to read?

12. *Affective Involvement:* This is the warmth factor and again need not be verbal. This represents the sense or expression of affection that the mediator conveys to the child. This is also a very culture-relevant factor, and assessors must become aware of how emotions are typically expressed within the culture of the child's family. What we look for here is some sense of enjoyment with being with the child, as well as positive affective expression, however subtle, toward to child.

INSTRUCTIONS

The assessment procedure requires a total of 30 min and is set up as follows. The caregiver is asked to interact with the child under three conditions: free play, teaching, and story reading. Beginning with free play also provides an opportunity for warm-up and relaxation for the dyads. For this condition, a standard set of toys, relevant to the child's background, is provided. The caregiver is asked to "play with your child as normally as you can with these toys." These should be about five or six toys that allow for a variety of interactions, such as play dough, a puzzle, a construction toy, crayons and paper, and some dolls. The teaching condition involves a set of Legos, and the caregiver is told to "teach your child to build a house with these Legos." For the reading condition, a small selection of books can be offered, and the caregiver is asked to "read one of these books with your child for a few minutes." Each condition requires 10 min, after which time the materials are removed and those for the next condition are introduced. The assessor completes a fresh MLERS protocol for each condition, scoring each as independently as possible. This allows not only for multiple samples of behavior, but for some judgment regarding the relationship of the nature of the task to the behaviors observed.

While interactions between primary caregivers and the child are the most likely to be included in an assessment, it is also possible to include the child's interactions with other family members, and even to combine interactions such as mother and father or mother and grandmother with the child for additional insight into the family's dynamics (this will obviously elicit interactions well beyond those involved in mediation).

During the course of the interaction, whether videotaped or not, the assessor should record as much description as possible about the nature of the interactions. With the 12 components in mind, it is recommended that the assessor make a running record on the back of the scoring sheet, adding cues for which component the behavior represents. How these components appeared in the mediator's behavior is very important to note, in addition to the child's responsiveness. There is a separate scale for recording child responsiveness to mediation, which is included in Chapter 5. When used for diagnostic purposes, the scale is useful primarily as a description of the interaction, not in the scores it yields. This is not a standardized, normed instrument, and we do not have the information to indicate the extent to which any specific behavior is "good" or "bad." Interpretation reflects our knowledge base regarding child development, particularly regarding what is appropriate for the age and nature of the child's disabilities. The scores allow us to develop a profile of the caregiver's mediational repertoire and to use this profile to compare the caregiver's development across time (in response to intervention), as well as to select targets for intervention.

Before engaging in this assessment procedure, it is very important for assessors to be trained to understand the nature of each component and to develop scoring reliability. Neither of these is very difficult, but they do require investment of at least 6 to 8 hours of formal training. Understanding of the components can be gained from careful reading of the protocol, from reviewing the material in Lidz (1991b), and from any of Feuerstein's publications on his dynamic assessment procedure (e.g., Feuerstein et al., 1979). To promote reliability, videotapes should be made of several caregiver-child interactions (these could involve colleagues), with some used for initial training and others for reliability testing.

SCORING

All of the MLE components are rated for each of the three caregiver-child interactions. That is, the full scale is applied to the free-play situation, to the teaching situation, and to the story situation (three full scales). All 12 components are rated as they apply to each interaction. Each component is rated from 0 (no evidence) to 3 (optimal). It is important to consider each component independently and to present the behavioral evidence in order to avoid positive or negative halo effect. There are some caregivers who just seem good, and it is easy to rate everything they do at a high level, whereas others just seem poor, and everything they do attracts a low rating. It is important to avoid making such overgeneralizations. Everyone has strengths and weaknesses, and the specific situation may not elicit some behaviors from some individuals. The assessor is just to record what is observed, without editing or editorializing. How the scale is interpreted is a separate matter.

INTERPRETATION

As just indicated, the MLERS is not a normed instrument. It is criterion-referenced in relation to the theory of MLE. All of the components together, at their highest level of rating, represent an operational definition of MLE. The extent to which any one component occurs at an optimal level reflects not only the mediator's repertoire but also the nature of the situation and the child's behavior or developmental level. One would expect the occurrence of transcendence, for example, to be very different in relation to a 2-year-old compared with a child of 5. Once a profile is developed, it is also necessary for the assessor to make a judgment about which components warrant selection for intervention. The caregiver may be low in a component that does not appear very critical under the circumstances, such as sharing, compared to the greater need to focus on responsivity and mediation of meaning. Feedback to the caregiver should emphasize strengths, and the experience of being observed and evaluated should be positive and supportive as well as informative (Bailey & Simeonsson, 1988; Farran et al., 1990). Embedding one or two areas of need within a larger context of supportive feedback is the most useful approach.

RESEARCH

There have been five studies involving the MLERS. The first, by Glazier (1986), included 24 African American mothers of 4-year-old Head Start children with low-normal IQ scores and above-average preschool achievement scores. Glazier found that interrater agreement for the components ranged between 50% and 75% for exact agreement and between 92% and 100% for agreement within one point. Internal consistency, as determined by Cronbach's alpha, was .83. The mothers in this study received their highest ratings on the components of intent and lowest ratings on the components of transcendence, praise/encouragement, and meaning. In looking at profiles of high compared with low mediators, the presence of transcendence, praise/ encouragement, and meaning produced the greatest differentiation between the two groups; that is, these components were observable in mothers who received high total ratings and absent or at very low levels in those with low total ratings. Multiple regression showed that IQ plus MLE explained more of the achievement variance than either IQ or MLE considered separately; however, both variables accounted for only a small proportion of the children's achievement levels.

Glazier's second study (Glazier-Robinson, 1990), with 30 Head Start African-American mother-child dyads, utilized an experimental and control group to investigate the feasibility of teaching parents the components of mediated learning. The training of the experimental group involved several steps that included viewing a video explaining each component, followed by provision of examples of each component along with peer coaching, followed by individual feedback regarding videotaped interactions of the mother with her child. Dyads in the control group received no MLE training but were provided with the same experience as the experimental group once the study was completed. In this study, the range of exact interrater agreement was 85% to 93%. There was no evidence of either age or gender effects of the child in the mothers' mediation. This study documented training effects for increased intent, meaning, transcendence, and goal directedness and planning (now represented as task regulation). The parents in this study also showed transfer of their learning from a structured teaching to a free-play situation. Within the short time of the study, it was not possible to demonstrate effects of the mothers' changes on the performance of their children.

Lidz, Bond, and Dissinger (1990) investigated the cross-situational consistency of the MLERS with well-educated Caucasian mothers of normally developing preschool children. These mothers, in contrast to the mothers of low socioeconomic status, received high ratings on the components of transcendence and praise/encouragement, as well as on the component of sharing, which was not observed during the interactions of the previous groups. Internal consistency of the scale determined by Cronbach's alpha was .78, and most of the components were significantly correlated with the total scale score. Interrater agreement (correlation coefficients averaged across the three situations) ranged from .48 to .95, with most exceeding .80. The exception was a very low correlation for intent, which was rated at the highest level for almost all of the participants, so that any disagreement produced a low correlation. The consistency of the mothers' mediation was variable across the three situations of two structured teaching and one free play. Mediation was most consistent, and in all cases significantly intercorrelated, for the components of sharing, praise/encouragement, control (modified in the current version of the scale), contingent responsivity, and affective involvement. That is, these components were least affected by the nature of the task. The components were also correlated with the perceptual-performance subtest score of the McCarthy Scales, yielding a significant positive relationship with transcendence. That is, the children of mothers who received high ratings on transcendence obtained the highest scores on the McCarthy Scales of Children's Abilities.

The fourth study, by Zambrana-Ortiz and Lidz (1995), included 26 dyads of both mothers and fathers (i.e., 26 children interacting at separate times with their mother and father) in both teaching and play situations. These were normally developing 3- to 5-year-olds enrolled in Head Start in Puerto Rico. For both parents' combined scores, ratings on the components of intent and affective involvement were high, whereas ratings on the components of transcendence and praise/encouragement were low. Interrater reliability was estimated by correlation coefficients and ranged from .88 to .99 for total scores and from .43 to 1.00 for components. Internal consistency, estimated by Cronbach's alpha, was .93 for mothers' aggregated scores (.91 for both play and teaching) and .72 for fathers' (.87 for play and .93 for teaching). Internal consistency was also estimated with correlations of each component with the total score, and these were significantly positive in all cases (with the exception of the child's reciprocity, which is separated from the scale).

Because this study also included two situations, teaching and play, there was an opportunity to look at cross-situational consistency. In this study the parents were most consistent within gender groups, that is, mothers teaching compared to mothers playing, and fathers teaching compared to fathers playing. Mothers playing and mothers teaching also correlated significantly, though not as strongly, with fathers teaching; fathers playing did not correlate significantly with any condition except fathers teaching. Cross-situational consistency of the components was moderate but highly significant in all cases for the fathers and, in most cases, for the mothers; exceptions for the mothers included transcendence and contingent responsivity. Ratings for the mothers were higher for transcendence during play, and ratings were higher for the mothers for contingent responsivity during teaching.

The Zambrana-Ortiz and Lidz (1995) study also investigated the criterion validity of the MLERS in relation to the HOME (Caldwell & Bradley, 1978). The results differed for mothers as compared with fathers. For mothers, there were significant relationships between HOME and MLE for the total scores of both measures. Components of psychological differentiation and affective involvement were significantly related to HOME total score; meaning and transcendence were related to the HOME modeling score. For fathers, meaning related to academic stimulation on the HOME, and transcendence related to modeling; both sharing and contingent responsivity related to the HOME score of physical environment.

Of particular interest in the Zambrana-Ortiz and Lidz (1995) study were the relationships between MLERS ratings and demographic variables. In general, mediation was negatively correlated with the number of children in the home and the mothers' ages and positively correlated with mothers' education and fathers' income. This is typical of research results looking at similar variables (Kellaghan, Sloane, Alvarez, & Bloom, 1993).

As this was one of the few studies that did not equate "parent" with "mother" and looked at differences in the mediation of mothers and fathers, these relationships are of interest as well. Mothers and fathers showed differences in their mediation of meaning, transcendence, and praise/encouragement. In most cases, mothers obtained higher ratings on these components. The mediations of mothers and fathers showed differential relationships with the child's functioning in school, as estimated by their teachers' completion of a Spanish version of the Vineland Adaptive Behavior Scales (VABS). Mothers' mediations related most strongly to the Daily Living Skills subtest of the VABS, and these relationships were evident for three components plus the total MLE score. In the case of fathers, only the component of transcendence showed a significant relationship, but in this instance it was with the Peabody Picture Vocabulary Test (Spanish version), as well as with all of the VABS subtests and total score (with the exception of motor). Thus, although mothers received higher scores on the component of transcendence, the fathers' mediation of transcendence correlated with the child variables. This finding of the differential impact of the interactions of each parent is similar to those of Sigel, Stinson, and Flaugher (1991), who found that even though both parents were using what the authors call *distancing strategies* (equivalent to Feuerstein's meaning of transcendence), it was the father's use of these strategies that had the significant relationship with the child's academic achievement.

The fifth study was conducted by Weinblatt in 1993. He rated 32 mothers during the course of play interactions with their 3- to 4-year-old children with mild to moderate disabilities. The ranges of education and income level of the mothers were wide, with most being single and working parents. The types of children's handicaps included speech impairment (over two thirds of the sample), emotional disturbance, mental retardation, learning disability, and autism. This study focused on furthering understanding of mediational interactions between mothers and their children with handicaps and the relationship between their mediations and the development of competence in the children. The mothers were observed in five conditions of interaction, and there was highly significant consistency in the mediation ratings among the five situations, varying from .62 to .86. The components of sharing and change were rarely observed in these interactions. This study documented a significant positive relationship between the mothers' MLE and their children's success in solving the tasks of the study. The MLE components that showed the strongest relationship with the children's success were task regulation, praise/encouragement, challenge, psychological differentiation, and contingent responsivity. There were also significant, though more moderate, correlations between the mothers' mediation ratings and their children's IQ, which is a possible confounding factor, because there was also a significant relationship between IQ and the child's reciprocity. Therefore, mothers were more mediational with children who were more responsive and who had higher IQ scores. In the multiple regression, child reciprocity was the strongest predictor of the child's task performance, followed by the MLE components of task regulation, challenge, and contingent responsivity, which made independent contributions.

The Weinblatt (1993) study also offered some interesting culture-related information. Mothers who were born in the United States and who had higher levels of education obtained higher MLERS scores. In addition, the mothers of the study showed higher levels of mediation with boys than with girls; however, they were more directive in their interactions with the girls.

Not only do these studies generally support the reliability and validity of the MLERS, but they also document the complexity of parent-child relationships. Any interpretations of the data generated by this approach to assessment must be very cautious and mindful of the circumstances of the interactions, as well as of the experiences and perceptions brought to the interaction by the participants. The complexity of these data is a likely reason that many assessors avoid applying these procedures, but such a search for simplicity is at the risk of ignoring or distorting reality.

SOME CONCLUDING THOUGHTS

Individuals and families each have unique stories. As professionals, much of what we learn to do is to listen. However, listening is particularly difficult when we deal with families because our own lives are so embedded within our own histories. We need to work hard to listen to the stories of the families with whom we work, to let them tell their stories, and to listen with as few preconceptions as possible. We then need to use this information to understand their unique contexts and to help them find ways to cope with their challenges.

SUMMARY

This chapter highlights the importance of assessing children's most important context: their families and the interactions that take place within this context. Families have contexts as well, and the beliefs and values that they develop within these contexts affect not only parenting interactions but also attitudes and behaviors toward children with special needs. Suggestions for working with families from diverse cultural backgrounds are reviewed. The chapter provides details of the MLERS as a direct observation tool for assessing caregiver-child interactions that affect children's development, and the research to support the reliability and validity of this procedure is reviewed.

SUGGESTED ACTIVITIES

SCHOLARSHIP

Select a component of mediation and conduct a research literature review of the relationship between this component and children's development.

APPLICATION

1. Informally observe a variety of parents interacting with their preschool children in a variety of spontaneous circumstances, such as on a playground or in a supermarket or restaurant. Describe the interactions and try to fit these within the MLE components. How would you rate them, and what effect do you think these will have on the child's development?
2. Assuming that MLE is a good thing and that parents can be taught to do it, outline a parenting program that would help parents learn to become more mediational.

Chapter Four

---- ♦ ----

Assessment of Play

---- ♦ ----

A frequently used metaphor in discussions about assessment of play is "window" (e.g., Eisert & Lamorey, 1996; Vig, 1997–1998; Vondra & Belsky, 1991). And indeed play does provide a window to all aspects of the child's functioning, including cognitive, social-emotional, fine and gross motor, and language development. Assessment of play is an especially important diagnostic tool for early childhood, and it is difficult to envision a comprehensive assessment of a young child without it.

Our discussion about play assessment highlights the difficulty of dividing the child into domains or functions. Play is so complex, rich, and comprehensive that it virtually straddles all developmental categories and approaches. This chapter extends the discussions of observation in Chapter 2 and parent–child interaction in Chapter 3 and links with the presentation of dynamic assessment in Chapter 6. Play is an activity that the child may do with objects (independently or with peers or adults) or in social interaction with peers. In this chapter we shall discuss the child's play with objects and focus on the information that this yields for informing the assessor about the child's developmental levels. This is justified by the fact that a high proportion of the very young child's experience is in interaction with objects, gradually yielding to increased interpersonal interactions (White, 1973). Object play is most characteristic of the play of children in early preschool years, whereas social and sociodramatic play increases in importance toward the later preschool years. The assessment approach used here begins with taking a running record of all of the child's actions and interactions during the course of the semistructured observation and estimating the levels of function under both independent and facilitated conditions.

RELEVANCE OF PLAY

But first let us pause for some discussion about this fascinating activity. What is play, and why do we care about it as an assessment focus? On one thing we can all agree: Play is what young children do. They do not require pleading to embark on it. They do not require reinforcement to continue it. And they may even need firmness and contingencies to terminate it. Play is the spontaneous activity of young children. When they do not play, there is cause for concern.

Beyond the fact that play is what young children do, there are several other advantages to including play assessment in our repertoire. Assessment of play offers a naturalistic context in which to observe the child's development across a number of domains. We often advocate for context-based, ecologically valid assessment, and play is when this is most easily realized. Even when conducted out of the home under so-called laboratory conditions, it is possible to approximate and sample the natural and spontaneous interactions of young children. Play offers a rare glimpse into the process of development and is one opportunity to view both product and process (Pelligrini, 1998).

Furthermore, children who are difficult to assess with other procedures are often amenable to assessment through observation of their play. This is critical because many children referred for psychological assessment are those who manifest developmental delays or who are disorganized behaviorally and will not respond to a structured test-like situation. One reason children with developmental problems are more amenable to play assessment relates to the fact that they remain in control. The assessor may select materials and apply a scoring system but otherwise remains an observer who avoids imposing a specific agenda on the child's activities.

Finally, play is universal, and the general sequential progression crosses cultural boundaries (Bornstein, Haynes, Pascual, Painter, & Galperin, 1999; Sigman & Sena, 1993; Sutton-Smith, 1980). This makes play an excellent candidate for assessment of children from diverse cultural backgrounds; however, the assessor must gain information about cultural attitudes and expectations regarding play to avoid mistakes that could affect interpretation of content, selection of play objects, and the child's freedom to display play activities.

Vandenberg (1978) suggested that organisms play to the extent that they are born with mechanisms for adaptation to the environment. Because these coping mechanisms need to develop, play provides the context for this development. Nevertheless, it is important to note that symbolic play is not necessarily universal. Some researchers claim that symbolic play is characteristic of Western middle-class societies and that children from other cultures and other Western backgrounds show less or no evidence of this type of object interaction. However, Weinberger and Starkey (1994) documented pretend play in American children of low socioeconomic status that was high in quality, though low in quantity, during their observed episodes.

There is some speculation that pretend play exists to the extent that the children in the culture are not full participants in the culture during their childhood years, and that those who have a prolonged childhood without full participation therefore need the play time to practice the skills needed for full participation (Karpov, personal communication April 10, 2001). This would support the Vandenberg (1978) observation just stated, in that children without full early participation require more time to adapt and to learn coping mechanisms for which play provides the practice. However, this would account for only one of the major functions of play.

HISTORICAL PERSPECTIVE

There is so much interest in children's play and such an abundance of play assessment approaches today that it is difficult to imagine a time when this was not the case. In fact, children's play was not taken seriously until the late 19th century (Gitlin-Weiner, Sandgrund, & Schaefer, 2000). The surge in attention to children's play activities was largely attributable to the development of the child study movement of the 1920s and 1930s (Sponseller, 1982) and to the theories and practices of psychoanalysts, including both Sigmund and Anna Freud, Melanie Klein, and Margaret Lowenfeld (for a full and excellent history of play and its assessment, see the introductory chapter in Gitlin-Weiner et al., 2000). Early writing regarding play tended to be in the form of developmental description, and it was the psychodynamic writers who fleshed out a theoretical foundation for play.

There was a lull in attention to play during the rise of interest in behaviorism because these researchers found play difficult to explain (Sponseller, 1982). It was primarily the work of Piaget (1962) that turned attention from the psychodynamic interpretations of the contents of children's play to its cognitive developmental implications. It became increasingly clear that play not only conveyed thematic content but also followed a predictable developmental course that paralleled cognitive and social-emotional development. Vygotsky (1966) suggested that play provided not just insight into the child's cognitive development, but a context for this development as well. According to Vygotsky, during play, children create a zone of proximal development that promotes acquisition of higher mental functions. Vygotsky viewed play as the leading activity in the development of the preschool child. Through adherence to implicit rules within play schemes, the child develops the capacity for self-regulation, because during play the child has to suppress impulsivity to comply with these rules. Also, engagement in imaginative play by definition decontextualizes meaning from perception and lays the foundation for abstract thought.

Attempts to assess play began essentially with the work of Parten in the early 1930s; however, Parten's system described categories of social play, which are discussed in Chapter 8 (unoccupied, solitary/independent, onlooker, parallel, associative, and cooperative; in Gitlin-Weiner et al., 2000). However, these categories have not been found to represent a developmental sequence (Smith, Takhvar, Gore, & Vollstedt, 1985). Smilansky also described play categories (functional, constructive, dramatic, and games with rules) that have been included in a number of research studies (Rubin, Watson, & Jambor, 1978).

The surge in development of play assessment procedures took place primarily in the 1970s and 1980s and continued to the point of Linder's (1993a) *Transdisciplinary Play-based Assessment* (TBPA), which represented an accumulation of most of what had been learned up to the time of that book's publication. Linder's approach emphasized developmental implications of play across all functional domains, including cognitive, social-emotional, fine and gross motor, and communication. Play procedures provide developmental descriptions that may or may not reflect a theory and therefore are developmentally referenced rather than norm or curriculum referenced (Wolery, 1989).

CHARACTERISTICS OF PLAY

Any attempt to assess play needs to find a balance between preserving the spontaneous characteristics of this behavior and the need to impose some structure for the purpose of facilitating interpretation. The spontaneity of children can usually be counted on, given sufficiently attractive and developmentally appropriate materials. The need for structure or standardization is usually accomplished through the use of predetermined materials and developmentally referenced or normed scoring systems (or both). In this way, the structure is imposed on the assessor, and it is hoped that spontaneity within the child is preserved. However, interpretation of thematic content remains relegated to the artistic aspects of theory-based clinical experience and insights, all the while maintaining awareness of the potential consequences of social-cultural contexts and attitudes. Most play assessment relies heavily on approaches developed for behavioral observation, regardless of theoretical bases for interpretation of thematic content. It is of primary importance in conducting play assessment that assessors generate accurate, reliable behavioral observations. What these may or may not mean is a relatively separate issue.

What play is and what it is not is not a straightforward issue. Usually, a play assessment procedure represents a specific definition or determination of the researcher's ideas about play. These may or may not overlap with the ideas of other researchers.

Several researchers have presented the characteristics most frequently associated with play. For example, Garvey in 1977 and Piaget in 1962 (in Gitlin-Weiner et al., 2000) suggested that play is "(a) pleasurable; (b) spontaneous, voluntary, intrinsically motivated; (c) flexible; and (d) a natural product of physical and cognitive growth" (p. 5). McCune-Nicolich and Fenson (1984) offered the following criteria: Play is

(a) pursued for its own sake;

(b) focused on means rather than ends;

(c) directed toward exploring objects in order to do something with the objects;

(d) not considered a serious endeavor because no realistic result is expected;

(e) not governed by external rules; and

(f) characterized by active engagement of the player (p. 5).

Developmentally, play shifts during the first two years from

1) undifferentiated activity toward simple objects . . . to 2) behavior that is modified to fit the characteristics of individual objects (i.e., functional play) and ultimately 3) functional play involving the interrelationships between objects. . . . Subsequently, 4) decontextualized and symbolic use of objects is displayed, first employing individual objects . . . and then involving multiple objects. (Bond, Creasey, & Abrams, 1990, p. 113)

We need to be aware that there is considerable evidence for gender differences in play—especially regarding toy preferences—that affect sociodramatic play in particular but may also be evident in object interaction (e.g., Fein, 1981; O'Brien & Huston, 1985). These appear to reflect the interaction of genetic predisposition and parental reinforcement. When selecting toys for observation of children's play, and when interpreting their play behaviors, we need to keep these in mind, as they occur very early in development. For example, boys are more likely to be interested in transportation and active, aggression-related materials and to engage in more rough-and-tumble play, whereas girls tend to gravitate toward dress-up and more passive sociodramatic play. These tendencies are of course overlapping, and some parents make a concerted effort to avoid stereotyping their selection of play materials.

EXPLORATION VERSUS PLAY

A number of authors differentiate between exploration and play. The child's interaction with objects is called *exploration* when the activity informs the child about what the object does. The interaction becomes *play* when the interaction provides a forum for determining what the child can or wishes to do with the object. A number of researchers (e.g., Garvey, 1977; Pelligrini, 1998; Ruff & Saltarelli, 1993) pointed out the importance of discriminating between children's play with familiar and unfamiliar objects. Interactions with unfamiliar objects at any developmental level (including adults) tend to be exploratory. The first order of business is to discover what the object can do—how it works. The next order of business is to use it, based on these discoveries. For very young children this difference may not always be clear (Smith et al., 1985). For example, when a child bangs a spoon on a cup, is this exploration or play? In such cases, it is necessary to query the child's history to find out the degree of the experience the child has had with the objects. Ruff and Saltarelli found that infants' attention is more focused and sustained during exploration than at other times, and the degree of focus and sustenance relates to later cognitive functioning. However, the ability to disengage attention to focus on a novel stimulus is important as well.

The differentiation between exploration and play is important with regard to its implications for play with familiar versus unfamiliar objects (Fewell & Glick, 1993). The behavior of the child with familiar versus unfamiliar objects is indeed different, with imagination being more appropriately applied to use of objects once their properties have been explored. Both types of behavior may involve pleasure, intrinsic motivation, and spontaneity; therefore, whether one or both are "play" depends on the definition. The research of Switzky, Ludwig, and Haywood (1979) documented how exploration preceded play in their participants and, with increased time, decreased while play increased. In their study the nature of exploration differentiated children with and without mental retardation, as retarded children spent more time exploring simple stimuli, whereas nonretarded children spent more time exploring complex stimuli. Vandenberg (1984) showed that interest in complexity is also a function of age (older age, higher interest).

DEVELOPMENTAL ASPECTS OF PLAY

Although there is no firmly fixed age at which play behaviors develop, there is a general developmental sequence with age estimates and approximations that is characteristic of most typically developing children. These appear in Table 4.1 and are derived from a number of sources, including Bond et al. (1990), D. Cole and LaVoie (1985), Fewell and Kaminski (1988), Garvey (1977), Largo and Howard (1979), Linder (1993a), McCune (1986), Rogers (1982b), Vondra and Belsky (1991), C. F. Westby (1980), and White (1973). It is important to be aware that this sequencing highlights only the development of new capacities. The previously developed behaviors do not disappear, with the possible exception of the lowest level of undifferentiated behaviors such as mouthing, throwing, and banging (Belsky & Most, 1981).

By the age of 3 years, the typically developing child is a rather sophisticated player. By this age the child is capable of demonstrating knowledge of the function and appropriate use of familiar toys, combining these toys appropriately (e.g., brush with comb, cup with saucer), developing sequences to portray a complex scheme (e.g., eating), combining schemes to act out a story, and using materials symbolically when necessary, that is, when the functional object is not present (e.g., use a block for a cup or comb).

According to Li (in Hughes, 1998), symbolic or make-believe play tends to develop in the following sequence:

Table 4.1   DEVELOPMENTAL PROGRESSION OF PLAY BEHAVIORS

Age	Play Behaviors
Birth to 9 months	Visual scanning inspection
	Mouthing
	Visual/motor manipulation
	Undifferentiated object interaction
	Combines two objects
9 to 12 months	Manipulations relate to object features
	Distinguishes color, shape, size
	Differentiates familiar/unfamiliar
	Object combinations relate to function
	Self-directed pretend
12 to 18 months	Differentiated object interaction according to real functions
	Pretend with real objects or activities
	Other directed pretend
	Exploratory play; explores cause and effect
	Functional play dominant
	Begins object substitution
18 to 24 months	Capable of deferred imitation
	Can follow adults' instructions
	Simple scheme combinations
	Representational play dominant
	Sequential schemes begin
2 to 4 years	Can use objects in representational/symbolic way
	Multiple substitutions and combinations
	Can apply previous learning to new experiences
	Can use reasoning for problem solving
4 to 5 years	May engage in rough-and-tumble play
	Can engage in constructive play, including drawing
	Can create imaginary characters and role-play
	Dramatic play with multiple sequences, complex themes
	Mixes real and symbolic as needed or available
	Evidence of metaplay (plans in advance, assigns roles)
> 5 years	Participates in games with rules

1. Object-related (one pretend action sequence)
2. Play with a scene that is decided in advance
3. Play with a theme and action sequence
4. Play with a story that is sustained and verbalized

The fact that the child is capable of representational play does not mean that the child is always engaged in symbolic play, just as the child's capability of sharing play with others does not mean that this becomes the child's sole modality. The implication is that this capability has emerged and is now accessible. The child's increasing ability to adapt play, that is, show flexibility, is an important hallmark of maturing development and is a reflection of cognitive functioning. Repetitive, stereotyped play is an indicator of atypical development and signals a cause for concern regarding the child's cognitive and social-emotional development.

There are three general concepts that are particularly important to understanding the development of play (Bond et al., 1990). These are the increasing *decentration* and *decontextualization* during the first 2 years and the increased *integration* from age 2 through 5 years. Decentration describes the change in direction of focus from self to others, where the child no longer performs actions solely in relation to himself but includes others and play characters as well. Decontextualization refers to the child's ability to use objects detached from their real contexts, so that the child can play at eating or sleeping without being in the kitchen or bedroom. Integration describes the increase in appearance of sequential themes in the child's play that continue to develop in complexity throughout the preschool years.

Linder (1993a) summarized the research that documented the importance of play for children. These include

- Play as an arena for problem solving
- The association of play with the ability of children to discriminate between relevant and irrelevant information
- The relationship of play to the development of mastery motivation and to task persistence
- The opportunity of play to broaden (and solidify) children's experiences and thereby increase their response repertoires
- The potential for play to increase or promote creative thinking
- The association of play with higher levels of academic development, including development of the concepts of classification, spatial reasoning, symbols, and sequential memory
- Play as a forum for practicing and developing social skills and language (see Chapter 8)

Thus, play is not only what children do, but also what they need to do for optimal development, particularly for development of higher mental functioning. Play is good for children.

Increasingly complex themes and sequences of interrelated schemes continue to develop, mixing functional with representational use of materials. Interpersonal interactions during play are of increasing importance, and these are discussed in Chapter 8. The presence of a play facilitator can help children to function at a higher developmental level (Smolucha & Smolucha, 1998). However, children who are referred for psychological assessment are often not typically developing, and the levels of their play development remain considerably lower than the complex increased decontextualization described earlier, reflecting their delayed levels of cognitive and social-emotional development. Nevertheless, children with delays are more likely to reveal their capabilities during play—particularly under facilitated conditions—than during standardized procedures, and many who will not respond at all to traditional tests will happily engage in play.

CHILDREN WITH DISABILITIES

One important issue for practitioners and researchers to address is whether children with disabilities play differently than do those without disabilities. Garvey (1977) cited a number of prerequisites that need to be in place for children to engage in object play. These include visually directed grasp, eye-hand coordination, object permanence, differentiated action patterns (motor planning), memory, and symbolic capacity. Wieder (1996) also noted that "even the simplest use of a pretend object requires numerous sensory and motor pathways or functions, combined with gestures or words retrieved from earlier experiences to convey comprehension"

(p. 268). Because many of these cannot be taken for granted in children with sensory disabilities, motor disabilities, or both, adults need to engage in deliberate interactions to facilitate their development (Yawkey, 1982). Conversely, when low levels of play are evident in children with disabilities, it is necessary to explore the opportunities for development of these prerequisites in the child's interpersonal experiences.

Hughes's (1998) review suggests that there are few meaningful qualitative differences in the play of children with disabilities compared to typically developing children, with some exceptions for children whose functioning would be described in terms of autism spectrum disorders (Rogers, 1988). Children with cognitive, sensory, and motor handicaps do play, and their play parallels that of children without disabilities, depending on their opportunities. For example, the play of a child who is blind depends greatly on individuals' making toys available to the child and presenting them in a way that the child can interact with them. When children with disabilities show delays in play, these delays tend to appear similar across types of disability in that the levels of play are delayed, the repertory of material exploitation is limited, and restricted imagination and symbolic thinking are evident (Brooks-Gunn & Lewis, 1982). However, there is little that distinguishes one disability from another (Mindes, 1982).

Malone, Stoneman, and Langone (1994); McCabe, Jenkins, Mills, Dale, and Cole (1999); and McLoyd (1988) reminded us that the type and level of play elicited from children relates very much to the nature of materials with which they interact and the contexts in which they play. Therefore, if we wish to assess capacity for symbolic play, we need to select materials that have the potential to elicit this type of behavior. Conversely, before we conclude that a child has not shown evidence of symbolic thought, we need to be sure that the opportunity to do so was available and that we consider the conditions surrounding the request for the child to play.

There do tend to be thematic differences in play for children who have experienced physical and sexual abuse (Hughes, 1998). The child who has been physically abused tends to show aggression and violence in play, whereas the child who has been sexually abused will often be passive and restricted.

ASSESSMENT OF PLAY

Most play assessment procedures have been developed for research purposes and are not readily accessible to professional consumers. Among these, most are appropriate for children functioning below the age of 3 years. Because of developmental delays, many of these remain relevant to preschool children who are referred for assessment, but it is more optimal to utilize procedures that extend beyond the age of 3 in order to provide an adequate ceiling and to be able to monitor the child's progress over time. Because of the paucity of procedures, the two texts authored by Schaefer, Gitlin, and Sandgrund (1991) and Gitlin-Weiner et al. (2000) have made a significant contribution in collecting detailed descriptions of a wide variety of useful procedures that previously were not easily accessible to practitioners.

Two procedures that deserve special mention are the Play Assessment Scale (PAS) designed by Fewell (e.g., Fewell & Kaminski, 1988; Fewell & Rich, 1987) and TPBA, designed by Linder (1993a, 2000; Linder, Holm, & Walsh, 1999). The PAS is appropriate for children between the ages of 2 months and 36 months and includes 45 developmentally sequenced items. The assessor assembles eight sets of preprescribed toys and presents the child with the sets that are most appropriate for the child's developmental level. Each child should interact with several sets in order to provide sufficient opportunity to observe the child's repertory. Observations are of both independent and facilitated play, and the assessor scores the occurrence of all play behaviors offered by the child, resulting in calculation of a developmental age. The PAS has been included in a number of research studies establishing its high level of concurrent and predictive validity, as well as interscorer reliability (e.g., Eisert & Lamorey, 1996; Fewell, Ogura, Notari-Syverson, & Wheeden, 1997; Harrison & Kielhofner, 1986). Although it is appropriate for infants and toddlers, it is mentioned here because the functioning of many of our referred children falls within these age ranges, and it is helpful for the assessor to have a sense of the full developmental sequence of play behaviors.

Linder's (1993a, 2000) TPBA is a lengthy, complex procedure that applies to children whose level of developmental functioning ranges between the ages of infancy and 6 years. The procedure is carried out by a transdisciplinary team with a minimum of three professionals and extends over several phases from independent spontaneous play to facilitated play to peer interaction. The total time required for this is about 1.5 hr. Each functional domain (cognition, communication, motor, social-emotional) is itemized by Linder and is intended for observation and scoring by the appropriate professional. This is not a normed or standardized procedure, although Linder does provide guidelines that estimate the typical ages at which each capability emerges. One major advantage of the TPBA is that it is a package not of toys, but of scoring forms, training tapes, and, of course, administration guidelines. Although the manual and tape are reusable, the scoring forms are not.

Myers, McBride, and Peterson (1996) provided positive evidence of the social validity of the TPBA. They found that the procedure was associated with favorable parent and staff perceptions, reports that were evaluated as useful, and strong relations with developmental ratings. According to Bagnato et al. (1997), the TPBA "provides a good foundation for program planning; [is] highly individualized, natural and functional, . . . [and] allows for discussion of observations and transdisciplinary assessment" (p. 308). Despite the limited data regarding efficacy available at the time of writing, these authors rated the procedure at a high level.

Although I think that every psychologist working with young children should read Linder's books and become familiar with her approach, I find it unrealistic to carry out the full procedure as described in the book (Linder, 1993a). I would, however, strongly suggest that all assessors secure a copy of the book containing suggestions for intervention (Linder, 1993b), as this allows true linkage between the assessment and intervention and is not tied to any specific assessment procedure.

SUGGESTED GUIDELINES FOR OBSERVING PLAY

What we will seek during the course of assessment of children's play combines insights into the child's developmental status in the cognitive, motor, communication, and social-affective domains, as well as hypotheses regarding the content of the child's thoughts and concerns. We will view play as multidetermined, serving the purposes of developing competence and mastering new learning, reviewing past learning, and playing out areas of conflict and concern. Play is both a venue for assessment and a forum for intervention; it provides a link between assessment and intervention. We need to work from a key that provides a basis for developmental interpretation of what we observe and to apply good behavioral observation practices. We need to inform ourselves about the attitudes and practices of the child's family and ethnic community.

We need to be alert to thematic content and check out our hypotheses regarding its meaning, without jumping to conclusions in our interpretations.

Finally, although qualitative analysis is appropriate and indeed necessary, as psychologists we also appreciate the need for quantification, at least as derived from behavioral observation, so that we can use the results to describe, as well as to monitor, the child's functioning. Therefore, my approach offers opportunities to record and track the child's behavior to permit the gathering of both types of information.

Form 4.1 provides guidelines for the psychologist's observations of children's play. This is an informal procedure that allows description and monitoring of the child's object interactions during play during both independent and facilitated conditions with both familiar and unfamiliar materials. This approach differs from other approaches regarding inclusion not only of independent and facilitated play, but also comparisons of play with both familiar and unfamiliar objects. One section includes behavioral observations, whereas the second section promotes analysis and interpretation of these observations. It is very important that the assessor write out descriptive observations and language samples to provide the qualitative features of these observations; quantitative analysis is not sufficient to promote understanding of these complex behaviors. The assessor is also encouraged to note incidences and evidence of both explicit and internalized self-talk, differentiating between task-relevant and non-task-relevant talk. Such information reflects current knowledge about children's cognitive development, particularly in the area of development of self-regulation.

For this procedure the assessor needs to assemble a standard toy set and select one toy that is familiar and one that is unfamiliar to the child. These selections can be from within the toy set, or the caregiver can be asked to bring one of the child's favorite toys from home; however, it is necessary that this toy be able to elicit a variety of interactions and not be just a transitional, "hug"-type toy. A typical standard toy set might include play dough, a construction toy, miniature family figurines, crayons and paper, a puzzle, a book, a bang or hit type of toy, and another that inspires search and exploring kinds of behaviors.

The assessor would proceed in the following sequence:

1. Familiar/independent
2. Familiar/facilitated
3. Unfamiliar/independent
4. Unfamiliar/facilitated
5. Toy set/independent
6. Toy set/facilitated

The first four situations would be allotted 5 min each, and both toy set conditions would be allotted 10 min each.

The instructions for the single toy conditions are, "Here is a toy; go ahead and play with it for a few minutes." For the toy set, the assessor says, "Here are some toys; go ahead and play with them for a few minutes." For the facilitated conditions, the assessor says, "Now I'm going to play with you for a few minutes with this (these) toy(s)." Appropriate encouragement should be offered the children if they hesitate in playing under any of the conditions. It is also recommended that the parent act as facilitator; when this occurs, the interactions can be viewed in terms of mediated learning experiences (MLEs) as described in Chapters 2 and 3.

When the assessor is the facilitator of the child's play, the assessor functions within the realm

Object Play Observation Guide

This procedure is a guide to observations of young children's play under conditions of independent and facilitated interactions with materials, as well as comparisons of the child's interactions with both familiar and unfamiliar toys. Determination of familiarity is best derived from consultation with the child's caregivers. For the familiar situation, the caregiver or program staff person should be asked to provide a toy with which the child is familiar and with which the child enjoys playing. However, this toy should provide opportunities for a variety of interactions and should not be just a "hug me" type of toy.

An unfamiliar toy can be selected from among the assessor's standard toy set in consultation with the home or program caregiver, or it could be selected from the program's repertory.

Recommended toys for "Toy Set" condition:

- Play dough
- Age-appropriate puzzle
- Crayons and paper
- Age-appropriate construction toy
- Set of small family figures
- "Hit" and "bang" type of toy
- Age-appropriate book
- Bubbles
- Cause-effect type of toy (e.g., jack-in-the-box)

Proceed with the assessment in the following order of conditions:

1. Independent/familiar
2. Facilitated/familiar
3. Independent/unfamiliar
4. Facilitated/unfamiliar
5. Toy set/independent
6. Toy set/facilitated

Provide directions as follows: "Here is a (or another) toy to play with for a few minutes." For the facilitated conditions, ask the caregiver to "play with your child the way you would play at home (or in the program)." You may also be the facilitator, in which case you would function according to the principles of the mediated learning experience. When the caregiver is the facilitator, this is an opportunity to observe the nature of these interactions within the framework of mediated learning experience (see relevant chapters in this text, as well as Lidz, 1991).

First make a running record of the child's interactions under all conditions, and then record the sequence in which the child interacts with the materials (e.g., touches [1], manipulates [2], pretends block is a chair [3], looks [4], and so on). For each, estimate (count to yourself) the amount of time spent on each behavior. The single toy conditions are allotted 5 min each, and the toy set conditions are allotted 10 min each.

VERY IMPORTANT: Record language samples whenever offered by the child, and record descriptive notes about the child's behavior that are not covered in the scoring form. Do not rely on the categories provided; add information to describe what you see. Refer to the developmental table (Table 4.1) for age-level estimates.

Form 4.1

Child's Name: _____ **C.A.:** _____ **Date:** _____
Location: _____ **Assessor:** _____
Facilitator: _____ **Toys:** _____

Independent *Language Sample* *(indicate Ind. or Fac.)*	Familiar (5 min) Toy: *(indicate order and length of* *time for each)* Mouths: ___ Looks: ___ Touches: ___ Manipulates: ___ Function use: ___ Imaginary use: ___ Symbolic use: ___ Other (specify): ___ Affect state: _____	Unfamiliar (5 min) Toy: *(indicate order and length of* *time for each)* Mouths: ___ Looks: ___ Touches: ___ Manipulates: ___ Function use: ___ Imaginary use: ___ Symbolic use: ___ Other (specify): ___ Affect state: _____
Facilitated *Language Sample* *(indicate Ind. or Fac.)*	Mouths: ___ Looks: ___ Touches: ___ Manipulates: ___ Function use: ___ Imaginary use:___ Symbolic use: ___ Other (specify): ___ Affect state: _____	Mouths: ___ Looks: ___ Touches: ___ Manipulates: ___ Function use: ___ Imaginary use: ___ Symbolic use: ___ Other (specify): ___ Affect state: _____
Toy Set (list toys) Language Sample	Independent (10 min) Mouths: ___ Looks: ___ Touches: ___ Manipulates___ Function use, single: _____ Function use, combine: _____ Imaginary, single: ___ Imaginary, combine: ___ Symbolic, single: ___ Symbolic, combine: ___ Function/symbol combine: ___ Simple theme: ___ Complex theme: ___ Other (specify): ___	Facilitated (10 min) Toy Mouths: ___ Looks: ___ Touches: ___ Manipulates: ___ Function use, single: ___ Function use, combine: ___ Imaginary, single: ___ Imaginary, combine: ___ Symbolic, single: ___ Symbolic, combine: ___ Function/symbol combine: ___ Simple theme: ___ Complex theme: ___ Other (specify): ___

Form 4.1 (*continued*)

Child's Name: _____ Birth Date: _____ Age: _____

Assessor: _____ Date of Assessment: _____

Describe typical play style/sequence.

Describe range of levels of play from lowest to highest level with age estimates and within contexts of independent/facilitated, familiar/unfamiliar, single/multiple toys.

Describe language and evidence of self-talk and internalized speech.

Describe interpersonal interactions with assessor and facilitator (if not assessor).

Describe content of any play themes.

What held the child's attention the longest? (For how long?) And what were the child's toy/play preferences?

Describe the child's affective state during play.

IMPLICATIONS OF ABOVE FOR INTERVENTION:

Form 4.1 (*continued*)

of MLE. The assessor should interact in a warm, responsive, encouraging manner. Similar to many of the facilitating behaviors described by Linder (1993a), the assessor tries to follow the child's lead and offers imitations, models, and elaborations as appropriate. The assessor also serves as a language source for the child, narrating the child's behaviors and thinking aloud about the assessor's own behaviors. The assessor asks questions and poses problems that can be jointly addressed by the dyad under the assessor's guidance. The assessor should have in mind the types of behaviors that it would be useful to explore. This requires awareness of the developmental levels demonstrated during independent interactions so that the assessor can capitalize on these to create zones of next development to see if the child will show higher levels of functioning with some encouragement and support. For example, if the child does not seem to know how to operate a specific toy or has not paid attention to a toy, the assessor would help the child notice and explore the object's properties. If the child has not fully exploited a toy or tends to move from one toy to another after only seconds and minimal interaction, the assessor would work to prolong the child's engagement by modeling what can be done with it and talking the child through more elaborate interactions. If the child has shown no evidence of pretend play, the assessor would try to promote this by starting an interaction sequence. Finally, if the child has demonstrated only simple pretend sequences, the assessor would try to increase the length and complexity of these.

Scoring involves sequential notations of the children's behaviors as they interact with the toys. The assessor notes not only the sequence but also the amount of time (counting seconds to self) of each behavior. This information permits graphing of the child's functioning and monitoring of the child's play behaviors over time. It will also provide quantifiable data amenable to research. The assessor should add descriptive notes to try to capture the qualitative nature of the child's play. It is recommended that the play behaviors of the child first be recorded as a running record and then entered onto the score sheet immediately following the session. The assessor needs to have the scoring categories and descriptions in mind while taking notes for the running record in order to facilitate the final scoring.

This procedure is designed for use in the typical assessment situation in which the assessor evaluates the child during a private session. It can also be used to guide observations of the child's object interactions within a program. However, a separate observation of social play guidelines is described in Chapter 8, and this other approach would be more appropriate under these circumstances. It is often the case in the assessment of young children that they are not yet involved in a program but are being assessed to determine their programming needs. In this case, Form 4.1 is quite appropriate.

GENERAL ASSESSMENT CONSIDERATIONS

As always, we need to be cautious about the conclusions we reach from any single source of data, including play. Although there is a strong tendency for play to follow a developmental sequence and for these levels to be positively associated with other sources of evidence regarding cognitive and social-emotional functioning (Becher & Wolfgang, 1977; Bradley, 1986; Christie & Johnsen, 1983; Pelligrini, 1998; Tamis-LeMonda & Bornstein, 1993; White, 1973), there is never a perfect correlation in these relationships, and there are researchers who have not found such strong, clear-cut association (e.g., Steele, 1981). For example, Fein's 1981 review pointed out that the issue of causative relationships between play and language and cognitive development had not yet been resolved.

In addition, there is variability in the assignment of specific levels of play to developmental ages across instruments, with occasionally wide age spans for these levels along with significant overlap. Furthermore, evidence regarding reliability and validity of specific approaches, though available, remains limited, and the effects of cultural background are insufficiently explored (Athanasiou, 2000). The good news is, when developmental delays are identified through observation of children's play, these weaknesses are amenable to intervention; facilitation can work to promote higher levels of mental functioning (e.g., Saltz & Saltz, 1986).

Finally, we need to keep two principles of good assessment firmly in mind:

1. Conclusions should be based on hypotheses derived from multiple sources of information.
2. It is always possible to be more secure in drawing conclusions about what the child does do than about what the child does not do.

SUMMARY

This chapter reviews issues and procedures for the assessment of object play of preschool children as an approach that is particularly appropriate for this age level and that is especially helpful for use with children who are difficult to assess. Play provides insights into the child's functioning within all domains of development. The characteristics of play are reviewed, as well as the ways in which play differs from exploration. Issues of assessing children with disabilities are discussed. The chapter provides details regarding the approaches to play assessment designed by Fewell and by Linder and outlines an approach that includes both independent and facilitated play, as well as play with both familiar and unfamiliar objects.

SUGGESTED ACTIVITIES

SCHOLARSHIP

1. Compare and contrast the theories of play of Piaget and Vygotsky.
2. Document and critique the relationship between play and cognitive development.

APPLICATION

1. Observe a preschool child playing; record and summarize your observations according to Form 4.1.
2. Observe a preschool child's independent play with the same materials on two separate occasions. Compare and evaluate your observations.
3. Observe a preschool child's independent play with different materials during the same or different occasions. Compare and evaluate your observations.

Chapter Five

♦

Development-, Curriculum-, and Performance-Based Assessment

♦

When we say a test is "-referenced" or "- based," we are making a statement about both its design and its interpretation. Norm-referenced tests inform us of the individual's standing in relation to a representative group of individuals of similar age or grade (or both), that is, the norm group. Criterion-referenced or domain-referenced tests inform us of an individual's degree of mastery of a representative sample of content from a specific domain such as language, mathematics, or motor skills. Curriculum-referenced or curriculum-based tests are a subdivision of the more general criterion-referenced testing, and they provide information regarding the individual's mastery of content within a specific curriculum, not just a general domain of functioning. That is, curriculum-based tests are more specific than is a sample of the general domain of, for example, language, and are from the actual curriculum that the child is learning within the child's program. However, our understanding can be further confused by the fact that there are at times blurred boundaries between curriculum- and criterion-referenced procedures, as curriculum-referenced tests can be further subdivided into curriculum-embedded and performance-based procedures. In this case, the term *curriculum-based* refers to curriculum content that transcends a specific curriculum and instead is typical of, for example, general or typical preschool curricula. Curriculum-embedded, then, samples a specific curriculum, and performance-based describes the method of data collection for this content-related information. For example, one curriculum-based test may assess a child's mastery of language objectives such as vocabulary, syntax, and pragmatics. That child's curriculum may target specific vocabulary words that the child is expected to learn, so a curriculum-based or curriculum-embedded test would need to sample these specific vocabulary words. To test the child's mastery of these words, the assessment tool may be performance-based because the basis for the assessment is a language sample collected by tape-recording the child's verbalizations during spontaneous play interactions with peers using a standard set of play props to elicit the target vocabulary words.

To further complicate matters, it is possible for a test to be both norm- and criterion-referenced, for example, the Battelle Developmental Inventory (Newborg, Stock, Wnek, Guidubaldi, & Svinicki, 1984). Tests such as the Battelle include items that are designed to reflect knowledge or activities that a typically developing child is expected to master, and the objectives that these items represent are therefore potential targets for teaching. Assessment using these items also provides information that compares the child's level of functioning with that of other children of the same age and similar background so that the assessor has an idea of whether it is reasonable to expect a child of this age and background to master this activity.

The one curriculum-based approach that has not yet been applied to early childhood is *curriculum-based measurement* (CBM). This refers to measures of rate and fluency of basic academic tasks, developed by researchers from the University of Minnesota (Deno, 1989; Fuchs & Fuchs, 1997; Marston, 1989; Shinn, Nolet, & Knutson, 1990; Tindal, 1988). CBM involves 1-min probes of reading, mathematics, or spelling that are timed and administered on a weekly basis for monitoring of the student's progress. Although not developed for use with young children or with so-called preacademic tasks, it would be possible to develop such measures for early childhood. For example, according to the Zill and West (2001) study, which delineates what most American children know when they enter kindergarten, this knowledge base could be assessed for rate of response and fluency in a manner similar to CBM procedures. The children would be asked to name as many of the items as possible until told to stop after 1 min or just timed to see how long it takes to complete the task. Such an approach could include reciting the alphabet, reading the letter names of randomly placed letters of the alphabet, counting to 10, naming randomly placed numerals, naming randomly placed basic shapes (circle, square, triangle, rectangle), or naming randomly placed colors. Because this information knowledge base needs to be automatized, the child's acquisition can be further tested by challenging those who have mastered the basics by asking them to count backward from 10 or forward by 2s and by asking for the letters and numbers before and after specified letters and numerals and by naming both attributes of shapes with colors (red circle, blue triangle, etc). As the children move along in the curriculum, they could then be asked to write their names, write the alphabet, and write out the numerals. Basic expressive vocabulary and concept development could similarly be sampled by randomly selecting items from popular picture vocabulary tests and administering them in a rate-fluency manner, having the child go through the items as quickly as possible with the teacher recording, but not correcting, errors. This type of assessment would require development of local norms so that the teachers would have an idea of an appropriate rate to expect to determine mastery and readiness to move on.

When a test is developmentally referenced, the content refers to behaviors that are characteristic of a typically developing child at specific ages. These are hierarchically ordered according to the sequence in which they occur during the course of development. In the case of children from birth through the preschool years, the available assessment tools tend to combine developmental milestones and curriculum to the point that the milestones are the curriculum. This is both the good news and the bad news.

The positive aspect of using development as curriculum is that there is a general universality to the sequence of normal development that is more or less built into the human, assuming appropriate interactional opportunities that are likely to be available in a "healthy" environment. There are several limitations, however. First of all, because certain behaviors tend to develop in a given sequence does not necessarily inform us about the implications of behaviors that fail to develop in this manner. (What about those of us who never did go through a crawling stage?) Moreover, the fact that a child can do something at a particular age does not necessarily imply that the child needs to do this in order to develop properly; that is, this behavior is not necessarily a precursor to later developing important behaviors. A frequently cited example is the child's ability to stack blocks. This follows a developmental course, but we know precious little about block stacking as a precursor to later behaviors. Nevertheless, we include this on most tests of young children, and teachers target this skill as a necessary teaching objective. Considerably more research is needed about developmental precursors before we recommend that teachers spend important instructional time on a skill. An example of work that is being done is the study by Bornstein and Haynes (1998), who found that vocabulary competence at 20 months, as an indictor of language competence, was a good predictor of both verbal and performance IQ at 48 months.

Perhaps the most serious challenge to standardized, as well as developmentally referenced, procedures (which are "normed" in the most concrete sense; i.e., they reflect the sequence of "normal" development) and an argument for approaches such as dynamic assessment, which is discussed in Chapter 6, is that these procedures represent results of group performance, which reduces performance to single points that simultaneously represent everyone and no one. This kind of information is not appropriate for in-depth diagnostic understanding of the learning of individual children. Siegler (1996) pointed out that the performance of any individual is highly variable, but particularly when considering the development of young children. Conclusions regarding how children develop over time tend to reflect trends abstracted from large data sets, which look very different from the performances of any of the individuals within these sets. When we assess a child in relation to standards based on abstractions of typical performance of peers, we are setting a standard of a single level of performance, around which actual performance of any individual varies considerably. This makes it very hazardous to attempt to determine a developmental level because, in fact, there is a wide range of developmental levels, and we would need a combination of multiple samples, as well as optimization of performance to derive a valid impression of the capabilities of a single child. We are again reminded of the issue that positive results can be trusted more than negative or no results, as well as of the need to be cautious regarding drawing conclusions about what children cannot or do not do. This issue also relates to the inconsistencies in assignment of age levels to skills from test to test and the effect this can have for determination of so-called developmental delays (Barnett, Macmann, & Carey, 1992).

The primary argument for the development and use of curriculum-based procedures with young children has been the need for closer linkage between assessment and intervention, as well as for the employment of more authentic measures (Gickling & Rosenfield, 1995; Hargis, 1987; Salvia & Hughes, 1990; Shapiro & Derr, 1990). The employment of curriculum-based tests is usually referred to as curriculum-based assessment (CBA). Gickling and Rosenfield captured the nature and purpose of CBA when they defined it as "a system for determining the instructional needs of a student based upon the student's on-going performance within existing course content in order to deliver instruction as effectively and efficiently as possible" (p. 587). The CBA approach provides a response to the "what" questions of assessment; that is, What does the child know? What does the child not know? At what point is it best to begin to teach? At what point is it appropriate to move on?

CBA procedures are the most appropriate to use for monitoring the child's progress within a preschool program (i.e., the educational setting in which the child is enrolled). Assuming that the child has a list of objectives to accomplish and that these objectives reflect the curriculum used to teach the child the objectives, these objectives can then be sampled to determine the child's degree of competence. Looking at the accomplishments of all of the children enrolled in the program provides information about the adequacy of the program in meeting the needs of the children enrolled. CBA provides assessment-program linkage and authenticity because these procedures are actual samples of the program and the tasks are very real in the same sense—of being close to the program. Again, this is both good news and bad news, as these procedures have limitations in generalizability if they are too curriculum embedded as well as limitations regarding generalizability if they are not.

In addition, while these approaches are the best for providing responses to the "what" questions, they do not provide responses to the "how" or "why" questions. Again, it is necessary for assessors to understand their tools and the information provided by these tools. It is not a just criticism of CBA that it does not provide answers to all questions, just as it is not a just criticism of standardized assessment that it does not inform instruction. Each of these approaches is appropriately used for its designed purpose. The criticism is justly applied to assessors who use their tools inappropriately, such as using a hammer to turn a screw or, in this case, using a curriculum-based procedure to try to determine the cause of a child's problem or the most appropriate approach to teaching the child.

Although CBA is what all teachers need to be doing, psychological assessors also need to be informed about CBA approaches for the purposes of both consultation and direct assessment. As consultants, psychologists can help teachers select procedures or develop their own, as well as design a system for recording and utilizing results. There are standards for these types of measures, just as there are standards for other approaches, and these include design, as well as reliability and validity. When used for monitoring, it is helpful to graph children's performance. Psychologists can help teachers with this and can also help them develop other rubrics and approaches for systematic recording and tracking of results.

Psychologists can take any of three general approaches toward the direct assessment of children. First, if the child is already enrolled in a preschool program and there is an Individual Education Plan (IEP) or IEP equivalent in place, it is possible just to use the IEP objectives for assessment purposes. In this case, each objective can be turned into a test item. For example, if the IEP specifies that the child "will name the colors red, blue, green, and yellow four out of five times when shown crayons of each color," then the assessor does just this. This approach is particularly useful when parents have concerns about the child's progress in a program. In this case, the assessor may decide to determine early in the assessment whether the child is making progress. The best source for this information is to assess the child's accomplishment of IEP objectives. It can be sadly surprising to discover that this has never been done prior to the assessment. Second, there are now a number of developmentally-based curriculum-referenced procedures distributed by major publishers, and a sampling of these are discussed in this chapter. If these can be determined to be a reasonable match for the curriculum (or future curriculum) of the child, then using one of these would be the easiest route. The third possibility again applies to a child who is already enrolled in a program or who is about to be enrolled in a known program; in this case, the assessor would go directly to the curricula used within that program and use the already embedded assessments or, if not available, take a sample of the objectives and create a test. In any case, it is important to understand what any curriculum claims it will address and to sample these, while also determining the developmental appropriateness of these skills and tasks for the referred child.

The purpose of using a CBA procedure is to inform instruction. The results should give teachers an idea of where to begin teaching the child, what kinds of experiences the child needs, and the framework for monitoring the child's progress on these tasks. Without monitoring, it is difficult to discern whether the child has learned, even though the content may indeed have been taught. Too often, teaching and learning are equated. Teachers may present material to the children, but whether the children learn this material is another matter.

Assessors need to be aware that the child's ability to perform a task is a function not only of the child (including the child's prior experiences) but also of the task itself and of the multiple sources of variables related to the task (e.g., directions, materials, presentation). Any interpretation of whether the child did the task must be made within that context, with the implication that "under these circumstances" the child did not do it, avoiding the equation of "did not" with "could not." Further exploration of the "did not" conclusions is a matter for dynamic assessment, which is discussed in the next chapter.

STANDARDS

In Lidz (1981) I listed a number of criteria for evaluation of criterion-referenced assessment measures that would also be relevant for curriculum-based procedures, when formally designed. There is rarely evidence of application of these criteria in the procedures that are available. There is a tendency to perceive a procedure as good on the basis of its apparent content validity ("apparent," because this is rarely formally determined). Nevertheless, it is important for psychologists to be aware that it is possible to evaluate these procedures and that they are not good just because they are linked with a curriculum. It is an interesting exercise to search for the technical information for some of the most widely used curriculum-based procedures.

The Lidz (1981) checklist for evaluation of criterion-referenced measures included the following questions:

1. Do the authors specify the manner in which the domain objectives were generated? (e.g., by what methods: logical? empirical?)
2. Do the authors specify the manner in which the items were generated? (e.g., random sample? random stratified sample?)
3. What methods of item analysis were used?
4. What is the evidence of reliability: internal consistency? reliability of decisions made on the basis of the scores? number of items representing each objective?
5. What is the evidence of validity? How well do the items represent the domain? Do scores discriminate between masters and nonmasters (i.e., those who have mastered the objectives and those who have not)? What methods were used for determining validity, such as the judgment of experts or pre- and postinstruction administration?
6. Is there normative information in addition to the criterion- or curriculum-referenced information? For what level of ability or development is the measure appropriate?
7. Under what conditions, and for what populations, are the scores valid?
8. Is there any attempt to systematize errors for diagnostic purposes?

These standards are not easily addressed, and really adequate responses to the questions would be a costly investment for a publishing company, even more so for a smaller agency or individual. The point of listing them here is to suggest that *curriculum-based* assessment should not be *standards-free* assessment.

SPECIFIC PROCEDURES

DEVELOPMENT-BASED TESTING

Bagnato and Neisworth (Bagnato, 1981b; Bagnato, Neisworth, & Capone, 1986; Neisworth & Bagnato, 1986) have been the most vocal supporters of what they call the curriculum-based developmental approach to assessment. In this approach the developmental landmarks become the instructional objectives, although each of the landmarks requires further task analysis to refine and break down the steps involved in mastery, the prerequisite skills needed, and the developmental hierarchy involved. Evaluation generally estimates the degree to which these skills are mastered, emerging, or not mastered. Although mastery is traditionally defined in terms of an 80% level (i.e., 80% of the objectives mastered; Salvia & Hughes, 1990), one could question whether it is acceptable to conclude that a child has mastered the alphabet if, for example, the child can recite only 80% of it. Alternatively, mastery can be set as correct performance 80% of the time.

Examples of procedures that are both development- and curriculum-based include the Learning Accomplishment Profile–Diagnostic Standardized Assessment 1992 Revision and Standardization (LAP-D; Sanford & Zelman, 1981) and the Hawaii Early Learning Profile (HELP) for Preschoolers (VORT, 1995). The Developmental Observation Checklist System (Hresko, Miguel, Sherbenou, & Burton, 1994) is an example of one of the better assessment tools that can be used for multiple purposes: to screen children between the ages of birth to 6 years to determine risk for developmental problems, to target areas of need for intervention, and to monitor the children's response to intervention. This is a standardized, normed procedure that depends on ratings by caregivers. There are three components: a developmental checklist, a behavior adjustment checklist, and a parent stress and support checklist. The items on these scales represent a more updated review of the research literature than is available from most scales, and the authors also attempt to target behaviors that are important for future functioning, not just those that describe current status. The inclusion of the parent stress and support information also reflects current awareness of the importance of these factors to children's development, as well as the increased emphasis on ecological validity of the measures, supporting the need to address family issues more comprehensively. The domains of the developmental checklist include language, social, motor, and cognition. The authors present strong positive evidence regarding reliability and validity. Although making no specific claims for the scale as the basis for a curriculum, these items and domains are as relevant or even more so than are those included on scales that are the basis for many development-based preschool curricula, which often date back (uncritically) to the information gathered by Gesell and his collaborators (Ames, Gillespie, Haines, & Ilg, 1980; Knoblock & Pasamanick, 1980), which were selected essentially because they were easy to test and characterized typical, but not necessarily important, behaviors of children.

A procedure that was designed to reflect both developmental milestones and early childhood curriculum objectives is the Developmental Rainbow (Mahoney & Mahoney, 1996), which is applicable with children between the ages of birth through 5 years. The content represents the authors' review of other developmental instruments and curricula, with an attempt to include items that represented a consensus or median level from these sources. There are five domains: cognition, language, social-emotional, motor, and self-help, and the assessment records observations of children's behavior while engaged in the program's activities. Behaviors included in the scale were intended to be representative of the capabilities of typically developing children, as well as behaviors that are easy to elicit, rather than offering a comprehensive reflection of development. The behaviors are hierarchically ordered, although the authors admit that this is not always appropriate for all domains at all ages. Assessors who use this instrument should be aware that it is not a normed test. The normative information is taken from other procedures, some of which were never normed, and the age levels were not empirically determined either for this or for many of the sources. Nevertheless, there is in many cases a general consensus (and significant discrepancies) among the instruments, as well as in the child development literature, to support the placement of many of the behaviors. The cognitive functioning domain of this instrument is particularly strong in its inclusion of higher mental functioning and symbolic thought. The procedure does not include specific classroom activities to address the items, but the authors intended to provide items representing behaviors that were easily observed during the course of classroom activities, for example, placing graduated sizes in order, completing color patterns, constructing complex puzzles, obeying adult requests, labeling feelings, and taking care of toileting needs.

CURRICULUM-BASED TESTING

A good example of a curriculum-based approach to assessment of preschool children is the Carolina Curriculum for Preschoolers with Special Needs (CCPSN; Johnson-Martin, Attermeier, & Hacker, 1990), which is an upward extension of the program developed for infants and toddlers. Addressing the domains of gross motor, fine motor, cognitive, language, and social/ self-help, the authors devised items in the order that they should be taught, without attempting to represent developmental milestones or align the items with specific age levels. As is typical of curriculum-based approaches, the "items included in the sequences were drawn from the clinical experience of the authors, the research literature, and a variety of published assessment instruments" (p. 3). The authors acknowledge the inevitable overlapping of task demands among the domains and downplay the assignment of a skill to a particular domain. Therefore, it is important for assessors to be able to analyze the possible bases for item failure, as it is not possible to conclude that a failed item in, for example, the fine motor domain is necessarily a reflection of the child's fine motor ability. Any complex behavior can have more than one cause, which argues for the need for well-trained professional diagnosticians to be involved in these assessments. These items are intended as guidelines, and many may need to be modified to accommodate the special needs of individual children, whereas others may need to be omitted if not appropriate.

To promote the alignment of assessment with teaching, the CCPSN provides a form called "Assessment Log and Developmental Progress Chart," and the bulk of the text offers recommendations for teaching the item content. Each item is accompanied by scoring criteria, and teaching suggestions address both individual and group situations. As is typical of these procedures, there is no technical information available.

Another very popular curriculum-based procedure that has been used for many years in many programs for preschool- and school-age children is the Brigance Diagnostic Inventory of Early Development (Brigance, 1978). More recently, the author of these procedures has developed an array of screening devices (restandardized in 1995), including one called the Preschool Screen, which is appropriate for children between the ages of 2 years, 9 months, through 4 years, 8 months. Unlike with the other Brigance instruments, technical information is available for these screening devices, including information regarding standardization, reliability, and validity. The Preschool Screen samples the domains of general knowledge/comprehension, speech/language, gross motor, fine motor, and math. According to information distributed by the publisher, a research study completed by Glascoe in 1991 with 408 children between the ages of 2 years and 6 years in widely dispersed sites reported that the hit-rate score regarding identification of children who would need further assessment was 75%. Although this can be interpreted as moderately high, it also means that one fourth of the children who require further study are missed, resulting in a rather high number of false negatives. For a screening measure used for identifying children for further assessment regarding eligibility for benign, nonintrusive services, it is usually better to err on the side of false positives (i.e., identifying too many rather than too few). The same study reported a somewhat higher (80%) hit rate for correct identification of children who did not require further assessment.

Similar to other curriculum-based measures, the content of the full Brigance measures is based on review of other existing procedures and related literature. It is important for assessors to be aware that any age estimates assigned to items are just that—estimates. These are not normed procedures, and age-related information should not be derived from them. The content is intended to represent teaching objectives and instructional content only; interpretation of results can be made only in terms of the child's degree of mastery of the domain content. This procedure, like the CCPSN, would be considered curriculum-based if the content serves as both the assessment and the curriculum and criterion-referenced if used as an assessment of progress or status in relation to another curriculum.

The High/Scope Child Observation Record (High/Scope Educational Research Foundation, 1992), which is applicable for children between the ages of 2 1/2 years through 6 years, is an example of a curriculum-embedded assessment. In this case, the curriculum came first, and the assessment tool was designed to record the progress of the children who participated in it. Unlike the others, the items on the assessment are not themselves the curriculum objectives, but are an attempt to tap the curriculum objectives, for example: tries to solve own problems, chooses own play materials or activities, engages in play that involves many steps, is able to work with others to solve a problem. The teacher first keeps an anecdotal record of the children's activities in the six domains and then periodically (two or three times a year) rates the children on the 30 items based on these records. The domains include initiative, social relations, creative representation, music and movement, language and literacy, and logic and mathematics. Even though this scale is embedded in the High/Scope curriculum, the authors consider it appropriate for use with any "developmentally appropriate" curriculum. The technical data show strong factorial validity for the domains. Evidence regarding internal consistency, interscorer agreement (teachers with assistant teachers), and concurrent validity is available and generally supportive.

Another well developed curriculum-relevant standardized test is the Developmental Tasks for Kindergarten Readiness–II (Lesiak & Lesiak, 1994; see Test Review 5.1), which samples actual curriculum demands such as color naming and alphabet and number knowledge. Finally, the two reigning tests of basic concepts, the Boehm-3 Preschool (based on the Boehm Test of Basic Concepts–Third Edition) and the Bracken Basic Concept Scale–Revised (see Test Reviews 5.2 and 5.3), specifically target language concepts associated with basic curriculum demands and, while yielding normed scores, are also intended for direct instruction. The Bracken has an associated intervention program, and the Boehm-3 manual includes guidelines for intervention.

Test Review 5.1

Test Name

Developmental Tasks for Kindergarten Readiness–II (DTKR II) (1994)

Authors

Walter J. Lesiak and Juki Lucas Lesiak

What the Test Measures

The DTKR II assesses skills relevant to school curriculum, based on review of curriculum guides specifying instructional objectives for kindergarten. There are 13 subtests as follows: social interaction, name printing, body concepts-awareness, body concepts-use, auditory sequencing, auditory association, visual discrimination, visual memory, visual motor, color naming, relational concepts, number counting, and number use. The purpose of the test is to identify instructional competence and need. The manual provides suggested intervention strategies for each domain tested.

Age Range

4 years 6 months through 6 years 2 months

Administration Time

20 to 30 min, plus 20 min for scoring

Publisher

PRO-ED

8700 Shoal Creek Blvd.

Austin, TX 78757-6897

800-897-3202

www.proedinc.com

Norms

The DTKR II was normed on 2,521 children, selected to be representative of the U.S. population as reflected in the 1990 Census with regard to variables of race, ethnicity, gender, and geographic area.

The DTKR II yields scaled scores for each subtest with a mean of 10 and *SD* of 3. There are also three factor scores (mean of 10, *SD* of 3)—scores for acquired knowledge, verbal-conceptual ability, and visual skills—plus a composite quotient with a mean of 100 and *SD* of 15.

Reliability

Percentage of interscorer agreement exceeded 90% for the four areas assessed: name printing, body concepts-use, auditory association, and visual motor. Test-retest reliability with a 2-week to 1-month interval ranged from .82 to .97 for subtests and .93 for the composite score, with 11 of the 15 coefficients exceeding .90. Internal consistency alphas ranged from .38 (color naming) to .98 (alphabet knowledge). The authors attribute the lowest score to low variability of scores on this test. Other subtest alphas are at least .60.

Validity

Evidence to support predictive and construct validity is offered.

Test Review 5.2

Test Name

Boehm-3 Preschool/Boehm Test of Basic Concepts–Third Edition (2001)

Author

Ann E. Boehm

What the Test Measures

The Boehm-3 Preschool assesses receptive comprehension of basic spatial, quantitative, and temporal concepts. The test can be used to identify children who require special language services, as well as to provide curriculum-based information regarding specific targets for instruction. The test may also be used to monitor children's responses to intervention. One unique feature of the Boehm-3 Preschool is its double testing of each concept. There is also a Spanish edition. A parent form describes the test, lists the concepts tested, and provides information about the child's performance. Finally, there is a test summary and ongoing observation and intervention planning form to allow teachers and therapists to note the child's progress. The manual includes general guidelines for intervention.

Age Range

3 years to 5 years 11 months

Administration Time

15 to 20 min

Publisher

The Psychological Corporation
PO Box 839954
San Antonio, TX 78283-3954
800-211-8376
www.PsychCorp.com

Norms

The preschool sample consisted of 660 children, with information compiled in 6-month age bands. All children were able to take the test without modifications, and children with IQs below 80 were excluded and placed in the clinical sample. The norm group is approximately representative of the 1998 U.S. Census on variables of race and ethnicity, geographic region, and parent education level. Items showing bias were eliminated.

   Concepts included on the test were derived from research, from test customers, and from review and frequency counts of concepts used in curriculum guides and test directions. The final list was submitted to a bias review panel with regard to gender, ethnicity, social class, cultural background, and regional use. Scores are in percentiles, and there is a list of the concepts that most children from each age range are able to identify.

Reliability

Internal consistency alphas ranged from .85 to .92. The standard errors of measurement range from 2.08 to 2.88. Test-retest stability with an interval of 2 to 21 days ranged from .90 to .94.

Validity

Evidence to support content, concurrent, and discriminant validity is offered.

Test Review 5.3

Test Name
Bracken Basic Concept Scale–Revised (1998)

Author
Bruce A. Bracken

What the Test Measures
The Bracken is designed to assess the development of basic concepts in young children. There is an English and Spanish version assessing receptive comprehension of 308 concepts on 11 subtests, the first six of which comprise the School Readiness Composite and tap concepts directly related to educational attainment: Colors, Letters, Numbers/Counting, Size, Comparison, Shapes. The other subtests tap areas of Direction/Position, Self-Social Awareness, Texture/Material, Quantity, and Time/Sequence. This test is both norm-based and curriculum-based, and the concepts that the child does and does not know can be communicated to teachers and parents. Learning of the concepts can be reinforced through the related intervention program.

Scores derived from the Bracken include scaled scores for each subtest (mean of 10, *SD* of 3), standard scores for the total (mean of 100, *SD* of 15), percentile ranks, and concept age equivalents. There are also mastery scores in percentages. The items are hierarchically arranged for difficulty level and allow for determination of basal and ceiling levels. The categorical arrangement of the subtests provides an advantage over other receptive vocabulary and concept tests and allows for determination of strengths and weaknesses. Another strength is the inclusion of guidelines for instruction and remediation. There are scaled scores for zero raw scores.

Age Range
2 years 6 months through 7 years 11 months

Administration Time
30 min for the whole test, 10 to 15 min for the School Readiness Composite

Publisher
The Psychological Corporation
555 Academic Court
San Antonio, TX 78204-24988
800-211-8378
www.PsychCorp.com

Norms
There were 1,200 children in the standardization sample, selected to represent the 1995 U.S. Census on parameters of gender, race and ethnicity, geographical region, and parents' level of education. The children had to comprehend and speak English and be able to take the test without modification. For children who require modifications or who are out of age level for the test, it can be used as a curriculum-based measure, and a concept development age can be derived; however, the scaled or standard scores cannot be used.

The Spanish edition is not normed and can be used only as a curriculum-based test. However, reliability and validity evidence is offered for this version. The same stimulus materials were used, but the directions needed to be changed in some cases to accommodate language differences.

(*continued*)

Reliability

Information is provided regarding internal consistency, standard error of measurement (SEM), and test-retest stability. The average internal consistency for the total test is .98 with a range for the subtests from .91 to .97. The only coefficient within the age ranges to drop below .80 is the School Readiness Composite at age 7. The SEMs are generally below 1.0, with an average SEM for the total test of 2.0 and a range of 0.5 to 0.9 for the subscales. Test-retest stability for a selected group of children from the standardization sample with a 7- to 14-day interval (age groups of 3, 5, 7) was .94 for the total test and greater than .80 for all subscales except Quantity (.78) and Time/Sequence (.78).

Validity

Information is presented for content, criterion, concurrent, predictive, and construct validity. There is a strong relationship between the Bracken and major measures of IQ: in one case higher with verbal than nonverbal, and, in the other case, the opposite. There are strong positive relationships between the Bracken and other receptive vocabulary tests. The Bracken successfully discriminates between children with and without language disorders, as well as between children with and without developmental delay. The floors are shown to be adequate for all age ranges, with the ceilings adequate for all but the oldest children.

Test Reviews 5.1 through 5.5 provide an overview of a number of these curriculum-based procedures.

PERFORMANCE-BASED TESTING

The Work Sampling System (WSS; Dichtelmiller, Jablon, Dorfman, Marsden, & Meisels, 1994; Meisels, 1993, 1995, 1997; Meisels, Liaw, Dorfman, & Nelson, 1995) is an example of the combination of development- and performance-based approaches to assessment, designed for application in classrooms from preschool through fifth grade. There is a developmental checklist covering seven domains that is completed by teachers three times per year. The performance-based component is a portfolio of the children's work that is to be systematically compiled to represent their growth on both core content and work that is specifically representative of the child. The core areas include language/literacy, mathematical thinking, scientific thinking, social studies, and the arts. Only the core items are preplanned, and the total number of items collected per year is 45. How and what are collected are worked out by the teachers with the children. The portfolio information, as performance, can be collected in a variety of ways, including videotape and audiotape, photographs, drawings, and work pages; how the performance is represented would reflect the nature of that performance (e.g., drawings for visual arts). Finally, the teachers complete a summary three times per year that incorporates the information from both the developmental checklists and the portfolios. This includes ratings of the children's progress in the core areas, plus personal-social and physical development, and this summary serves as the report card that is shared with the parents.

The WSS is an example of an assessment procedure that is installed in the classroom and is compatible with a variety of curricula; that is, the assessment procedure does not inform the assessor about the specific curriculum used by the teacher. An assessor working with a child

Test Review 5.4

Test Name

Learning Accomplishment Profile-Diagnostic Standardized Assessment 1992 Revision and Standardization (LAP-D)

Authors

Aubrey D. Nehring and Emma F. Nehring, Project Coordinators; John R. Bruni Jr. and Patricia L. Randolph, Statistical Consultants

What the Test Measures

This test is divided into a hierarchy of developmental skills in four domains with two subscales for each domain: fine motor manipulation, fine motor writing, cognitive matching, cognitive counting, language naming, language comprehension, gross motor body movement, and gross motor object movement. The purpose is to determine mastery of instructional goals. The content is based on a task analysis of the domains, with item analysis of a sample of 2,723 children from the full age range.

Age Range

30 to 72 months

Administration Time

45 to 90 min

Publisher

Kaplan Press
Kaplan School Supply Corporation
PO Box 609
Lewisville, NC 27023-0609
800-452-7526

Norms

The standardization sample totals 792, closely approximating the 1990 U.S. Census on variables of ethnicity and gender. There are 100 or more in each age group, with the exception of the oldest and youngest. There are basals and ceilings to increase efficiency, and both subscale and domain scores are available. The test yields standard scores, percentile ranks, z scores, T scores, age equivalents, and normal curve equivalents.

Reliability

Reliabilities reported for internal consistency (split-half) generally exceed .80, with the exception of writing at 30–35 months; fine motor manipulation at 48–53 months, 54–59 months, and 66–72 months; language naming at 36–41 months; and object movement at 60–65 months. Standard error of measurements are generally low, with the exception of writing, and a tendency for greater impact at younger ages.

Validity

Evidence is presented for content, concurrent, and construct validity. Content validity was established through review by a panel of experts. Concurrent validity was investigated through correlations with three other tests showing significant but moderate results. Construct validity was shown through intratest correlations with age partialed out.

Test Review 5.5

Test Name

AEPS Measurement for Three to Six Years

Authors

Diane Bricker and Kristie Pretti-Frontczak, Editors

What the Test Measures

The AEPS comes in two volumes: one for assessment and one for curriculum. It is criterion-referenced and intended for use by direct service personnel including teachers and specialists, with the goal of developing Individual Education Plan (IEP) and Individualized Family Service Plan (IFSP) objectives to be used in conjunction either with its own curriculum or with others such as the Carolina Curriculum for Preschoolers with Special Needs. Several forms are also available, including data recording, family report, family interests, and child progress record; a set of IEP-IFSP goals and objectives is included in an appendix. The content taps functional skills in the domains of fine motor, gross motor, adaptive, cognitive, social-communication, and social development. Data are gathered through observation of children in their natural environments. Adaptations for children with disabilities may be made as needed. The intended use is for children who are at risk for or who have disabilities. The items are hierarchically arranged, and the procedure can be administered by various team members within their domains of expertise. The procedure and its curriculum are activity-based so that multiple domains can be addressed within any single activity. Family participation is assumed and built in.

The fine motor domain includes manipulation of objects and prewriting. Gross motor includes balance and mobility in standing and walking as well as play skills. Adaptive includes dining, personal hygiene, and dressing and undressing. Cognitive includes participation, demonstration of understanding of concepts, categorizing, sequencing, recalling events, problem solving, play, premath, and prereading. Social communication includes social-communicative interactions and production of words, phrases, and sentences. Social includes interaction with others, interactions with environment, and knowledge of self and others.

Scoring indicates passes consistently, inconsistent performance, or does not pass. There are notations to be made regarding assistance provided, behavior that interfered, as well as modifications and adaptations made.

Age Range

3 to 6 years

Administration Time

Varies with assessor's familiarity, but estimated to be between 1 to 2 hours for initial assessment and much less for reevaluations and monitoring

Publisher

Brookes Publishing
PO Box 10624
Baltimore, MD 21285-0624
800-638-3775
custserv@brookespublishing.com

Norms

This is not a normed procedure.

Reliability

Interobserver correlations for 53 children, half with disabilities and half without, ranged from .60 for social to .94 for fine motor and .94 for total test. A second study with 82 children reported higher interobserver correlations: .99 total test, .75 for fine motor, .82 for adaptive, .83 for gross motor and social, .95 for cognitive, and .96 for social-communication.

Test-retest reliability for 18 children yielded Pearson coefficients of .86 for fine motor, .07 for gross motor, .13 for adaptive, .91 for cognitive, .77 for social-communication, .50 for social, and .91 for total test.

Validity

Concurrent validity for 18 children in relation to the McCarthy Scales of Children's Abilities was .35 and .06 for the fine and gross motor domains, respectively, .66 between the McCarthy General Cognitive Index and AEPS cognitive domain, and .72 between the McCarthy's Verbal Scale and AEPS's social-communication.

Three-year-olds were found to perform significantly higher than 4-year-olds, but there was no significant difference between the performance of 4- and 5-year-olds on total test scores. In another study, the reverse was found: 5-year-olds scored higher than both 3- and 4-year-olds, but there was no difference between 3- and 4-year-olds.

All domains were found to contribute significantly to the total test score. Supportive data regarding discriminant validity are presented.

from this type of classroom can learn a great deal about the child by reviewing the three components of the system, as well as the child's understanding of the components of the portfolio. Asking the child to carry out samples of tasks from the portfolio would greatly help the assessor to gain insight into how the child approaches the tasks, as well as the nature of the errors made. Because the items in the portfolio are likely to be samples of the child's best and corrected efforts, it would be helpful to try to elicit a wider range of examples of the child's approach to the tasks targeted for the assessment. The items in the portfolio help to inform the assessor about the teacher's expectations of performance, as well as the content covered within the program. It would be relevant to compare the portfolio of the referred child with that of another, nonreferred, adequately performing child.

A second example of a performance-based approach to assessment, and perhaps the most clearly performance based of all, is the group of activities developed for Howard Gardner's and David Feldman's Project Zero, published under the title of Project Spectrum (Krechevsky, 1998). This is also a curriculum-embedded, classroom-based approach. The assessments involve 15 information sources tapping the eight domains of movement, language, mathematics, science, social, visual arts, music, and working styles. Some of the assessments are games; others are longitudinal portfolios; and others are teacher-completed checklists. Within each domain, based on the expertise of the designers, a number of core capacities were identified. For example, core capacities for math included counting, simple calculation and notation, adherence to rules, and strategy formation (p. 5). A Working Styles Checklist is completed for each activity to describe the more qualitative aspects of the child's engagement. The activities are scheduled at different times during the year, and some, such as the art portfolios, are collected throughout the program year. There are scoring criteria for each. Information from all of the sources is compiled at the end of the year into a profile that describes the child's strengths and interests and range of abilities. For the psychologist-assessor, it would be important to review the scoring sheets, portfolios, and teacher's notes and checklists, as well as to try to observe whatever assessments are in process at the time. It would also be possible to try to duplicate the setups for areas of interest to provide direct observation of the domains of interest.

LE PLUS ÇA CHANGE . . .

The French saying that "the more things change, the more they remain the same" is all too true of education and its related and supporting fields. I wrote a short article back in 1979 in response to the pervasive embracing of criterion-referenced assessment. At the time, this seemed like the answer to all our assessment dreams, and even then I was aware of education's tendency to become involved in fads and bandwagons and felt the need to warn against uncritical acceptance of this approach. With CBA as a variation on criterion-referenced assessment, we have not come all that far, and there is just the occasional hint that CBA is the ultimate answer to all of our assessment prayers. Not only does such a point of view leave psychologists wondering just what it is that they have to offer in the educational arena other than indirect service, but—more seriously—it also suffers from the same superficiality that characterized early versions of behaviorism (of the "fundamentalist" variety), leaving the consumer with the idea that all we really need to know is what we observe at the time of observation.

There is no question that, as diagnosticians, we need to determine where the referred child stands in relation to the task demands of the instructional situation. Engaging in both criterion- and curriculum-referenced assessment will provide information that relates to that issue. However, most children who are referred for psychological assessment do not stand very tall in relation to the task demands of the classroom, and both the teacher and the parent are telling us when they make their referrals that the child is not a competent learner. We need to be able to do more than reassure them of the correctness of their perceptions. Does CBA belong in the psychologist's assessment repertory? I would offer a strongly positive response. Do psychologists need to engage in other assessment approaches as well? I would offer an even more strongly positive response. As one piece of a complex puzzle, CBA has much to offer.

SUMMARY

This chapter defines, describes, and differentiates among criterion-referenced, curriculum-based, performance-based, and development-based approaches to assessment. These all provide information regarding what the child knows in relation to specific curriculum content and objectives. Specific procedures are reviewed, criteria for their evaluation presented, and the limitations of this approach discussed. The primary limitation of this approach is that these procedures do not provide information about what may be obstructing the child's ability to respond to instruction or information about the interventions that may help the child overcome obstacles to learning, and they were not designed to respond to these issues. When used appropriately, these procedures make an important contribution to assessment by informing assessors about the child's degree of mastery of specific domains of learning and development.

SUGGESTED ACTIVITIES

SCHOLARSHIP

Compare and contrast norm-based assessment and CBA in terms of test design, reliability, validity, and interpretation.

APPLICATION

Select a subdomain from one of the major preschool curricula and devise a curriculum-based test of this domain. Administer this to two children: one who is identified as having difficulty with learning and one who is learning adequately.

Chapter Six

———— ◆ ————

Dynamic Assessment

———— ◆ ————

In this chapter I discuss an approach to assessment that is relatively new but has attracted a good deal of attention, particularly in relation to issues of cultural diversity and attempts to link assessment with intervention (Lidz, 1997). The motivation for the development of dynamic assessment derives from both positive and negative sources (Baek, 1994; Stagg, 1988). On the positive side, there is a history of attraction to approaches to assessment that include a learning component (Lidz, 1987). There is a certain logic to the assertion that the best way to assess learning is to involve the child in a learning situation. Validity is, after all, increased by increased similarity between the nature of the assessment and its criterion. On the more negative, reactive side, is the frequently stated feeling of dissatisfaction with traditional standardized approaches to assessment—particularly assessment of intelligence and cognitive functioning—primarily in relation to individuals from diverse backgrounds (Tzuriel & Haywood, 1992). There are also frequently stated or covert impressions regarding the lack of relationship of psychological assessments to instructional and intervention situations.

With the political trend toward more inclusive education for children with special needs, there has been some downplaying of the need for assessment results to be used for determination of eligibility to programs, with a corresponding increase in the need for assessments to inform instruction and to estimate children's responses to interventions. This has led to a search for alternative approaches (e.g., Fewell, 1984; Losardo & Notari-Syverson, 2001). Although curriculum-based and performance-based approaches have been among the most popular of these alternatives, the information from these is still not sufficient for children with learning disorders or for those from diverse backgrounds. It is not enough, in these cases, to document what the children can or cannot do. Interventionists also need information regarding the nature of the obstructions to more optimal performance, as well as suggestions regarding how to overcome these challenges.

Standardized, psychometric testing has been most successfully used for determining risk and for informing decisions regarding program eligibility. The validity of standardized procedures is determined largely by their success in predicting future failures and successes in relation to academic achievement criteria. We can no longer be satisfied with such successes. We can no longer be content to predict that a child will fail. As Lyon, Moats, and Flynn (1988) observed, normative data "yield only indirect and nonspecific information regarding the nature of the child's problem as it is manifested in his learning context. The test data do not address motivational factors and their impact on learning, nor do they inform the teacher or clinician about the child's spontaneous use of strategies or procedural knowledge in learning" (p. 137).

Use of standardized tests with very young children presents serious problems, and many have cautioned against this practice, particularly for high-stakes decisions that may have a lasting impact on the child's life (Bredekamp & Rosegrant, 1995; Kagan & Shepard, 1998). Those who have cautioned against the relevance of standardized tests with this population have found much of promise in dynamic approaches, and dynamic assessment has developed considerably since these publications have been available.

By optimizing or scaffolding performance, such as is the case for dynamic assessment, children are pushed to perform at their ceiling level, or just beyond, which would be expected to decrease their variability and thereby decrease the so-called error of measurement. This is one supporting factor for dynamic assessment, and there is evidence that dynamic assessment has this effect (e.g., Guthke, 1982). Furthermore, dynamic assessment has been documented to provide unique information to tests of intelligence in accounting for the achievement variability, as well as superior prediction of future learning, compared to traditional tests of intelligence (Guthke & Beckmann, 2000; Lidz, Jepsen, & Miller, 1997). In fact, there is rapidly accumulating documentation to support the validity and reliability of these procedures (Lidz, 1996; Lidz & Elliott, 2000a).

Despite these issues, dynamic assessment is not presented here as an alternative to standardized assessment, and this discussion is not intended to generate either-or thinking about application of these models. To the contrary, as has been emphasized throughout this text, the issue for assessors is to be clear about what information they need to address referral issues, to understand what information each of their tools provides, and to select tools that provide the data to respond to the assessment questions and decisions to be made.

With all this in mind, we can now consider what dynamic assessment is and how we should apply it with young children.

DEFINITION AND CHARACTERISTICS

Dynamic assessment is most frequently characterized by the inclusion of interaction for the purpose of optimizing the functioning of the learner during the course of the assessment. Most dynamic approaches follow a pretest-intervention-posttest format, although some proceed without the pretest and move directly into intervention. Dynamic assessment approaches also tend to emphasize learning processes rather than products; that is, the focus is on how learners approach tasks, as well as on the mental process obstructions to more competent performance.

Dynamic assessment is neither limit testing nor trial teaching. It differs from limit testing in both intensity and intent: Not only are more time and effort extended to facilitate changes in the learner's functioning, aiming to reduce the capacity-performance gap, but also the intent is well beyond exploring the child's ability to do a little better on an otherwise standardized test if given more time or in response to modified directions. It differs from trial teaching in the process, compared to content or product focus. Although there is interest in exploring what types of teaching approaches work, there is also the diagnostic issue of investigating the underlying process-based obstructions to learning and addressing these with the interventions selected for intervention during the course of the assessment.

When used for diagnostic purposes, dynamic assessment should yield information regarding the learner's ability to profit from intervention, the intensity of intervention needed to facilitate the learner's competence, the nature of the processes obstructing more optimal performance, and the types of interventions that show promise for promoting the learner's mastery of the task.

HISTORICAL-THEORETICAL ROOTS

The most generally recognized roots for dynamic assessment are the works of both Vygotsky and Feuerstein, although there is a longer history of expressions of discontent with standardized psychometric approaches and suggestions for incorporation of "learning" into assessment of cognitive functioning that extends back at least to the early 20th century (Guthke & Wingenfeld, 1992; Lidz, 1987). It was the Russian psychologist Vygotsky (1978) who suggested that a child's functioning cannot be fully understood without knowledge of the zones of both actual and proximal development, and Feuerstein who, working independently, operationalized these ideas into an assessment procedure and described the specific nature of interactions that would create a zone of proximal development.

According to Vygotsky, the zone of actual development (ZAD) is what the child is able to do independently, without support, whereas the zone of proximal (next) development (ZPD) is what the child is able to accomplish with the assistance of a more experienced collaborator (e.g., parent, teacher, peer). The ZAD represents yesterday, whereas the ZPD represents tomorrow. It is not difficult to understand the relevance of the ZPD for the instructional situation, as it can also be conceptualized as the instructional zone and describes the target of the educational process (I have also called this the *challenge zone*). I find it helpful to view standardized and curriculum-based procedures as informing us about the ZAD and dynamic assessment as informing us about the ZPD. An important implication is that we need both (Lidz, 1995). The problem is that we have been overfocused on—one could say, obsessed with—the former (Haywood, Tzuriel, & Vaught, 1992).

Feuerstein's academic roots were in Geneva, where he worked with Piaget's collaborator, Andre Rey. When faced with the responsibility of helping to socialize and integrate traumatized children who immigrated from Europe and North Africa to Israel, Feuerstein found that he had to develop an alternative approach to assessment to resolve the discrepancies he perceived between what he thought the children could do academically and socially versus what his test results suggested. To this end, he and his collaborators (Feuerstein et al., 1979) adapted a number of Rey's tests, as well as others such as those of Raven and Arthur, and added an interactive component that worked to facilitate the child's competence and looked at the child's responses to these interactions. This became the battery titled the Learning Potential Assessment Device (LPAD). Not content just to assess, Feuerstein and his collaborators also developed an intensive program of intervention that aimed to induce lasting changes in the levels of the children who showed deficiencies of cognitive functioning; this program is called Instrumental Enrichment (Feuerstein, Rand, Hoffman, & Miller, 1980).

PREVAILING MODELS

Although there are now a number of greatly varied dynamic assessment procedures and a wide variety of approaches (Lidz & Elliott, 2000a), most of them fit within four model types described in Lidz (1991b). Each model is represented within the research and writing of its historically primary developer. These include Feuerstein's (Feuerstein et al., 1979; Lidz, 1987, 1991) highly intuitive and clinical approach, Budoff's standardized procedure (in Lidz, 1987, 1991b), Campione and Brown's (in Lidz, 1987, 1991b) graduated prompts, and Lidz's curriculum-based dynamic assessment.

Feuerstein typically launches directly into intervention while working with his clients. He analyzes learner performance in relation to evidence of a number of possible cognitive deficiencies to which he addresses his mediations during the course of the interactions around his extensive battery of LPAD tasks. While having a basic repertory of interventions for each task, Feuerstein follows the responses of the learner, offering the type of intervention he discerns is needed as the learner proceeds to solve the various problems. This approach to dynamic assessment is highly intuitive and clinical and requires in-depth familiarity with Feuerstein's theory of cognitive modifiability and, particularly, with his concepts of mediated learning experience (MLE; see Chapter 3 for a detailed discussion), his extensive listing of cognitive deficiencies (e.g., blurred and sweeping perception; inability to select relevant vs. nonrelevant cues; impulsive, acting-out behavior), and the demands of each test task. Nevertheless, the frequently dramatic improvements that learners experience during the course of such an interaction are not restricted to the expertise of Feuerstein and his associates; it is possible for others with good interaction abilities, who do their theoretical homework, to generate similar results. However, for those who want to prefer quantitative over qualitative or descriptive information, this is not the approach of choice except when adapted to yield more scorable outcomes. What is gained from this approach is evidence of the learner's responsiveness to interaction on a descriptive level, as well as information regarding the types of interactions and mediations that yielded positive effects and the intensity of effort involved in eliciting learner modifiability. Feuerstein's interest is in demonstrating and uncovering the learning potential of the clients with whom he works.

Budoff (in Lidz, 1987) designed his standardized approach for a specifically psychometric purpose: to classify students as mentally retarded with greater accuracy. Working in the early to mid-1970s, Budoff was concerned about the misclassification of students who lacked the background experiences that were assumed to be in place by the major tests used for classification purposes. His procedures were therefore designed to discriminate between children who were mentally retarded and those who were more accurately labeled as "pseudo-retarded." Budoff did this by administering tests similar to some of those in Feuerstein's LPAD battery, according to the pretest-intervene-posttest format; however, the intervention was predesigned and standardized to teach the basic principles and strategies of task solution. All students received the same intervention, at times administered in groups, and the results were analyzed in terms of students who made significant gains from pretest to posttest versus those who did not. The standardization made this approach much more amenable to research, and Budoff was able to generate a good deal of evidence regarding the validity of his approach. His procedure remains in use in a number of places, including the Philadelphia, Pennsylvania School District, for identification of culturally diverse gifted students.

Campione and Brown (in Lidz, 1987) developed their graduated prompting procedure from yet another point of view. Their theoretical interest in dynamic assessment derived from the work of Vygotsky and his colleagues and students, and they sought to operationalize Vygotsky's concept of the ZPD. They did this through development of a rubric for counting the number of hints the students needed to solve problems. These hints provide a sequence of approximations to task solution, termed *graduated prompts.* Following an error, the assessor offers a hint and increases the hints following further errors to provision of full problem solution. In this model, it is the task, not the student, that is analyzed. The learner is described solely in terms of the quantity of help needed for problem solution. Again, because such an approach is quantifiable, the authors have been able to generate a good deal of data to demonstrate the validity of their approach. Campione and Brown have also worked to link their dynamic assessment with basic academic achievement tasks.

My curriculum-based approach reflects my work as a school psychologist practitioner, as well as the need for practitioners to link assessment with meaningful intervention that informs instruction. Not satisfied that other approaches to dynamic assessment made this link sufficiently clear, and not convinced that curriculum-based approaches per se provided adequate information for diagnostic purposes, I decided to link the assets of the two models with processing and intervention components. From curriculum-based approaches, I chose tasks directly from the classroom, reflecting referral concerns, but began the assessment where most procedures terminated: at the ceiling level. If reading was the referral issue, then reading was the assessment task. From dynamic assessment, I incorporated the interactive approach within the pretest-mediation-posttest format, using Feuerstein's conceptualization of MLE to guide development of the interventions, convinced that this would optimize generalization through addressing metacognition. However, rather than analyzing the learner in terms of cognitive deficiencies, I chose the route of neurological processing, asking the question of what mental processes needed to function in the child while learning and what processing demands were made on the learner by each task. This approach allows optimal individualization and diagnostic exploration and also permits the creation of rubrics so that both quantitative and qualitative information can be generated. The details of this approach are elaborated later in this chapter because the approach applies to children of all ages and is certainly appropriate for use with preschoolers.

Dynamic assessment procedures have been developed by an impressive international array of researchers (e.g., Hamers, Sijtsma, & Ruijssenaars, 1993; Lidz & Elliott, 2000a; Van der Aalsvoort, Resing, & Ruijssenaars, 2002). Most of the procedures apply to school-age children, as well as adults. However, Kahn (2000) developed an approach for use with infants and toddlers, and Tzuriel's (2001) procedures are appropriate for use with children in the lower primary grades. Except for Lidz and Thomas's (1987) adaptation of subtests from a standardized test, and the introduction to curriculum-based dynamic assessment in Lidz (1991b), there has been a gap in the availability of dynamic assessment procedures relevant for use with children of preschool age. Exceptions to this are procedures that tap early literacy (e.g., Spector, 1992) and language (e.g., Gutierrez-Clellan & Quinn, 1993; L. Miller, Gillam, & Peña, 2001; Olswang, Bain, & Johnson, 1992), but the observation remains true in the area of more general cognitive functioning within the realm of psychological assessment.

The information in the following sections addresses this gap and provides suggestions for applying the concepts of dynamic assessment to preschool-age children. The first approach, a review of the curriculum-based dynamic assessment model, has no age-range restrictions. It is a generic approach that applies virtually to all ages because the specific content involves selection of material directly from the learner's curriculum or program. The second approach is a more packaged, curriculum-based dynamic assessment procedure that offers preselected tasks and predesigned interventions.

A GENERIC APPROACH TO CURRICULUM-BASED DYNAMIC ASSESSMENT

Figure 6.1 outlines the steps of the curriculum-based dynamic assessment procedure (CBDA). Based on referral issues and assessment questions, the assessor selects content from the child's program or curriculum. If this is not readily available, I recommend selecting items from the developmentally referenced or curriculum-referenced procedure that may have been administered to the child as part of a screening or comprehensive assessment. These should be items at

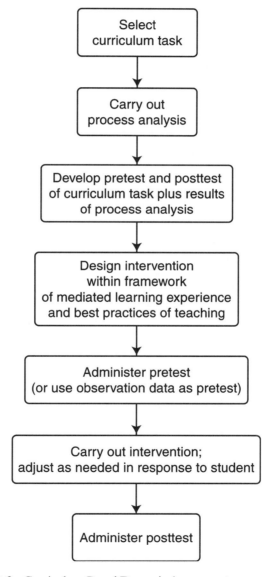

Figure 6.1   Flowchart for Curriculum-Based Dynamic Assessment

the ceiling level that the child has not already or not fully mastered. If the procedure has already been administered, then this will serve as the pretest and need not be repeated. If the assessor selects content from the program, a pretest and posttest will need to be constructed unless the program has its own predesigned curriculum-based test.

Following the acquisition of information about what the child is able to do independently and at what point the child can no longer succeed, the assessor then needs to engage in a process analysis of the task demands (the task targeted for assessment), as well as in an error analysis of the child's performance based on observations, work samples, and pretest performance. The processes to guide these observations appear in Form 6.1. It is very important to determine the child's prerequisite knowledge and skill base prior to or at least during the course of the assessment. The assessor may discover, as the assessment proceeds, that it is necessary to back up to teach some of this prerequisite knowledge or, in fact, even to reframe the assessment objectives if the assessment task requirements are beyond the child's ZPD and instead are at a frustration level.

Engagement in a successful dynamic assessment requires creating a ZPD in interaction with the child, and this zone needs to extend just beyond the child's zone of actual (independent) development. One of the important outcomes of this approach to assessment is to define the child's ZPD for a particular task, as it is all too common that teaching in the program is occurring well beyond this. Good dynamic assessment according to this model requires understanding the task's processing demands, the learner's processing capabilities, and the nature of the match or mismatch between the two. For example, if a task has a high memory processing demand and the learner shows significant problems with maintaining information in working memory, then there is a mismatch that needs to be addressed in the intervention. The focus of the intervention would be to work with the learner to develop more effective memory strategies for the type of domain with which the child is experiencing problems.

Each process and its remediation are discussed in considerably more detail in Lidz (1991b) than can be devoted to this topic here. However, the following offers a brief overview of these processes.

1. *Attention* involves recognition that a stimulus has impinged on the nervous system through an increased state of alertness (orientation), followed by continuation of this alertness (focus) to allow time for processing, maintaining neural excitement restricted to these stimuli while suppressing reactivity to competing stimuli (selective attention), and maintaining this responsivity for the time needed for full processing of the information (attention span).

2. *Perception* refers to a search-detect-sort process in which the stimuli coming in to the nervous system are recognized, attributed meaning, and compared with other stimuli; much of this process is done on the basis of the noting of the distinctive features of the attributes of the stimuli, with some attributes being more salient than others and some of the salience being related to developmental level.

3. *Memory* involves holding information in consciousness for a short period of time, placing it in storage for a longer period of time, and distributing it to the appropriate areas to await retrieval as needed for future conscious mental activity.

4. *Metacognition* describes the executive activities that include planning, self-regulation, evaluation, and memory retrieval. Metacognition is involved with all of the aforementioned processes and adds the strategic, voluntary-control aspect to this processing. It is largely through metacognition that we can affect these processes, as it is mostly strategies and prin-

Instruction-Related Process Analysis

The Learner: _____ **The Task:** _____ **Date:** _____

Describe the learner with regard to: What are the task demands regarding:

---

1. **Attention**   **Attention**
   - Orienting
   - Focus
   - Maintenance
   - Response inhibition
   - Attention span
   - Selective attention

---

2. **Perception**   **Perception**
   - Recognition/meaning
   - Modality effects
   - Distinctive features
   - Pattern detection
   - Comparisons

---

3. **Memory**   **Memory**
   - Short-term
   - Working memory
   - Placement in long-term
   - Retrieval from long-term

---

4. **Knowledge Base**   **Knowledge Base**
   - Vocabulary
   - Skills
   - Concepts
   - Experiences

---

5. **Conceptual Processing**   **Conceptual Processing**
   - What if . . .
   - Cause/effect
   - Comprehension of logical sense

Form 6.1

6. **Metacognition**   **Metacognition**
   - Problem recognition
   - Problem definition
   - Strategy determination
   - Strategy application
   - Planning
   - Evaluation
   - Response to feedback from evaluation
     (flexibility)
   - Self-regulation

Summary:

Describe the processing demands of the task:

Describe the processing areas of the learner that are intact and in need:

Describe how you will address these processing needs in your assessment:

Form 6.1 (*continued*)

ciples of problem solution that we teach when we offer interventions. However, each of the processes can be targeted through its metacognitive connections so that it is possible to conceive of interventions that specifically address attention, perception, and memory. For example, for attention, children can be helped to become more self-regulating; for perception, features of materials can be manipulated to increase their salience, and learners can be helped to improve their ability to notice these distinctive features. In addition, in the case of memory, specific strategies can be learned.

If assessors are to be effective mediators and education consultants, they need to be aware of the literature regarding how to enhance learning and learning processes, and this literature is constantly growing.

The design of the intervention combines what is currently known about best teaching practices regarding the cognitive processes involved in the task with MLE. This approach to dynamic assessment views the interactive segment of the model as an opportunity to involve the child in an optimal MLE as the means of creating a ZPD with the child. Although all 12 components of MLE (see Chapter 3 for definitions of these) should be evident during the course of the interaction, it is necessary to preplan for only four of these, specifically, intentionality, meaning, transcendence, and task regulation. We shall assume that the assessor shows additional evidence of intentionality not only by making a clear statement of the purpose for the interaction but also by engaging and maintaining the child's involvement in the interaction. We shall assume that MLE components such as affective involvement, contingent responsivity, psychological differentiation, and praise/encouragement will automatically occur, and we will assume that the assessor will mediate change, sharing, joint regard, and challenge as an inherent aspect of the interaction.

An outline for preplanning the three components that do require forethought appears in Form 6.2. A statement should be made to the child at the beginning of the task regarding precisely what it is that the child will be doing and what it is that the child is expected to learn from this activity (intentionality). This should be stated in as process-oriented a way as possible, for example, "We're going to work together today. I will ask you to listen to a story and tell it back to me when I'm finished. Then we will work on learning how to be good at remembering stories."

The mediation of task regulation includes thinking about how to provide directions to the child in a way that the child will understand and in a way that will maximize the child's chances of success. Thinking about how to select and present the materials is part of this, as well as considering the principles and strategies of task solution. What does the child need to know to become competent with this kind of work? What are the principles and strategies that will generalize to other tasks such as this? What does the child need to notice about the materials in order to succeed (meaning)?

Finally, the assessor needs to think about possible bridges for the processing demands of the task (transcendence). If the primary process is memory, the assessor might ask the child to think about why memory is important. Was there a time at home when it was important to remember something? Was there something the child really wants his or her parents to remember? How can the child help them remember that important thing?

One of the important pieces of information that emerges from engaging in a dynamic assessment concerns the child's responsiveness to the intervention. This can be recorded both quantitatively and qualitatively. One source of this information is the change in scores between

Planning for Dynamic Assessment Mediation

Child's name: _____ Date of assessment: _____

Assessor: _____

What is the task? What are the goals of this task? What is it that the child is to learn? What are the processes the child needs for this task?

What materials will you use? What instructions will you give? What principles of task solution are relevant? What strategies are appropriate?

How will you mediate meaning?

How will you bridge the *processes* involved in this task?

Form 6.2

the pretest and the posttest. This *gain score* information has a controversial history in the psychometric world (Cronbach & Furby, 1970) because of the unreliability of the scores and the dependence of the posttest score on the pretest. One way to make the gain score more legitimate and acceptable is to have information about the test-retest studies and the error of measurement statistics of the pretest and the posttest. If the obtained score outpaces either of these, there can be more confidence in the significance of the gain, and the issue of practice effects can be ruled out. Of course, this can only be used when a formally constructed instrument is being employed. When the CBDA relies solely on informal tests, the significance of the gains can only be qualitatively described. Another possibility is to use only the posttest score (Guthke & Wingenfeld, 1992). Other approaches that have been prescribed for dynamic assessment have included latent trait modeling (Embretson, 1987), linear regression analysis (Schottke, Bartram, & Wiedl, 1993), and normed posttests (Klauer, 1993), but it is not reasonable for the practitioner to apply these to this informal model because of the demands on time and mathematical expertise.

Assessors need to be aware that even reference to information such as test-retest results can be misleading when applied to children with significantly handicapping conditions such as mental retardation or cerebral palsy because standardized tests rarely if ever include these children in their norms, and it remains unknown just how much of a gain is significant. In reality, a very small positive change may be highly significant for an individual child. Assessors must use their clinical judgment and should also try to determine baseline data regarding the rate of the child's progress prior to exposure to intervention.

Another source of information about the learner's responsiveness is to use a rating scale to describe the nature and degree of these behaviors. Of course, this information is subjective, but at least these observations are quantified, and assessors can explore issues of rater reliability and validity within their own work situations. Lidz developed a preliminary version of such a scale, called the Response to Mediation Scale (see Form 6.3), that has yielded interesting and useful results in studies carried out in the Netherlands (Van der Aalsvoort & Lidz, 2002).

The items in the Response to Mediation Scale were selected to reflect aspects of learner behavior that would be expected to be responsive to mediation. This scale, considered to be an experimental or research version, can be used informally to describe the learner during the course of the dynamic assessment, just as the Mediated Learning Experience Rating Scale can be used to describe the assessor. In this way, there are guidelines to help with interpretation of the results of the assessment. The task is described in terms of the process demands; the learner is described in terms of both processing and responsiveness; and the intervention is described in terms of mediation and task-related, process-based practices.

Following is an example of a CBDA designed to reflect the generic model. The task is story retelling, and the objectives for the child include the following:

- Correct statement of 80% of story elements
- Statement of elements in correct order to match the story
- Communication of the story with a beginning, middle, and end
- Oral statement of the story without visual support

Prerequisite knowledge for this task includes the following:

- Vocabulary used in the story
- Familiarity with language syntax and semantics of the story

Response to Mediation Scale

Child's Name: Age: Rater: Location:

Date: Task/Activity:

This scale is designed to describe the response of individual children to mediational interactions with teachers, assessors, or parents. The scale is intended to complement the Mediated Learning Experience Rating Scale and should be completed following an observation of at least 10 min during an activity shared between the child and the mediator. The
scale describes the child's contributions to the interaction, as well as changes in the child in
response to changes in mediational experiences. The child is rated on all components for
each observed activity.

The intended outcomes of a mediated learning experience are the child's development of
self-regulation, strategic problem solving, active learning, and representational thinking.
This scale is designed to reflect these outcomes. [This is a research edition; feedback from
researchers is welcome.]

A. Self-regulation of attention
    1. Unable to maintain attention to task
    2. Fleeting attention to task even with input from adult
    3. Maintains with significant input from adult
    4. Maintains with occasional input from adult
    5. Maintains with no input from adult
    * Does not apply

B. Self-regulation of motor activity
    1. Impulsive to point of disruption
    2. Impulsiveness needs significant restraint from adult
    3. Impulse control needs moderate restraint from adult
    4. Impulse control needs minimal restraint from adult
    5. No evidence of difficulty with impulse control
    * Does not apply

C. Self-regulation of emotions
    1. Extreme emotional lability; difficulty self-calming
    2. Significant emotional lability; difficulty self-calming
    3. Minimal emotional lability; able to self-calm
    4. Rare emotional lability; able to self-calm
    5. No evidence of emotional lability
    * Does not apply

Form 6.3

D. Strategic problem solving
 1. Does not engage in any organized manner with task
 2. Engages, but uses trial and error approach
 3. Pauses for seeming momentary reflection before proceeding
 4. Some evidence of planful, organized task involvement
 5. Clearly planful and well organized approach
 * Does not apply

E. Evidence of self-talk when working on challenging task
 1. No evidence
 2. Makes noises, but these express effort, not task
 3. Verbalizes, but content is not task related
 4. Makes task-related comments
 5. Task-related comments guide efforts at task solution (this includes comments that may be muttered and not totally clear)
 * Does not apply

F. Interactivity with the mediator
 1. Does not engage in turn-taking communications
 2. Minimal engagement in turn-taking communications
 3. Moderate engagement in turn-taking communications
 4. Comfortable, frequent engagement in turn-taking communications
 5. Initiates and responds appropriately and expansively in several chains of conversational interactions
 * Does not apply

G. Responsiveness to initiations of mediator
 1. Resistive to mediator's initiatives
 2. Passive noncompliant
 3. Passive, minimally responsive
 4. Consistently responsive
 5. Enthusiastic and responsive
 * Does not apply

H. Comprehension of the task
 1. No evidence of task comprehension
 2. Willing imitator, but needs model, demonstration, or move through
 3. Slow to comprehend, but does eventually get it
 4. Average comprehension of task
 5. Quick to comprehend task
 * Does not apply

Form 6.3 (*continued*)

I.   Response to challenge
     1. Refuses, cries, or tantrums in response to challenge
     2. Begins, but quickly gives up
     3. Persists, but with significant encouragement from adult
     4. Persists and completes task, with minimal adult encouragement
     5. Energized by challenge; enjoys the challenge
     * Does not apply

J.   Use of adult as a resource when child needs help
     1. Does not refer to adult
     2. Nonverbally, passively signals need for help
     3. Nonverbally actively seeks help
     4. Verbally asks for help
     5. Actively seeks help and seems to appreciate help provided
     * Does not apply

K.   Interest in activity materials
     1. Shows dislike of materials
     2. Neutral reaction to materials
     3. Minimal interest in materials
     4. Fluctuating interest in materials
     5. Consistently strong interest in materials
     * Does not apply

NOTES:

Form 6.3 (*continued*)

- Understanding of storytelling pragmatics
- Familiarity with most story referents
- Intact auditory and visual functioning (this can be modified to accommodate children with sensory deficits, e.g., using sign language for children who are deaf or three-dimensional toys for children who are blind)

Process analysis for this task includes the following:

Attention: The length of the story is appropriate for the audience. The children vary in their ability to maintain attention, regardless of the length. Ability to focus and maintain attention for the length of the story is relevant.

Perception: Deriving meaning from the language of the story and from the supporting pictures is relevant to this task.

Memory: Maintaining the story elements and their order in short-term and working memory is relevant to this task, as are matching the auditory and visual perceptual elements to long-term storage of prior experiences and retrieving them into working memory.

Conceptualization: Understanding the logical flow of the story; comprehending the ideas of beginning, middle, and end; and making cause-effect and inferential connections are relevant to this task, as is the ability to separate fantasy from reality.

Metacognition: Regulation of attention and emotional reactions, monitoring self-understanding, and asking questions to clarify or expand, as well as the ability to say "don't know" in response to a question, are all relevant to this task.

Based on this process analysis, a short checklist can be made to indicate at which points the child to be assessed is experiencing difficulty; this would be a behavioral scale to accompany both the pretest and posttest, which would be based on the story itself. For the pretest and posttest, the number of elements recalled would be reported, as well as an indication of the sequencing of the story. It would be best just to make a verbatim recording of what the child says and to analyze it following the assessment. A sample behavioral rating scale would look as follows:

Rate each item from 4 (optimal) to 1 (poor).
Write descriptive notes for each item.

Prerequisite knowledge base:
Hearing:	4	3	2	1
Vision:	4	3	2	1
Vocabulary:	4	3	2	1
Language comprehension:	4	3	2	1
Story pragmatics:	4	3	2	1
Story referents:	4	3	2	1

Attention:
Focus:	4	3	2	1
Maintenance:	4	3	2	1
Span:	4	3	2	1

Perception:
Auditory:	4	3	2	1
Visual:	4	3	2	1

Memory:
Short-term:	4	3	2	1
Working memory:	4	3	2	1
Retrieval from long-term:	4	3	2	1

Conceptualization:				
Story logic:	4	3	2	1
Comprehension of beginning/middle/end:	4	3	2	1
Cause/effect:	4	3	2	1
Inferential thinking:	4	3	2	1
Fantasy/reality distinction:	4	3	2	1
Metacognition:				
Regulation of attention:	4	3	2	1
Regulation of emotional reactivity:	4	3	2	1
Clarifying/expanding questions:	4	3	2	1
Awareness of self-knowledge:	4	3	2	1

With this information in mind, the pretest and posttest can now be designed. This might look like the following:

I'm going to read you a short story. Does anyone read to you at home? This is a story about a child who goes to the beach. Do you know what a beach is? Do you ever go to the beach? Now listen carefully. When I'm all done, I want you to tell me the story. Here it is. (Read story slowly and with expression.)

All done. Now you tell me the story. Tell me what you remember. (Record story verbatim. Provide encouragement, but no specific clues, as needed.)

Based on what has occurred thus far, it is possible to record the number of story elements, as well as to derive some evaluation of their sequencing (you can make a rating scale for this similar to the scale for processing). You can also rate the child on a number of the process rating scale items. For those items that are not readily observable, specific questions can be devised, such as the following:

1. Why do you think that happened?
2. What else could he or she do?
3. What do you think will happen next?

Although it is better testing practice to use a new story for posttesting, my experience with this type of task is that expecting the child to be able to transfer learning onto a completely new story is too far a reach. It might appear to be near transfer, but for very young children it actually seems to be far transfer. Therefore, my recommendation is to use the same story for the posttest. For children who are high functioning and who do relatively well on the pretest, the change of stories for posttesting would be the better choice, or it could be used for testing the limits.

Alternatively, and perhaps preferably, the pretest could consist of a story read to the class by the teacher, with the assessor's observations recorded based on this context. The same story could then serve as the posttest. With this information, let us suppose that the assessor develops hypotheses that the observed or referred child experiences difficulty with this task because of limited attention span and difficulty with regulation of attention. The assessor then designs an intervention reflecting this hypothesis, representing the assessor's knowledge about how to improve attention. The assessor may decide to try out a package of interventions that includes shortening the story, enhancing the perceptual qualities of the experience, and providing more physical support for the child. With this in mind, the intervention includes a reduced version of the story, asking the child to "show me the . . ." (something related to the story) in each of the pictures accompanying the story, using more voice inflection while reading and slowing the pace somewhat to promote processing, and providing physical contact for the child such as a lap or a chair with a back and arms to sit in while listening. The assessor observes the child's response to these interventions and makes adjustments as needed to see what, if anything, improves the child's ability to attend to the story. The posttest would consist of asking to child to retell the story, independently, without cuing from the assessor, following supported practice with the intervention accommodations in place. As a near transfer task, the assessor could ask the child to retell the story without picture cues, and as a far transfer task, the assessor could ask the child to retell a new story, keeping the accommodations in place. However, assessors must keep in mind that what is near or far transfer for any individual children may differ and not be readily apparent prior to the assessment.

THE APPLICATION OF COGNITIVE FUNCTIONS SCALE

Because a CBDA procedure such as the previous example can be time-consuming to prepare and because assessors inexperienced with dynamic assessment are sometimes uncomfortable trying to use a procedure that is so very different from the standardized approaches with which they are familiar, there seemed to be a need to design a more packaged approach that would ease assessors into application of dynamic assessment with young children. The other very important agenda was the need to have a procedure that involved some degree of standardization so that it could be scored and used for research, as well as for monitoring of children's progress. These were some of the thoughts that led to the development of the Application of Cognitive Functions Scale (ACFS), a curriculum-based dynamic assessment procedure for use with children functioning between the ages of 3 and 5 years (Lidz, 2000; Lidz & Jepsen, 2000).

The ACFS is curriculum-based in the sense that the content reflects typical processing demands of most American preschool programs. These are processes that go beyond specific content such as learning colors or letter names; that is, they are processes that are basic to cognitive development and that lay a foundation for higher mental functioning. To this end, six processes are represented in the tasks of the subtests, and each subtest is administered in a pretest-intervene-posttest format. The child's performance on each subtest is scored in a curriculum-based fashion in terms of mastery of the steps of the task, and the child's behavior is rated during each pretest and intervention phase on the same parameters that represent primarily metacognitive, interactive functions that are apparent within the situation. Scores are available for pretests, posttests, and behavior ratings. The subtests include the following:

Core:

- *Classification:* grouping blocks according to three possible attributes
- *Visual Memory:* recall of pictures of common objects
- *Auditory Memory:* story retelling
- *Pattern Sequencing:* completion of a pattern of sequenced tangrams

Supplementary:

- *Verbal Planning:* communicating a plan for carrying out a common activity
- *Perspective Taking:* teaching the assessor how to draw a simple picture by using a visual cue of that picture

Although a number of these subtests have significant verbal loading, none requires a high level of verbal skill. However, the ACFS is not an appropriate procedure for a child who has no expressive communication. Sufficient evidence documents that the tasks are appropriate for children between the ages of 3 through 5. Assessors need to keep in mind that the purpose of the assessment is to create a ZPD and that the child should not enter the assessment situation with the ability to do these tasks independently; the tasks were deliberately designed to induce a need for mediation so that the assessor can be in the role of helping the child move to a higher level of functioning. It is the child's response to these efforts that is the primary focus of this procedure.

As just indicated, the child's behavior is rated during the course of the pretest and intervention for all subtests. This occurs on the same seven dimensions across tasks, enabling comparison of the child's behavior in relation to task demands, as well as in relation to independent versus collaborative situations. These behaviors are as follows:

- Self-regulation
- Persistence
- Frustration Tolerance
- Flexibility
- Motivation
- Interactivity
- Responsiveness

The total time required for the ACFS is approximately 1.5 to 2 hr, and it is typically administered in two sessions of three subtests each. However, it is possible to select subtests and not administer the entire procedure. It is my experience that the children enjoy the experience. It does not feel like a test, but more like an instructional conversation. The interventions are predesigned to reflect best practices in relation to the tasks, but they are not fully scripted so that the assessor does not sit and read the instructions to the child. When the ACFS is used for diagnostic and not research purposes, assessors are encouraged to explore interventions beyond those provided, that is, to test the limits of this procedure.

Several studies have now been completed to document the reliability and validity of the ACFS (Lidz, 2000). There is evidence of significant gains between pretests and posttests, and these gains can be attributed to the mediation and not to practice effects. There is also evidence that the ACFS significantly predicts the child's cognitive functioning on alternative measures and that it discriminates between children with and without documented special needs. A study with the behavior rating scale used by itself showed good agreement between the researcher's ratings and those of the classroom teacher and speech therapist.

SOME EDITORIAL REMARKS

I have frequently heard it said (or seen it written) that among the so-called limitations of dynamic assessment is the perception that it takes a lot of time and requires expertise and training. I feel that it is necessary to comment on both of these issues, as the reader who may wish to engage in dynamic assessment may hear the same comments from those who hold decision-making power over their practices.

It may well be true that dynamic assessment requires more time; however, this is only true if the assessor continues doing everything else just the same way and adds dynamic assessment to this. In fact, dynamic assessment can require as short a time as 30 min or as long a time as 3 to 5 days, depending on what is done and how it is used. In my experience, dynamic assessment is used to supplement and extend a comprehensive assessment that includes a wide variety of approaches and procedures. There is information provided by dynamic assessment that is simply not available from other procedures, and I feel this addition (usually requiring from 30 to 60 min) is necessary. In other instances, the assessor may only do dynamic assessment, such as in the circumstances of instructional consultation when there are no issues of determining risk or eligibility but, rather, information is needed for instructional planning and monitoring of progress. When added to file review, interview, and observation, dynamic assessment requires only an additional 1 to 2 hr.

I have been in the situation of being asked to do only dynamic assessment with children who have already experienced a great deal of traditional psychometric testing. In these cases, the parents found the information from these traditional approaches very meager and not particularly useful. I had the moving experience of a parent's telling me that she cried after reading my report, feeling for the first time that she recognized her daughter and found something meaningful said about her. These parents, often of young children, may compile an inch-thick, sometimes indexed portfolio of assessment reports. Some professionals would dismiss these parents' efforts as shopping for a diagnosis. To the contrary, I view these parents as shopping, perhaps, but looking for some meaningful information and guidelines about what to do to help their children. In our field's cost-containment frenzy and obsession, we at times ask the wrong questions. The question of "how long will this take" may be valid but is not necessarily primary, and at times it is very shortsighted. The more important questions are, How will this promote the child's learning? What information will be generated? How will this inform instruction? In other words, what bang will we get for our buck?

For the second recurring comment—that dynamic assessment requires training and expertise—I have no apologies. Yes, it is true: Becoming a good dynamic assessor does require skill, training, supervision, and experience. It is interesting that this same comment is not considered a criticism of therapy or teaching or, for that matter, of IQ test administration. It seems that if an assessment cannot be administered by a paraprofessional, scored by a computer, and read verbatim from a manual, some consider it to be limited. As to the more relevant question of whether it is worth doing: The answer is a matter of research, experience, and attitude. The research is accumulating, and an increasingly vast literature is now available for those who wish to inform themselves (e.g., Hamers et al., 1993; Haywood & Tzuriel, 1992; Lidz, 1987, 1991b; Lidz & Elliott, 2000a). Certainly, there is need for more research and for an increasing number and variety of dynamic assessment approaches.

SUMMARY

This chapter defines and discusses dynamic assessment procedures that typically embed interventions within an interactive approach to assessment. The historical and theoretical roots, primarily related to the work of Vygotsky and Feuerstein, are elaborated, and the prevailing models of Feuerstein, Budoff, and Campione and Brown are reviewed. Process-based CBDA is detailed and offered as a generic procedure that can be applied to any content and with children of any age. Finally, a more structured, standardized approach for use with preschool children, the ACFS, is described.

SUGGESTED ACTIVITIES

SCHOLARSHIP

Select one of the processes outlined in the process analysis Figure 6.1. Review the literature regarding effective approaches to intervention that address this process.

APPLICATION

Select an item from a developmentally-referenced, curriculum-based procedure such as the Carolina Curriculum for Preschoolers with Special Needs or the Hawaii Early Learning Profile for Preschoolers and design and carry out a CBDA procedure with a preschool child.

Chapter Seven

--- ◆ ---

Standardized Testing

--- ◆ ---

Standardized testing of young children comes with a warning label: Beware of trying to quantify the unquantifiable! (Or what Sarason, 1976, referred to as the issue of *premature quantification* [p. 588].) There are a number of standardized tests now available for application with young children, and there is useful information that can be generated by these procedures. Standardized tests allow comparison of children over time, provide the basis for determining the extent of deviation from typical development, and serve as a ticket for meeting program eligibility requirements (Bondurant-Utz & Luciano, 1994). However, we must remind ourselves of the basic principle of assessment that tells us that positive results can be trusted more than negative results or absence of results. That is, we know that a child has the capacity to do what in fact the child does, but we do not know the child's capacity to perform tasks that are not performed or that are performed poorly.

Young children often do not understand the assessor's need to have them sit still, attend for prolonged periods of time, and provide responses to scripted directions (and also experience prolonged periods of failure before moving on to easier requests). In fact, in Bagnato and Neisworth's (1994) national survey of preschool psychologists, almost half of the children referred for assessment were described as untestable with standardized procedures.

Contrary to some professional assertions, the child does not need the test; the assessor does. However, when we can gain the child's cooperation or become creative and patient enough to elicit scorable performance from the child, we can use these results for decisions regarding determination of risk, program eligibility, and, in many cases, areas in need of intervention.

We should also be mindful of another principle of good assessment that informs us that high-stakes decisions should be made on the basis of multiple sources of information and that we should never rely on the results of a single measure. This caveat applies to all approaches to assessment discussed in this book, but it seems particularly necessary to highlight it in this chapter, as it is very tempting to be impressed with information that bears a numerical value. Numbers seem more like "real" science. I like to refer to this as the *illusion of precision* (I am apparently not the only one, as I found that Bagnato and Neisworth used this term in their 1994 article, so perhaps I liked it so much I absorbed it as my own!).

A number of professionals working with young children are uncomfortable with the use of standardized tests with this population. Neisworth and Bagnato (1992) have been among the most outspoken against this practice, although their remarks primarily target early intervention. However, there is overlap in the application of their concerns to the preschool population. These authors framed their remarks in terms of putting intelligence tests on trial and finding them guilty of violating six major assumptions. They concluded the following:

- There is a lack of definition of intelligence in most tests, and a lack of a theoretical basis for most.
- Any score means different things for different individuals; and particularly for children with disabilities, developmental skills do not covary.
- Predictions are poor because early tests assess mainly sensorimotor status, whereas later tests rely to a greater extent on language.
- The floors of most tests are inadequate.
- Most tests, which reflect group data, lack instructional utility for individuals.

This chapter discusses procedures developed for application to young children that have been standardized and normed. Those that are administered by psychologists usually focus on cognition or intelligence (Paget, 1989). Issues related to attempts to measure intelligence in individuals of any age are tremendous, and many of these issues relate to the difficulty of defining the concept. For example, Sternberg and Grigorenko (2001; see also Hale, 1982) concluded that the definition of intelligence "depends upon whom you ask, and it differs widely across disciplines, time, and place" (p. 344). Because of this, most current test developers caution against interpreting their results as innate capacity and suggest a more conservative interpretation of the scores as samples of currently developed abilities. As Goodwin and Driscoll (1980) reminded us some time ago, "IQ test scores are merely descriptive, not explanatory" (p. 148).

When a procedure is standardized, it needs to be administered to all individuals in exactly the same way as it was administered during the determination of norms (Stone, 1995). Although some instruments have room for slight flexibility, any significant deviation from the standardized administration precludes the ability to apply the normative information.

The determination of norms provides the basis for interpreting the scores of these procedures. Scores are usually made to fit the assumed normal curve, yielding a mean score of 100 and a standard deviation of 15 (or 16, in the case of the Stanford-Binet Intelligence Scale–Fourth Edition and the McCarthy Scales), and the individual child's score is interpreted in relation to the level of performance of other children of the same chronological age. Establishment of norms requires adequate sampling of the population with which the test will be applied. Usually, typically developing children are sampled, and very few children with disabilities are included. When this is the case, the application of the norms for children with disabilities is of questionable use (Goodman, 1990). The individual child's score is compared with this typically developing group to permit inferences regarding degree of match or deviance from expectations of what the normative-group children can do. Significant negative deviation from average suggests that the child is at risk for developmental problems, and this is the usual indicator for determining eligibility for intervention programs.

Not only is it important to have adequate sampling of the normative group, but it is also important to have a good sample of the content domains that are assessed, such as language or cognition, as well as subdomains within these. Determination of the goodness of the content sampling is usually made in terms of item analysis (items fall into a hierarchy from easy to hard and from younger to older), discrimination among individuals who are high or low as determined by another, independent criterion, and indicators of psychometric reliability and validity. Assessors need to be aware that results from standardized tests tend to be less reliable for young children (particularly those with special needs; K. N. Cole, Mills, & Kelley, 1994), and it is all the more important to report scores in ranges, as well as to engage in testing the limits (Stone, 1995).

The psychometric approach to assessment was developed to maximize objectivity, particularly with regard to determinations of eligibility and selection, which, historically, were important issues for adults entering the armed services (or, further back in time, for selection for civil service jobs; Laosa, 1977). The assessment approach was gradually extended downward, reaching into the early childhood years during the design of early longitudinal studies, and then more recently transferred into procedures released for professional practitioners with special impetus from Head Start in the United States. The main point to be made from these remarks is that most of what we now know as standardized early childhood assessment procedures either are downward extensions of instruments designed for much older populations or are reflective of developmental measures designed for research projects that followed children over time. That is, they were not designed to link assessment with intervention or instruction, and the downward extensions were not redesigned to reflect the developmental characteristics of young children.

When selecting a norm-based test for administration, it is important for assessors to have criteria for guiding their choices. The following criteria are abstracted from the more in-depth discussion by Alfonso and Flanagan (1999), who suggested that a procedure is "adequate to good" if it

- Has a sample of at least 1,000 to 2,000 in the total norm group
- Has a minimum of 100 in each age group of at least 1 year span
- Has data that have been collected within at least the last 20 years that match the demographics of the U.S. population on at least three to five variables, including gender, race, and socioeconomic status (Lehr, Ysseldyke, & Thurlow, 1987, set 15 years as a maximum)
- Offers norm tables with age divisions with a maximum of three to four months
- Presents evidence of reliability and has internal consistency and test-retest stability no lower than .80 (Lehr et al., 1987, set .90 as a minimum for instructional planning and placement decisions for individuals and .80 for screening)
- Offers floors so that a raw score of 1 is at least -2 SD below the mean and total score at least -2 SD below the mean
- Presents evidence of content, criterion, and construct validity

In addition to these recommendations, Bracken (2000b) offered the additional criterion regarding the need to consider the adequacy of the test's item gradient, so that there are only small standard score changes per raw score changes—specifically, no more than a 1/3-SD alteration per single raw score.

Alfonso and Flanagan (1999) outlined other parameters that are important to notice about the procedures beyond these psychometric characteristics. For example, the test manuals should offer a description of the theoretical basis for the test and be clear regarding the abilities assessed. The manual should offer guidelines for interpretation as well as for interventions. The materials and instructions should be developmentally appropriate, with basic concepts within the young child's comprehension and with materials that can hold the child's attention. Most modern tests also offer opportunities to teach the tasks to the children and have discontinue rules that minimize the child's frustration.

In their review of the major norm-based procedures currently available, Alfonso and Flanagan (1999) observed that they generally had good to adequate psychometric properties but inadequate floors, particularly for young and lower functioning children. A test is not good when the child's ability is represented by scores that may reflect essentially four to six items completed successfully. There are still some psychometric tests that can be said to "measure the dead" because it is possible to obtain a scaled subtest score with a raw score of zero, suggesting that it is not necessary to be present to obtain a score! Many of the tests available for young children that include older children and adults tend to measure different factors at the younger ages than at the older ages, and assessors must read the manuals carefully to determine what the test is measuring at the age of the child being assessed. For example, the Stanford-Binet Intelligence Scale–Fourth Edition, which has three to four factors for older ages, typically shows only two factors at the preschool level. It is also very important to look at the reliability information, particularly regarding test-retest, for the specific age of the child being assessed, as some subtests tend to be reliably unreliable at these very young ages (e.g., tests of motor functioning).

Good practice in the case of any test evaluation is to ask the question, What do the authors say they are doing in designing the test? Next ask: How well have they done it? For example, if the Bayley Scales are not intended to be a measure of intelligence, but only of accomplishment of developmental milestones, then they should not be evaluated as a measure of intelligence. If the various Wechsler scales do not purport to offer guidelines for program development, then they should not be evaluated as such. Therefore, the first item on the agenda when evaluating a procedure is to determine its intent: What is it designed to do?

EXAMPLES OF STANDARDIZED TESTS FOR YOUNG CHILDREN

Test Reviews 7.1 through 7.10 briefly summarize a large selection of standardized tests now available for young children. Both the Stanford-Binet Intelligence Scale and the Wechsler Preschool and Primary Test of Intelligence were in the process of revision at the time of this text's publication but were not yet released; however, preliminary information is included in these reviews.

As can be seen from these reviews, there are now a number of standardized tests available for young children—all, by the way, with hefty price tags. Standardizing tests is a very expensive enterprise (and a very big business). Assessors must carefully select those with the best match for their purposes, and to do this succesfully, assessors must be clear about their purposes. A test may look good on paper but not work well in application to a particular situation, so teams must evaluate the usefulness and accuracy of their selections after they have gained some experience with their use.

Test Review 7.1

Test Name
Bayley Scales of Infant Development: Second Edition (1993)

Authors
Nancy Bayley and James S. Gyurke (project director)

What the Test Measures
The Bayley assesses developmental functioning with three scales: Mental, Motor, and Behavior Rating. The Mental Scale includes memory, habituation, problem solving, early number concepts, generalization, classification, vocalizations, language, and social skills. The Motor Scale includes gross and fine motor control and movements. The Behavior Rating Scale includes test-taking behavior in the areas of attention/arousal, orientation/engagement toward task/examiner/caregiver, emotional regulation, and quality of movement.

Items are in developmental hierarchy, and content is "theoretically eclectic." The primary purpose is to contribute to identification of children with developmental delays.

Age Range
1 month to 42 months

Administration Time
25–35 min for below 15 months; up to 60 min for above 15 months

Publisher
The Psychological Corporation
555 Academic Court
San Antonio, TX 78204-24988
800-211-8378
www.PsychCorp.com

Norms
The norms are representative of the 1988 update of U.S. Census regarding race and ethnicity, child gender, parents' education, and geographic location of child. There are basals and ceilings, and content has been submitted for bias review. Norms included 1,700 cases with 100 in each of 17 age groups.

Scores include standardized index scores and developmental age equivalents. Percentiles for Behavior Rating Scores are in monthly intervals up to 36 months and then are in 3-month intervals thereafter to 42 months.

Reliability
Internal consistency was determined through alpha coefficients, all above .80 for the Mental and Motor Scales, except for Motor for 30 and 42 months. Behavior Rating alphas range between .73 to .92, except those for attention/arousal, which range between .64 and .82 and are applied only during the first 5 months. Standard error of measurement averages 5.21 for the Mental Scale and 6.01 for Motor. Test-retest stability ($n = 175$ at ages 1, 12, 24 and 36 months with interval of 1 to 16 days with mixed gender and ethnicity) is .87 for Mental Scale for all ages and .78 for Motor Scale for all ages. Interscorer agreement was found to be high, with stronger agreement for the Mental than for the Motor Scale.

(*continued*)

Validity

Data are reported for content, construct, concurrent, predictive, and discriminant validity. The scale was submitted for expert review for content analysis and submitted to correlational analysis to document intratest relationships. The Behavior Rating Scale yields different factors at different ages: Motor Quality and attention/arousal prior to 5 months and emotional regulation, orientation/engagement, and motor quality after 5 months.

Correlations with other tests show generally positive and moderate results, including the relationship with the early Bayley. The correlations tend to be stronger between the Mental Index and Verbal portions of other tests

Test Review 7.2

Test Name
Cognitive Abilities Scale: Second Edition (CAS-2) (2001)

Authors
Sharon Bradley-Johnson and C. Merle Johnson

What the Test Measures

The CAS-2 was designed as a measure of current level of intelligence or achievement, with content selected to reflect classroom demands. The authors state that it is a measure of achievement when current functioning is of interest and a measure of intelligence when future functioning is predicted. The test yields a General Cognitive Quotient (GCQ; all accumulated points) and a Nonvocal Cognitive Quotient (NVQ; points from items not requiring vocalization). The Preschool Form includes five areas: Oral Language, Reading, Mathematics, Handwriting, and Enabling Behaviors (imitation and memory). The test was designed to enable identification of children with cognitive deficiencies related to program eligibility, and individual items are intended for instructional planning. The test can also be used to evaluate the child's response to instruction. The items are not hierarchically ordered and therefore do not represent a developmental progression; instead, they are clustered to sample mastery of the domain being assessed.

Scores include the GCQ and NVQ, which are standard scores with a mean of 100 and SD of 15. In addition, there are percentile ranks and age equivalents. The authors note that when used for instructional planning, it is the skill area that is to be taught, not the test item.

Age Range
3 months to 3 years 11 months

Administration Time
20 to 30 min

Publisher
Pro-Ed
8700 Shoal Creek Boulevard
Austin, TX 78757-6897
800-897-3202
www.proedinc.com

Norms

The norms reflect the 1997 U.S. Census, presented in 1-month intervals from 3 through 12 months, 2-month intervals from 13 to 20 months, and 3-month intervals from 21 through 47 months. The norms include 5.5% of children with physical or mental impairments with no effects of gender or race.

The total norm group numbered 1,106, reflecting the U.S. population on the variables of geography, gender, race, residence, ethnicity, educational attainment of parents, disability status, and age in months.

The GCQs range from 55 to 145, and the NCQs range from 55 to 140, with some variation depending on age. Standard scores are not assigned to raw scores of 1 with the exception of the NCQ at age 24–26 months. There is a big jump in the implications of items passed as the age moves to the next level; for example, 42 items correct at age 33–35 months yields a GCQ of 80, but the same number correct at age 36–38 yields a GCQ of 74. This can fall into the category of "what a difference a day makes" for the child whose birthday is at the end of an age span.

Reliability

Internal consistency alphas range from .89 to .94, with low standard errors of measurement. There were two test-retest studies of the preschool population, both with a 2-week time interval, one group of 2-year-olds and one group of 3-year-olds. All correlations exceeded .90.

Validity

Content validity was established through research literature evidence as well as through item analysis. Concurrent validity is demonstrated through correlations with three major texts, yielding coefficients from .67 to .82 for the GCQ and all above .80 for the NCQ. The test shows discriminant validity between the performances of children with typical compared with deficient development. Criterion validity is evidenced through correlations exceeding .80 between the CAS-2 and tests of early reading and mathematics.

Test Review 7.3

Test Name

Differential Ability Scales (DAS) (1990)

Author

Colin D. Elliott

What the Test Measures

The author's intent is to provide meaningful profiles of children's abilities to portray reliable indications of strengths and weaknesses. Composite scores reflect subtests that access conceptual and reasoning abilities. The test provides floors and ceilings with assessment of exceptional children in mind. The design goal was to provide a flexible tool for cognitive assessment. The primary purposes are both classification and placement and diagnostic profiling. The DAS is a revision of the earlier British Ability Scales.

There are two preschool levels, the first of which is for children 2-6 to 3-5 and involves four core subtests that yield a composite score (Block Building, Verbal Comprehension, Picture Similarities,

(*continued*)

and Naming Vocabulary); two diagnostic subtests can be added to these (Recall of Digits and Recall of Objects). The second level ranges from 3-6 to 5-11 and involves six core subtests yielding a composite score (Verbal Comprehension, Picture Similarities, Naming Vocabulary, Early Number Concepts, Copying, and Pattern Construction); five diagnostic subtests can be added to these (Matching Letter-Like Forms, Recall of Digits, Recall of Objects, Recognition of Pictures, and Speed of Information Processing).

The preschool tests were not downward extensions of those designed for older populations, but were conceptualized specifically for application to young children.

Subtest raw scores are converted to *T* scores (called Ability Scores), with a mean of 50 and *SD* of 10. The core subtest *T* scores are then summed and converted to a standard score with a mean of 100 and *SD* of 15. These can also be interpreted in terms of percentiles, as well as age and grade equivalents. When additional floors and ceilings are needed, out-of-level testing can be carried out to further tailor the subtests for the child.

The DAS results are interpreted in terms of three levels that describe cognitive functioning: the General Cognitive Ability (GCA), or most general, Conceptual and Reasoning Ability; the Cluster, or intermediate level, Verbal/Spatial/Nonverbal Reasoning Abilities; and the Subtest, or least general, Specific Abilities/Processes. At the preschool levels, the DAS assesses two clusters: verbal and nonverbal. Items are hierarchically ordered in terms of difficulty. The test was submitted to a panel for review regarding cultural fairness.

Age Range
2 years 6 months through 17 years 11 months

Administration Time
25 to 65 min

Publisher
The Psychological Corporation
555 Academic Court
San Antonio, TX 78204-24988
800-211-8378
www.PsychCorp.com

Norms
The total norm sample numbered 3,475, with 175 at each 6-month age group up to age 4 years 11 months. Children with significant disabilities were not included, although children in special education who were able to take the test were not excluded. Sample selection followed the 1988 U.S. Census proportions on variables of race and ethnicity, parent education, and geographic region; genders are equally represented. Children from rural backgrounds are somewhat underrepresented; children classified as gifted were somewhat overrepresented, whereas those with exceptionalities negatively impacting their learning are somewhat underrepresented.

Reliability
Evidence is provided regarding internal consistency, standard error of measurement, test-retest stability, and interrater reliability. Internal reliabilities for the preschool subtests range from .68 to .90, with the cluster coefficients ranging from .86 to .90 and the composite coefficients ranging from .89 to .94. The standard error of measurement is somewhat wide for subtests (about 1/2 *SD* as a rule) but lower, as expected, for clusters and composites. Test-retest stability with a 30-day gap (random

sample of 100 from each of three age groups of standardization sample) ranges between .56 (Picture Similarities) and .81 (Verbal Comprehension for core subtests, with .84 for Verbal Ability and .79 for Nonverbal Ability). Interrater reliabilities available only for the Copying subtest at the preschool level were .96 and .95 for two groups of 50.

Validity

Information regarding factorial, concurrent, predictive, and discriminant validity is presented. Confirmatory factor analysis supports a general and two-factor cluster interpretation at the preschool level; however, Recall of Objects loads weakly on the Verbal factor at the upper preschool level, and Early Number Concepts load weakly on Verbal for the full preschool age span. Correlations with other tests of cognitive ability are moderate and significant, supporting the concurrent validity of the DAS; the DAS composite score tends to be slightly lower than the others, which is typical when a test with more recent norms is compared with those with older norms.

Test Review 7.4

Test Name
Kaufman Assessment Battery for Children (K-ABC) (1983)
(The revision is scheduled to be published in 2004.)

Authors
Alan S. Kaufman and Nadeen L. Kaufman

What the Test Measures
The K-ABC presents a genuinely different model of intelligence, reportedly derived from the neuropsychological descriptions of Luria. This test offers assessment of both intelligence and achievement, with the former, called Mental Processing, tapping Simultaneous and Sequential processes. The test was designed to offer a strong theoretical basis for the assessment of intelligence and to link assessment of mental processing with remediation of school achievement.

The authors of the K-ABC also sought to minimize the effects of cultural differences. There are sample and teaching items for all mental processing subtests, and the assessor is granted considerable flexibility to ensure that the child understands the task. The items were subjected to a variety of examinations regarding bias, and test result differences related to race have been greatly reduced.

The preschool battery for children between the ages of 2-6 and 3-11 consists of five subtests, with two added from the age of 4 years on. The achievement battery for preschoolers is limited, with two subtests for children between the ages of 2-6 to 3-11 and four subtests for children ages 3 and 4 years. Children age 5 years are administered two additional mental processing tests and one more achievement test.

Age Range
2-6 through 12-6 years

Administration Time
45 to 50 min

(continued)

Publisher
American Guidance Service, Inc.
4201 Woodland Road
Circle Pines, MN 55014-1796
800-328-2560
www.agsnet.com

Norms
The standardization sample of 2,000 was selected to reflect the 1980 U.S. census on variables of age, gender, geographic region, community size, socioeconomic status, race and ethnicity, and parental occupation and education. Children with disabilities were included in the norms in the proportion to which they were represented in the population.

Reliability
Test-retest stability with an interval of 2 to 4 weeks yielded coefficients for the Mental Processing Composite of .83 at the preschool level. Split-half reliability for the composite scores ranged from .86 to .93. Internal consistency means vary from .86 to .91 for the Mental Processing global scales and are .93 for Achievement.

Validity
Evidence is presented regarding construct, concurrent, criterion, and discriminant validity. Factor analysis supports two mental processing factors at each age level. There are moderate and significant correlations with other major tests of intelligence.

Predictive validity in relation to a number of major achievement tests has been demonstrated. Factor analysis produces two factors for children ages 2 and 3, with Achievement emerging as the third factor at age 4, and the placement of the subtests is supported by the analysis. The K-ABC was also shown to have good discrimination between average- and high-risk preschoolers.

Test Review 7.5

Test Name
Leiter International Performance Scale–Revised (1997)

Authors
G. H. Reid and L. J. Miller

What the Test Measures
This is a nonverbal measure, completely revising and updating the original Leiter Scales. There are 20 subtests with four domains: Reasoning, Visualization, Memory, and Attention. Derived scores include standard scores, percentile ranks, and grade and age equivalents. The items are hierarchically ordered. This test is used frequently with children with significant disabilities as well as with non-English-dominant individuals. The scale's intent is to assess nonverbal intelligence. There are four rating scales for completion by the examiner, parent, the individual being assessed, and the teacher. Scaled scores have a mean of 10 and *SD* of 3, and the composite has a mean of

100 and *SD* of 15. There is also a Brief IQ Screener comprised of four subtests from the Visualization and Reasoning subtests; the same subtests are used for screening individuals at all ages.

There is a separate set of six subtests for children between the ages of 2 and 5 years. The primary purpose of the battery is for identification and placement decisions. The Attention and Memory batteries are available for additional diagnostic and neuropsychological information and include options of brief screening or more comprehensive diagnosis. These were normed on a representative sample of 763 children with typical development. Every first item of all the subtests includes opportunities to teach the task.

Guided by Carroll's model, the major factors assessed at the preschool level are Fluid Reasoning (Repeated Patterns, Sequential Order, and Classification), Fundamental Visualization (Matching, Picture Context, Figure Ground, and Form Completion), and Attention/Memory (Attention Sustained, Associated Pairs, and Forward Memory); Recognition Memory (Immediate Recognition and Delayed Recognition) is introduced at 4 years. The number of factors increases with age. The authors refer to theirs as a "hierarchical 'g' model" that reflects both the multiple facets of intelligence as well as its global aspect. There are basals and ceilings to promote efficiency. Examiners are encouraged to make accommodations to facilitate the child's ability to respond.

The rating scales tap the areas of attention, activity level, organization and impulse control, sociability, sensory reactivity, emotions, anxiety, and mood.

Zero raw scores are assigned scaled scores, but the authors provide cautions regarding their interpretation.

Age Range
2 years to 20 years 11 months

Administration Time
Under 40 min for the full battery, 25 min for the screener

Publisher
Stoelting Co.
620 Wheat Lane
Wood Dale, IL 60191
630-860-9700
www.stoeltingco.com

Norms
The standardization sample includes 1,719 individuals stratified to reflect the 1993 U.S. Census. The Northeast is somewhat underrepresented. Norms are presented in 6-month groups between the ages of 2 and 5 years.

Reliability
Evidence is presented regarding internal consistency, test-retest stability, standard error of measurement, and decision-making consistency. The alphas for the Visualization-- Reasoning composites for ages 2 to 5 years all exceed .80 except at age 5 (.78). Spatial Orientation is the only subtest with alphas consistently below .80 for this age group. The attention and memory coefficients exceed .80 except for Associated Pairs. Standard error of measurement is generally below 1.0 for both the examiner and teacher rating scales, with internal consistency coefficients above .90 for these same groups. For the parent

scale, internal consistency exceeds .80, and standard error of measurement remains below 1.34. The self-rating scale does not apply to preschoolers. Standard errors of measurement for the Visualization-Reasoning Battery were generally low, below 1.75 for subareas and an average of 4.24 for the composite score. Standard errors of measurement for the Attention/Memory battery were below 1.44. The alphas for the main battery all exceed .87. Test-retest stability for a sample of preschool children selected from the standardization population shows correlations above .80 for all subareas and .90 for Full IQ. The coefficients are lower for the Attention/Memory battery, with a range of .61 to .85 for the composites. The test-retest coefficients for the Examiner Rating Scale for preschool children all exceed .85. The consistencies regarding identification of children with cognitive delay for the screener and full battery were .90 and .95 respectively.

The Leiter-R was reviewed regarding item bias, with items discriminating among groups removed.

Validity
Evidence regarding content, criterion, and construct validity is presented. Item analyses and feedback from tryout versions were used for content analysis.

Discriminant analysis was conducted for application to a number of special groups, including gifted, hearing impaired, learning disabled, traumatic brain injury, and attention-deficit/hyperactivity disorder. Correlations of the Leiter-R with another major IQ test showed substantial relationships, for example, .85 for Full Scale, Verbal, and Performance IQ. Correlation with an achievement battery showed a range of .63 (Arithmetic) to .83 (Math Composite) for the Brief IQ and .62 (Arithmetic) to .82 (Broad Reading and Broad Mathematics) for the Full IQ.

Factor analysis supported a four-factor model for ages 4 to 5: Fluid Reasoning, Visualization, Attention, and Recognition Memory. The Sequential Order subtest loaded more strongly on Visualization than on Reasoning. At ages 2 to 5 the subtests with the highest g loadings were Figure Ground, Form Completion, Matching, Sequential Order, Picture Context, Classification, Associated Pairs, Forward Memory, and Attention Sustained.

Test Review 7.6

Test Name

McCarthy Scales of Children's Abilities (1972)

Author

Dorothea McCarthy

What the Test Measures

This scale is one of the early attempts to provide a normed instrument for young children, allowing systematic observation of cognitive and motor behaviors specifically in the areas of Verbal, Perceptual-Performance, Quantitative, Memory, and Motor functioning, with derivation of a General Cognitive Index (GCI). Manipulative tasks were designed with the intent of discriminating among developmental ages and between children functioning at the lower and upper ends of the developmental continuum.

The content was selected on the basis of the author's clinical experience. There are a total of 18 subtests administered to all children, with basal and ceiling scores to facilitate efficiency. The Memory tests are embedded in subtests from the three primary abilities (Verbal, Perceptual Performance, and Quantitative) that make up the GCI, and the Motor Scale is a mixture of independent tests, with overlap with the Perceptual-Performance subtests.

The GCI has a mean of 100 and *SD* 16, and the index scores for Verbal, Perceptual-Performance, Quantitative, Motor, and Memory have means of 50 with *SD* of 10. For children over 5 years, the assessor can also establish lateral dominance.

Age Range

2 1/2 through 8 1/2 years

Administration Time

45 to 50 min

Publisher

The Psychological Corporation
555 Academic Court
San Antonio, TX 78204-24988
800-211-8378
www.PsychCorp.com

Norms

Scaled scores are available for the GCI and six scales but not for the 18 component tests. However, means and *SD*s for the component tests are presented to aid interpretation.

The stratified sample was determined in relation to the 1969–1970 U.S. Census on the variables of age, gender, color (considered as White/non-White, with Hispanics considered in terms of racial background), geographic region (including urban vs. rural), and father's occupation. Norms are presented for 6-month age intervals up to 5 1/2 years and for 12-month intervals thereafter. The total number of cases was 1,032 with at least 100 at each age level. The sample included only children with normal development and with English language dominance. GCI scores range from 50 to 150. Additional scores include percentile ranks and mental ages.

(*continued*)

Reliability

Reliability information includes test-retest stability, internal consistency, and standard error of measurement. These results are generally strong, especially for the GCI and Verbal Indexes. The Memory and Motor Scales are relatively weaker but are still in an acceptable range.

The test-retest group consisted of 104 children at six age levels from the norm group who were reassessed after an average interval of 1 month. The GCI yielded .90 stability, and the results for the other scales ranged from .75 to .89. The Motor Scale was the least reliable, at .69.

Validity

The author cites factor analytic support for three factors that are consistent across age groups: a general cognitive, a motor, and a memory factor. Verbal, quantitative, and perceptual-performance abilities were supported, but not consistently for all ages.

Predictive validity of the McCarthy in relation to the Metropolitan Achievement Tests (MAT) is significant for the Perceptual-Performance, Quantitative, and General Cognitive Scale but not for the Verbal and Motor scales and evident for Memory only for mathematics and total MAT score. However, the levels, though highly statistically significant, are weak with regard to variance accounted for because the maximum relationship is .54, and most are below this level.

Comment

The McCarthy is an attractive scale for young children in terms of its appeal; children generally become easily involved. However, the norms are now considerably out of date, and a more serious concern is its tendency to underestimate children of lower functioning. In other words, this should not be the only major cognitive test to diagnose mental retardation, as the scores are likely to be lower than those obtained from other measures. See Lidz and Ballester (1986) for a literature review and additional data regarding this issue.

Test Review 7.7

Test Name

Mullen Scales of Early Learning: AGS Edition (1995)

Author

Eileen M. Mullen

What the Test Measures

The Mullen assesses cognitive abilities in the domains of visual, linguistic, and motor functions and distinguishes between receptive and expressive processing. The five specific scales are Gross Motor (birth to 33 months only), Fine Motor, Visual Reception, Receptive Language, and Expressive Language. Normed scores are provided for each scale, as well as a composite; the scale scores are T scores with a mean of 50 and SD of 10. The Early Learning Composite, derived from the T scores, has a mean of 100 and SD of 15. In addition, percentiles and age equivalents can be determined. The information is intended to reflect the child's developmental level, to profile the child's strengths and weaknesses, and to provide a basis for intervention programming. A large number of manipulative materials are provided, but the assessor needs to supply some items such as cereal, crayons, and coins.

The theoretical underpinnings of the Mullen rely essentially on the author's clinical experience and the attempt to represent discrete but related abilities that characterize the early development of children. There are basals and ceilings, as well as recommended starting points. Items are hierarchically ordered in terms of level of difficulty.

Age Range
Birth to 68 months

Administration Time
Estimates are 15 min for 1-year-olds, 30 min for 3-year-olds, and 60 min for 5-year-olds.

Publisher
American Guidance Service, Inc.
4201 Woodland Road
Circle Pines, MN 55014-1796
800-328-2560
www.agsnet.com

Norms
The total sample for the Mullen numbered 1,849, with data collected over a period of 8 years. The norms reflect the 1990 U.S. Census regarding variables of gender, geographic region, race and ethnicity, community size, and socioeconomic status.

Zero scores at the younger ages are assigned scores. The bands of error tend to be wide, in some cases exceeding 1 *SD*. At the older preschool ages, the floors appear adequate, but the ceilings do not.

Reliability
Information is presented regarding internal consistency, measurement error, test-retest stability, and interscorer reliability. Median split-half internal consistency coefficients exceed .80 for all subscales and the composite, with the exceptions of Visual Reception (.79) and Fine Motor (.75). The standard error of measurement medians range from 4.1 (Gross Motor) to 5.0 (Fine Motor), which is on the high side considering the standard deviation of 10 for the *T* scores. Two test-retest studies with intervals of one to two weeks show coefficients exceeding .80 for the younger group (1 to 24 months) and all in the .70s for the older group (25 to 56 months). The trend was for a slight gain at the second testing, most noticeable for Visual Reception. Interscorer reliabilities all exceed .90.

Validity
The manual offers evidence of construct, concurrent, and criterion validity. Construct validity is supported by demonstration of score increases with age. Factor analysis yielded one *g* factor per age group, with Receptive and Expressive Language loading highest on this factor (perhaps better called a language factor rather than *g*?). Correlations between the Mullen and Bayley range between .30 (Gross Motor) and .70 (Composite) for the Bayley Mental Developmental Index, with other subscale scores in the .50s. Correlations with the Bayley Psychomotor Development Index range from .76 (Gross Motor) to .28 (Visual Reception), with others scattered; the correlation for the Mullen Composite was .43. The language scales were correlated with a major language test and yielded .85 for Receptive, .72 for Expressive with the other test's Auditory Comprehension, and .72 for Receptive and .80 for Expressive with the other test's Verbal Ability. Similarly, correlations between the Mullen's motor scales and another major motor test range between .65 and .82 for different age ranges.

Criterion predictions related to a readiness scale show correlations ranging from .35 (Expressive Language) to .47 (Fine Motor) for Pre-Reading and between .35 (Visual Reception) and .50 (Fine Motor) for Quantitative.

The author also describes a study documenting discriminant validity between children of low versus normal birth weight.

Test Review 7.8

Test Name
Stanford-Binet Intelligence Scales–Fifth Edition (SB5) (in press)

Author
Gale H. Roid

What the Test Measures
This latest edition of the Stanford-Binet represents a major revision. The test yields Verbal, Nonverbal, and Composite IQs with mean of 100 and *SD* of 15 and subtest scores with means of 10 and *SD* of 3.

The SB5 also yields scores on five dimensions representing major cognitive factors: reasoning, knowledge, quantitative reasoning, visual-spatial processing, and working memory, each with a mean of 100 and *SD* of 15. All dimensions are assessed with both verbal and nonverbal subtests.

Subtests for preschool children include more toys and manipulables than are in the previous version.

Age Range
2 years to 90 years

Administration Time
45 to 60 min

Publisher
Riverside Publishing Company
425 Spring Lake Drive
Itasca, IL 60143-2079
800-323-9540
www.riversidepublishing.com

Norms
The test uses a national stratified sample of 4,900 individuals reflecting the 2000 U.S. Census.

Reliability
Not available at time of publication.

Validity
The items have been reviewed for gender, ethnic, cultural, regional, and socioeconomic bias.
Other information not available at time of publication.

Test Review 7.9

Test Name

Wechsler Preschool and Primary Scale of Intelligence (2002)

Author

David Wechsler

What the Test Measures

There are 15 core and optional tests with eight subtests that are new to this revision: Picture Naming, Receptive Vocabulary, Concept Grouping, Matrix Reasoning, Picture Concepts, Word Context, Symbol Search, and Coding. This will allow comparison of receptive and expressive vocabulary, as well as verbal and nonverbal fluid reasoning and a separate factor of processing speed. All items have teaching and practice opportunities, with minimal demands on speed and accuracy for the nonverbal items.

The primary purpose of the test is to identify exceptionality in young children, from mental retardation through giftedness. There is overlap in the norms at the upper limit with the Wechsler Intelligence Scale for Children–Revised, so clinicians must decide which is the more appropriate instrument based on the need for an adequate ceiling or floor. The scale is not appropriate for children with sensory or motor handicaps.

This WPPSI revision is organized to yield Verbal, Performance, and Full Scale standard scores with a mean of 100 and *SD* of 15. There are six Verbal subtests (Information, Comprehension, Arithmetic, Vocabulary, Similarities, and Sentences) and five Performance subtests, with the sixth being optional (Object Assembly, Geometric Design, Block Design, Mazes, Picture Completion, and Animal Pegs).

Age Range

2 years 6 months through 7 years 3 months

Administration Time

30 to 45 min for ages 2 years 6 months through 3 years 11 months; 60 min for ages 4 years through 7 years 3 months

Publisher

The Psychological Corporation
555 Academic Court
San Antonio, TX 78204-24988
800-211-8378
www.PsychCorp.com

Norms

The total norm group includes 1,700 children, stratified to represent the most current U.S. Census with regard to age, gender, region, parent education, and race.

Reliability

Not available at time of publication.

Validity

Items were reviewed for ethnic, gender, regional, and socioeconomic bias, and those presenting problems were modified or dropped. Further information not available at time of publication.

Test Review 7.10

Test Name

Woodcock-Johnson, Third Edition (WJ III) (2000)

Author

Kevin S. McGrew, Richard W. Woodcock, and Nancy Mather

What the Test Measures

The WJ III assesses three categories of cognitive functioning: verbal ability, thinking ability, and cognitive efficiency. There are seven tests in the standard battery (Verbal Comprehension, Visual-Auditory Learning, Spatial Relations, Sound Blending, Concept Formation, Visual Matching, and Numbers Reversed), three supplemental tests (Incomplete Words, Auditory Working Memory, and Visual-Auditory Learning-Delayed), and ten tests in the extended battery (General Information, Retrieval Fluency, Picture Recognition, Auditory Attention, Analysis-Synthesis, Decision Speed, Memory for Words, Rapid Picture Naming, Planning, and Pair Cancellation), for a total of 20 subtests.

The scores provide information regarding general intellectual ability, as well as clusters (Verbal Ability, Thinking Ability, and Cognitive Efficiency) and cognitive factors (Comprehension-Knowledge, Long-Term Retrieval, Visual-Spatial Thinking, Auditory Processing, Fluid Reasoning, Processing Speed, and Short Term Memory). There is also information regarding clinical clusters (Phonemic Awareness, Working Memory, Broad Attention, Cognitive Fluency, and Executive Processes). Analysis of intracognitive discrepancies allows for profiling of strengths and weaknesses.

Some of the achievement tests can be administered to preschool children, including Letter-Word Identification, Story Recall, Understanding Directions, Spelling, Passage Comprehension, Applied Problems, Story-Recall Delayed, Picture Vocabulary, Oral Comprehension, Quantitative Concepts, and Academic Knowledge.

Test items are hierarchically ordered according to difficulty; basals and ceilings are determined for efficiency, and subtests can be selected to tailor the testing for the individual.

Age Range

2 years to 90 years

Administration Time

Not clearly specified because this varies with selection of tests, but assessors should expect to spend about 45 to 60 min on this battery

Publisher

The Riverside Publishing Company
425 Spring Lake Drive
Itasca, IL 60143-2079
800-323-9540
www.riversidepublishing.com

Norms

The preschool sample included 1,143 children. The WJ III was co-normed with the WJ III Tests of Achievement. The entire sample was selected to reflect the 2000 U.S. Census on variables of geographic region, community size, gender, race and ethnicity, parent education, and type of school (private, public, home).

Reliability

Reliability information includes measurement error, interrater agreement, and test-retest stability. For younger children (ages 2 to 7 years) with an interval of 1 to 2 years, the test-retest coefficients range between .57 (Memory for Words) and .91 (Letter-Word Identification); 10 out of 15 exceed .80. Most cluster reliabilities are .90 or higher. For preschool children on the standard battery, the standard errors of measurement appear best for Verbal Comprehension and Visual-Auditory Learning, moderate for Spatial Relations and Sound Blending, and fairly high for Concept Formation and Visual Matching.

Validity

Information is presented regarding construct, content, and concurrent validity. The batteries were submitted to review and analysis for bias. For preschool children, the WJ III Standard Scale correlations with WJ III Achievement clusters range from .27 (Passage Comprehension) to .79 (Oral Language), with an average of .55. These relationships were found to be stronger than for other major cognitive measures. Correlations between the WJ III and other major tests for preschool children ranged between .53 and .67. Studies with the preschool population are limited.

Comment

Although an advantage of the WJ III is the continuity provided across the ages, the same tests are administered across age levels; that is, there are no tests developed specifically for preschool children. All tests are presented in two-dimensional format, with audiotapes used for some. There are no manipulable materials. Therefore, it is necessary for a young child to have the ability to attend to the presentation format of this test. The WJ III differs from other major cognitive batteries primarily regarding the specificity and breadth of its factors.

STANDARDIZED TESTING AND ISSUES OF CULTURAL AND LINGUISTIC DIVERSITY

Padilla (2001) pointed out that there are an estimated 14% of children living in the United States who come from non-English-dominant families and that some states have a proportion of non-English-dominant speakers as high as one third. Virtually all of the existing procedures, norm-based as well as others, can be criticized in relation to their relevance for children from diverse cultural backgrounds. Lopez (1995) found the use of normed tests even more problematic than other approaches to assessment when used with children with limited English language proficiency. Even tests translated into other languages may not offer the dialect of the referred child and may be offered within a context that is unfamiliar to the child (Garber & Slater, 1983). This is further complicated by the fact that families from many minority backgrounds are disproportionately poor (De Barona & Barona, 1991). For example, Johnson and McGowan (1984) found that scores of preschool children on both the Stanford-Binet Intelligence Scale–Fourth Edition and the McCarthy Scales were weak predictors of later school achievement for Mexican American children of low socioeconomic status. Test results of children from nonmainstream backgrounds are, to a significant extent, measures of the degree of the family's acculturation (Ortiz, 2001). From this point of view, low levels of performance on these tests would be a cue for the assessor to consider both the barriers to the adjustment of the family and the child and the needs of the family for services that will facilitate their adaptation (McEvoy & Barnett, 1988).

Specific procedures vary in their degree of relevance for culturally diverse learners, as some are more flexible in their application, whereas others are more sensitive to cultural variables. Nevertheless, the assessor must always be mindful of the appropriateness of applying a procedure to a child and must evaluate the validity of interpretations made in relation to the various contexts of the child and family (Taylor & Lee, 1990). It is important to keep in mind that families differ in their degrees of adaptation to the mainstream culture and that there is great heterogeneity within any group (Laosa, 1977; Walton & Nuttall, 1999).

Ascher (1990) discussed issues relating specifically to assessment of bilingual children, who, like children in other culturally diverse contexts, have tended to be overidentified as mentally retarded, and their ability to learn has frequently been underestimated. There is still much we do not know, not the least of which is "how to measure the extent to which one of the languages of the bilingual student influences the other, or even how to describe bilingual competence" (Ascher, 1990, p. 2). According to Ascher, bilingualism can affect testing results in several ways:

- *Code switching,* in which bilinguals tend to move back and forth between languages, related to factors such as the content, the circumstances, and the people involved
- Slow processing in the less familiar language
- Anomalies that are difficult to explain, such as the tendency for Spanish-speaking bilinguals to do better with digits backward than forward
- Increased distractibility with limited English mastery
- The need for up to 7 years for full mastery of English (an issue for preschool children who are by definition younger than seven years)

Ascher (1990) described five options that are commonly used for testing limited English speakers, all of which have limitations:

1. *Use of nonverbal tests:* These have poor predictive validity for bilinguals and are not immune to the effects of language. The study by Lidz and Macrine (2001), for example, documented the lack of advantage provided by nonverbal tests for identifying children from culturally diverse backgrounds for a gifted program.

2. *Translated tests:* This creates a new test; translation of the language changes the difficulty level of the items, and tests that are translated are rarely renormed for the translated version. Furthermore, some concepts are not translatable into other languages, and in other instances information related to the answer may be contained in the question of the translated item (similar to asking who is buried in Grant's tomb).

3. *Use of interpreters:* There is uneven training of interpreters and very little research of the effects of using interpreters on test results (see also Cheng, 1991).

4. *Use of bilingual assessors:* This has the advantage of enabling the assessor to determine the child's competence in both languages through language samples in other environments; however, bilingual assessors tend to rely on standardized tests that all have limitations for bilingual students.

5. *Alternative approaches:* Ascher was particularly impressed with the promise of dynamic assessment for use with bilingual students, and there has been further development of these approaches since the publication of her article. Dynamic assessment is discussed in detail in Chapter 6. The research of Peña and her associates has been particularly pertinent to the application of dynamic assessment with bilingual preschool children (e.g., Kester, Peña, & Gillam, 2001; Lidz & Peña, 1996; Peña, Iglesias, & Lidz, 2001).

Lopez (1995) and Gonzalez, Brusca-Vega, and Yawkey (1997) highlighted the need for multiple sources of data for children from limited English backgrounds and recommended greater reliance on observations, interviews, checklists, rating scales, and informal procedures than on standardized tests. Lopez also emphasized the importance of determining the child's level of language acquisition in both languages.

CONCLUDING COMMENTS

Both Sarason (1976) and Hilliard (1989) bemoaned the fate of Binet's original test and the thoughtfulness underlying its development. Sarason minced no words when he claimed that "school psychology was born in the prison of a test" (p. 587) and when he wrote that "the God-dards' and Termans' . . . concerns for rigor and precision in measurement were uncluttered by the thoughtfulness of a Binet" (p. 583). Hilliard provided a left punch when he commented that "IQ tests are and have been rationalized and justified on the basis of their psychometric properties, not on the basis of their contribution to pedagogical services" (p. 126). We certainly must be careful not to throw the baby out with the bathwater, but perhaps we also need to consider occasionally changing the bathwater to ensure that our tools are serving their intended purposes.

Standardized tests are one among many tools of the psychological assessor. As with any tool, a test's characteristics and strengths and weaknesses must be understood so that it can be used appropriately. Standardized tests can be invaluable aids for determination of risk and program eligibility, but use of these tests should not be a substitute for good judgment and thinking. If the results of the test fail to make sense, then the results should be challenged with additional data. Direct observation and reliable reports from parents and teachers should be weighed heavily against questionable standardized test results. Information about the educational level of the parents, as well as their child rearing practices, should count heavily toward predictions (Lytton, Watts, & Dunn, 1986). The numbers from standardized tests reflect assumptions about normal distribution and analysis of large groups. The performance of any individual may or may not be well described by these comparisons. The experience and good judgment of the human assessor is still a valued asset in protecting clients from abuses of test-driven decision making.

A word should be said about the use of age equivalence scores because of the considerable discussion among professionals about this issue. Age equivalents are appealing because of their apparent consumer friendliness. However, there is some danger in taking such a common-sense route to test interpretation. For very young children, a case can be made for the content validity of developmental ages, when it can be demonstrated that the item content is truly typical of the sequence of developmental progress on meaningful dimensions for specific ages. The problem is that many children do not follow the rules and often obtain their total raw scores in an annoying variety of ways. One child may obtain a raw score of 8 by passing items 1 through 8. Another child may obtain the same raw score by passing items 1, 4, 7, 8, 10, 12, 14, 15, and so on for innumerable combinations. Yet both children will receive the same age equivalent (and, by the way, the same scaled score). Age equivalents are merely the median scores obtained by children of certain ages on the test. Age equivalents are neither ratio nor interval scores, and an age equivalent at one age cannot be compared with an age equivalent at another age; in addition, delays at one age have a very different implication from delays at another age (consider the meaning of a 6-month delay at age 2 years versus 16 years). Furthermore, one cannot conclude that a 5-year-old child who obtains an age equivalent of 2-0, for example, has the mind of a 2-year-old. It can only be concluded that the child succeeded on the same number of items as did a child of 2-0. Certainly a child of 1-6 who obtains an age equivalent of 2-0 has a very different "mind" from a child of 5 who obtains the same score. What the score means requires further interpretation and analysis. Assessors should be cautioned to use these scores very judiciously, if at all, and to be very careful about how they are explained to parents and teachers.

SUMMARY

This chapter reviews issues of using standardized tests with young children and provides many cautions and warnings that need to be applied with this population, particularly with regard to interpretations of scores, applications with children from culturally and linguistically diverse backgrounds, and predictive validity. The chapter reviews a number of standardized tests that have been developed for use with preschool-age children, as well as criteria for evaluating these instruments. Standardized tests can be useful when used for the purposes for which they were designed, namely, to estimate level of risk, as well as to determine eligibility for special education services.

SUGGESTED ACTIVITIES

SCHOLARSHIP

Select one of the major standardized tests and write a comprehensive review, updated with review of literature conducted since the publication of the manual.

APPLICATION

Select two of the major standardized tests and administer them to three children, and include a supervised review of the procedure, scoring, and interpretation. If it is not possible for the trainer to do a direct observation of the test administration, submit a videotape of at least one example of administration of each test for critical review (the trainer may prefer to conduct a role play session). Note that for those who struggle with accurate determination of chronological age, American Guidance Associates provides a free downloadable age calculator at their Web site, www.agsnet.com.

Chapter Eight

◆

Social-Emotional Functioning

◆

This is the only chapter that focuses on a function rather than an assessment approach. It is difficult to explain the rationale for this; it boils down to "feeling right" (how appropriate for this chapter!). However, this is an area, along with cognition, that is considered a specific domain of the psychologist, and there is no single approach to its assessment. We will draw on material presented in earlier chapters, such as observation and play. Cognitive functioning and social-emotional functioning are both separable and inseparable. Children may have strengths or weaknesses in one and not the other, although there are certainly strong developmental relationships and "causal" influences. The chapters on standardized tests and even dynamic and curriculum-based assessment could be delegated to a cognitive emphasis, whereas observation and play are clearly in both domains; however, cognitive tasks include social-emotional components and vice versa.

Assessment of social-emotional functioning of young children relies to a significant extent on rating scales completed by adults who are intensively involved with the child, such as caregivers and teachers. Whereas older children are able to communicate about their feelings through interview and self-report measures, very young children are limited in their ability to respond to these approaches. Reliance on the reports of others means that the information that is provided informs assessors about both the child and the reporter. The content is the child's behavior as it is perceived and experienced by the rater. For this reason, we can anticipate discrepancies between raters, as well as between the ratings of any of the adults and what we might find through direct observation. Where is the truth? The truth, of course, appears in all of the results, and we must be able to weigh and interpret the findings in relation to the sources and to the many other bits of assessment information we gather. Rating scales remain the most efficient sources of data, and the perceptions of the raters are valuable; however, they should never be used in isolation (R. P. Martin, 1986, 1988a, 1991).

SOCIAL-EMOTIONAL DEVELOPMENT

Children of preschool age are capable of many complex emotions, such as empathy, shame, and embarrassment, and they are rapidly learning the cultural rules of emotional display. Because this learning is in process, they are also more prone to show their emotions and are able to make immediate causal connections for their own most basic feelings, although they struggle more with attributions of emotions and causal relationships regarding others, particularly if the causes lie in the past (Denham, 1998). Children of preschool age are also beginning to be aware that emotions can be controlled, and they are beginning to learn strategies for emotional regulation. All of these developments relate very much to their social interactive experiences in their caregiving environments (Denham, 1998; Thompson, 1993).

Emotions are at the threshold between the individual and the environment and appear to function as a next step following arousal that alerts the person to the occurrence of an event. Emotions energize the individual's attempts to cope with both internal and external stimulation that is sometimes pleasurable and sometimes stressful (Campos, Campos, & Barrett, 1989). The integration of perception, cognition, and emotion serve an evaluative function that determines the degree of pleasure-stress of these events and the nature of the most appropriate behaviors with which to respond. How the individual responds also relates to memory, which contributes to the evaluation and attribution of meaning to emotion-inducing events; it is meaning that connects with the type of emotion and motoric behavior that responds to the stimulation. When children behave in a way that we would interpret as emotionally disturbed, we can infer that there has been some event, internal or external, that has caused stress and that their behaviors are their attempts to cope with this stress (Lidz, 1983). What makes this behavior disturbed is usually that these attempts to cope are not effective, or, if effective for the child, result in negative consequences for the child's social or object environment. Underlying such inappropriate displays of emotion (inappropriate often by virtue of timing or intensity) is the child's struggle with the development of emotional regulation (Thompson, 1993). It is also possible that these behaviors are merely learned from a nonnormative environment. Determination of the source in this case would have direct implications for intervention. Emotional functioning, as any behavior, occurs within a social context.

Children are programmed for social interaction. They are born to interact and, in fact, must do so to survive (Grief, 1977; Schiefelbusch, 1986). Their dependence requires it, and their responsiveness inspires it. As babies, humans interact primarily with adults and, within these relationships (as well as with siblings, extended family members, and alternative caregivers), develop the cognitive, language, and motor skills that will gradually enable them to interact with peers. The attachments and social skills developed within the home lay the foundation for their interactions in other settings (LaFreniere & Sroufe, 1985; Lieberman, 1977; Sroufe, 1989). Secure attachment, which rests on a foundation of development of trust (Hodapp & Mueller, 1982), relates to good emotion regulation that in turn provides a foundation for successful social interaction (Kuebli, 1994; Raver & Zigler, 1997). Good emotion regulation depends to a significant extent on language skills that also have a developmental spurt during preschool years, and development of good language skills relates to social interaction experiences within the primary caretaking contexts (Kopp, 1989). Emergence and integration of these functions allow expression of the "emotional thinking" that characterizes the developmental stage of the optimally developed preschool child (Greenspan, 1992).

By age 3, typically developing children are able to initiate and sustain friendships (Hartup,

1989). Behavior within these friendships differs from behaviors in relation to nonfriends with regard to reciprocity, cooperation, time spent in negotiation, and elaboration of play (Hartup, 1989); thus the development of friendships seems to play an important developmental role. Whether with friends or acquaintances, the typically developing child is engaging in associative or cooperative play by the time of preschool, or, if not interacting, the child is likely to be playing independently. It is unusual at these ages for children without developmental delays to be unoccupied or in an onlooker role (except in the service of gaining entry to play) or to be involved in parallel play (Parten, 1932; Rubin, 1986).

It is no surprise that social development is a critical developmental task during the preschool years. This is the time when the development of executive functions that underlie self-regulation make a significant spurt in the brain. Freud may have correctly anticipated later theories and discoveries of brain organization in his descriptions of id, ego, and superego, which might be viewed as grossly representing the primary, secondary, and tertiary (according to Luria) areas of the brain. Infants and toddlers can be viewed as dominated by the limbic (emotional or id) areas, gradually developing their cognitive functions (posterior cortex) and, finally, their executive control mechanisms (anterior cortex). The great variability from one individual to another in the rate and nature of these developments is a valuable source of assessment information and is useful for predictions of children's adjustment to formal instructional environments and to life in general. Good social interaction requires considerable "executive" skill, as well as adequate development of the underlying cognitive, language, and motoric functions. These functions need to be integrated, coordinated, and appropriately applied. Social-emotional development is no easy task. The good news is that a significant portion of this development is sensitive to environmental input and therefore is amenable to intervention, particularly if this intervention takes place during this time of rapid development. The bad news is that a significant portion of this development is sensitive to environmental input and therefore is amenable to the influence of potentially debilitating interactions that are difficult to overcome. Children differ in their degrees of resilience to these negative experiences.

Although there are an increasing number of assessment procedures tapping social skills, relatively little in the assessment repertoire allows asessors to represent the increasing executive control over social-emotional functioning of preschool-age children in a formal way. The primary data derive from research and procedures used for research related to temperament and adaptive behavior or coping (discussed later).

In designing the Application of Cognitive Functions Scale (ACFS), described in detail in Chapter 6, Lidz and Jepsen (2000)* decided to include a behavior rating scale that would capture these qualitative aspects of children's executive functioning as they were in the process of problem solving the six tasks of the procedure. Aranov (1999) subsequently investigated the utility of this scale as a stand-alone instrument and obtained significant agreements between the assessor and classroom teacher, between the assessor and speech therapist, and between the classroom teacher and speech therapist of young children involved in a treatment program for developmental delays. Because school psychologists often make inferences about the child's behavioral capacities based on brief observations of their behavior within the assessment situation, including limited classroom observations, the findings of such agreements with professionals working with the child over more prolonged periods of time were very encouraging. A copy of this scale as modified by Lidz for completion by teachers and therapists appears in Form 8.1.

---

*This procedure has experienced a number of modest revisions, and some studies have used previous versions.

Behavior Observation Rating Scale

(adopted from the Application of Cognitive Functions Scale by Lidz & Jepsen, 2000)

Please rate the *typical behavior* of the child whose name appears below. The rating should characterize this child's behavior *when you are trying to teach her or him something new.* Provide these ratings only if you have known this child for at least four months. Please add any comments you wish to explain or elaborate your ratings.

Child's Name: _____ Rater: _____ Position: _____

Date of Rating: _____ How long have you known this child? _____

	Consistently	Inconsistently	No Evidence
1. The child controls her or his own behavior.	2	1	0
2. The child completes most tasks.	2	1	0
3. The child continues to work when tasks become challenging.	2	1	0
4. The child tries alternative solutions or self-corrects when solving tasks (i.e., doesn't get stuck on one solution when it doesn't work).	2	1	0
5. The child shows enthusiastic reactions to tasks and/or interest in materials.	2	1	0
6. The child shows willingness/openness to "receiving" teaching.	2	1	0
7. The child is able to engage in reciprocal social interactions, that is, turn-taking behavior and conversation.	2	1	0

Total Score: _____

Thank you! Please return by _____ to _____

Lidz, Carol S. *Early Childhood Assessment.* Copyright 2003, John Wiley & Sons.

Form 8.1

Form 8.1 can be completed by any professional who is involved with the child, such as teachers and other support service staff. That is, the same form can be completed by different individuals for the same child. This information allows the assessor to look for patterns of agreement or disagreement regarding the child's developing executive skills across contexts. Most important, the scale provides insight into behaviors that are otherwise rarely tapped during the course of assessments of young children, as it is often incorrectly concluded that children do not have executive capacities at such young ages (see Chapter 9 for further elaboration of this issue). This scale may also be useful for monitoring the child's responsiveness to treatment, as one important outcome of any treatment for children with social-emotional disorders is the development of increased self-regulation and ability to become a good social partner.

Linder's (1993a) play-based observation approach provides useful guidelines for operationalizing social-emotional development as well as the other major developmental domains. If we look at the age ranges associated with the components she provides for social-emotional functioning, we can derive some reference point for expectations for the typically developing child so that we can be alerted to significant deviations from these parameters. For typically developing children between the ages of 3 to 5 years, we would look for the following (Linder, 1993a, pp. 150–152):

Mastery Motivation

• Prefers challenging tasks when given a choice between relatively easy and difficult tasks

Attachment, Separation, and Individuation

• Can answer whether he or she is a boy or girl
• Separates from parent without crying
• Joins other children in play
• Can explore neighborhood unattended (this would vary considerably with background)
• Has a strong sense of family and home and quotes parents as authorities

Development of Humor

• Laughs at concrete, perceptually incongruent events and distortions of familiar sights
• Laughs at multiple meanings of words

Social Relations with Peers

• Plays spontaneously with other children in complicated verbal communication
• Increased rough-and-tumble play (for boys)
• Begins cooperative play
• Replaces parallel play with group play
• Prefers playing with other children to playing alone unless engrossed in the project
• Has peer interactions characterized by talking, smiling, laughing, and playing
• Begins group games with simple rules
• Shows concern and sympathy for others in group

These behaviors represent a profile of the social-emotional functioning of the preschool child even though they tend to emphasize social behavior rather than emotional expression or regulation. Assessors must always bear in mind that lack of evidence of any of these behaviors does not necessarily imply an absence of the capacity to develop them. Social-emotional functioning is an area that is particularly sensitive to home and cultural influences, and the parents' expectations with regard to emotional displays and social interactions will make significant contributions to the child's development of these behaviors. Needless to say, a caring parent is unlikely to allow a child to explore a dangerous neighborhood freely, as is suggested by one of the items on the preceding list. Furthermore, the manner in which emotions are displayed varies considerably across and within cultures; for example, even within Western cultures, these expectations differ considerably for boys compared with girls.

The Linder guidelines are not alone in emphasizing social interaction with relative oversight of emotional expression and functioning. This is an area that is very difficult to capture in most assessment procedures. In research, emotion is usually assessed with physiological measures such as heart rate, blood pressure, and glandular systems change, but these measures are not very good at discriminating among the specific types of emotions (Yarrow, 1979), only suggesting that emotional response has occurred. Furthermore, the equipment involved in these procedures is an unlikely candidate for the toolbox of the school psychologist (try carrying an electrocardiograph up three flights of stairs and stuffing it into a closet-sized testing room!).

The only scale that attempts to assess the emotions of young children with any significant detail is the Scales of Socioemotional Development, authored by Lewis and Michalson (1983); this requires the assessor to observe the child throughout an entire day in a day care setting. The items assess the child's emotional responses to a number of commonly occurring situations such when the parent arrives and departs, when another child is crying, when another child grabs a toy away, and when the caregiver teases or acts silly. Completion of this scale yields a profile of the child on the dimensions of fear, anger, happiness, affiliation, and competence.

A number of rating scales with normative references that tap parameters of social-emotional functioning are discussed later. One scale that assesses more molar aspects of social development than most others is the Devereux Early Childhood Assessment (DECA; LeBuffe & Naglieri, 1999), detailed in Test Review 8.1. The DECA differs from other scales in its focus on positive behaviors and resilience and with regard to its design specifically for preschool-age children. It also contains a scale for screening behavioral concerns. With this information, the assessor can also provide consultative services by helping to design programming for children identified as at risk for development of adjustment problems as a preventive measure, rather than waiting until problems occur.

The Ages and Stages Questionnaires: Social-Emotional (ASQ:SE; Squires, Bricker, Heo, & Twombly, 2001) is a new scale that relies on ratings by parents or caregivers. A description of this appears in Test Review 8.2. The ASQ:SE was developed specifically for use with very young children and for continuity of assessment from infancy through preschool years. The test represents behaviors that characterize adaptive and malaptive behaviors at each of eight age groups from 6 through 60 months.

The Early Screening Project (Walker, Severson, & Feil, 1995) provides another approach that allows for efficient identification of children at risk for developing emotional problems by screening entire classrooms. Based on evidence of the stability of the two parameters of internalizing and externalizing disorders (Merrell, 1996), the teacher is first asked to nominate three children who show the most extreme behaviors within each category. The teacher then completes a rating scale for only these six children. Based on the results of this scale, the parents of

Test Review 8.1

Test Name
Devereux Early Childhood Assessment [DECA] (1999)

Authors
Paul A. LeBuffe and Jack A. Naglieri

What the Test Measures
The DECA is based on a model of resilience and assesses both within-child protective factors and emotional and behavioral problems of preschool children. It is therefore possible to view behavioral concerns in the context of protective factors. The DECA rating scale can be completed by teachers or parents and includes three subscales within the Protective Factors domain (initiative, self-control, and attachment), as well as a Behavioral Concerns score. It is a 37-item scale that rates the child regarding occurrence of each behavior from never to very frequently. It is intended as a screening device to identify children in need of attention, as well as a source of information regarding programming. The package includes a Classroom Strategies Guide, a Classroom Observation Guide, and a parent booklet with recommendations for fostering resilience, in addition to the rating scale.

Age Range
2 years to 5 years 11 months

Administration Time
No time requirement provided, but it should not require more than 10 to 15 min

Publisher
Kaplan Press
1210 Lewisville-Clemmons Road
Lewisville, NC 27023-0609
800-334-2014

Norms
The Protective Factors sample included 2,000 children, with teachers rating 1,017 and parents rating 983. The sample approximated the 1991 U.S. Census data on variables of gender, geographic region, race, ethnicity, and socioeconomic status. Age groups are in 1-year increments with more than 100 in each group.

There were 1,108 children in the Behavioral Concerns Scale sample, with 541 rated by parents and 567 rated by teachers. There were approximately an equal number of males and females in each group, with the numbers in each age group exceeding 100.

Reliability
Internal consistency, determined by Cronbach's alpha, was .91 for the Protective Factors Scales parent raters and .94 for teacher raters, with subscale alphas ranging from .71 to .90, with a median of .80 for parent raters and .88 for teacher raters. Test-retest stability with a 24- to 72-hour interval ranged from .55 to .80 for parent raters and from .68 to .94 for teacher raters; only one teacher rater coefficient fell below .87. Interrater reliabilities ranged from .21 to .44 for parent raters, from .57 to .69 for teacher raters, and from .19 to .34 for parents compared with teacher raters.

Validity
Evidence supportive of content, criterion, and construct validity is presented.

Test Review 8.2

Test Name

Ages and Stages Questionnaires: Social Emotional (ASQ:SE) (2002)

Authors

Jane Squires, Diane Bricker, and Elizabeth Twombly

What the Test Measures

These are a series of eight questionnaires to be completed by parents or caregivers. There is a separate questionnaire for each of the eight ages, including 6, 12, 18, 24, 30, 36, 48, and 60 months. These are available in both English and Spanish, and the questionnaires may be photocopied. There are 22 to 36 items per questionnaire, with choices of most of the time, sometimes, and rarely or never. The areas tapped include self-regulation, compliance, communication, adaptive functioning, autonomy, affect, and interaction with people. Items were selected to be culturally sensitive and were written so as not to exceed a sixth-grade reading level.

Age Range

6 to 60 months

Administration Time

10 to 15 min

Publisher

Brookes Publishing
PO Box 10624
Baltimore, MD 21285-0624
800-638-3775
www.brookespublishing.com

Norms

There were 3,014 children in the norm group, with over 300 at each age level and an approximately equal number of males and females (there were fewer families than children, since some completed questionnaires for more than one child). Compared to the 2000 U.S. Census data, the norm group had a somewhat higher proportion of mothers with higher levels of education; somewhat lower proportions of Caucasians, African Americans, and Hispanics; and a higher proportion of children of mixed ethnicity. Compared to the 1999 U.S. Census, the income level of those in the norm group was lower, although this information was missing from a number of the questionnaires. Children with developmental and social-emotional disabilities were included.

Reliability

Internal consistency alphas ranged from .67 to .91, with an overall alpha of .82. Alphas were at the highest levels for the older preschool ages. Test-retest stability with an interval of 1 to 3 weeks yielded agreement between the two scores of 94% for the classifications of risk or no risk. A study by Squires et al. (2001) reports test-reliability of .94.

Validity

Significant gender differences were found at 30, 36, 48, and 60 months. Cutoff scores are available for boys but need to be revised for girls. Data are presented to support concurrent and discriminant validity. The authors also determined the utility of the questionnaires and reported feedback from the parents that most could complete it in less than 10 minutes, that it was easy to understand, and that the content was appropriate. They also reported finding the questionnaires interesting and thought-provoking regarding their children.

Underreferral ranged from 2.4% at 60 months to 4.7% at 12 months, and overreferral ranged from 3.0% at 18 months to 8.6% at 30 months.

The Squires et al. (2001) study reported a sensitivity range from .75 to .89, with overall sensitivity of .82; specificity ranged from .82 to .96 with an overall specificity of .92.

the children who manifest degrees of behaviors of concern would be asked to complete a rating scale, and further assessment would follow as needed.

Two scales that are particulary useful for offering information regarding general social-emotional functioning are the Behavior Assessment System for Children and the Conners' Rating Scales, presented in Test Reviews 8.3 and 8.4. Another very useful scale, but one that is very specific to one type of disorder, is the Children's Autism Rating Scale, presented in Test Review 8.5.

Most scholars and practitioners agree that using projective or associative techniques such as inkblots, drawings, or storytelling approaches are not appropriate for preschool-age children. For example, their typical responses to pictures are one-word descriptions. Not only are the fine motor, cognitive, and language demands of these techniques too difficult for most, but very young children's responses to them tend to be unreliable. Nevertheless, I have found what I call *affect drawings* to be useful with older preschoolers who possess more well developed fine motor coordination, especially for those who have difficulty accessing their emotional concerns. Affect drawings involve asking the child to draw a series of pictures: a happy, sad, angry, scared, and "just any" picture. The assessor provides a set of crayons in just the primary colors. The directions are to "draw a happy (etc.) picture; something happy (etc.; and the assessor makes a facial expression to represent the affect)." The assessor should be careful not to make the request more specific, such as asking the child to draw a "happy face." These are not assumed to be projective in the sense that projective techniques are interpreted with older individuals. These are used merely to provide an alternative means of communication for the child. Once the picture is drawn, the assessor then asks the child to tell what the picture shows, and then the assessor can ask for expansions in a manner similar to other queries used for drawings; however, it is not usually helpful to stray too far from what was portrayed. The information from these drawings includes first of all the central theme: What does happy, sad, angry, or scared elicit from the child? What do these emotions mean to them? Are some emotions easily elicited and others only with more difficulty? Are some well elaborated and some more restricted? It is also possible to note the appropriateness of the emotions portrayed, as well as how differentiated each is from the other. I have frequently found that children have difficulty distinguishing between sadness and anger, which generates a hypothesis within me that their angry or aggressive behavior may be an expression of their sadness because they may be having difficulty distinguishing these feelings within themselves. Such a hypothesis needs to be explored further with them. Although I have no data to justify my inference, I also take note of how the child uses the colors red and black. The placement of red in the picture alerts me to an area of possible conflict or concern, and the use of black appears to support traditional psychodynamic interpretations of sadness, stress, or anger, depending on how it is used. (It is not a far inference to interpret anger or at least a "problem" when a child draws a well-articulated house and then scribbles over it with black crayon so that it is totally obliterated.) Again, these are hypotheses that need to be followed up with the child, family, or both through further interviewing and observation. Because children of this age are not good candidates for formal interviewing, conducting interviews in the contexts of play and drawing provides props that facilitate communication for them; it is up to the assessor to be able to read these cues and use them as a basis for conversation with the child. Sharing a hypothesis with the child and listening carefully to the child's response can be enlightening. As is the case with any procedure, assessors must be aware of the potential cultural influences on the child's responses. For example, LaVoy et al. (2001) demonstrated that differences between the drawings of children from the United States and Japan reflect each culture's attitudes toward

Test Review 8.3

Test Name
Behavior Assessment System for Children (BASC) (1998)

Authors
Cecil R. Reynolds and Randy W. Kamphaus

What the Test Measures
For preschool children, there is a parent and teacher form to rate behaviors, thoughts, and emotions. The scales tap adaptive and problem behaviors, as well as those related to attention-deficit/hyperactivity disorder (ADHD). The packet also includes a structured developmental history form. The purpose of the BASC is to aid in the diagnosis and classification of children with emotional and behavioral disorders. There are versions in both English and Spanish. Both the teacher and parent scales have a form specifically applicable to preschool children. The Composite areas and respective subscales assessed include externalizing problems (aggression, hyperactivity, conduct problems), internalizing problems (anxiety, depression, and somatization), school problems (attention and learning), other problems (atypicality and withdrawal), and adaptive skills (adaptability, leadership, social skills, and study skills). There is also a behavioral symptoms index score, as well as a form for recording direct observations of behaviors using a time sampling method.

Age Range
2 1/2 to 18 years

Administration Time
10 to 20 min for rating scales

Publisher
AGS
4201 Woodland Road
Circle Pines, MN 55014-1796
800-328-2560
www.agsnet.com

Norms
Standard scores are in the form of T scores, with a mean of 50 and SD of 10. There are four norm samples available for each rating scale: general, female, male, and clinical. The general norms reflect a representational national sample on variables of gender, race and ethnicity, classification, and, for the parent form, parent education. High scores on the adaptive scales are positive, and high scores on the clinical scales are negative regarding risk. There are also scales to indicate the validity of the ratings.

Items that behaved differently with regard to gender or race or ethnicity were dropped. There are separate norms for ages 2-6 through 3-11. With some overlap regarding individuals who completed the forms, the total number in the sample for the teacher scale was 2,401 and for the parent scale, 3,483.

Children with special education classifications are included in the norms, but only for ages 6 and older.

Reliability
Internal consistencies for the teacher scale average .80 (.82 for ages 4-5).

Test-retest stability with an interval of 2 to 8 weeks was .89 for the preschool level. Test-retest stability over an interval of 7 months for children aged 6-11 was .69. Interrater reliability in one study yielded a median of .83, and in another study, between .63 and .71 for the teacher form.

Validity

The content was selected to reflect clinical experience, review of other scales, and frequently used constructs. Information was gathered from mental health professionals, teachers, and students.

A three-factor solution for children between the ages of 4 to 5 was supported: externalizing problems, internalizing problems, and adaptive skills. Subscales loading on the School Problems factor at the older ages load on different factors at the youngest ages. Data are also presented to support concurrent and discriminant validity.

For the parent form, internal consistency scores ranged from the mid .80s to low .90s, and the Behavioral Symptoms Index ran with a 1-month interval from .88 to .94. The test-retest stability median scores for the preschool level were in the high .80s. Interparent agreement for the preschool level was .46, with the highest agreement regarding externalizing problems. Factor analysis supported a three-factor interpretation for all ages: externalizing problems, internalizing problems, and adaptive skills. Evidence is presented to support concurrent and discriminant validity.

Test Review 8.4

Test Name
The Childhood Autism Rating Scale (CARS) (1986)

Authors
Eric Schopler, Robert J. Reichler, and Barbara Rochen Renner

What the Test Measures
The CARS offers 15 items intended for the diagnosis of autism, designed to be consistent with five major diagnostic systems. It was especially designed to help differentiate children with autism from those with other developmental delays such as mental retardation. The child is rated from 1 to 4 on each item, ranging from normal to severe and yielding a final score indicating nonautistic, mildly to moderately autistic, or severely autistic. The items reflect relating to people, imitation, emotional response, body use, object use, adaptation to change, visual response, listening response, taste-smell-touch response and use, fear or nervousness, verbal communication, nonverbal communication, activity level, level and consistency of intellectual response, and general impressions. Because a severe rating on any of the behaviors would be atypical at any age, this would be considered a criterion-referenced rather than a norm-referenced procedure.

The scale can be completed by a clinician or teacher or parent, based on observations of the child's behavior.

Age Range
Appropriate for all ages, including preschool

Administration Time
Not provided, but should not require more than 15 to 20 min

(continued)

Publisher
Western Psychological Services
12031 Wilshire Boulevard
Los Angeles, CA 90025-1251
800-648-8857
www.wpspublish.com

Norms
The information presented in the manual reflects research from North Carolina that was collected through Project TEACCH. The sample reflects the treatment population of over 1,500 predominantly male children, most of whom entered the program when younger than 6 year. About two thirds of the children were White, and about one third were Black; most have IQs below 70, but the range reaches above 85.

Reliability
Internal consistency (alpha) was reported as .94. Interrater reliability averaged .71, and test-retest stability with a 1-year interval was .88. Agreement of results regarding the same child evaluated over time was .64.

Validity
Evidence to support criterion-related validity is presented.

Test Review 8.5

Test Name
Conners' Rating Scales (1990)

Author
C. Keith Conners

What the Test Measures
There are two Conners' Scales, one for parents and one for teachers. There are short and long forms, which were separately developed and have separate content and norms. The long form of the teacher rating scale has 39 items, rated to reflect frequency of occurrence of the behaviors, including hyperactivity, conduct problem, emotional overindulgent, anxious-passive, asocial, and day dream and attention problems. The teacher short form has 28 items with similar 0 to 3 ratings for behaviors including conduct problem, hyperactivity, and inattentive-passive. The parent long form contains 93 items, rated from 1 through 4 for behaviors of conduct disorder, anxious-shy, restless-disorganized, learning problem, psychosomatic, obsessive-compulsive, antisocial, and hyperactive-immature.

The parent short form has 48 items, rated from 0 through 3 for behaviors including conduct problem, learning problem, psychosomatic, impulsive-hyperactive, and anxiety. The parent long form is not appropriate for preschool children. All forms include a hyperactivity index, which is made up of the 10 items that are most sensitive to drug treatment effects (this is not the same as the Hyperactivity Scale within the rating scale).

The Conners' was initially designed for research regarding drug effects on children with attention-deficit/hyperactivity disorder (ADHD) but has been revised to identify a number of problem behaviors. The forms are partially self-scoring.

Age Range
3 through 17 years or 4 through 12, depending on the form

Administration Time
CPRS-93, 30 min; CPRS-48, 20 min; CTRS-39 and 28, about 15 min

Publisher
Multi-Health Systems, Inc.
908 Niagara Falls Boulevard
North Tonawanda, NY 14120-2060
800-456-3003
www.mhs.com

Norms
The normative sample for the teacher long form totals 9,583 Canadian children between the ages of 4 and 12 years. The norms for the teacher short form total 383 children between the ages of 3 and 17. Norms for the parent long form apply to children between the ages of 6 and 14 years. The norms for the parent short form reflect data from a sample of 578 children between the ages of 3 and 17, with separate norms for boys and girls.

The scores are in terms of *T* scores with a mean of 50 and *SD* of 10.

Reliability
For the CTRS-39, one-month test-retest reliability ranges from .72 to .91, with 1-year interval from .33 to .55. Interrater reliability correlations are reported from .30 to .94 for teacher ratings, from .46 to .57 for parent ratings (between mother and father), and between .24 and .49 for parent-teacher ratings. Internal consistency alphas range from .61 to .94, with most over .80.

Validity
The scales have been used in hundreds of studies, and the author concludes that, based on these, there is evidence of strong predictive, concurrent, construct, and discriminant validity. Factor analysis of the CTRS-28 supports a three-factor interpretation: conduct problem, hyperactivity, and inattentive-passive with five items not loading on these factors. Factor analysis of the CPRS-48 supports a five-factor interpretation: conduct problems, learning problems, psychosomatic, impulsive-hyperactive, and anxiety.

displays of emotion and attention to details. The drawings of the Japanese children were notably more restrained (lacking smiles) and detailed than were those of the U.S. children. Because both of these factors affect interpretations regarding emotion and intelligence, we must be very aware that what we observe to a significant extent reflects socialization practices of the family rather than some culture-free trait of the child.

TEMPERAMENT

Temperament describes meaningful within-child predispositions that interact with environmental experiences to produce behaviors that describe the "hows" or styles of observable behavior (Keith & Campbell, 2000). Despite claims of diverse definitions, there actually is a fair degree of consensus among those who provide definitions of temperament—for example, "a characterization of fundamental elements of behavioral organization, constitutional in origin and persistent over extended periods of time" (Hertzig & Snow, 1988, p. 134), or, "those psychological qualities that display considerable variation among infants and, in addition, have a relatively, but not indefinitely, stable biological basis . . . even though the inherited physiological processes mediate different phenotypic displays as the child grows" (J. Kagan, 1989, p. 668). There is general concurrence that aspects of temperament are relatively stable, genetic in origin, descriptive of qualities of emotion and central nervous system arousal and regulation, not immutable, and the result of complex organism-environment interactions (R. P. Martin, 1983).

Evidence for these dimensions in the biology of the child is rather robust, but biology does not have the final word, as most researchers concur with the authors of the New York Longitudinal Study regarding the importance of goodness of fit (Hertzig & Snow, 1988; J. Kagan & Snidman, 1991). That is, the ultimate trajectory and outcome of these behaviors are a function of their consequences for environmental interactions. Not only do adults and peers interact differentially in relation to children with different patterns of behavior (R. P. Martin, 1983), but these same interactive agents also have preferences for certain constellations of behavior. For example, some adults very much like working with slow-to-warm-up children and enjoy helping them accommodate to new situations, whereas others find these children very unappealing and difficult to work with. Nevertheless, some constellations of temperament seem to place some children at risk for both adjustment and academic disorders (Caspi, Henry, McGee, Moffitt, & Silva, 1995; Hertzig & Snow, 1988; Jewsuwan, Luster, & Kostelnik, 1993; R. P. Martin, Drew, Gaddis, & Moseley, 1988). These predictions do not apply solely to the negative aspects of development but include positive aspects of resilience as well (Teglasi, 1998). Early evidence of temperamental variables of low persistence, high distractibility, and high activity level are associated with low academic functioning, and early evidence of variables of high emotional intensity, as well as poor adaptability, seem to put children at risk for later behavior dysfunction (R. P. Martin, 1983). The study by Keogh and Burstein (1988) suggested that temperamentally based behaviors differentiated children with and without disabilities and that these variables related to the nature and frequency of their peer and teacher interactions. In their study, children with disabilities were lower in task orientation and flexibility and showed greater extremes of reactivity (both under and over).

Although interest in temperament can be dated as far back as ancient Greece (Hertzig & Snow, 1988), attention to temperament peaked when the findings from the New York Longitudinal Study (A. Thomas & Chess, 1977; A. Thomas, Chess, & Birch, 1968; A. Thomas, Chess, Birch, Hertzig, & Korn, 1963) were published. The conceptualization of temperament as described by these authors has been a powerful influence on subsequent research and scale development. This study generated a list of nine variables that described temperament and that have subsequently been used on a number of rating scales. These included the following categories, which were evident in infants as young as 2 months: activity level, biological rhythmicity, approach/withdrawal in new situations, adaptability to new or altered situations, sensory threshold of responsiveness to stimuli, intensity of reaction, quality of mood, distractibility, and attention span/persistence (Hertzig & Snow, 1988). These dimensions derived from content analysis of mothers' descriptions of their children's behaviors. When later subjected to factor analysis, some of these showed overlap and weak support, so the original nine have been collapsed to three to six for some scales (Presley & Martin, 1994).

Based on the considerable research that has occurred subsequent to the New York Longitudinal Study, Rothbart and Jones (1998) offered the following dimensions, based primarily on factor analytic studies. These dimensions occur early in the child's life and show both stability and predictive utility:

- Positive affect/approach
- Negative emotionality/fearfulness, tendency to withdraw from novelty
- Irritability/frustration, with negative affect, showing in response to failure to attain goals and possibly manifested in aggressive behaviors (in infancy, this shows as a separate factor, but it combines by school age with negative emotionality)
- Attention span/effortful control (self-regulation)

These authors also note that some studies have shown separate, weaker factors for rhythmicity and threshold, but they did not include these factors in their work.

Temperament is a particularly meaningful concept for infants, toddlers, and preschool children because although its direct effects appear to dissipate (or become increasingly complex) over time, there seems to be a strong influence of temperament on parent-child and teacher-child interactions that affects the child's development, particularly with regard to social competence. These effects can also impinge on early development of attachment with caregivers (Cassidy, 1994).

The stability of temperamental variables increases and becomes reasonably more predictive of later behavior during the preschool years (McDevitt, 1988). The most stable parameters appear to be the more extreme clusters, and the New York Longitudinal Study researchers identified three: the easy child (characterized by regularity of biological rhythms, positive approach to new situations, high adaptability, mild mood or moderately intense mood, and predominantly positive affect); the difficult child (the converse of the easy child); and the slow-to-warm-up child (mild intensity and slow adaptability despite repeated contacts).

Clearly, however, temperament does not account for all of behavior, but some dimensions impinge more reliably than others on how well the child is likely to develop, particularly the extreme constellations, and most specifically those that have been shown to characterize difficult children. In the New York Longitudinal Study, although not all children who started off as difficult developed behavior disorders, 70% of those who manifested the cluster of difficult behaviors during their early years developed behavior disorders that resulted in their parents' seeking clinical intervention, compared to 22% of the general study population. However, Kagan and Snidman (1991) have also found considerable stability for the dimensions of shyness and inhibition. The accumulating data on temperament remind us that behavior is characterized by both consistency and change (Chamberlin, 1981).

Although three possible approaches to the assessment of temperament are available, including direct observation, interview, and questionnaire or rating scales, the last is by far the most frequently used in applied settings (Teglasi, 1998). Two of the available ratings scales appear in Test Reviews 8.6 and 8.7.

Rating scales are the easiest and most efficient of the methods; however, there is concern with interrater agreement, internal consistency, test-retest stability, and convergent validity (i.e., the extent to which similar scales are measuring the same construct; Hertzig & Snow, 1988; R. P. Martin, 1983). Teachers and parents may differ in their ratings not only because of differences in their perceptions of the child but also because of differences in their opportunities to observe the child's behavior. In addition, McDevitt (1988) pointed out the difficulty of us-

Test Review 8.6

Test Name

The Temperament Assessment Battery for Children (TABC) (1988)

Author

Roy P. Martin

What the Test Measures

This rating scale has three forms: parent, teacher, and clinician. Ratings reflect frequency of occurrence, on a 7-point scale, of six of the temperamental variables researched in the New York Longitudinal Study: activity (motoric vigor), adaptability (early/speed of adjustment to new circumstances), approach/withdrawal (in relation to new social situations), emotional intensity (vigor of affect expression), distractibility (disruptibility of attention by minor events), and persistence (attention span; tendency to stay with challenging learning or performance situations).

Age Range

3 years through 7 years

Administration Time

10 min (clinician); 15 min to complete and 10 min to score (teacher/parent)

Publisher

PRO-ED
8700 Shoal Creek Blvd.
Austin, TX 78757-6897
800-897-3202
www.proedinc.com

Norms

There are no representative national norms for the TABC. However, there are some large samples from varied regions throughout the United States. The parent form norms are based on a sample of 1,381 individuals from New Jersey, Georgia, South Carolina, and Colorado. The teacher form norms are based on a sample of 577 individuals from states in the Southeastern and Rocky Mountain regions. The norms for the clinician form are based on the results from the Preschool Clinic in the University of Georgia in Athens, Georgia. Results are in terms of T scores, with a mean of 50 and SD of 10.

Reliability

Internal consistency (Cronbach's alpha) for the parent form ranges from .65 to .86; for the teacher form, from .69 to .86; and for the clinician form, from .54 to .81. The teacher form shows the most consistent internal consistency, with all but one of the coefficients exceeding .80. Interrater reliability for the teacher form ranges from .06 to .42, and for the parent form, from -.21 to .64; there is considerable variability for the rater agreements across samples.

   Test-retest stability for the parent form with a 1-year interval ranges from .42 to .70, and for a two year interval, from .31 to .75. Stability of scores for the teacher form for the same rater with a 6-month interval ranges from .69 to .87, and for different raters with a 12-month interval, from .07 to .67.

Validity

A number of validity studies are presented. For example, correlations between the TABC and observed behavior ranged from the .40s to .60s for the appropriate variable. Relationships have also been found between TABC and both intelligence and achievement, as well as psychopathology.

   Data are presented for both item analysis and factor analysis. The factor analysis supports three factors: emotionality (primarily activity-positive relationship and emotional intensity), persistence (primarily activity-negative relationship, distractibility, and persistence), and sociability (primarily adaptability, approach/withdrawal, and persistence).

Test Review 8.7

Test Name

The Temperament and Atypical Behavior Scale: Early Childhood Indicators of Developmental Dysfunction (TABS) (1999)

Author

John T. Neisworth, Stephen J. Bagnato, John Salvia, and Frances M. Hunt

What the Test Measures

The TABS is a norm-referenced checklist intended to identify children who are at risk for atypical development. There are two forms, a 15-item screener and the full 55-item form. The full form provides a space to record whether the child exhibits the behavior and whether the reporter (usually caregiver) needs help regarding the behavior. There are four factors: detached, hyper-sensitive/active, underactive, and dysregulated, yielding a total Temperament and Regulatory Index. The TABS is also intended to provide the basis for program planning, as well as a vehicle for monitoring the child's progress. The respondent replies yes or no to each item, indicating whether the behavior is in evidence. The authors provide research-based suggestions for interventions for each item on the scale.

Age Range

11 through 71 months

Administration Time

5 min for the screener and 15 min for the full TABS

Publisher

Paul H. Brookes Publishing Co.
PO Box 10624
Baltimore, MD 21285-0624
www.brookespublishing.com

Norms

The sample of children with and without disabilities was gathered from almost 200 service provider agencies and organizations. Because the items were designed to represent neurobiologically based atypical behaviors, the authors did not feel it was relevant to have a nationally representational sample. There were two samples: one with and one without disabilities. The final norm samples totaled 621. There were no gender or age effects. The range of disabilities was wide, including attention-deficit/hyperactivity disorder (ADHD), pervasive developmental disorders (PDDs), autism, cerebral palsy, Down syndrome, fetal alcohol syndrome (FAS), and a number of others. The standard scores have a mean of 100 and SD of 15. High scores on the TABS reflect atypical functioning.

Reliability

Split-half correlations for children at risk range from .49 to .63 for subdomains and .72 for total index, and for children with disabilities, from .68 to .86 for subdomains and .91 for total index. Test-retest stability after 2 to 3 weeks showed a slight but consistent decrease in the scores, but generally high correlations, ranging from .73 to .92 for subdomains of children not at risk and .91 for their total index, and from .78 to .91 for subdomains of children with disabilities and .93 for their total index. The internal consistency (alpha) for the screener was .83.

(continued)

Validity

The TABS was developed using an empirical approach of reviewing the research literature, existing scales, and clinician opinion regarding behaviors that were considered atypical, aberrant, or undesirable. Items that were developmentally immature or learned were eliminated. The authors focused on behaviors with a neurobiological basis that served as markers for atypical development.

The screener shows a hit rate of 83%, with a higher likelihood of false positives (14.5%) than false negatives (2.4%). Therefore, there is some tendency to over-identify children as at risk, but this should be followed by completion of the full scale.

The authors present evidence that the scores act according to expectations and evidence to support discriminant validity.

ing temperament scales for children with developmental delays, as behavioral expressions of temperament tend to vary with age, and the wording of some items may not be appropriate (e.g., the use of the word "infancy" in relation to a delayed child who is not an infant but is functioning at a very low level).

Best practice in the assessment of temperament would be to secure ratings from all adults who are intensively involved with the child; to follow these with interviews to review, clarify, and expand on the rating information; and to observe the child across contexts.

Some reasons to include assessment of temperamental variables are (a) to help caregivers and teachers understand the child and to acknowledge with them that children are not blank slates, (b) to ameliorate caregiver feelings of guilt or self-blame in the case of difficult children, and, most of all, (c) to promote attempts to develop goodness-of-fit interventions so that difficult younger children do not become difficult older children and so that the "easy" and "other" children do not develop difficulties (McClowry, 1998). Children with different temperamental predispositions require different approaches to management. For example, children with high activity levels may profit from time for energy release and movement built into their program, whereas slow-to-warm-up children may need time to adjust and acclimate, with low-keyed encouragement, and possibly the presence of a caregiver when being introduced to a new situation. The goal of intervention is not necessarily to change the temperamental variable (although some modification may be desirable for some variables), but to optimize the outcomes regarding adjustment and competence for the child. Although further research is warranted in this area, McClowry reviewed existing studies that provide evidence of parent satisfaction and reports of improved interactions with their children in response to temperament-based interventions.

ADAPTIVE BEHAVIOR AND COPING

The concept of adaptive behavior has two primary roots, the first involving the attempt to reduce reliance on IQ tests for determination of mental retardation and the second involving the attempt to reduce the perceived bias of special education eligibility determinations (Witt & Martens, 1984). The development of adaptive behavior measures has a history of well over 50 years, with very few changes in their structure or conceptualization. Almost all of these procedures rely on information from adults in close relationship with the child, that is, primarily caregivers and teachers. A number of researchers in this area point out that adaptive behavior, in the form of social competence, predates use of IQ tests as the basis for determination of mental retardation (Coulter & Morrow, 1978; P. L. Harrison & Robinson, 1995; Nihira, 1999). When IQ tests were introduced, it was with the thought that these provided a more objective and more efficient basis for classification of mental deficiency than did judgment-based impressions of social competence. This assumption was challenged in the 1960s and 1970s through lawsuits and legislation related to evidence of disproportionate placement of children with minority backgrounds in special education classes. In 1961 the American Association for Mental Deficiency (AAMD) began to include adaptive behavior as part of its definition of mental retardation (Reschly, 1982), and the inclusion of adaptive behavior along with measures of cognitive functioning is now mandated for determination of this condition and for determination of eligibility for access to special education services for students with this classification (Tassé & Craig, 1999).

These issues have primarily concerned children diagnosed with "mild" mental retardation, and one of the outcomes of this debate has also been to tighten and lower the IQ scores used for determining eligibility for special education services (Reschly & Gresham, 1988). At the same time there has been increasing reliance on evidence of out-of-school functioning, assessed through measures of adaptive behavior to mitigate against the phenomenon of the "six-hour retarded" child (i.e., the child who is considered retarded only in relation to academic functions within the school setting). Reschly and Gresham pointed out that one issue contributing to this debate is the underlying assumption of standardized procedures that traits such as IQ are stable. When IQ tests were initially introduced into the United States early in the 20th century, it was with the idea of determining the existence of this within-person trait as something that resides within the person, defines that person in relation to others, and remains relatively immutable over time. One of the contributions of the use of adaptive behavior procedures has been the concern that they represent with linking assessment with programming and the targeting of domains for instruction with the ultimate goal of increased normalization (P. L. Harrison & Robinson, 1995). One of the problems these procedures have had is that they too are based on psychometric assumptions, which tends to work against the goal of modifiability (Leland, 1983).

P. L. Harrison and Boan (2000) described adaptive behavior in terms of "the skills needed for successful life functioning . . . based on the degree to which an individual takes care of himself or herself and gets along with others" (p. 124). These authors list the skill areas identified within the domain of adaptive behavior by the American Association of Mental Retardation as follows: self care, communication, social, health and safety, leisure, home living, community use, self-direction, functional academic, and work. Identification of individuals as mentally retarded requires administration of both a major cognitive test and an adaptive behavior procedure to mitigate against classifying individuals as retarded based solely on their functioning within an academic setting, when they may function quite adequately within their home and community.

Despite claims of vague and disparate definitions of adaptive behavior, comparisons of the many adaptive behavior scales that are available tend to yield a number of common domains that greatly overlap and reflect those listed by AAMD. The emphasis is on independent self-care and independent functioning within and participation in the social community (Knoff, Stollar, Johnson, & Chenneville, 1999). Adaptive behavior measures increasingly reflect the cultural-relatedness of expectations in their rhetoric, although it is difficult to find this issue represented in the actual items; therefore, interpretation of the results of use of these measures must be very cautious when employed with children from minority backgrounds.

There are a number of adaptive behavior scales available, and most of them begin at birth or at very young ages and cover the age span through adult years. Two of the most frequently used procedures are the Vineland Adaptive Behavior Scales (VABS; Sparrow, Balla, & Cicchetti, 1984a, 1984b; see also P. L. Harrison, 1985) and the Scales of Independent Behavior-Revised (Bruininks, Woodcock, Weatherman, & Hill, 1996). These are reviewed in Test Reviews 8.8 and 8.9.

P. L. Harrison and Boan (2000) noted the moderate to low correlations between scores from adaptive behavior scales and IQ tests and commented that whereas adaptive behavior adds little to the variance of academic functioning accounted for by IQ, it does add considerably to the variance of life functioning. Witt and Martens (1984) noted that one of the problems of finding significant correlations between IQ tests and adaptive behavior measures is the diversity of the latter, so that the relationships found differ considerably depending on the measure used.

Because the content of most adaptive behavior measures has changed imperceptibly over time (except with regard to improved psychometric properties and norms) and is increasingly difficult to differentiate from measures of general development for young children (Leland, 1983), I am particularly fond of the Coping Inventory: A Measure of Adaptive Behavior (Zeitlin, 1985), which was designed specifically for use with young children and attempted to capture variables of functioning that are process- and temperament-based, rather than just performance-based. Described in Test Review 8.10, the Coping Inventory takes the concept of self-regulation seriously and expresses this rapidly developing capacity in terms of how the child relates both intra- and interpersonally. The Coping Inventory is also very intervention oriented (Zeitlin & Williamson, 1994).

Although the thinking behind the development of adaptive behavior measures has been productive in addressing issues of classification and the need to use the assessment information to promote normalization, the reality of many of the measures is that they are limited in their usefulness for planning instructional interventions for children (Reschly & Gresham, 1988). Other limitations include their reliance on third-party report, so that, as has been discussed in relation to other rating scales, the results must be interpreted in terms of reflecting the reporter's perceptions, and the reporter's reliability is also an important factor. None of the major approaches includes direct observation of the child, and to be valid, this would have to be carried out across a variety of settings, in and out of the school or program. (For older children, direct interview would also be an option; as discussed earlier, this would not be appropriate for preschool children.) Reschly and Gresham (1988), among others, have also pointed out that the measures tend to reflect typical, rather than optimal, performance and, therefore, do not necessarily represent the individual's capacity to perform the skills assessed.

Adaptive behavior needs considerably more thought in relation to the functioning of preschool children. The concept has more meaning in relation to school-age and older children and adults because there is more of a split between their functioning in academic and nonacademic settings. However, even in the case of older populations, some suggest that it does not make sense to separate adaptive behavior from intelligence, but, alternatively, that the conceptualization of intelligence should be broadened to include social competence, and the settings and contexts for expressions of social competence would cross all boundaries (Schalock, 1999).

Test Review 8.8

Test Name
Scales of Independent Behavior-Revised (SIB-R)(1996)

Authors
Robert H. Bruininks, Richard W. Woodcock, Richard F. Weatherman, and Bradley K. Hill

What the Test Measures
The SIB-R assesses adaptive behavior in the four domains (14 areas) of motor skills, social interaction and communication skills, personal living skills, and community living skills. In addition, the SIB-R provides information regarding three behavior clusters (eight areas), including internalized maladaptive, asocial maladaptive, and externalized maladaptive. It can be administered as either a structured interview or a checklist. The focus is on estimating the ability of individuals to function independently in various settings, including home, school, and community.

The individual is rated on each item from 0 (never/rarely) to 3 (does very well or always/almost always) regarding degree of independence on the task.

The Early Development Form applies to children from infancy through age 6 years (or older individuals through age 8 functioning within this range). It includes 40 items selected from the total test that are relevant to this age group.

Scoring is as complex as most of the Woodcock-related tests, involving cluster scores, and is best carried out through computer. Age equivalents can be determined directly on the protocol. Other scores available include Relative Mastery Indices and Adaptive Behavior Skill Levels as well as percentile ranks and standard scores (mean of 100; *SD* of 15).

In the case of the problem behaviors, there are Maladaptive Behavior Indices.

Age Range
Infancy to 80+ years

Administration Time
15 to 20 min for the Early Development form and short form; 45 to 60 min for the full scale

Publisher
Riverside Publishing
425 Spring Lake Drive
Itasca, IL 60143-2079
800-323-9540
www.riversidepublishing.com

Norms
The SIB-R was normed on 2,182 individuals stratified to reflect the 1990 U.S. Census regarding characteristics of gender, race, occupational status/level, geographic level/region, and type of community.

Reliability
Split-half reliabilities for Early Childhood (1–4 years) on the Early Development Form range from .55 to .88, with 10 out of 16 exceeding .80. Split-half reliabilities for the four cluster scores all exceed .80.

(*continued*)

Test-retest stability with an early childhood sample and 7- to 14-day time gap yielded a correlation of .97 for the Early Development Form, .85 to .90 for the Problem Behaviors, and .92 for the General Maladaptive Index.

Interrater reliability for the Early Development Form comparing the independent ratings of teachers and aids yielded a correlation of .91 for the Early Development Form, .68 to .83 for the Problem Behaviors, and .78 for the General Maladaptive Index.

Validity

Evidence is presented to support construct, concurrent, criterion, and discriminant validity. For example, using the Early Development Form, there were significant differences between children with and without disabilities regarding early development, as well as Internalized Maladaptive and General Maladaptive (not Asocial Maladaptive or Externalized Maladaptive). Correlations of the Early Childhood clusters with the Woodcock-Johnson Cognitive Ability scores range from .27 to .33, with a correlation between Broad Independence and the Woodcock of .34.

These are well below the correlations between these measures for children between the ages of 5 to 12, and well above those for individuals between 13 and 90.

Test Review 8.9

Test Name

Vineland Adaptive Behavior Scales (VABS) (1984); Vineland Adaptive Behavior Scales, Classroom Edition (1985)

Authors

Sara S. Sparrow, David A. Balla, and Domenic V. Cicchetti; Classroom Edition: Patti L. Harrison

What the Test Measures

There are three forms: the Interview Edition–Survey Form, the Expanded Form, and the Classroom Edition. The first contains 297 items and is administered by semistructured interview to the primary caregiver. The second has 577 items, including all those in the survey form, and is also administered by semistructured interview to the caregiver; this form is intended to serve as a basis for program development. The Classroom Edition has 244 items, in questionnaire format, completed by the teacher. The domains covered by all three include Communication (receptive, expressive, written), Daily Living Skills (personal, domestic community), Socialization (interpersonal relationships, play and leisure time, and coping skills), and Motor Skills (gross and fine). A tape is available for training for the semistructured interview. There is an optional Maladaptive Behavior domain. The VABS yields subdomain scores, as well as an Adaptive Behavior composite.

Four scales from the VABS (Interpersonal Relationships, Play, Leisure Time, and Coping Skills) have been abstracted to form the Vineland Social-Emotional Early Childhood Scales (Vineland SEEC).

Age Range

Both interview forms begin at birth, and the Classroom Edition starts at 3 years and goes through adult. The Vineland SEEC is appropriate for children from birth through 5 years 11 months.

Administration Time

Interview/Survey: 20 to 60 min; Expanded: 60-90 min; Classroom: 20 min; the Vineland SEEC requires between 15 and 25 min

Publisher
American Guidance Service
4201 Woodland Road
Circle Pines, MN 55014-1796
800-328-2560
www.agsnet.com

Norms
The norm group total was a national sample of 3,000 individuals stratified regarding age, race, gender, region, parental education, and community size. There were 200 individuals for each of 15 age groups. The standard scores for each domain and the composite score are based on a mean of 100 and *SD* of 15.

Reliability
Split-half means for the Survey Form domains range from .83 to .90 and for the Composite, .94. Split-half means for the Expanded Form domains range from .91 to .95, and for the Composite, .97. Mean Cronbach alphas for the Classroom Edition range from .80 to .95 for the domains, and .98 for the Composite. Test-retest means for the Survey Form range from .81 to .86 for the domains, and .88 for the Composite. Mean interrater correlations for the Survey Form range from .62 to .78 for the domains and .74 for the Composite.

Validity
The manual reports confirmation of the organization of the domains by factor analysis. Evidence is provided in the manual with regard to content, construct, criterion-related, and discriminant validity. Correlations between the VABS and intelligence tests tend to run in the low to moderate range (e.g., .30 between the Composite and the Binet).

Test Review 8.10

Test Name
Coping Inventory: A Measure of Adaptive Behavior (1985)

Author
Shirley Zeitlin

What the Test Measures
The Coping Inventory consists of 48 items providing information about the child's ability to cope with self and environment. Each of these categories is divided into the three dimensions of productive, active, and flexible. The rater must be an individual who knows the child well, usually a teacher, and rates the child on scale from 1 to 5, indicating the degree of effectiveness of the child in relation to each item. The items are all positive statements of effective coping. The scale yields an adaptive behavior summary (coping with self compared to coping with environment), as well as a coping profile (ratings on each of the three dimensions). There is a sheet to record the most and least adaptive behaviors, which would serve as the bases for instruction.

(*continued*)

Age Range
3-16 years (there is an Early Coping Inventory for infants and toddlers)

Administration Time
Not provided, but estimated to require about 15 to 20 min

Publisher
Scholastic Testing Service, Inc.
Bensenville, IL 60106-1617
800-642-6STS
www.ststesting.com

Norms
The sample totaled 1,119 children with typical development as well as handicaps from 16 locations of various sizes in Texas, New Jersey, and New York. At the preschool level, there were approximately equal numbers of males and females, from predominantly White middle-class backgrounds for the older preschool group, but approximately equal number of low socioeconomic families for the younger preschool group. Blacks and Hispanics were represented.

Reliability
Internal-consistency alpha coefficients ranged from .84 to .98 for the subscales.
Interrater reliability coefficients ranged from .78 to .94 for children with handicaps and from .78 to .89 for children without handicaps. All but one coefficient for both groups exceeded .80.

Validity
The items were based on the research literature as well as clinical judgment as representing behaviors that reflected the concept of coping, looking at temperament as an aspect of coping.
Factor analysis supports a single "general coping" factor.
 Evidence is presented to support concurrent and criterion related validity.

PEER RELATIONS

The ability to interact with peers is a critical developmental task of early childhood (Guralnick, 1992, 1993; Odom & McConnell, 1989). Peer relationships differ from children's relationships with adults in their mutuality and egalitarianism, which provide opportunities for development that differs from that with adults (Hartup, 1979; Hartup & Moore, 1990). Such opportunities include the need to compromise, to negotiate, and to resolve conflicts, as well as to share mutual interests. Peer relationships are also more motor involved than are the more verbally dominated interactions of children and adults (Hodapp & Mueller, 1982).

A number of authors differentiate between social skills and social competence. *Social skills* usually refer to what individuals do, whereas *social competence* refers to how well they do it (S. N. Elliott & Ershler, 1990). There is ample evidence to document a relationship between social competence during preschool years and later school and life adjustment (Asher & Parker, 1989; Creasey, Jarvis, & Berk, 1998; Gresham, 1984; Hartup & Moore, 1990; Levy-Shiff & Hoffman, 1989; Parker & Asher, 1987; Rubin, 1986). However, it is important to note that even though most poorly adjusted adults have a history of poor early social competence, not all early social incompetence results in adult maladjustment (Hartup & Moore, 1990). However, this relationship is particularly strong with regard to aggressive and impulsive behaviors and interactions, which are discussed later.

The ability to interact with peers requires complex integration of brain functions, whose development makes a spurt at this age and therefore varies considerably from individual to individual. Good social interactors must be able to take the perspective of another, inhibit impulsive responding, read both verbal and nonverbal cues of others, respond appropriately both verbally and nonverbally, verbally and motorically participate in sociodramatic play episodes, and both generate and apply appropriate problem-solving strategies (Kemple, 1991). Socially competent children must also be flexible and adaptable, able to evaluate their successes and modify their unsuccessful behaviors. They must also show reciprocity to the overtures of others (Howes & Matheson, 1992; Strain & Shores, 1977).

Development of social competence is a very demanding task for young children, and there will inevitably be many who come to these skills at a slowed pace or not at all (without intervention). It is a wonder, in fact, that so many children develop so well in this area. Deficits in social interaction skills cut across all disabilities, as deficits in any domain can impinge on development of competence in this area (Bailey & Simeonsson, 1985; Beckman & Lieber, 1992; S. N. Elliott & Ershler, 1990; Guralnick, 1980, 1992; Guralnick & Groom, 1987a, 1987b; Odom et al., 1999).

Peer interaction is an area where "the rich get richer," as involvement in social interactions and the opportunities for practice and feedback from these interactions lead to enhancement and further development of social skills and, thereby, social competence. According to Piaget, peer interactions serve to reduce the child's egocentrism because of the demands on perspective taking (Shantz, 1975), and according to Vygotsky, play with peers serves to improve the child's self-regulation because of the necessity of observing the rules of the roles (Elias & Berk, 2002). Peer interaction provides opportunities to practice and adjust social skills involved in conflict management and problem solving (Creasey et al., 1998).

Development of social skills is associated with a number of factors, including experiences within the family; intrachild variables such as cognitive level, language development, and temperament; and experiences within out-of-family caretaking situations (Grief, 1977; Hartup & Moore, 1990; Saunders & Green, 1993). Positive early attachment history and authoritative parenting interactions and models appear to promote social competence in children, which, in turn, interacts with the child's temperamental variables.

Because these skills are to a significant extent learned, there is optimism regarding the possibilities for teaching these behaviors (Creasey et al., 1998). However, it has been considerably more difficult to document successful outcomes from intervention, particularly regarding lasting effects, than it has been to find associations between likely causative or predisposing factors (DuPaul & Echert, 1994). To date, the most effective interventions have involved peer mediation rather than direct teaching of social skills (Odom et al., 1999; Strain, 1986). With peer mediation, the target child (the one who shows deficiencies) is paired with a highly socially competent child who is coached by a trained adult to engage in a number of interactive initiations. However, this has been most successful with shier, more withdrawn children. There has been evidence of success with impulsive, acting-out children with the Shure and Spivak (1979) "I Can Problem Solve" approach, in which children are taught to think of and apply alternative strategies; however, the extent to which these effects are generalized remains equivocal (Rickel, Eshelman, Loigman, 1983). Other promising approaches include reading stories with prosocial themes to children, followed by interactive activities related to the themes (Bhavnagri & Samuels, 1996), and changing environmental consequences such as responses and reinforcements by others (DuPaul & Echert, 1994). S. N. Elliott and Ershler (1990) noted that the elements of successful social skills training appeared to include opportunities to interact, reinforcement of appropriate behavior while ignoring or punishing inappropriate behavior, modeling of appropriate behavior along with coaching, and built-in facilitation of generalization, such as cross-situational practice and fading. *Cross-situational practice* means that the behaviors need to be practiced in as many contexts as possible, and *fading* means that the cues for positive behaviors need to be gradually withdrawn so that the child learns to carry these out independently.

Because play is the most likely forum for social interaction of young children, observations of children engaged in play are therefore a frequently used and ecologically valid and appropriate assessment approach. Observation of peer interaction during play has been found to be positively associated with teachers' ratings of children's general social competence (Howes & Matheson, 1992). Studying how well children initiate and respond to, as well as sustain, play interactions provides meaningful descriptions of their social skills and interactive repertoire. Observation approaches are described in Chapter 2, and behaviors related to peer interactions that are of concern can be used as the content for these observations. The specific types of behaviors related to social competence that are likely and useful targets for observation are outlined by Guralnick (1992) as follows:

- The purpose, frequency, and success of social initiations
- The responsiveness of the child to others
- Forms of expression, including use of verbal abilities, intelligibility, and quality and quantity of verbal exchanges
- Setting and play themes and the circumstances associated with the social interactions
- Developmental domains, especially cognitive level, language, and sensorimotor skills
- Strategies related to obtaining compliance from others, gaining entry, resolving conflicts, and sustaining play

Guralnick (1992) pointed out that successful entry to a play group involves observing play for a period to gain understanding of the theme and content of the play, making comments relevant to the content, engaging in nonintrusive nonverbal behavior such as carrying out the same play activity in close proximity, and timing the actual attempt to move in. Failure of first attempts to gain entry is high, and children need to be able to modify their behaviors as well as be persistent; they must also be able to resolve the potential conflict that may arise from the process, which includes negotiation, compromise, and provision of alternative suggestions.

Form 8.2 offers a format for recording and summarizing informal observations of children's peer play, following the parameters described by Howes and Matheson (1992). Howes and Matheson found early emergence of complex play to be a good indicator of later social competence; complex play, which involves role taking and role reversal, as well as metaplay (organizing and planning), emerges between the ages of 42 to 48 months in the typically developing child. This form can be used to write descriptions of the child during the course of the child's involvement in play with peers.

A number of rating scales assess social interaction skills of young children. Three of the more well known of these (the Preschool and Kindergarten Behavior Scales by Merrell, 1994; the Social Competence and Behavior Evaluation: Preschool Edition by LaFreniere & Dumas, 1995; and the Social Skills Rating System, or SSRS, by Gresham & Elliott, 1990) are presented in Test Reviews 8.11, 8.12, and 8.13.

Guidelines for Describing the Complex Peer Play of Preschool Children

(based on Howes & Matheson, 1992)

Describe child's behaviors in the following categories:

Play setting/themes:

Initiation of play:

Entry to ongoing play:

Response to peer initiations of play:

Integration of affect and action during play:

Resolution of conflicts:

Response to suggestions of others during play:

Ability to engage in role taking and role reversals:

Evidence of metaplay (articulation of planning of play themes and content):

Form 8.2

Test Review 8.11

Test Name
Preschool and Kindergarten Behavior Scales (PKBS) (1994)

Author
Kenneth W. Merrell

What the Test Measures
The PKBS yields scores on two dimensions: Social Skills and Problem behavior, with a total of 76 items. Social Skills includes behaviors that are characteristic of well-adjusted children, whereas the Problem Behaviors describe children who experience adjustment problems. All items are rated on a 4-point scale indicating frequency of occurrence. Social Skills include social cooperation, social interaction, and social independence. Problem Behaviors include self-centered, explosive behaviors, attention problems or overactivity, intimidation/harm to others, social withdrawal, and anxiety/somatic problems. The scales are completed by parents or teachers.

Age Range
3 through 6 years

Administration Time
8 to 12 min

Publisher
PRO-ED
8700 Shoal Creek Blvd.
Austin, TX 78757-6897
512-451-3246
www.proedinc.com

Norms
The norm group consisted of 2,855 preschool and kindergarten children representing communities in four geographical regions: West, North Central, Northeast, and South, including 16 states. There were weak gender differences, but the authors decided not to separate scoring by gender. According to the 1990 U.S. Census, there was a slight overrepresentation of Whites and slight underrepresentation of other racial groups. Children with developmental delays were included in the norms, with 8.4% already identified and another 2.6% in the process of assessment. There was slight overrepresentation of parents in the managerial/professional group, and stronger overrepresentation of parents in the operator/fabricator/laborer group than the national census. Standard scores have a mean of 100 and SD of 15. Norms are provided for two groups, ages 3 to 4 and ages 5 to 6.

Reliability
Cronbach's alpha scores ranged from .81 to .97, and split-half correlations ranged between .94 to .97. Standard errors of measurement are generally low. Test-retest reliability with a 3-week interval ranged from .58 to .87, and, with a 3-month interval, from .63 to .78 (with .36 for anxiety/somatic problems). Ratings for problem behaviors tended to be somewhat more stable. Agreements regarding ratings between teachers and teacher aids ranged from .36 to .61, and between teachers and parents, from .13 to .57.

Validity
Items were designed to reflect the research literature regarding both normal and abnormal development and were subsequently reviewed by early childhood professionals.

Factor analysis yielded three Social Skills factors: Social Cooperation, Social Interaction, and Social Independence. Factor analysis of the Problem Behaviors was "more complex, ultimately supporting Externalizing Problems and Internalizing Problems, but leading to the dropping of some items." The externalizing problem behaviors were further divided into self-centered/explosive, attention problems/overactive, and antisocial/aggressive. The internalizing problems were further divided into social withdrawal, and anxiety/somatic.

There were gender and disability status effects in the results of the ratings, with females and children without disabilities showing significantly stronger social skills and significantly lower problem behaviors.

Test Review 8.12

Test Name

Social Competence and Behavior Evaluation: Preschool Edition (SCBE) (1995)

Authors

Peter J. LaFreniere and Jean E. Dumas

What the Test Measures

There are eight basic scales and four summary scales that describe the child's manner of emotional expression, social interactions with peers and teacher-child relations (two scales for the last). Each basic scale has 10 items, with a total of 80. There is a composite scale called the General Adaptation Scale. Each item is rated on a 6-point scale of relative frequency of occurrence.

Age Range

30 to 78 months

Administration Time

15 min

Publisher

Western Psychological Services
12031 Wilshire Boulevard
Los Angeles, CA 90025-1251
800-648-8857
www.wpspublish.com

Norms

Norms totaled 1,263 children from two states, Indiana and Colorado. There were a total of six sites within these states. The sample had somewhat lower level education than the national census (1991), with a higher percentage of Black and Asian children and a lower percentage of Hispanic. Scores are T scores with a mean of 50 and SD of 10.

Reliability

Interrater agreement correlations ranged from .72 to .89, with internal consistency according to Cronbach's alpha, between .80 to .89.

Validity

The items were designed to reflect research evidence regarding successful social interactions and emotional expression of young children. Factor analysis yielded three principal factors of Social Competence, Externalizing Problems, and Internalizing Problems, supporting the three summary scales.

Test Review 8.13

Test Name
Social Skills Rating System (SSRS) (1990)

Authors
Frank M. Gresham and Stephen N. Elliott

What the Test Measures
The SSRS includes three sets of forms for completion by parents, teachers, and students. The national norms extend from preschool through secondary level, with the self-ratings available only for school-age children above preschool level. The scales assess both positive (cooperation, assertion, responsibility, empathy, and self-control) and problem (externalizing, internalizing, hyperactivity) behaviors. Each item is rated with regard to both frequency of occurrence and perceived importance to the rater. The items that indicate problems and are considered important for the student can be selected for inclusion in an intervention plan. At the preschool level, there are 40 items on the teacher scale and 49 items on the parent scale. The social skills items differ between the forms to apply to the specific location (home/school), but the problem behaviors are virtually the same.

Age Range
Preschool Forms for teachers and parents of children 3 years to 4 years

Administration Time
10 to 25 min

Publisher
American Guidance Service, Inc.
4201 Woodland Road
Circle Pines, MN 55014-1796
800-328-2560
www.agsnet.com

Norms
The norm sample included over 4,000 children between the ages of 3 through 18 years, stratified to match the U.S. 1988 Census on variables of age, gender, race, geographic region, parent education, and community size. The norms include 17% of children with handicaps, and there are separate norms for boys and girls.

Reliability
Internal consistency of ratings of social skills ranges from .93 to .94 for teachers and from .87 to .90 for parents. Ratings for problem behaviors range from .82 to .86 for teachers and from .73 to .87 for parents.
   Test-retest stability for social skills is .85 for teachers and .87 for parents. For problem behaviors, the stability is .84 for teachers and .65 for parents.

Validity
Evidence to support content, construct, concurrent, and factor analytic validity is presented. The items have been analyzed for cultural bias.

The results of any rating scale reflect the perceptions and experiences of the raters and must be interpreted as such. For this reason (as well as for ecological validity), it is particularly important to solicit ratings from more than one individual (e.g., parents and teachers; mothers and fathers) to allow comparison of the perceptions of the child's behaviors across contexts. Because these ratings may or may not correspond with the child's actual behavior, it is also important to carry out a direct observation of the child, but saying this is not to diminish the importance of tapping the perceptions of those important figures involved with the child. Any intervention carried out with the child is also aimed at the caregivers, and assessment of changes in their perceptions is important and relevant outcome information regarding the success of treatment.

A further issue in using rating scales is that although there may be some significant correlations among them, these relationships are rarely very strong or consistent. Two scales that may claim to measure the same processes may in fact yield very different results. This becomes readily apparent when reviewing the concurrent validity evidence for any of the scales. When constructing a scale, it is desirable to have only moderate positive correlations with other measures within the same domain. However, from the point of view of clinical practice and intervention, these moderate relationships (e.g., a statistically significant and relatively strong correlation of .50 in fact indicates only 25% shared variance) present a challenge to decisions about which scale to use. It is therefore imperative for assessors to read and digest the information in the test manuals and to have a clear idea of the variables they wish to assess so that they can determine how well the measures reflect these variables. Demaray et al. (1995) compared and evaluated six of the major social skills rating scales and concluded that the SSRS was the most comprehensive because of its multisource approach and linkage with intervention.

One scale that is still in the process of development but for which there is considerable accumulating research is the Penn Interactive Peer Play Scale (PIPPS; Coolahan, Fantuzzo, Mendez, & McDermott, 2000; Fantuzzo, Coolahan, Mendez, McDermott, & Sutton-Smith, 1998; Fantuzzo & Hamptom, 2000; Fantuzzo, Mendez, & Tighe, 1998), which is specifically designed for use with preschool children from urban environments of low socioeconomic status. The PIPPS has separate forms for teachers and parents, as well as for preschool and kindergarten. Each of the 32 items on each scale represents a behavior that has been associated, through direct observations, with the interactions of children who are either socially successful or unsuccessful. The rater scores on a Likert-type scale the degree of frequency of occurrence of the behavior during the previous two months. Factor analysis of the scales yields three factors, each of which has shown internal consistency above .80. The authors also conducted research to document concurrent and predictive validity.

When interpreting the results from rating scales, it is important to consider cultural variables, especially when comparing the ratings by teachers and parents who may come from different backgrounds (Fagan & Fantuzzo, 1999; Powless & Elliott, 1993). Cultural values, expectations, and child-rearing practices are likely to affect the results, and the responses to the scales must be interpreted with these issues in mind; that is, the implications of the scores do not necessarily have the same meaning for individuals from all cultural backgrounds.

One of the most frequently used approaches to assessment of social status and degree of social likability has been sociometry (Odom & McConnell, 1989). Sociometric procedures are more reliable for 4- and 5-year-olds than for 3-year-olds (Denham & McKinley, 1993; Eisenberg & Harris, 1984). There are basically two approaches to sociometry: peer nominations and peer ratings. Although both provide useful information, peer ratings have been found to show more reliability and validity (Olson & Lifgren, 1988), particularly regarding prediction of future cognitive and social functioning (Denham & McKinley, 1993; Howes, 1988; Ironsmith & Poteat, 1990; LaFreniere & Sroufe, 1985; Poteat, Ironsmith, & Bullock, 1986). In contrast to peer nominations, peer ratings provide information regarding every student in the class but require more time to administer. With peer nomination, children are usually asked to name (point to the picture of) three children with whom they like to play and three with whom they do not like to play. For preschoolers in both approaches, there is usually a board with all the photographs of all of the students in the class, and the child is first asked to name each child; when the child does not know a name, it is provided. In the case of peer ratings, the children are then trained to sort pictures of various foods into three categories: those they really like, those they sort of (kind of) like, and those they do not like. The sorting is done by placing the pictures into boxes with faces drawn on the front that include a smile, neutral or no expression, or frown. The children are then given the randomly ordered photos of the children in the class to sort in the same way. Children who are placed in the smile box are assigned a score of three; those in the neutral box, a two; and those in the frown box, a one. The scores for all of the sorts from all of the children in the class are then averaged to determine social status of each child. Some of the researchers then further classify the children, by determining cutoff scores, into those who are popular, rejected, neglected, or controversial (sometimes given positive ratings, sometimes negative; Chan & Mpofu, 2001).

There is an ethical dilemma regarding the use of negative nominations or assignments because the effects of making negative ratings are as yet unknown (Chan & Mpofu, 2001). At the same time, however, the determination of "rejected" is the most powerful and stable predictor of future status and is very effective in determining children who are at risk for conduct disorders and other behavioral deficits (Kemple, 1991; Parker & Asher, 1987).

Children who are rejected are typically characterized by both aggressive and impulsive behaviors. Children who are popular are characterized by cooperative behavior and friendly demeanor, with a good ability to comply with suggestions of others and expand on their reasons when they do not wish to comply. Rubin (1986) found that isolated, nonaggressive children articulated fewer problem-solving strategies and were less likely to modify their unsuccessful strategies than were the more popular children. The isolated children were not necessarily disliked, but they would tend to assume submissive roles during play and were often rebuffed. The social status of these children was stable over time, and Rubin saw them as at risk for developing internalizing disorders, whereas the rejected children were at risk for developing externalizing disorders.

Assessors using sociometry need to be aware that young children are likely to choose others of the same gender as those they like (Guralnick & Groom, 1987b; Vaughn, Colvin, Azria, Caya, & Krzysik, 2001), and ethnicity and cultural background may also affect choices, depending on the circumstances (Raver & Zigler, 1997), for example, whether the children from other cultures are a distinct minority or are very different in socioeconomic status.

There is general agreement that the best approach to assessment of social interaction in preschool children is a multidimensional one that combines direct observation in natural settings with both teacher and parent judgment-based rating scales with the sociometric technique of peer ratings (Gresham, 1981, 1984; McConnell & Odom, 1999; Odom & McConnell, 1985). We must always keep in mind that these procedures provide descriptions and normative comparisons, not explanations for social interactions.

FUNCTIONAL BEHAVIOR ASSESSMENT

The phrase "new wine in old bottles" (Ervin, Ehrhardt, & Poling, 2001, p. 173) applies to functional behavior assessment (FBA). We could also phrase this as, Who put the F in ABC? Behavioral assessment and concern with the functions of these behaviors have been around for a long time. However, recent special education legislation (P.L. 105-17) requires that an FBA be considered for special education children with severe behavior disorders and mandates that it occur for students (including preschool students) who are to be suspended in excess of 10 days or who are to be moved to an interim alternative educational setting (Drasgow & Yell, 2001); there has therefore been a rush to produce documents and formats for these procedures. The federal government provides only general guidelines, and it is up to each state to prescribe the specifics of the procedures outlined in the federal regulations. The most positive outcome of this phenomenon is that psychologists are forced to enter classrooms to observe children's behavior.

Actually, the FBA is only a part of the larger entity that emphasizes positive behavioral supports incorporated into the Behavior Intervention Plan (BIP) for which the FBA is the data-gathering process (Drasgow & Yell, 2001; Sugai et al., 1999). The addition of the F to the ABC approach to behavioral assessment (see Chapter 2, which discusses observation procedures) changes the focus from almost exclusive consideration of environmental variables (assumed to be controlling or causative) to inclusion of intraindividual variables, including biological and intrapsychic, although these tend to be downplayed in most of the research literature and discussions of this approach. The focus on "function" introduces concern regarding the purpose the behavior serves for the individual (i.e., in what way is this behavior representing the individual's attempt to adapt or cope with the stimulus [trigger/antecedent] events?). The typical array of choices for functions are social attention, access to tangible materials or preferred activities, escape from aversive tasks or activities, escape from or avoidance of other individuals, or internal stimulation (Gresham, Watson, & Skinner, 2001). The primary goal of the positive behavioral supports built into the BIP is to devise strategies to help the student meet these needs in a more socially acceptable way. Strategies must be generated through a team-based problem-solving process that addresses the setting events (predisposing factors, which include within child variables), antecedents (triggers), consequences, and direct teaching of skills that the student may lack.

Interventions that target antecedents attempt to diminish the student's exposure to triggers that precipitate the problem behaviors. Interventions that target the problem behaviors attempt to promote the development of alternative behaviors (or teach them if not in the child's repertoire). Interventions that target the consequences attempt to change these consequences so that the problem behaviors are not reinforced (Nissen, Blader, Fleiss, Kurtz, & Courtney, 2000). These strategies must also be system-focused, that is, not apply just to the student, but address changes that need to be made in the school, the classroom, and the home. Furthermore, the strategies must be proactive and preventive when possible, as well as nonaversive, that is, not include pain, humiliation, or tissue damage (Sugai et al., 1999).

According to the guidelines developed by the Office of Special Education Programs (Sugai et al., 1999), FBA is defined as "a systematic process of identifying problem behavior and the events that (a) reliably predict occurrences and non-occurrence of those behaviors and (b) maintain the behaviors across time" (p. 12). The information for this task is to come from multiple sources, including file review, interviews of caregivers and teachers (and students, in the case of older ages), rating scales, experimental manipulation of antecedent, consequent conditions, or both, as well as direct observation. Nowhere is it suggested that the child be directly tested except for administration of curriculum-based measurement procedures (Sugai et al., 1999); the clear emphasis is on contextual rather than within-child variables. Thus, FBA differs from functional analysis in its comprehensiveness and multiplicity of data sources, as functional analysis is limited to direct behavioral observation (Vollmer & Northup, 1996). Intra-individual issues are handled primarily with the concept of "setting events or establishing operations," such as biological conditions or aspects of family history that may impinge on the state of the individual and influence responsiveness to environmental triggers and consequences (Gresham et al., 2001).

As a comprehensive process, the FBA should consist of the following components (Drasgow & Yell, 2001, p. 247):

- Review of files
- Interviews of teachers, caregivers, and others who have intensive contact with the child
- Multiple direct observations of the child in a variety of settings
- Experimental manipulation of variables, if necessary
- Development of summaries of the hypotheses about the likely functions of the problem behaviors
- The entire FBA process conducted in a timely manner
- Development by the Individual Education Plan (IEP) team of a BIP based on the information from the FBA
- Monitoring and documentation of the effectiveness of interventions, and modification as needed

The purpose and outcome of the interviews (actually the whole procedure) is to identify and define operationally the target behaviors, identify antecedent and consequent events, determine the probable functions of the behaviors, and identify appropriate replacement behaviors (Gresham et al., 2001; see also the interview format presented in Chapter 2).

Historically, FBA was developed primarily to detect symptoms such as self-injury in individuals with severe mental retardation. Although research with higher functioning individuals is gradually accumulating, based necessarily on single case studies, its usefulness with low-frequency behaviors (e.g., carrying a weapon to school, which may occur just once) requires further study (Ervin, Radford, et al., 2001; Nichols, 2000). There are potentially many instances when "the hypothesized functions that drive the entire process are nonobservable elements in the domain of thoughts and feelings" (Nichols, 2000, p. 394; see also Miller, Tansy, & Hughes, 1998). In these instances, the manipulation of antecedents and consequences within the classroom or school setting will not affect the primary behavior of concern, although some of the experiences of the child, such as rejection by peers that may be occurring in a potentially observable way and that may relate to the primary problem behavior, can be addressed, and the child's interpretations and behaviors that serve as stimuli or responses to these events may also be addressed. After reviewing more than 100 articles applying FBA in school settings, Ervin, Radford, et al. (2001) concluded that the "existing FA [functional analysis] technology [on which a good deal of FBA relies] was not developed to deal with verbally mediated responses controlled by distal contingencies" (p. 208).

Recognizing that traditional psychometric criteria are not entirely appropriate, Shriver, Anderson, and Proctor (2001) offered standards that are relevant for determining the validity of FBA. One of the most important of these, and one that "should" apply to other procedures as well, is the determination of the assessment's relationship with the effectiveness of treatment that is based on this assessment. Such determination is much more easily said than done, and applied settings such as schools would need to build this kind of data collection into their special education procedures and value (require!) this type of research in order to justify their practices. Needless to say, this is not the norm. This is an area in which the school psychologist can make a potentially important contribution. Determination of treatment effectiveness is not only desirable; it is now required by federal (and, therefore, state) regulations. Much time and money can be saved in relation to due process hearings if these data become a built-in part of the FBA-BIP process. (Chapter 10 addresses this issue.)

The issue of interpretation of controlling variables as causal is an interesting one. First of all, in my experience it is not easy to establish reliable patterns of triggers and consequences for complex behaviors. Second, these triggers, as others have pointed out, may be triggers because of distal events that have their effect through the development of the child's perceptions and beliefs. What makes a trigger a trigger is rarely discussed by writers in this area. I distinctly recall an early experience in Head Start, when I was given my own class to teach (because, at that time—1964 and 1965—that seemed easier than trying to figure out what a mental health consultant was supposed to do). In this class there was a boy who could almost be described as a feral child with regard to the development of his social skills. He had none; he had reactions, but no skills. One of the expressions of his social interaction problems was that any attempt by another child to touch him precipitated an aggressive response. The consequence was that the children avoided him. This was a reliable antecedent-behavior-consequence sequence. However, my strategy, which I think worked, was cognitive rather than strictly behavioral. My hypothesis was that the cause was in his mind and experience. On the one hand, it was likely that touch in his experience was aversive; on the other hand, it was also likely that he had not developed good social interaction skills related to this (and to limited exposure to peers; tactile defensiveness did not seem to be the issue, although it needed to be considered). My strategy was to address the trigger and consequence based on an intrachild hypothesis. I kept reinterpreting the meaning of the attempt to touch to him: that the touching was meant to try to be a friend and not to hurt him. Likewise, I encouraged the child who touched him not to withdraw, but to persist in attempts to connect. In this case, the touch was the antecedent, and the function might be inferred as his wish to avoid social interaction, although I am not so sure of that. I suspect that he was exercising his limited response repertory and that he was clueless about social interaction with peers as something to approach or avoid. That is, his behavior was almost a conditioned response, and the strategy was to introduce some mediating thought between stimulus and response. Was the consequence maintaining the behavior? If we interpret this in a functional way and say that his need or desire or the purpose of his behavior was to avoid social contact, do we then devise strategies for him to accomplish this goal through alternative behaviors? This and other situations challenge some of the thinking behind the FBA model because it was not initially developed for the (potentially) "thinking" child with a relatively intact cortex. As J. Miller, Tansy, and Hughes (1998) suggested, much of the research on this model has been from an operant theory perspective. It is still possible to preserve the intent and procedures of the FBA process and proceed from a more diverse theoretical basis.

Except when mandated, the decision to conduct an FBA is left to the discretion of the IEP team. The team is only told that it "must consider" an FBA when students engage in behaviors that impede their learning or the learning of other students. Because there is no requirement for the participation of a psychologist on this team, despite the psychologist's relative specialized training and expertise in this social-emotional domain, it is legal and possible (unless otherwise legislated by individual states) not to include the psychologist in this process. Therefore, it is important for psychologists to become knowledgeable about the FBA process, including the interventions that have demonstrated research-based effectiveness, and to be assertive about their relevance to guiding and participating in these procedures. Because the ongoing effectiveness of interventions outlined in the resulting behavioral plan must be documented, it is particularly important that the psychologist's expertise in research design and implementation be tapped.

In conclusion, the area of social-emotional functioning is arguably the most complex of all developmental domains, to a large extent because it involves all domains, including cognition, language, adaptive, and motor functioning. The issue of emotional regulation has become increasingly central to understanding the nature of the child's functioning, as well as for a target of intervention (Lemerise & Arsenio, 2000; Wittmer, Doll, & Strain, 1996). One of the basic principles of the functioning of the human organism (and all others) is homeostasis, or the restoration of equilibrium and balance. Survival homeostatic mechanisms are built in and do not require conscious regulation. However, this basic principle seems to apply to higher level, more cortically controlled functions as well. Emotions represent an arousal system that creates disequilibrium (sometimes actively sought), and cognitive strategies, developed through social interactive experiences, serve to restore balance (or seek further stimulation). Initially, although the infant shows very rudimentary behaviors that work to reduce stress and disequilibrium, the more complex, conscious regulation occurs externally and becomes increasingly internalized in optimal, development-inducing environments and in typically developing children. This internalization process can be disrupted from any number of sources, and these disruptions affect the individual's development of social skills, and, thereby, social competence. Human survival depends on social interaction, and social competence is therefore a basic need. We are currently in a state of greater understanding of how competence and incompetence develop than we are with regard to provision of intervention once this complex process has gone awry. There are some promising approaches to intervention, but the most effective approach to date appears to be individualized problem solving based on careful data collection with conscientious monitoring of outcomes.

SUMMARY

This chapter discusses what is possibly the most complex and challenging area of assessment: the social and emotional functioning of young children. The chapter begins with an overview of the developmental characteristics of this domain. This discussion includes the topics of temperament, adaptive behavior, peer interaction, and FBA. Temperamental characteristics are particularly influential during the preschool years and can affect the future course of the child's development through the effects on interactions with both adults and peers. Assessment of adaptive behavior is problematic during the preschool years because of the difficulty of differentiating it from assessment of general development. Peer relations represent an area of rapid development during this time period and can offer significant predictive value regarding the child's risk for future social-emotional problems. FBA has become a mandated approach for evaluating children with significant social problems.

SUGGESTED ACTIVITIES

SCHOLARSHIP

1. Select a dimension of one of the prevailing social skills rating scales and review the relevant literature. To what degree does the literature support or refute the choice of items on this dimension?
2. Research and discuss the construct of adaptive behavior in relation to young children.

APPLICATION

1. Compare two social competence or skills rating scales with regard to the dimensions that they share. Consider the evidence of validity regarding their degree of relationship and try to account for the extent to which they agree and disagree.
2. Give the appropriate forms of one of the rating scales to at least two adults who know the selected child well. Compare the ratings and interpret and discuss the results.
3. Ask a child's teacher to complete one of the major behavior rating scales. Conduct a direct observation of the same behaviors covered in the scale (if there are too many, select some that are representative). Compare and discuss the results.

Chapter Nine

♦

The Neuropsychological Functioning of Young Children

♦

Everything that has been written in this book has implications for the neuropsychological functioning of children. We are social beings. We are individuals. We are the product of the interactions of our individuality and our experiences, and we are also a bundle of brain-behavior relationships. Some of us focus more intently on the behavior, whereas others focus more on the nervous system. In this chapter I discuss aspects of the neuropsychological functioning of young children that relate to their assessment. Of all the topics that have been discussed so far, this may be the least fully developed or explored area of assessment. Therefore, to many, this may be the most exciting area to consider. Children bring their families, their cultures, their communities, and their experiences to an assessment. They also bring their nervous systems. If we wish to understand why and how children develop learning and behavioral disorders and how we should approach interventions with inclusion and attention to the so-called black box of the brain, then we need to consider their neuropsychological functioning. Indeed, Hynd and Willis (1988) concluded that "behavior and neurology are inseparable" (p. 4). However, we also need to be aware that there is no necessary direct correspondence between the behaviors we observe and their underlying neurology (or vice versa) and that, according to research evidence, any relationships that do exist are likely to show gender differences because of the differences in organization of the brains of males and females (Aylward, 1988; Bigler, 1988; Kalverboer, 1976).

Those who claim that all that is necessary to help children is to understand and control the antecedents and consequences of the observed behaviors need only to think about children who are referred for difficulties with attention and impulsivity. It is not difficult to understand how different the interventions would be and how relevant it is to determine likely "cause" if these observed behaviors were associated with attention deficit disorder, anxiety about poor school work, anxiety about an impending parental divorce, exposure to a shrieking teacher, inadequate mastery of

This chapter assumes some basic knowledge of the brain that most psychology majors would have covered in a physiological psychology course.

the language of the classroom, and so on. Gathering evidence based on hypotheses remains the never-ending quest, and some of these hypotheses will address brain-behavior relationships.

All psychologists to some extent need to be neuropsychologists (Byrnes & Fox, 1998). We need to be aware that there are implications of behavior for nervous system functioning and, to some extent, what these might be, if only to be able to make appropriate referrals (e.g., Dawson, Meltzoff, Osterling, & Rinaldi, 1998; Glaser, 2000). The psychologist working with young children may be the first professional to engage in careful observation and assessment of the child beyond developmental and health concerns addressed by the pediatrician. As psychologists we also receive referrals of children who have been diagnosed with neurological conditions, and we then function as assessors to determine how these conditions are manifested within the school or learning context and as consultants to help teachers and parents facilitate their learning and coping in both home and school. The referrals we receive of very young children are even more likely to involve neurological issues than are those for older children (Deysach, 1986).

When I was trained as a school psychologist, the primary issue related to neuropsychological assessment was the attempt to determine whether there were signs of what was then called *organicity* (i.e., an "organic" basis for the behavior). We administered tests to try to infer the existence of an organic basis for symptoms and conditions, and the primary source of this information was the Bender Gestalt (well, perhaps along with a figure drawing). We acted as if organicity were some singular, meaningful entity. Some of us went a little further and began to learn some neurological screening procedures, but the issue was still the same: to respond to the question of organicity on a yes or no basis. Today, responses to the question of neurological involvement need to be considerably more detailed and specific, and the tools of assessment must be considerably more complex and sensitive. Certainly one test cannot serve as a meaningful data source (Bigler, 1988).

THE "NEURO" IN NEUROPSYCHOLOGICAL ASSESSMENT

What makes an assessment "neuro" psychological is to some extent an issue of data interpretation, as well as systematic sampling of functional systems. However, there is more, and the components of a typical neuropsychological assessment as outlined by Reynolds and Mayfield (1999, pp. 112–114) include procedures that inform the assessor regarding the following:

1. Educationally relevant cognitive skills or higher order processing skills
2. The relative efficiency of the right and left hemispheres
3. Both anterior and posterior regions
4. Specific deficits
5. Acuteness versus chronicity
6. Intact complex functioning systems
7. Affect, personality, and behavior

The limitation of any such list is that it typically reflects assessments of adults and that categories such as specificity and chronicity, and even laterality, do not necessarily have the same meaning for young children as for adults because the former's brains are not fully developed (Aylward, 1988).

In any assessment it is first necessary to take a careful history from the caregivers, including information about the child as well as about close relatives. Certainly, information about development is important, as well as the child's birth and delivery, but the assessor also needs to know about history of trauma (accidents as well as emotional), health, sensory systems, medications, and seizures. Assessors need a careful review of the history of members of the immediate family regarding health and learning, and a review of medical and previous assessment records is essential. These should be requested prior to the assessment, as it often takes some time for them to be prepared and released, although some parents do keep reasonably complete records. Review of this information has been incorporated into Form 1.1.

The assessor then needs to observe the child's physical characteristics and interactions with both the object and the social environment as described in Chapter 2. Many syndromes are associated with dysmorphic facial features, such as lowered ears, spacing of eyes, location of hairline, and size of head. The assessor's intuitive feeling of "funny-looking kid" needs to be transformed into detailed observations of what appears to be unusual in the child's features or mannerisms. As in any ecologically valid approach, the child should be observed within as many contexts as possible—certainly within the child's preschool program, and optimally within the home and in interaction with primary caregivers.

Finally, the assessor engages in direct testing to sample systematically the child's functions both quantitatively and qualitatively. As discussed earlier, quantitative assessment is especially challenging for very young children because of issues such as cooperation, developmental variability, and developmental access to relevant information (e.g., prognostic indicators of future intellectual functioning are not necessarily apparent in the accessible behaviors of very young children, although they are more so than in infants; Aylward, 1988). With regard to neurological issues, the functions that are most adequately assessed during early childhood are those that are the most fully developed and that follow a predictable sequence of development, namely, sensory, perceptual, and motor functions. Those that are developing, such as higher mental processes and the executive functions, are considerably more elusive and less reliable because early childhood is a period of developmental spurts (Epstein, 1978; Rourke, Bakker, Fisk, & Strang, 1983); needless to say, all children do not "spurt" in the same way or in exactly the same time frame. Determination of the intactness of sensory, perceptual, and motor functions is a relevant assessment endeavor, as long as this is conducted with caution and humility. This dynamic aspect of development is also what makes it considerably more easy to rule in evidence of an ability than to rule it out, as we can always be more secure in concluding that a child can do something (that they in fact have done) compared to concluding that they cannot based on what has not been observed or elicited. Similarly, it appears easier to predict intact functioning on the basis of preschool neurological screening than it is to predict later occurring disorders (Lindahl, Michelsson, & Donner, 1988). This point was made earlier but bears repeating as a basic principle of assessment.

THE MENTAL STATUS EXAM

A comprehensive psychological assessment can also be viewed as an extended and comprehensive mental status exam. Most neurologists and neuropsychologists conduct a mental status exam as part of their intake procedure to provide an overview of the neurological systems of the client. This typically involves information gathering regarding the following (Wiederholt, 2000):

- Level of consciousness (including attention)
- Orientation (regarding time, place, and person)
- Speech (voice, tongue, prosody, volume)
- Sensori-motor functions (vision, hearing, fine/gross motor)
- Language (receptive, expressive, fluency, writing)
- Memory (short-term, working, long-term)
- General information (age and background relevant)
- Calculation
- Abstraction and judgment
- Other skills (demonstrating how to use objects, following multistep directions)

However, most mental status exams were developed for use with adults so that all normally functioning adults would be expected to be able to perform all items on the exam successfully. Children are by definition in a state of change, and preschool children in particular are in a period of rapid development and are very context dependent for items such as knowledge and language. However, the mental status exam just outlined does provide reasonable guidelines for designing an assessment battery and for making detailed observations to assure that these areas are addressed. These procedures should yield information tapping each area, and by using well developed procedures and astute observations, assessors should be able to provide considerably more comprehensive conclusions than is possible with the typical screening approach described previously.

NEUROPSYCHOLOGICAL ASSESSMENT OF YOUNG CHILDREN

Until recently, very little research was available to aid the psychologist-assessor to address the neuropsychological functioning of the young child in areas other than language and sensorimotor functioning. The approach to neuropsychological assessment of young children was basically a downward extension of procedures developed for use with adults (Lyon et al., 1988). Among the problems with this approach was that the model of brain functioning was that of the adult, which significantly differs from that of the young child, for example, regarding the issue of focal (adult) versus more diffuse (child) manifestation of disorders (Kemp, Kirk, & Korkman, 2001). These adult-based procedures also had poor ecological validity for children, as the contexts in which they function differ significantly from those of adults. Finally, the norms that were available were not appropriate for the younger populations, particularly for children below the age of 5 years.

We now have the NEPSY: A Developmental Neuropsychological Assessment (Korkman, Kirk, & Kemp, 1998), which, though not perfect, allows for some systematic sampling of the child's functional systems and provides opportunities to observe the child's qualitative functioning as well. This, along with the guidelines for neurological referral outlined in Form 9.1, should provide a reasonable basis for drawing conclusions regarding the child's level of risk for neurological disorder so that appropriate referrals can be made. The general rule would be, "When in doubt, refer," as many signs and symptoms can be very subtle, and the assessor is sometimes working more on intuition than on hard data; it would be much preferable to err on the side of overidentification in the case of neurological disorders. However, it is also necessary to let the caregivers know that you are just being cautious and thorough so that they are not panicked by the thought that their child many have some dreaded nervous system disorder.

Guidelines for Neuropsychological Referral

Name: _____ Date(s) of Observation: _____

Age: _____ Assessor: _____

Record potential risk factors from historical review:

  Regarding child:

  Regarding family:

  Regarding cultural/community contexts:

Describe child's physical appearance:

Administer the Following Screening Directly with Child:

For Children Age 3 [and 4] Only:

  Tandem Gait*: Walks heel to toe on tape without stepping off.   P/F

  Touch Localization: With closed eyes, shows or tells where touched by assessor:
  top side of one hand, then the other, then both   P/F

For Children Ages 3 [4], and 5: [1]

  Walk on toes*: Walks across room on toes of both feet.   P/F

  Walk on heels*: Walks across room on heels of both feet.   P/F

  Restless Movements: Sits motionless for at least half of a 1-min period, with
  feet off the ground and hands in lap.   P/F

  Hand Coordination*: 3 cycles of each hand carrying out rapid pronation,
  supination movements.   P/F

For Children Age 5 Only:

  Tandem Gait Backward*: Walks heel to toe backward, keeping feet on tape.   P/F

  Downward Drift: Stands with eyes closed, hands outstretched palms down for
  20 s without any arm drift (help child into position)   P/F

  Hopping*: Hops on each foot twice   P/F

  Hopping: Hops on each foot ten times   P/F

  Alternate Tapping*: Tap five times with right index finger, then five times with
  left index finger, then alternative right/left index fingers four times   P/F

  Complex Tapping*: Child taps two times with left, two times with right and
  repeats this pattern for five cycles; child then taps once with left index finger
  and twice with right index finger, continuing pattern for five cycles.   P/F

Score for Risk:
Age 3: three or more failures [Apply to age 4 also]
Age 5: four or more failures

Note: Since this procedure was conducted only on children ages 3 and 5, in the case of 4-year-olds, just administer the procedure for 3-year-olds.
[1] This information is based on the study by Huttenlocher, Levine, Huttenlocher, & Gates, 1990
* Assessor demonstrates
Lidz, Carol S. *Early Childhood Assessment.* Copyright 2003, John Wiley & Sons.

The screening in Form 9.1 is a reformatting of the procedure researched by Huttenlocher, Levine, Huttenlocher, and Gates (1990), which in turn was an abstraction of the more extensive Touwen and Prechtl (1970) procedure. Huttenlocher et al. applied the screening to middle-class suburban children aged 3 and 5 years, with a follow-up of the 5-year-olds when they were 7. The items of the screening represent those that showed the greatest discrimination between children with and without risk for developmental disorders (otherwise determined), as well as those that showed acceptable reliability and ease of administration and scoring. Scoring is pass-fail with cutoff scores. The results for the 5-year-olds who were followed up 2 years later showed a −.55 correlation with Full Scale IQ (from the Wechsler Intelligence Scale for Children–Revised), −.42 with Verbal IQ (strongest relationship with Arithmetic), and −.48 with Performance IQ (strongest relationships with Picture Arrangement and Coding). Almost all of the children who were later placed in special education were correctly identified. These results were comparable to the team screening procedure offered within the school that involved an arena (transdisciplinary) assessment, a much more time-consuming and expensive approach. Determination of risk should include a detailed history in addition to any procedure such as this.

The NEPSY represents a compilation of frequently used neuropsychological assessment procedures that offers the advantages of simultaneous standardization of all tests on a single normative population as well as normative information that extends between the ages of 3 and 12 years. Prior to this, it was necessary for assessors of young children to create a loosely configured battery of tests that either had no normative references or had a different set of norms for each test. Earlier versions of the NEPSY have a long history of development, application, and research in Finland, Denmark, and Sweden, and extensive piloting in the United States was conducted in order to select the most effective and efficient subtests. The materials are visually attractive and appealing to children and relatively easy to administer and score (with some significant exceptions) for assessors.

Recognizing the developmental differences of very young children, the authors of the NEPSY included some subtests that were appropriate just for children between the ages of 3 and 4, whereas some subtests apply throughout the entire age range, thereby providing some continuity to allow for monitoring through serial testing.

The NEPSY subtests assess the domains of Attention/Executive functioning, Language, Sensorimotor, Visuomotor, and Memory/Learning. Selection of subtests was not determined or confirmed by factor analysis but was derived from traditional neuropsychological theory and practice, as well as research evidence regarding nervous system areas tapped by the test's processing demands. Because each of these areas is complex and represented differentially in the central nervous system, the subtests within each domain tend to tap different aspects of the domain and often do not correlate strongly with other subtests within the domain. Therefore, interpretation of the NEPSY is best done at a subtest, rather than domain, level, and the assessor must be adept at process, task, and error analysis to maximize the information from this procedure. However, assessors need not be neuropsychologists, as the authors state that meaningful interpretation can be done at a processing level without necessarily making inferences about the nervous system.

Assessors seeking some unitary measure of processes such as memory and attention will not find one in this test largely because these are not represented in the nervous system as unitary processes. Therefore, assessors cannot interpret the information from the NEPSY in terms of conclusions about memory, attention, and so on, without qualifying what this means in terms of type and nature of the process, its context, and its relationship with other sources of evidence.

The NEPSY includes core tests that sample each domain and are administered to all children. When there are weaknesses or questionable areas, these can be further explored with the expanded subtests. The closest to a theory base for the NEPSY is the work of Luria—both his observations about the organization of neurological functions and his approaches to their assessment. However, Luria worked primarily with adults and addressed localization of lesion issues, which is less of a concern for neuropsychological assessment today and is less relevant to the nature of young children's functioning. Korkman (1999) also noted that Luria's conclusions regarding primary and secondary deficits may not apply to children, who are more accurately described in terms of strengths and weaknesses of functions and processes. The NEPSY authors also changed Luria's pass-fail scoring to a psychometrically normed approach but preserved Luria's hypothesis-testing approach by including subtests that extend beyond the core battery that can be used to verify hypotheses and further explore areas of weakness.

LURIA'S CONTRIBUTIONS

Luria (1973) described the organizational structure of the central nervous system as a bottom-up development involving three functional units. The first (primary) concerns regulation of tone, as well as waking and mental state. The second (secondary) receives, analyzes, and stores information, and the third (tertiary) programs, regulates, and verifies (evaluates) mental activity. The first unit is located essentially in the brain stem and just above this in the diencephalon areas, concerns survival functions, and is not lateralized. The second area includes visual and auditory functions and is located primarily in the parietal, temporal, and occipital areas, that is, the posterior regions of the cortex. This area is most active in its development between the ages of 2 and 5 years. The third area is located in the frontal, particularly prefrontal, areas of the cortex and shows heightened development from the age of 4 years. Both secondary and tertiary regions are lateralized in the adult (i.e., they show dominance regarding specific functions), but although there are areas of specialization, there is no strict localization. With evolutionary development of the prefrontal cortex, which contains executive capacities, what is most characteristic of the human brain is its interconnectedness: Everything except the most basic survival functions is connected with the prefrontal cortex and vice versa. The areas where the lobes of the cortex interconnect are particularly important for intermodality analysis, and the area that researchers most closely associate with assessed intelligence and academic learning is the posterior association area, which contains the boundaries of the occipital, temporal, and parietal regions. How these functions are regulated and applied is a matter for the prefrontal lobes.

In neurology, the terms primary, secondary, and tertiary have an overlapping but more specifically regional reference, as well. These differ somewhat from Luria's uses of the terms, which tend to extend over broader areas of the brain and are more function based, whereas these referents are more structure based, specifically those structures in Luria's secondary zone. According to common neurological parlance, primary zones "are modality specific and receive input from the senses or control motor activity"; secondary zones "lie adjacent to primary . . . and integrate modality-specific information into perceptive information"; and tertiary zones "are associative, supramodal areas encompassing the borders of parietal, temporal, and occipital zones as well as the vast prefrontal region with its abundant cortical and subcortical . . . connections" (Risser & Edgell, 1988, pp. 49–50).

Although the anatomical structures are in place in the newborn, the full organization and potential of dendritic (branches from the central axonal cells) connections are not, and the brain will be developing these connections and myelination (glial cell "white matter" covering and insulating neurons, promoting speed and efficiency of communication) for many years. It is experience that will promote these connections and determine what stays and what goes during the normal process of neuronal pruning. Just how this experience becomes registered within the brain seems not only to encourage the sprouting of axons (the main cell body), dendrites (the branches from the main cell), and synapses (the connections among the cells) but also to alter neural transmitter synthesis and release, as well as metabolic activity (such as blood flow; Nelson, 1999). In addition, just how well higher levels of cortical development function depends on the intactness and integrity of the lower levels, so problems occurring prior to birth or very early in the child's development can disrupt development of later functions because the brain is not sufficiently well organized to compensate for these disruptions. Localization does matter to some extent, particularly as it is involved in the more primary aspects of complex functions, and particularly if a primary function is damaged (i.e., bottom-up influence rather than top-down from the prefrontal lobes; Byrnes & Fox, 1998).

FIVE IMPORTANT POINTS

What is it important for us as psychological assessors to know about the neuropsychological functioning of young children? Five points are particularly important.

First, it is during the preschool and early elementary years that children are in their most plastic (and thus most vulnerable) state and are therefore most optimally receptive to learning and intervention. Although the peak of frontal-lobe neuron density occurs between the ages of 12 and 24 months, there is no significant decline until after the age of 7 years (Bronson, 2000). It is during this period that the principle of "use it or lose it" particularly applies (Bronson, 2000; K. W. Fischer & Rose, 1994); that is, cells that are not tapped for use may die off. It is experience that both activates neuronal connections and strengthens those that already exist. Experience has the strongest impact on regions that are in the process of developing.

Because of the numerous educational publications discussing brain-based learning, many people are now aware of the pruning that takes place in the brain when the central nervous system rids itself of cells that it either does not need or has not used (Thompson & Nelson, 2001). Although pruning is necessary for the efficient functioning of the nervous system, along with it goes the organism's capacity to adapt and to reprogram itself (Segalowitz, 1994). So-called "blooming and pruning" takes place in different areas of the brain at different times. In the preschool child, these phenomena have already taken place in the sensory and perceptual areas but are very much in process in the frontal areas (Thompson & Nelson, 2001). Therefore, guided stimulation of children—particularly regarding development of metacognitive and self-regulatory processes—is especially important during this period of time.

The related issue of critical periods applies to areas that are at their height of blooming, when it is presumed that optimal development requires certain environmental interactions. However, most of the conclusions about critical periods derive from research with animals, and it is thought that this idea, more correctly termed *sensitive periods,* applies more correctly to functions of vision and language than to cognition or social-emotional development (with the possible exception of attachment; Shonkoff & Phillips, 2000). Even in the case of attachment, the "period" may be broad and somewhat flexible (Thompson & Nelson, 2001).

Second, related to the first point, during the preschool years children begin to develop their prefrontal, executive-metacognitive capacities, which, with the aid of speech and language, will develop the functions that, according to Luria (1973), allow them to engage in intentioned, regulated, and evaluative activities. From ages 2 through 4 years there is a large increase in the metabolic rates of the prefrontal cortex, associated with the development of private speech in children between the ages of 3 and 5 years (Bronson, 2000). It is not just private speech, but language in general, that shows a dramatic increase in development during ages 3 to 4 years (K. W. Fischer & Rose, 1994). According to Vygotsky (1978), private speech serves as an important mediator between the external and internal world of the child, functioning as the mechanism of internalization and the capacity for self-regulation. Private speech functions to promote self-regulation because it separates "affect from events and one's initial reaction to them so that the child can develop perspective and objectivity" (Bronson, 2000, p. 152).

These are the human functions that are most dependent on experience and also on a sound foundation of lower order functions that involve registration and processing of incoming stimuli. For children, the hierarchy of development is bottom-up, from brain stem to posterior cortex to prefrontal cortex. Once this sequence is fully developed, the control becomes more top-down. During the preschool years, the abilities to engage in top-down control, which interconnects with all other functions and participates in their regulation, is just emerging and is therefore malleable and fragile, as well as sensitive to modification by experience. The development of these executive or prefrontal lobe functions allow humans to plan their actions, anticipate the future, control their behavior to carry out these plans, and then evaluate the results and adjust their behavior in response to this evaluation.

Once this regulatory, or executive, functioning begins to develop, there are at least three neural loops that appear to be particularly important for the self-regulatory functions; these can be viewed as essential for successful adaptation to a complex, democratic culture. These include prefrontal connections with the brain stem, particularly the reticular activating system, regarding attention; connections with the limbic system in the midbrain region, regarding emotions; and connections with the motor system for activity level and impulse control (response inhibition). There are also important connections between the executive and the posterior association areas that are involved in what we conventionally call intelligence, as well as most academic tasks associated with literacy and numeracy. Another central feature of the executive is its access to and role in memory as it is represented throughout the cerebral cortex; the executive retrieves stored memories after they have been processed by the hippocampus (located in the limbic system in the lower area of the cortex, deep inside the brain, above the brain stem) and sorted to their relevant locations and maintains these memories into what we call working memory, which permits the carrying out of functions such as planning and evaluation.

These loops are bidirectional; therefore, dysfunctions in any of these areas impact executive functioning, just as dysfunctions in the executive impact these connections; however, in the case of the limbic (emotional) system, there are more connections to the prefrontal lobes than vice versa, suggesting that emotions play a particularly important role in guiding behavior. As mentioned earlier, the most central feature of the executive is its interconnectedness, so a fully mature central nervous system is a complex and fully integrated organ, while simultaneously maintaining regions of specialization, particularly regarding primary and secondary functions.

Even though the prefrontal cortical areas show a surge during the preschool years (Sega-lowitz, 1994), the frontal lobes do not begin their functions at this age but have connections with other areas of the brain even at the time of birth (Parmelee et al., 1994); these connections seem particularly to involve attention, and the early regulation of attention has turned out to be a reasonably good predictor of later development. According to Parmelee et al. (1994), based on their longitudinal data, "Those infants who have well integrated neonatal state organization and attention are likely to have more successful interactions with the environment, and therefore to be at reduced risk for later developmental problems" (p. 547); these authors clearly recognize the importance of interactions between the organism and the environment.

Contrary to the thinking of some, the prefrontal lobes are not the seat of intelligence; rather, they provide the management and controls for intelligence to function properly. What we refer to as intelligence is more properly assigned to the posterior association area of the cerebral cortex, which also is the region most highly involved with literacy and numeracy tasks of reading, spelling, writing, and math. For those who wish to consult their neurology texts, Hynd and Willis (1988) specified the occipital cortices, the region of the angular gyrus, Wernicke's area, the left planum temporal, the arcuate fasciculus, Broca's region, and the supplementary motor areas (p. 102) as the location of the functional system for reading. Reading, as math, is represented in many locations, depending upon the specific task demand. For example, Byrnes (2001) suggested involvement of the bilateral parietal area as associated with the semantic knowledge involved in numbers, and the left-cortical pallidum-thalamic loop for the verbal sequences involved in arithmetic facts.

A third important general point is that although we have tended to assume that cerebral dominance, related to brain laterality, develops during the preschool years, it has become increasingly clear that the brain shows some degree of lateralization much earlier. This may have the most significant implications for the emotional component of temperament. Thus, just as capacities for organization, meaning, remembering, strategizing, and exploring appear to be built into the genetic programming of the organism, there also appears to be some prewiring for temperamental dispositions such as approach and avoidance in unfamiliar situations or with novel objects. Davidson's (1994) studies with infants found that "asymmetry in the anterior cortical regions is significantly associated with emotion and emotional reactivity" (p. 534). His studies looked at infants who cried or did not cry in response to maternal separation and at toddlers who reacted with approach or avoidance, as well as proximity to their mother, when introduced to a toy robot. In these studies, right frontal activity was activated in the inhibited children, and their left frontal lobe was underactivated; in the uninhibited children, the opposite was found.

Related to the issue of lateralization is the observation that despite decades of conviction that evidence of mixed laterality has serious negative implications for intelligence and learning ability and despite the fact that most neuropsychological batteries continue to include assessment of lateral dominance among their subtests, the evidence to support this conclusion is at best equivocal (Sulzbacher, Thomson, Farwell, Temkin, & Holubkov, 1994).

The fourth major point is that, in addition to language and executive capacities, the child's ability to engage in representational thought shows a developmental spurt during ages 3.5 to 4.5 years (K. W. Fischer & Rose, 1994). This was discussed in more detail in Chapter 4, and these capacities become most easily observed during the course of children's play. These developments reflect the increasing myelination of brain regions, which tend to mature (myelinate) in bottom-up sequence, with the higher level and evolutionarily newer areas maturing later and more gradually.

Finally, it is important to point out that preschool children are often at the point of "growing into" their disorders (Hooper, 1988; Rourke et al., 1983). Not infrequently, parents report that the child experienced historical risk factors, and might even have had seizures or been involved in an accident but was medically checked and was found to be "just fine." These parents are not necessarily in a state of denial. The consequences of these incidents may be quite subtle and may not become apparent until the task demands tap into the affected areas of the nervous system. There are, after all, no dyslexics in nonliterate societies. Thus, the child may indeed be "just fine" in terms of functioning successfully within the demands of home and community but may begin to show signs of learning-related disorders when placed in the formal instructional situation.

Thus, children of preschool age are at a critical juncture in their development—a juncture that moves them into uniquely human capacities and a juncture that plays an important determining role in their ultimate developmental destinies. Furthermore, the so-called Kennard principle (Aylward, 1997) suggesting that younger is better in terms of the consequences of brain injury does not necessarily hold, as "brain damage during development has its greatest impact upon those cell populations and/or individual growth parameters that show the greatest rate of development at the time of the insult" (Risser & Edgell, 1988, p. 52). Therefore, the impact of an injury to the brain during early childhood would depend on a number of parameters, including location, severity, and timing (Rourke et al., 1983); the state of organization of the brain is a very important issue. Also, as noted earlier, disruptions at lower levels of development have consequences for development at higher levels that cannot always be anticipated and may not become observable until demands are made on activation of these areas. To further complicate the issue, interactions with the environment, particularly with caregivers (which interact with parameters associated with socioeconomic level), play an important role in outcome. In any case, young children "seem to show their deficits primarily through attention problems" (Rourke et al., 1983, p. 106), reflecting the more diffuse, less integrated state of the young child's brain. Impairment in young children tends to have more diffuse, general effects on cognitive and perceptual functioning rather than resulting in specific, localized symptoms (Ernhart, Graham, Eichman, Marshall, & Thurston, 1963), but as Dennis (1988) concluded, "The earlier the brain damage, the more extensive the potential functional consequences" (p. 99). These consequences may not be evident immediately following the insult but may emerge well afterward, as development unfolds.

ELECTROPHYSIOLOGICAL PROCEDURES

It is useful for psychologists who receive reports from medical agencies and who make referrals to these agencies to be familiar with the major electrophysiological diagnostic procedures that are likely to be used with children with neurological disorders. Those that are least invasive and hold the least amount of risk are as follows (information primarily from Hynd & Willis, 1988):

Computed tomography (CT scan): Plain or enhanced by radiopaque fluid, this method provides a view of soft tissues of the brain and spinal cord, including the ventricles. This presents some risk for individuals allergic to the fluid, as well as presenting exposure to radiation.

Electrophysiological electroencephalogram (EEG): Electrodes are placed on the scalp to record the electrophysiology of the brain; this method is used primarily to detect seizures.

Evoked potentials (Eps): These include auditory, somatosensory, visual, and event-related; electrodes are placed on the scalp to record brain-stem-level response to stimuli; this method is very useful for young children when hearing or visual defects are suspected but evidence from other sources is equivocal.

Magnetic resonance imaging (MRI): This is the least invasive procedure, and it provides clear images of soft tissue but produces static results.

More recently, functional MRI and positron-emission tomography (PET) scans have been available, and these allow views of the brain in the course of activity to look directly at processing. Although the fMRI is noninvasive, PET scans utilize radioactive materials. These two procedures are the methods of choice, but they have the significant disadvantage of being extremely costly. A second disadvantage is that tasks have to be performed while the patient lies down within a tubular chamber that makes clanging noises during the course of the procedure (Byrnes, 2001). Finally, they are especially difficult and in many cases inappropriate for young children because they require the patient to remain still for a period of at least 30 min (in a tubular chamber making clanging noises; Thompson & Nelson, 2001).

IMPLICATIONS FOR ASSESSMENT

So what does all this mean for the assessment of young children? Certainly one implication is that awareness of nervous system functioning is an important aspect of the psychologist's knowledge base. Second, it would be relevant for assessors to view the data from assessments as samples not just of overt behaviors, but of nervous system functions as well, keeping in mind that, though relevant, there is no necessary simple correlation. Third, it would be appropriate to include procedures in the assessment battery that are deliberately selected to sample the intactness of nervous system functions at least on a screening level, and these can follow the outline provided by the basic mental status exam (Deysach, 1986). Although all psychologists may not wish to become neuropsychologists, all psychologists would need at least to be educated consumers of the information rapidly generated by neuropsychological research in order to understand the functioning of children more fully. Armed with this information, we are in a better position to understand that such frequently and loosely used concepts as developmental lags and memory and attention are often inaccurate and inappropriate and that processes such as attention and memory are complex and multifaceted, involving many areas of the brain (Byrnes & Fox, 1998; Tramontana, 1988). As school and child psychologists, we would be in a better position to be informed advocates for the whole child.

SUMMARY

This chapter discusses the importance and relevance of the neuropsychological bases of behavior for assessing young children. The fact that preschool children are in a stage of rapid development of their neurological processes makes knowledge of these foundations for learning particularly important. The NEPSY procedure is reviewed in detail as the primary test available that assesses the neuropsychological functions of young children. Luria's conceptualizations of brain functions are described because his work provides the foundation for the development of the NEPSY. The chapter emphasizes the plasticity of young children, as well as the important contribution of experience (particularly language) to the development of higher level and executive functions. The chapter provides a brief overview of the major electrophysiological procedures that are most likely to be used by physicians for assessment of the brain.

SUGGESTED ACTIVITIES

SCHOLARSHIP

1. Write a full critique of the NEPSY.
2. Select an area of the brain and develop an in-depth paper describing its structure and functions.
3. Write a paper on a neurological disorder that might be encountered in young children. Include implications for learning as well as interventions and accommodations that might be needed.

APPLICATION

Administer and interpret three NEPSY protocols, along with the screening procedure in Form 9.1. Relate the findings from each procedure.

Chapter Ten

Assembling, Reporting, and Evaluating the Pieces

We are nearing the end of a journey that has taken us through many domains and techniques. With each approach to assessment we have considered the many sides: the applications, the advantages, and the limitations. We have taken a very complex process and pulled it apart to facilitate our perception and ability to derive meaning. Now we must reassemble these disparate parts into an integrated whole that facilitates the development of the children and families with whom we work and enhances the abilities of caregivers and program providers to meet their needs. No one said it would be easy. The challenges we now face are to abstract the meaningful data from the huge amount of information that we have inevitably assembled, to integrate this into some meaningful whole, to link the assessment with intervention, and to evaluate the effectiveness of this whole process. These are the greatest challenges for the beginning student who is still struggling with getting the words of test directions right, trying to remember to put the blocks inside the box lid, or trying to get through just one complete test while simultaneously managing a child who thinks the best place to interact is under the table (or dealing with a child who thinks, "Isn't it fun seeing how many times I can flick the light switch on and off in just a matter of seconds!" or, worse yet, who sits still with tears in his or her eyes and refuses to do anything, totally indifferent to the number of candies that are offered). The encouraging or discouraging news for the novice is that we all continue to struggle with this: using our assessments to generate genuinely helpful information that results in improved outcomes for our clients. Development of expertise is only relative and never absolute.

WRITING REPORTS

I have a confession to make. I have been a school psychologist for over 35 years, and I still hate to write reports. However, I now feel better about the reports and receive increasingly positive feedback about their readability and about the utility of the content.

The need to put assessment information in writing cannot be overemphasized. No matter what is shared verbally, this disappears once the people who heard it have moved on (or, in

205

some cases, turned their heads or averted their gaze). One of the important services we can render for children and families is to create a paper trail that documents the child's needs, creates a written history, and follows what has been done and how well it has worked. In addition, the sad truth of our litigious times is that we need to put everything in writing to avoid a legal disaster. The answer to the question of what are the three most important activities of the practitioner is, Document, document, document!

Document everything you tell someone and everything you do with regard to your professional activities. When you sit down to write your report, think of it as a way to document all of the hard work involved in data collection, and look at it as creating a historical document for the child (Surber, 1995). I still dislike writing reports, but I now write them with a sense of doing something important. We are documenting history.

The reports written by psychologists have generally not fared well with teachers (Bagnato, 1981a; Hulburt, 1995; Wiener, 1985). Parents seem more satisfied, as they find value in information that promotes understanding of their children even if they are not totally satisfied or fail to follow the recommendations; having your child assessed seems to be an intervention for some parents, who may find that their relationship with the child and the child's self-esteem have been enhanced by the experience (Ross-Reynolds, 1990). However, teachers want specific, instruction-relevant, and feasible suggestions (Hulburt, 1995). They want ideas for action, and they want these actions to work. The wise assessor-consultant will derive these ideas in collaboration with the teacher (as an antidote to the inevitable "yes, but . . ." response to concrete suggestions).

Through the process of assessment and the resulting report, the psychologist is expected to be able to pose specific, measurable referral questions; tailor assessment procedures to respond to these questions; integrate information to address these questions; and develop interventions to respond to these questions, reducing the gap between the child's current levels of functioning and areas of need and the system's expectations (Surber, 1995). Again, no one said it would be easy. This is not a job for a technician.

There are almost as many suggested formats for writing reports as there are practitioners and trainers who use them. In the end, how we format reports reflects where and with whom we work. My own formats tend to vary with the nature of the case, but I generally follow a fairly traditional outline. It is mainly the content and the way I arrive at the data that have changed over the years. Most recommendations regarding report writing emphasize the need for clarity, readability, and relevance (Bagnato, 1981a). Clarity is achieved by avoidance of jargon and use of a conversational tone. Readability is enhanced by good organization, a focus on interpreting the information in relation to its meaning for the child, use of descriptions of task demands rather than test names, and anecdotal descriptions of how the child approached the tasks. Reports that wear the reader down are filled with numbers and look like they are boilerplate documents in which you merely need to fill in the name, gender, and age of the child. Relevance is facilitated by addressing the referral issues throughout and by providing specific, instruction-related recommendations. Teachers and parents want to understand the child better and to know what to do to improve the child's functioning. If this information is not in the report, they are likely to be dissatisfied. Guidelines for a traditional but useful report format appear in Form 10.1, which includes suggestions for content within each area of the report. Again, this varies with the nature of the referral. The format offered is generic. I have included four examples of actual psychological reports (Reports 10.1 through 10.4) to provide several alternative styles and formats.

Suggested Format for Psychoeducational Assessment Reports

Psychoeducational Assessment Report

Name: Dates of Assessment:
Birth Date: Chronological Age:
Parent(s):   Program:
Address: Grade Level:
                                               Program Address:
Phone: Program Phone:
Referred by: Assessor: name/affiliation

Reasons for Referral:
[state concerns as expressed by referral source; enumerate specific referral questions]

Assessment Procedures:
(State: Test scores on last page)
[list full names of all procedures used]

Background Information:
[review developmental and educational history, including health and medical information; describe who is in the family and any history of developmental-learning disorders; indicate and briefly summarize previous evaluations; indicate cultural background and dominant language of the family; family history should contain "need-to-know information," avoiding potential embarrassment.]

Assessment Results:
[you may find it helpful to organize this section according to functional domains as follows; however, the information within these domains should be integrated and discussed in relation to the referral issues and questions and should describe the child, not the procedure; when referring to a procedure, talk about it in terms of the demands on the learner, not the names of the subtests]

Cognition [level of functions; strengths and weaknesses; processes of attention, perception, memory, problem solving, and self-regulation; responsiveness to interaction and feedback; manner of task approach]

Communication [effectiveness and clarity of verbal and nonverbal communication; pragmatics of communicative interaction; length, complexity, and syntax of sentences; level of vocabulary; receptive compared with expressive language; bilingual issues, if relevant]

Form 10.1

Social-Emotional [emotional expression, range, and self-regulation; nature and effectiveness of interactions with peers and adults; stress coping approaches; responsiveness to adult as teacher]

Sensori-Motor [intactness of sensory and motor systems, including visual, auditory, tactile; fine and gross motor, as well as cross-sensory integration and sensorimotor integration; responsiveness to verbal regulation; self-help skills; daily living skills]

Preacademic [early literacy, numeracy, prewriting, basic concepts, basic information]

Conclusions:
[integrate the child's overall strengths and areas of need, and specifically address what the assessment data reveal in relation to the referral questions; this section could include instructional goals and objectives derived from the assessment data]

Recommendations:
[these should include placement and referral recommendations, but the bulk of this section should offer specific program-related, instruction-relevant suggestions, based on what you have learned works for the child during the course of the assessment, as well as what you know (or will find out) are appropriate interventions for the child's needs]

Sign Report with your name, degree, and affiliation and any certificate, license information

Test Scores:
[list all scorable procedures and standard scores, with error of measurement ranges and percentile ranks; if it is a test with which other assessors may not be familiar, include the mean and standard deviation]

Note: In the case of students and noncertified professionals, all reports should be reviewed, approved, and counter-signed by a supervisor. Reports should have correct spelling and grammar and a professional appearance.
Lidz, Carol S. *Early Childhood Assessment.* Copyright 2003, John Wiley & Sons.

Form 10.1 (*continued*)

◆ *Report 10.1*

Child: Max

Age: 3 years 9 months

Reason for Referral

Max's parents were referred through X University's Department of Psychology for information to help them plan for appropriate intervention and educational programming. He is seen periodically for developmental evaluations at the University as part of a research project. Max has a history of developmental delay and Noonan's syndrome. The questions for this assessment are: What are Max's current educational needs, and what are some suggestions for meeting these needs within an educational program?

Procedures

- Parent interview and completion of the Developmental History Checklist for Children
- Goodman Lock Box (play assessment)
- Carolina Curriculum for Preschoolers with Special Needs
- Temperament Assessment Battery for Children (parent form)
- Vineland Adaptive Behavior Scales
- Selected subtests from the Stanford-Binet Intelligence Scales: Fourth Edition

Background Information

Max lives with his natural parents. His mother has two children from a previous marriage, ages 25 and 27, who live on their own. Pregnancy with Max is reported as uncomplicated, with the exception of mother's excessive weight gain. He was born 3 weeks early with birth weight of 8 lb 1½ oz. Hypotonia was apparent during his delivery, when it was difficult to get him through the birth canal, and suction was needed. He was slightly jaundiced but required no treatment, and his Apgar scores were satisfactory. Behaviorally, he was very irritable; everything seemed to bother him, and he seemed constantly uncomfortable. Some of this discomfort appeared to be related to frequent ear infections, and his behavior improved when he was given antibiotics. Max has had a myringotomy (ear tubes); one tube remains in place. His sucking reflex during nursing was weak. His developmental milestones were mildly delayed, with sitting accomplished at 7½ months. He never crawled but instead "scooted." He began walking at 18 months and learned to talk after 2 years. Toilet training is not yet accomplished; he will at times indicate his need.

Max has attended a private regular preschool program on a part-time basis, and has done well there. Previous attempts at therapy (e.g. occupational therapy) were not accepted by him, related to his low thresholds for sensory stimulation. He tends to have very low thresholds for sounds and touch, although his reactivity to these has greatly improved. His parents have been the primary interveners, and they have carried out the recommendations of the various specialists. They note a great deal of improvement and describe their son as a happy, sociable child, though still quite a challenge to manage. His behavior with peers varies between solo and parallel play, and his current preferred play objects are trains. He has progressed in his peer interactions from being a passive observer to more active follower. He does not present significant separation problems.

Issues of concern regarding Max include his poor motor coordination, intense reactivity, and language delays. A report from X University notes developmental scores between low normal to average, with a recent McCarthy Scales General Cognitive Index of 90 (average). They comment on Max's eagerness to interact and his strong curiosity, although he presented some challenges to management during the assessment.

Assessment Results

Max is an appealing, friendly, affectionate child who occasionally cooperated with attempts at formal assessment. In most instances, information was most reliably elicited either through his parents or from observations of his spontaneous interactions.

Max's speech is comprehensible, particularly within a known context. His communications vary between one-word labeling to two- to eight-word sentences, with most between two to four words. Some language samples include: "I can't reach it"; "Come off"; "Car go there"; "There two." He has a reliable yes-no response and labels pictures and objects very well (within average range for his age). Max also spontaneously seeks information from those around him, is able to engage in a conversational exchange, and is able to follow directions. He is a good listener and direction follower (one and two steps) as long as he does not have to be involved for prolonged periods of time. He is able to answer some "wh" questions such as what, who, where, and some why (e.g., Why do we go to the store? "Buy some cereal").

Max continues to have a low threshold for stimulation and is easily distracted by environmental sounds. It is important to know that at times when he is unresponsive or off target, he may in fact be responding to something in the environment that has captured his attention. He likes music, and music will hold his attention. He prefers soft music.

Max is able to keep himself occupied with play and has shown evidence of pretend play (e.g., pretending that he is his mother). At the moment, he is particularly enamored of trains and appears to be aware of different types of train engines, such as diesel versus coal-burning. During the assessment, his interaction with the Goodman Lock Box, a play assessment, was enthusiastic, and he succeeded in opening some of the more simple locks, with awareness of how to use the toys he secured from the opened areas. While he showed evidence of functional use of the toys, his play repertory appeared restricted, primarily in terms of the length of time he maintained his involvement. Many of the locks were too difficult for him (possibly related to his hypotonicity), and, while frequently returning to those that resisted his attempts, he tended to use an impulsive problem-solving approach. He showed his willingness to imitate, as well as his ability to understand and profit from verbal cues. The main obstructions to higher level of functioning on this task related to the motor challenge of the locks and to his nonpersistence and trial-and-error, impulsive problem-solving approach.

According to the information provided by Max's parents, his temperament is characterized by low activity (in terms of vigor of response), average adaptability to new social situations, high emotional intensity (particularly in expression of negative reactions), and low persistence, and he does not readily respond to attempts at distraction as a means of management. All of this portrays a picture of a sociable but not "easy" child. When he gets involved in a period of intense resistance, his parents have found it helpful to use quieting, calming approaches. Direct confrontation or insistence only exacerbates his resistance.

On the measure of adaptive behavior, completed by Max's parents, there is a significant difference between his generally low normal level of development in areas of communication, self-help, and socialization, compared with his deficient level of functioning in the motor area. Some of the depressions in self-help appear to be related to his lower level of motor functioning. For example, he is a messy, slow eater, and he does not like chewy food. The more "cognitive" the demand, the higher the level of his response; whereas the more "motor" the demand, the more deficient. However, even his higher areas are showing delays of at least 6 months, warranting attention from early intervention services, given the strength of his home background.

Max has developed a number of preacademic skills. He can name most colors and shapes and is able to count to five. He can match and can complete two-piece interconnecting puzzles and single-insert types of puzzles. He is very interested in books and will sit by himself and turn pages, looking through the books and naming and talking about what he sees. He has favorite books and recalls some stories from them. He can give some factual information about himself such as his name, age, and gender. Learning to play, share, and function in a group with other children is emerging. Again, related to his motor delays, prewriting skills appear to be slower to emerge. He will make marks on paper and is showing some right-hand preference, although he will use both. He will sometimes scribble and can be guided into making more deliberate directional marks but asks his parents to do this activity for him.

Conclusions and Recommendations

Max is a pleasant, affectionate child who has shown significant improvement in his functioning in response to the intensive intervention efforts of his parents. Though "mild," his continuing delays, particularly in the motor area, are sufficiently significant to warrant early intervention services from the public education system. There is no strong implication at this time for location of services, that is, whether he should be enrolled in an early intervention center or a less restrictive general preschool program with services offered on an itinerant basis. This would have to be determined in collaboration with his parents. The most important aspects would be that the environment be good in terms of high-quality early childhood programming, that the teacher be a good early childhood program provider who is willing to accommodate a child with special needs, and that the services needed are provided.

Special services that are recommended for Max would include both speech-language and occupational therapy. This would ideally combine direct with consultative services—consultative to both his teachers and his parents. Max is showing a cognitive strength and a motor weakness, and his motor limitations are serving to obstruct expression of his cognitive strengths. It is important to continue to stimulate his cognitive growth while intensifying intervention regarding his motor and sensorimotor functioning. His history of hypotonia and tactile defensiveness is also of relevance for occupational therapy.

Some specific recommendations within any program setting include the following:

1. Max is quick to say "I can't" when experiencing difficulty, and he will say this whether the problem is his limitation or the impossibility of doing what he is attempting. In this way, he overgeneralizes his own limitations and increases his experiences of failure. He needs help to evaluate the difficulty of what he attempts. He needs to substitute "it" for "I" when appropriate. For example, the adult could say something like, "No, Max; *it* can't be done; it really doesn't work that way; here's another way to do it."

2. Max tends to try to solve perceptual-motor problems with trial-and-error motor solutions (e.g., to open a lock by increased pulling or pushing). He should be encouraged to use his

eyes and think to see what needs to be done before acting. Encouraging him to "Stop, look, think" as a routine that he hears frequently enough to internalize is recommended. He can also be encouraged to "Use your eyes; what do you see?"

3. Utilization of a curriculum that promotes self-regulation and problem solving, such as Bright Start (Haywood, Brooks, & Burns, 1992; Watertown, MA), is recommended as an addition to a more content-oriented curriculum. This curriculum emphasizes the mediational role of adults with children, and this is elaborated in handouts that have been provided to Max's parents.

4. Increased attention to awareness of patterns and sequences is recommended. This would involve helping Max notice the features that make something a pattern and adding a verbal rhythm to it to emphasize the pattern-like nature of the sequence (e.g., adding voice inflection to UP down UP down UP . . .).

5. Max needs to work toward increasing his cognitive control over his motor movements. Again, this relates to inducing a "stop, look, think" habit but also involves having him learn to talk himself through challenging task solutions. Giving him some challenging tasks, interspersed with easy ones, would be likely to induce this kind of self-talk. Modeling of this kind of task-related talk by adults and asking him process-related questions ("What do you need to do first?") may facilitate this.

6. Max's task involvement is most successfully prolonged when working within his self-selected areas of interest. Continuing to expand his language and exploration of activities that attract his attention is supported.

7. Max has shown himself to be responsive to intervention and has made significant strides in his development. Up to this point, his parents have borne the brunt of provision of these services, partly because Max would not tolerate handling by others. It is now time for services and support to the family to be offered through the public education system. Initiation of this contact is recommended.

Some additional next steps on a curriculum include the following:

- Recall of rhymes and songs
- Increased recall of stories
- Development of comparative concepts
- Development of same-different concepts
- Development of themes in play
- Symbolic use of objects in play
- Anticipation of what might happen next in a story
- Describing features of objects
- Increased interactive play with peers
- Increased independence in toileting
- Development of ability to deal with fasteners in dressing

Test Scores

Temperament Assessment Battery for Children (Parent Form)

Activity (tendency to engage in vigorous, fast, gross motor movement): 8th percentile; low

Adaptability (ease and speed of adjustment to new social situations): 79th percentile; high average

Approach/Withdrawal (tendency to approach/withdraw from new social situations): 21st percentile; low average

Emotional intensity (tendency to express negative emotion with vigor): 93rd percentile; high

Distractibility (ease of management through distraction): 21st percentile; low average

Persistence (attention span and continuation of problem solving attempts): 1.1 percentile; low

Vineland Adaptive Behavior Scales: Interview Edition

	Standard Score	Percentile	Level
Communication	89 (83–95)	23	adequate
Daily Living	81 (75–87)	10	moderately low
Socialization	82 (75–89)	12	moderately low
Motor	60 (50–70)	0.4	low

Stanford–Binet Intelligence Scales: Fourth Edition

The following three subtests were worked on, with no ceiling reached; these are offered as estimated, baseline scores for comparisons for future assessments; performance on these subtests should be interpreted as "no less than . . ." (50 = average; s.d. = 8).

Vocabulary: 53
Quantitative: 49
Bead Memory: 46

♦   *Report 10.2*

Child: Carl

Age: 4 years 8 months

Reason for Referral

This assessment was carried out in response to concerns raised by Carl's preschool teacher with his parents about his language processing and attention regulation. He will at times answer questions irrelevantly, and he has difficulty maintaining his attention in his program, compared with the other children. The referral was from Dr. X., consulting psychologist to the preschool program. The questions for the assessment are, To what extent is Carl experiencing a problem, and what are some ideas for improving his current functioning?

Background Information

Carl is an only child who lives with both of his natural parents. There were no complications regarding his early developmental history, although his motor development appeared somewhat slower than average and he remains mildly clumsy. His language development is described as average, whereas his mental development appears advanced to his parents. Temperamentally, he is said to be active, sociable, affectionate, and happy. He has a history of low sensory thresholds and difficulty adjusting to change.

Carl has experienced no serious medical problems or hospitalizations. His early childhood diseases included chicken pox with no sequelae.

Carl has a special talent of early reading, which he accomplished on his own by the age of 3, without direct teaching by his parents. He simply surprised them one day when he read the newspaper headlines. He spontaneously enjoys playing with letters and words and is able to spell and provide definitions. On the other hand, his parents express some concern about his "constant flood of talk," that is, his tendency to talk about unrelated topics and his difficulty focusing his attention.

Observations

Carl was first observed within his home. He is a tall, attractive, red- (he insists orange-) haired boy of normal physical appearance. He responds in a friendly way, and his loquaciousness is immediately evident. He carries on a nonstop conversation (exaggerated by the presence of a stranger), with difficulty yielding "his turn." He has many toys, and his parents say that he plays well with them and is able to occupy himself. His conversation is filled with content related to things he has read.

Carl was able to answer questions accurately, but he also provided answers when he did not understand exactly what was said; at these times he sounded off-topic. That is, he would answer a question whether he knew the answer or not. He speaks clearly, complexly, and profusely.

Carl complied with his parent's request to get a book, and he sat close to me while showing how he could read. He reads with expression and accurate response to punctuation and is able to sound out words beyond his level of comprehension. He felt compelled to read to the end of a book but was able to learn to decide to stop before that, and then to make himself stop. The level of books he was reading was not known, but appeared to be at least third grade or higher. Although he does not respond immediately to questions about his reading, his parents note that he uses information gained from his reading in his conversations.

Carl was next observed within his preschool classroom. During free play he was very focused on a board design task and showed good conversational interchange with his teacher. He had the most difficulty with attention maintenance and self-regulation during large group circle time; this was the only occasion when there were periods of having to listen without any visual-motor involvement. He was not disruptive, although his peer neighbors found his movements into their space annoying (he did not appear to understand the cues made by the boy next to him, and moved closer instead of further away). He participates appropriately in songs and circle time routines, though at times responds out of turn.

Carl very much enjoyed the next class activity, a parachute game (the whole class grasps an edge section of a parachute and responds to the content of a story told to them); here he was able to anticipate the story lines. This appeared to be a good activity for practicing excitation and inhibition, that is, self-regulation. Although it was somewhat difficult for him to settle down after this activity, he did succeed in doing so. His teacher makes special efforts to elicit his attention before asking him a question and provides him some leeway without bringing too much attention to his tendency to move about somewhat more than the others in his group.

The last activity observed involved writing. Carl shows a right-hand preference with adequate pencil grasp. He could print his whole name and showed knowledge of the concept "top" (as in top of the paper). He is just learning to write his numbers and actively seeks a visual model for his copying. His level of functioning in this activity is similar to many others in his group.

From conversations with Carl's teacher and the consulting psychologist, the concerns center around Carl's difficulty with language processing and his need for individual attention within his classroom. There is an issue of the comparison group, as many of the children in this school come in hyper-prepared, and many go on to a very strict, academically oriented private academy.

Direct testing of Carl was not seen as necessary at this time. His parents were asked to complete two rating scales, in addition to the Developmental History Checklist for Children. On the first scale, the Coping Inventory, Carl is rated at a high level in his ability to cope both with himself and with his environment on the dimensions of Productivity and Activity; his ratings on the Rigidity-Flexibility dimension were somewhat lower, particularly with regard to himself. Items relating to productivity and activity include his capacity for fun, demonstrations of happy feelings, awareness of feelings and moods of others, and initiation of actions to get his needs met. The areas where he could use more attention include accepting substitutes when necessary, bouncing back after disappointment, and accepting new ideas or reformulations.

The second scale, the Parent Behavior Checklist, rates Carl's parents within normal limits regarding their expectations, use of discipline, and provision of nurturance, compared with other parents of children the same age. They show realistic expectations, low use of physical punishment, and high provision of nurturance.

Impressions and Recommendations

This assessment was conducted more in the format of a consultation than as a comprehensive direct assessment. Carl presents a picture of a combination of significant precocity as well as attention deficit. He appears to have very low thresholds for stimulation from both external as well as internal sources; that is, he feels compelled to respond to everything he sees and hears and has difficulty filtering this input. The primary direction for interventions would combine continued encouragement and appreciation of the things he does so well with more aggressive management of his difficulties with attention regulation.

Two services available through his regional special education services provider are recommended for him. First is speech-language therapy to address his pragmatics in terms of issues such as turn taking and to regulate himself to listen to the whole message before responding. Second is occupational therapy, which would address his mild clumsiness, as well as engage him in exercises that may enhance his ability to regulate his attention and raise the thresholds of his sensory responsiveness.

Within his classroom, some ideas for intervention include the following:

1. Have him seated closer to and in front of the speaker so that he has direct eye contact with reduced distractions.
2. While continuing first to get his attention before addressing him, try to teach him to ask for more time to process; say, for example, "Do you need more time to think?" or "Take some more time to think" and simply wait several seconds.

3. When he responds off target, interpret this as indicating that he did not get the whole message and is responding only to the part that he absorbed. In this case, repeat, rephrase, and reduce what was said. Also give him feedback that he lost his attention and that is what made it hard for him to understand the whole message.

4. Openly discuss and problem-solve Carl's struggle with paying attention and regulating himself, and try to get him to participate in problem solving about how to help this. For example, he could be asked, "Do you think it would help if we put these objects away and just kept this out?"

5. When sitting on the floor during circle time, Carl may do better with something to lean against or with a piece of rug to mark the boundaries of his space (however, all the children would need to be given a similar piece). The children near him could be coached to give him feedback that he is in their space, and he could be coached to read their cues that indicate he is bothering them. [The teacher could interpret this for him, e.g., "Jimmy is letting you know he wants you to move."]

6. He could be given something to put in his hands to fiddle with when he needs to listen—something like worry beads, although this would have to be on a trial basis to ensure that it does not become too distracting.

7. Provide as much visual and visual-motor involvement as possible, with reduced passive listening.

8. Deliberately practice topic maintenance and stop-and-switch behaviors. For example, he could be asked about something he did and then be encouraged to "tell me something else about that." If his second response is not related to the first, tell him, "No; tell me more about. . . ." For stop and switch, he could be given blocks for a building, for example, and asked to build something with only eight of the blocks, and guided into stopping when he gets to eight. When he has finished, he could be encouraged to think of something else to build, this time with just nine blocks, and so on. In the case of reading, he could be asked to read up to a predetermined page and then to stop himself to do another activity.

9. Be sure to cue him about changes in activities or schedules as much in advance and with multiple warnings, if possible.

10. Provide him with opportunities to read to the group.

Carl has another year in his preschool, and this will give him time to continue his adjustment to school routines and group interactions. His next placement needs to be carefully selected to fit his style of functioning, and this will require some visits to classrooms and discussions with teachers. Although he needs structure and routine, he also needs to be with teachers who are flexible and can appreciate individual differences in children. His classroom should include opportunities for movement and free choice, with teachers who actively interact with the children.

◆ *Report 10.3*

Child: Peter

Age: 5 years 10 months

Reason for Referral

Peter was referred by his parents, who are seeking guidance about his needs for educational services when he enters kindergarten in the fall. Specifically, they are asking what services, if any, are recommended for him. The school district has already provided psychological and educational assessments. Peter's parents are seeking an independent evaluation.

Procedures
- Interview of mother
- File review
- Mother-child play interaction
- Standardized procedures
  - Kaufman Assessment Battery for Children
  - Kaufman Survey of Early Academic and Language Skills
  - Oral and Written Language Scales (oral only)
  - Beery-Buktenica Developmental Test of Visual-Motor Integration
- Informal procedures
  - Test of Phonological Awareness
  - Sawyers Test of Awareness of Language Segments
  - Dynamic assessment of classification and story retelling
  - Miscellaneous neuropsychological screening
- Rating scales completed by parents
  - Behavior Rating Inventory of Executive Function
  - Behavior Assessment System for Children
  - Conners' Parent Rating Scale–Revised, Long version
- Rating scales completed by teacher
  - Behavior Assessment System for Children
  - Conners' Rating Scale

Background Information

Peter was adopted by his parents from a Romanian orphanage at the age of 3 years. No information is available regarding his early history except that the environment of the orphanage appeared to be benign, and he had a close relationship with one of the caregivers, who remains in touch with the family. His parents think that the reason for his availability for adoption, since the age of 18 months, related to economic conditions.

Peter lives with his adoptive parents and his 10-year-old sister, also adopted from Romania. They are not genetically related. Peter had been retained in preschool in response to encouragement from his teacher. His preschool teacher had recommended a psychological assessment, related to concerns about his lack of progress learning, as well as his high activity level. Peter has been diagnosed with attention-deficit/hyperactivity disorder (ADHD) by a developmental pediatrician and is currently medicated with Concerta (18 mg in the morning) and Tenex. His mother expresses some concern about the effects of the medication on his appetite and, eventually, on his growth.

Peter's mother mentions sensory integration issues for which he had received a short term of occupational therapy in the past (about four sessions). These mainly addressed Peter's issues regarding touch; he picks his chin until it bleeds, wishes for his belt to be buckled very tightly, and wants his shoes tied either very tightly or very loosely.

[Following in the original report are results of reports from evaluations by a neurodevelopmental pediatrician, preschool teacher, a previous psychological, and educational assessments. These are omitted here.]

Assessment Results

Peter is a physically normal, attractive boy, with a number of inflamed sores apparent on his chin. These sores remain inflamed because of his picking. He entered each assessment session (there were four) apprehensively and wavered between wanting his mother with him and letting her remain in the waiting area. Although eager to terminate after about an hour, he would continue through two hours with encouragement. When his mother was in the room, he would often seek to sit on her lap and wanted to be held very tightly by her; when she was not in the room, he squirmed a great deal in his chair and at times preferred to work while standing. By report and observation, Peter is English dominant, and any attempt to communicate with him in his native language (there was a student assessor present who spoke his native language) was vigorously rejected. On the last day of the assessment, Peter had not taken his medication, and we noted a significant difference in his behavior, with considerably less regulation than was evident in previous sessions.

Peter showed right-hand dominance for copying and drawing, with mature grasp and good control and posture, even though he did not like to draw; he draws infrequently at home by choice. He was clearly avoidant of writing-drawing tasks, although he obtained an average-level score on a design copying test and was able to write his first name. He refused to draw pictures. He did tend to fill in the page with scribbles, as his teacher described in her note, but rather than reflecting angry feelings as she suggested, we saw this as an issue of self-regulation. Once he had started this activity, he had difficulty stopping and just continued to make marks. This was also evident on a task in which he had to "march" his pencil up the page, connecting a series of targets. In this instance, he switched hands midway up the page and had some difficulty stopping, although did so with minimal cuing. Despite his refusal to draw, when paper and crayons were available, he could not inhibit the impulse to take the crayon and scribble to fill the page.

Because Peter had recently been tested within his school district, we* did not wish to repeat the measures they had administered. As a major standardized cognitive procedure, he was given the Kaufman Assessment Battery for Children, which is generally considered to be relatively more culture free than others. On this, he showed a significant difference between his average level "simultaneous" compared to borderline level "sequential" functioning. Simultaneous tasks require integrated thinking, taking many elements into consideration at the same time; these also tend to tap spatial processing abilities. With these nonverbal tasks, Peter showed considerable strength. He improved his performance within the tasks, was mobilized

---

* This assessment involved two graduate students and myself as both supervisor and participant.

to greater attention and effort by the increasing difficulty of the task, and did better with the more abstract levels. For example, with a perceptual construction task, Peter first paused to reflect on what to do, applied a relevant counting strategy, and learned quickly as he moved through the items. On a reasoning task, Peter's performance improved when the language demand decreased and moved on to abstract rather than pictorial stimuli. In contrast to this strong domain of functioning, he had much less success with rote recall tasks in which sheer memory of the order was important, and there was no context for integrating or giving meaning to the information. We also administered the expressive vocabulary subtest, which is appropriate for children below Peter's age, but we wished to see if he had at least mastered these words, and he had not. He could name most of the pictures but missed most of the more difficult labels. Another screening of his vocabulary also showed below-average functioning. On another of the achievement portions, the Arithmetic subtest, Peter obtained a low average score, again showing better performance with reduced language demand.

To further explore Peter's language competence, we administered a specific procedure that compared his listening comprehension with his oral expression, and we found a highly significant difference between the two, with average-level listening comprehension in contrast to borderline level oral expression. Thus, we find that Peter's apparent mastery of English is not yet deep. It is certainly functional for everyday purposes, but there are still issues of language for him. We further narrowed the testing to look at Peter's phonological awareness, and he seemed adequate in this, with average-level scores. He also shows adequate (low average) number and letter knowledge, suggesting that he has the foundation "readiness" skills for kindergarten.

Peter showed a number of instances of very positive responsiveness to adult support of his learning and his ability to profit from adult facilitation. For example, there was a marked difference in the level and duration of his play in interaction with his mother, as compared to his independent level. When on his own, he had difficulty sustaining more than momentary involvement with the materials and moved quickly from one item to the next. In interaction with his mother, he carried out a self-directed play dough activity for a full half hour. His mother generally followed his lead, providing elaborations on his verbalizations and ideas ("We can make designs on the cake"), supporting his themes, offering praise and encouragement ("I like your idea! I like the kind of cookies you made?"), and providing a model and occasional suggestions to improve his success ("Take a little at a time"). There was an interesting incident when Peter was nearing the finish of his play and lapsed into some shouting and heightened activity level; when left to his own devices, he was able to calm himself down and regain control. It seemed that the mere presence, without specific intervention, of the adults, was enough support for his self-regulation.

Two activities were carried out that involved a pretest-intervene-posttest format (dynamic assessment), again to explore Peter's responsiveness to instruction. The first task involved grouping of blocks by attributes of color, shape, and size. Prior to the intervention, Peter demonstrated some emergent ability to group. Without adult guidance, he was quick to try to use the blocks aggressively but was easily refocused on the agenda of the task. Following the intervention, where he was introduced to the various attributes and encouraged to change the basis for grouping based on these attributes, he was independently able to apply this information and classify the blocks at a higher level. When pushed for flexibility and asked to group them another way, he did change what he was doing (i.e., acknowledged the need to do something different) but did not get to the point of reclassifying the blocks.

The second task involved the retention and retelling of a short story read to him. Prior to the intervention, Peter retained very little of the story, omitting all but one character, scrambling some information, and retelling only the central action of the story. Following the intervention, where he was taught to build a visual-symbolic model and to read the symbols back to aid his narrative, he accurately recalled all of the central characters, unscrambled the order of the events, and again recalled the main action. Thus, there was a significant improvement following brief intervention that provided a visual model, required his active involvement in constructing the model, and provided supported repetition of the story elements.

Both of the parents' and teachers' ratings of Peter's behavior place him at a high level in the areas of hyperactivity with attention and conduct or oppositional behavior problems. His parents also give him a high rating in the psychosomatic area. On ratings tapping Peter's ability to self-regulate, his parents' ratings suggest concerns regarding his ability to inhibit, as well as regarding the shifting and monitoring of his behavior. He was rated as of less concern regarding emotional control and the ability to initiate activities and interactions. His working memory and organization were also rated as of concern. These ratings indicate the high degree of challenge that Peter presents both at home and in school, and they can serve as a baseline for monitoring his progress and his response to medication and programming.

Conclusions and Recommendations

Although Peter has shown improvement in his behavior and he has most of the foundation knowledge base for kindergarten, his continuing need for close supervision and individualized programming suggests the need for a classroom with fewer children than is typical for regular education. He is a responsive learner, but he has ongoing difficulty with self-regulation and needs close attention from and proximity to a teacher who is experienced in working with children with special needs.

Peter is showing a significant difference between his levels of functioning in the areas of language (lower) compared to spatial (higher) domains. He appears to be at risk for a learning disability in the area of language; however, because his first three years were in a Romanian environment, where his foundation for language was established, we cannot at this time rule out the influence of this bilingual exposure. Nevertheless, because he is currently functioning at a risk level in the language area, we recommend speech and language services, focusing on his language acquisition and development.

Peter's medication for ADHD appears to be helping him, but because of his parents' report of its effect on his appetite and sleeping, this needs to be reevaluated and closely monitored, with consideration of frequent time off medication, particularly when he is not in a formal school environment. This should be discussed with the prescribing physician.

Peter excels with tasks tapping his spatial abilities (e.g., construction types of tasks), and this seems to relate to his relatively good development of early numerical ability. Continued opportunity to engage in these types of activities is recommended not only because they are important developmental skills but also because his ability to succeed with them provides a foundation for feelings of competence. Looking for opportunities to associate language with spatial tasks would be a productive route for addressing his weaker language functioning. For example, getting him to construct stories and tell the narrative of a story from his construction would be a relevant activity.

Because of evidence and reports of possible tactile defensiveness, we recommend referral for evaluation by an occupational therapist who is experienced with treating this condition. Peter may have general difficulty with sensory thresholds (i.e., he would react to stimuli that others would ignore), and this could contribute to his ADHD. Therefore, occupational therapy may be helpful in addressing this as well.

Specific targeting of self-regulation (response inhibition) is also recommended, such as practice stopping when writing after he has completed the task, engaging in deliberate slow-fast movements while drawing lines or shapes or throwing or rolling a ball, playing stop-go games such as red light/green light, having him give instructions to another child who has difficulty doing something that he can do well.

A copy of the Lidz/Childers "Let's Think About It" parenting program has been given to the parents to provide some suggestions for activities that can be useful for developing foundation skills for learning and thinking. This may be useful to share with his teacher as well.

◆ *Report 10.4*

Child: Richard

Age: 6 years 1 month

Reason for Referral

Richard has been diagnosed with Noonan's syndrome, which has primarily medical and health implications but usually no specific psychological or learning-related sequelae. His parents are experiencing behavioral management difficulties with him and are seeking consultation regarding any possible effects of the syndrome on his behavior, as well as implications for his learning. They are seeking responses to the following questions:

1. To what extent are his difficult behaviors related to his condition and development versus just behavior management issues?
2. How much control does Richard have over his behaviors, or is he acting in a manipulative way?
3. What are the educational implications of his current functioning?

Background Information

Richard is the product of a full-term (37-week) pregnancy and had a birth weight of 6 lb 13 oz. He was delivered by Cesarean section, with Apgars 9 and 10. During the pregnancy, a procedure to drain a right pleural effusion was performed, and synthroid medication was prescribed. Otherwise, the pregnancy proceeded normally.

Following his birth, Richard received supplemental oxygen for three days but did not require additional hospitalization. His developmental milestones have been accomplished within normal limits (sat at 6–7 months, stood alone at 9 months, walked alone at 13–14 months). He is in the lower percentiles for height and weight, which is typical for Noonan's syndrome.

Shortly after his delivery, a heart murmur was noticed, in addition to concerns about his physical appearance (low-set right ear, widely spaced eyes). A left pulmonary artery branch stenosis was found, leading to the conclusion of a minor congenital cardiac anomaly, but this was thought to be benign, with the anticipation of spontaneous resolution, which in fact did occur. It was during this evaluation at 1 month of age that the possibility of Noonan's syndrome was first mentioned, and subsequently confirmed. A bone age study when Richard was 4 years 7 months revealed a bone age estimate of 2 years 8 months. Richard has had ear infections that did not require surgery, and his language development appears normal. He has no allergies.

Richard lives with both natural parents and his 7-year-old sister, who is advanced in learning and is a normally developed child. Both parents have college degrees and are employed full-time.

Richard attended a preschool program on a full-time basis from the age of 3 years to the present. Prior to this, he was cared for by a neighborhood caregiver in her home. He experienced no difficulties in preschool and was well liked by his peers.

Although Richard can be charming and outgoing, he tends to be slow to warm up with strangers and has difficulty separating from his parents. His interactions with peers can lapse into aggression, although he has had more success recently in sustaining play with his age mates. At home he enjoys playing baseball and soccer, and cooking ("he likes to mush things into goo"), riding his bike, and vacuuming ("almost obsessively"). He is described as an affectionate, happy child who can become overstimulated while playing, has a short attention span, and struggles with self-control.

Richard's parents estimate all areas of self-help at or above expectations for his age. Their ratings on the Behavior Assessment Scale for Children (BASC) show elevations in the areas of hyperactivity, aggression, anxiety, and withdrawal, with low ratings on adaptability. He is rated within the normal range in the areas of conduct problems, depression, somatization, atypicality, and attention; that is, he is not showing problems with these.

Procedures Administered
- Medical file review
- Parent interview
- Woodcock-Johnson, Third Edition
- NEPSY: A Developmental Neuropsychological Assessment
- Bracken Basic Concept Scale–Revised (School Readiness Composite only)
- Scales of Independent Behavior–Revised
- Behavior Assessment System for Children–Parent Rating Scales
- Dynamic assessment of
  —Human figure drawing
  —Copying a square
  —Classification subscale from the Application of Cognitive Functions Scale (Lidz & Jepsen, 2000)

Assessment Results
Richard's current levels of cognitive functioning are most consistently estimated within the low average range, with some degree of variability. One of the issues of standardized assessment, particularly of young children, is that they are continually pushed into performing at a frustration level because the items on each subtest have to be administered until they become too difficult for the child. This was not an easy experience for Richard, who early in the assessment agreed to do the work "only if it's not too hard." Well, there was some hard work, and he clearly did not like it, and was often resistant to persisting into his "challenge zone."

In contrast to this resistance to the standardized procedures, he was much more receptive to dynamic procedures, where he was taught the tools he needed to know in order to do the task. Thus, he was not resistant to being challenged within the teaching context of careful guidance into development of competence. This occurred during three opportunities, including teaching him how to draw a square, how to draw a person, and how to perform a classification (sorting) task with blocks. He was taught to draw a square by using the forms he could draw, both vertical and horizontal lines. Therefore, by drawing two vertical and two horizontal lines, each in parallel, he could avoid the difficult angle and successfully produce a square. For the drawing of a person, he was referenced to his own body and talked through thinking about what part to draw, what shape to use, and where each belonged. He remembered what he learned over the course of the assessment. On the last task, where he was asked to make groups with blocks, he spontaneously showed that he understood the concept of grouping and produced a good color-based group. He was receptive to the intervention that focused on "changing what we notice" in order to find other bases for grouping; under structured guidance, he could do this. However, during the posttest, in which he was again asked to do the grouping independently, he mixed up his original color-based grouping but did not change what he noticed for the purpose of grouping.

Difficulty with flexible thinking was a consistent and significant theme for Richard. He struggled with holding multiple bits of information in his memory and then working with that information. On the one hand, he became easily overloaded and then would crash and be unable to perform. On the other hand, he could not seem to take what was in his thoughts and manipulate that to go in different directions, such as was particularly evident when asked to repeat a series of digits backwards.

This scenario, of becoming overloaded by complexity and lacking flexible thinking, is a likely basis for the behavior difficulties he shows. He needs to enter a situation feeling that he has a chance for success. Once he evaluates it as too hard, he engages in avoidant behavior to escape the stress (fear of failure), and it is difficult to move him into reverse or onto an alternative course. However, it is not impossible, as attempts to teach him the aspects of some tasks that were difficult did often engage him, and he clearly enjoyed his successes.

Richard has strong language skills and very adequate phonemic awareness. He engages in good turn-taking conversation and demonstrates good verbal expression, comprehension, and excellent intelligibility, with only minor sound substitutions (e.g., *y* and *l*). This suggests that he has a good language-based readiness for literacy. He can recite most of the alphabet (with some gaps in the middle). He counts from left to right and is able to maintain 1:1 correspondence at least up to 15. Richard could identify virtually all of the colors presented to him, as well as all but one of the letters (*j*). He also knew all but three (long, thin, shallow) of the size concepts. He knew all but the most difficult shape names (diamond, curve, cube, pyramid, column, angle) and identified many comparative concepts, although this was his relatively weaker area (errors were match, alike, same, similar, and unequal).

Richard's fine motor functioning shows some mild delay. He is right-hand dominant, using an intermediate grasp for drawing. He can copy many basic shapes and learned quickly how to produce a square using four straight lines, but he is somewhat below expectations for his age in this domain. His greatest struggle was with finger manipulation tasks. These were laborious for him, were unevenly executed, and required his concentrated attention. He resisted carrying out tasks with his left hand, although he did with encouragement. He had difficulty forming a circle with his index finger and thumb, tending to perform finger tapping with extended fingers.

Although Richard showed good attention to directions and to storytelling, tests specifically tapping attention tended to overwhelm him. For example, although he could perform the more simple task of finding pictures of cats randomly scattered across two pages, he was unsuccessful when there were more items and more similar pictures of faces. It was only possible to get him to tackle the task when the number of items was reduced, as well as the amount of information he had to keep in mind during his search. Similarly, during an auditory attention task, when he had to coordinate hearing a target word with the motor act of selecting and placing a red square in a box, this again produced an overload condition, and he could not perform even though he succeeded during practice items and multiple rehearsals. Although all attention tasks have a speed component, the child is not usually as aware of this as when involved in this auditory task when the words just keep coming and coming. This demonstrates how necessary it is to control the amount of information with which Richard must deal. He is capable of carrying out these tasks if the quantity of information is controlled; once over his limit, he is unsuccessful. Thus, maintaining attention per se does not seem to be the issue; rather, the issue is more the quantity and speed of information to which he must attend. This is more of a combination of what would be called working memory (keeping a number of bits of information in mind) and executive monitoring, which relates to the flexible thinking issues mentioned above.

During play interaction with his mother, Richard made pancakes with play dough. Playing at cooking is one of his preferred activities. He was able to name some ingredients for his pancake, and, with encouragement, was able to move beyond "I mix it into goo," to produce more deliberate forms of a ball for a meatball and then an elongated oval for a hot dog. Richard's mother offers very nice mediation, including elaborations and connections between his activity and his other experiences. By report and observation, Richard's imaginative play appears to be somewhat restricted. He is recently engaging in thematic play with a peer, but this is an area that could use further development.

Conclusions and Recommendations

This has been Richard's first psychological assessment, and any findings must be considered preliminary and baseline, particularly because he was pushed to his frustration level in the standardized assessment and therefore found this to be a somewhat stressful experience. However, the data from this assessment are meaningful. We can certainly rule out mental retardation. Richard's cognitive functioning is within average expectations for his age, with good language skills and adequate readiness for his kindergarten experience. His cognitive weakness is primarily in executive functions, that is, his ability to self-regulate, plan, hold and retrieve, and manipulate information in working memory, as well as to shift his thinking. This appears to be the neurological basis for his current challenges to behavior management. Therefore, the responses to the first two questions of this assessment are that there does appear to be a neurological basis for these behavioral challenges. It is not possible to sort out what is or what is not attributable to Noonan's syndrome because the literature suggests no necessary implications of the syndrome for cognitive functioning; however, we can say that Richard is not merely willful. This is not to say that he is not capable of escalating his predispositions into behavioral difficulty that needs to be managed. It would be important to interpret moments of behavioral challenge as his attempt to cope with stress; he has not yet learned optimal ways to do this, which often ends up in struggles for control because he has difficulty backing off a course of action once it is begun. These behaviors are his attempt to reduce his own stress through avoidance of the situation that he feels threatens his self-esteem or competence.

With this in mind, the most helpful approach would be to function as a traffic manager to try to keep the flow of stimulation and information within what Richard feels he can manage. This means reducing amounts of materials, breaking down instructions into smaller steps, and providing adequate modeling and opportunities for repetition. While doing this, the adult needs to verbalize what is being done and why it is so that Richard eventually becomes capable of articulating what he needs for his own self-management. For example, he can be told, "I see this feels like too much to do right now. Let's back off and let me break it down for you. Try it this way and tell me if it helps."

Educational implications of this assessment include the following. Richard's difficulty with flexible thinking can be addressed first of all by trying to anticipate new situations and transitions and preparing him for these. Describe what will happen and mentally or physically walk him through it. Think about what could be done if "plan A" does not work, and go for alternative thinking ("What else could you do?"). Deliberately ask for "another way" to something that he does well.

Richard's delayed fine motor functioning and struggle with self-regulation may also be responsive to occupational therapy (OT). Referral for an OT evaluation is recommended.

His need for enhanced self-regulation can also be addressed by stimulation of his imagination during play, trying to facilitate development of themes and playing out sequences of stories. Imaginative play offers opportunities to develop thinking and practice problem solving in a safe pretend situation.

Involving Richard in the experience of interacting with a child who is functioning somewhat younger than himself can work to put him in a situation in which he is the more competent. Encouraging him to regulate the functioning of another child is thought to be helpful for the development of self-regulation.

In addition, when children work just beyond their levels of independent functioning, but not too far into their frustration levels, they are lead into the use of self-talk, which is also thought to contribute to the development of self-regulation. Yet another approach is to play simple games with rules with him. These should not be challenging regarding the skill needed to play, as the important element is the need to function within the rules of the game.

Richard does not show the need for support services other than OT at this time. However, he should be monitored as the demands increase so that he retains his ability to cope with new challenges. His needs for accommodations can be reevaluated at a later date if it seems necessary.

Test Scores

Woodcock Johnson III Tests of Cognitive Abilities

	Scaled Score	Percentile Rank
Verbal Comprehension	83 (77–90)	13
Visual-Auditory Learning	54 (48–61)	0.1
Spatial Relations	81 (77–85)	10
Sound Blending	96 (92–100)	40
Concept Formation	99 (94–103)	46
Visual Matching	73 (71–76)	4
Numbers Reversed	could not do	
Incomplete Words	105 (97–112)	62
Phonemic Awareness	99 (95–103)	46

NEPSY: A Developmental Neuropsychological Assessment

	Scaled Scores	Age Equivalent
Tower	9	5.0–5.5
Phonological Processing	9	5.6–5.11
Comprehension of Instruction	9	5.6–5.11
Fingertip Tapping	7	<5.0
Design Copying	6	4.6–4.11
Arrows	9	5.0–5.5
Memory for Faces	6	
Narrative Memory	10	6.0–6.5

Note: His responses to the Arrows subtest were random, and this score is not likely to be valid. Some tests were attempted, but could not be completed; these included Auditory Attention and Response Set, Delayed Memory for Names, and Visual Attention.

Bracken Basic Concept Scale–Revised

School Readiness Composite:
    Scaled Score: 8
    Percentile rank: 25
    Classification: average

Behavior Assessment System for Children: Parent Rating Scales

	T Scores	Percentile Rank
Hyperactivity	70	96
Aggression	69	95
Conduct Problems	56	78
Externalizing Composite	67	94
Anxiety	69	96
Depression	63	67
Somatization	36	3
Internalizing Composite	53	67
Atypicality	53	67
Withdrawal	69	96
Attention Problems	63	97
Adaptability	30	3
Social Skills	41	17
Leadership	34	6
Adaptive Composite	33	5

Scales of Independent Behavior–Revised

	Age Equivalent
Gross Motor	7-11
Fine Motor	6-9
Social Interaction	5-1
Language Comprehension	5-11
Language Expression	8-7
Eating	8-2
Toileting	5-3
Dressing	6-6
Self-Care	8-1
Domestic Skills	10-10
Time/Punctuality	5-8
Money and Value	7-0
Work Skills (habits)	4-7
Home/Community	6-3

These reports illustrate an accessible yet professional writing style that attempts to link referral issues and questions with assessment data and meaningful recommendations. Unfortunately, these reports are for evaluations of White boys from middle-class educated families (actual recent referrals that have not appeared in previous publications); however, one (Peter) does present issues of bicultural and bilingual background. Nevertheless, these reports illustrate acceptable formats and styles, if not diverse content (although the issues are certainly diverse within this group). Although these reports may suggest otherwise, I do not recommend occupational therapy for every child. There sometimes is a bias in this direction for young children, who are often referred with issues of fine motor development, low sensory thresholds, and difficulty with self-regulation. I have found the services from occupational therapists to be appropriate in these instances. Certainly, speech pathology is relevant for large numbers of children as well.

Some general guidelines for reducing the pain of report writing appear in Table 10.1. These guidelines are personal recommendations of what has worked for me.

LINKING ASSESSMENT WITH INTERVENTION

Linking assessment with intervention is one of those things we often say we need to do but rarely do—and even less often do it well (Ysseldyke & Christenson, 1988). It has not been the mission of this book to review in any significant detail methods of assessment that are associated with any specific type of disability. There are already several good sources of information for this type of information, such as Bracken (2000a); Culbertson and Willis (1993); Nuttall, Romero, and Kalesnik (1999); Sattler (2002); Simeonsson and Rosenthal (2001); and Wachs and Sheehan (1988a, 1988b). This type of information is well handled by an edited text. There are also excellent authored texts that address specific disabilities, such as Bradley-Johnson

Table 10.1   GUIDELINES FOR PAIN REDUCTION IN REPORT WRITING AND FOR
GENERATING MEANINGFUL REPORTS

- Develop clear referral questions and keep these in mind throughout the entire assessment process.
- Select your procedures to generate data that will address these referral questions.
- Continue to design and redesign your battery as you proceed and as new hypotheses and questions arise.
- As soon as you have collected the demographic and other background information, write this up to start your report. Do not wait until you have completed your assessment. Make sure that you have the correct birth date and use the age calculator from the American Guidance Service Web site (www.agsnet.com) to determine the child's age.
- Ask yourself how the background information will relate to your assessment in terms of procedure selection, interpretation, and recommendations.
- Following administration of each procedure, ask yourself what you have learned about the child from this procedure, and write this out in a way that may be appropriate to include in your report.
- Following administration of each procedure that is scorable, add this information to the test data sheet that will accompany your report. Do this as you proceed.
- At each step, ask yourself what you need to know and how you can best find out (this will determine what procedure to use).
- Constantly process what you observe in relation to its implications for intervention, and write down these ideas as you go. When it is time to write out recommendations, review these notes.
- Make copious observational notes that describe how the child proceeds with each task, and include language samples to reflect the child's language skills. Do not rely on test scores to describe the child.
- Write out brief impressions and behavioral descriptions immediately after you have seen the child. Do these in a way that may be appropriate for inclusion in your report.
- When you are writing out your procedure interpretations, process them in terms of what they contribute to the referral questions. Always ask yourself what might account for the child's performance.
- Make sure your report emphasizes positive coping and is not just a "can't do" report.
- Link your conclusions and recommendations to the referral questions. You can repeat the referral questions in your conclusion section and address each with your recommendations.
- Use a conversational tone in your report, as if you are communicating the feedback orally to a parent or teacher. Apply the golden rule: Communicate to others as you would wish them to communicate with you. Think of yourself as the parent who is hearing this information about your child.
- If you must use a technical word, add an explanation. Remember, what may not seem like a technical word to you may be one to the reader. In addition, do not use abbreviations unless you are very sure the reader will know what you mean (e.g., IEP is not a word!).
- Do not refer to subtests in the body of the report by the name of the subtest; refer to them in terms of the functions or activities involved (Vocabulary would be giving definitions of words; Object Assembly would be putting together puzzle-like pieces to construct a picture).
- Emphasize patterns of performance as they are represented across tasks.
- Proceed in a funnel-like manner from the more general to more specific. When describing results, begin with a general statement about level of performance, proceed to highlighting strengths and weaknesses, and then individualize the information with behavioral examples, quotations, or other observations.
- After each procedure and after asking yourself what you have learned from this, try to write out a statement reflecting what you have learned without looking at the test.
- When you have completed the assessment, ask yourself what the main conclusions and messages are about the child that you wish to communicate, and write these out to begin your "conclusions and recommendations" section (don't worry about not being finished with other sections). Look at each referral question and address each in terms of recommendations you would make based on your observations from the assessment, and fill these in.

Table 10.1   Continued

- Use headers in your report to represent the primary functional domains such as cognitive, social-emotional, preacademic, and sensory-motor functioning. If it is appropriate, you can use subcategories, such as attention, language concepts, perception, and memory for cognitive; interactions with adult, peers, temperament, and emotional regulation for social-emotional; literacy, numeracy, and written expression for preacademic; fine and gross motor and sensory thresholds. Pull together information that relates to each domain from multiple sources and integrate this information to emphasize the primary patterns and messages that you wish to convey.
- Consider not including a summary; if the body of the report is sufficiently tight, succinct, and to the point, you will not need a summary. Readers tend to jump to the summary and neglect reading the report.
- Develop graphs for any procedure for which this is appropriate; use the graphs that accompany the protocols of many procedures, and refer to these when you give feedback to parents and teachers.
- Your recommendations should address what teachers and parents can actually do and should not be restricted to issues of where to place or refer the child.
- Your recommendations should reflect what you have learned during the course of the assessment, what you know about evidence-based treatment approaches (if you don't know, then do your homework), and what is reasonable to expect others to be able to do. Do not necessarily be restricted to the limitations of the system, as the primary concern is to address the needs of the child, but do not make outrageous requests if they are not deemed absolutely necessary for the developmental progress of the child.
- Be prepared to help develop means of monitoring and evaluating the progress of the child's response to interventions that find their way into the Individual Education Plan.
- Solicit feedback regarding the satisfaction of parents and teachers with your assessment information.

(1994) and Bradley-Johnson and Evans (1991), and useful articles that discuss assessment with regard to special issues such as child abuse (Babiker & Herbert, 1998; Committee on Professional Practice and Standards, 1999). Rather, this book attempts to offer guidelines for an integrated assessment of all children of preschool age, regardless of presenting symptoms or disorders. Although sensorimotor and other biophysical challenges need to be addressed and accommodated, these children are children first, and most—if not all—of the approaches discussed in this book will apply.

Nor is it the mission of this book to suggest in recipe-like fashion specific interventions for each behavioral disorder. Good intervention flows in a logical way from the assessment process itself. If there is good problem clarification at the start of the assessment, and if the process proceeds in good hypothesis-generating, problem-solving fashion, then a repertory of interventions naturally unfolds. As I conduct an assessment, I am always processing my observations in terms of their implications for intervention, and I record these along with my notes describing my observations. It is also incumbent on the assessor to update awareness of intervention possibilities continually. I strongly recommend developing files of possible interventions for commonly occurring referral issues (e.g., Fowler, 1995; Karnes, Johnson, Cohen, & Beauchamp, 1986; Thomas & Tidmarsh, 1997). These days, the Internet is a major resource, and there are a number of Web sites relevant for school psychologists; one only need search for "school psychology" or the name of the disorder to access these or to reach the links through the Web site for the National Association of School Psychologists (www.nasponline.org). I strongly disagree with offering interventions in any formulaic way; what works for a group may or may not work for an individual. However, as social or practitioner scientists, assessors should be able to evaluate the evidence to support (or refute) the effectiveness of the interventions that are offered and should be suspicious of any that are offered as sure cures (McWilliam, 1999). It is difficult to be as current as a concerned and motivated parent with regard to available resources for any specific disorder, but the psychologist can offer the parent the scientific or professional eye for evaluating the evidence for any approach. There is increasing concern with provision of evidence-based interventions, and the professional psychologist needs to build a library of resources as these emerge. Some very helpful texts include Christophersen and Mortweet (2001), Linder (1993b), and Seligman (1998). The several best practices texts published through the National Association of School Psychologists are invaluable and are cited frequently throughout this text. One book that lays out the disorders and reasonable suggestions for intervention related to each disability is authored by Paasche, Gorrill, and Strom (1990), and a unique resource that compiles information regarding assistive technology for preschool children with disabilities is authored by Mahoney, Porto, Rosenshein, and Woolley (1995). Journal articles, particularly those from school psychology journals available through the National Association of School Psychology and Division 16 of the American Psychological Association, and others, such as those published by the Council for Exceptional Children (especially the Division for Early Childhood) and the National Association for the Education of Young Children, are also highly recommended. As there cannot be adequate research-based evidence for each and every intervention suggested for each and every child, it is also necessary to follow up the assessment with evidence collection for each child to document the child's response to the recommendations. It is also necessary for school systems to become more research minded so that the appropriate evaluative evidence can be collected (and psychologists and their organizations need to become advocates for this).

My approach to linking assessment with intervention is to do this concretely as I am developing the report on my computer. Any time I mention a concern in the body of the report, I make sure it is addressed in the recommendations section (or vice versa, as I often work backward!). I find most of these recommendations in the notes I have taken as I observe the child in various settings, and usually the most fruitful sources of these notes are classroom observations. For example, consider a young boy who has been referred because of aggressive behavior. From detailed interviews of his teachers and parents, as well as from direct observation, these concerns have been narrowed down to the domain of social interaction skills with peers and, more specifically, to poor development of play entry behavior. When this child wishes to join peer play, he either barges in and disrupts the play of those he wishes to join or grabs something with which they were playing and runs off to another section of the room. The hypothesis developed from this is that he does wish to join peers in play but has not learned how to do this in an acceptable way. It is then not a far inference to decide that one reasonable intervention would be to help him recognize what he is trying to do and the effects of what he is currently doing, and then coaching him through an alternative behavior that could get him what he wants. As would be compatible with a dynamic assessment approach, the assessor engages in some of this coaching and information sharing on a trial basis to see if there is any impact. Imagine that in this case the child is able to imitate the entry language modeled for him, seems to appreciate having his intentions recognized (while not being chastised for his behavior), and gets some short-lived positive results. However, it also becomes apparent that the other children need to be coached to recognize and react positively to these new behaviors from the referred child. This information then becomes part of the assessment recommendations, along with suggestions regarding how to monitor the outcomes and promote generalization.

Such meaningful and relevant interventions become possible when the assessor is constantly (and consciously) working to link assessment information with intervention. Assessors who administer a standard battery of tests and wait until they are completed to try to figure out what to recommend will inevitably fall short of such firm linkage. Ideas need to be generated while the referred behaviors are occurring, with, when possible, trial interventions offered or at least discussed (with the teacher, child, or parent) so that some beginning evidence of potential effectiveness can be developed. When this is not feasible, assessors need to consult their files and resources to brainstorm an array of possibilities. As Surber (1995) reminded us, "placement of a child in special education is not an intervention" (p. 166). The movement of a child from one location to another provides no information regarding what to do with or for the child following relocation. Although psychologists are motivated by hopes that moving the child into a smaller group and into closer proximity to a teacher who has specialized training to individualize programs to meet the needs of diverse learners will solve all of the child's problems, it is too much of an act of faith to hope or believe that this move alone will produce positive outcomes. Something has to be done within the setting, and we need to inform ourselves about the possibilities of what these might be. There is no homogeneity regarding children's needs or approaches to learning. If teachers are to individualize their programs, they need some guidance to inform them of the needs of the individuals within their domains.

Many psychologists are in a position where they are not considered to be a source for information about interventions, and I am convinced that this situation is based on a long history of teams being unaccustomed to receiving this kind of information from their psychologists. Once psychologists begin to offer useful suggestions, particularly when they show evidence of effectiveness, such information would become expected and solicited. However, before this can happen, psychologists need to expect it from themselves.

Barnett and Hall (1990) pointed out the importance of determining and considering the acceptability of interventions to those who must carry them out and to caregivers, whether or not they are the actual implementers. It would be expected that the interventions are more likely to be implemented if the teachers and caregivers were involved in their selection and design and if they viewed the interventions as acceptable and feasible. Keeping these interventions as nonintrusive as possible and providing advocacy for securing the needed resources to facilitate their application are important to consider as well. Finally, the assessor can provide an important follow-up service by helping program implementers to learn the interventions that are recommended and, related to this, to assess the treatment validity of the interventions (are they really being done as intended?). If the psychologist is not available to provide this service, it may be available from educators who participate on special services teams.

Barnett, Bell, and Carey (1999) offered several suggestions to guide determination of interventions:

1. Identify target variables, that is, those "predicted to change a problem situation in a desirable way" (p. 71).

2. Attempt to target keystone variables, that is, those "that, if changed, are likely to impact the largest set of other significant behaviors, perceptions, or problem environments" (p. 77).

3. Focus on increasing positive (replacement, enabling) behaviors rather than reducing the negative (however, do not ignore the latter).

4. Set priorities according to a safety first principle.

5. Consider the next educational environment, addressing skills that serve as precursors to what will be needed at the next level, particularly those considered to be survival skills.

6. Be aware of research evidence for interventions, but select an intervention in terms of the functional value for the individual.

7. Assess availability of resources.

8. Select interventions that are as naturalistic and nonintrusive as possible.

As mentioned previously (and see Barnett, Carey, & Hall, 1993), these authors also advocated the need for treatment acceptability and validity.

COMMUNICATING WITH TEACHERS AND PARENTS

Assessment information is obviously useless unless the results are communicated wisely and well. We have already discussed report writing, which serves as the permanent record of the assessment activities and their results. These results must also be communicated verbally to caregivers and to teachers or program staff who are involved in providing services to the child. The hallmarks of good communication are clarity and perceived usefulness. In conducting these feedback sessions, Wise (1986) highlighted the importance of following the golden rule: "Treat parents as you would want them to treat you."

For the novice or very young assessor, these sessions can cause anxiety, particularly if the caregivers are older or more experienced than the assessor, or both. (One compensation of the aging process is that eventually you become older than your clients!) I have found it useful to remain focused on the client and to avoid thinking about myself; we assessors should be thinking about what the experience is like for the family, what their needs are at this time, and how we can be helpful to them. We can help them by providing straightforward, honest information that helps to clarify the child's needs and points the child and family in a direction for meeting these needs.

A general outline for conducting a feedback session could be as follows:

1. Decide who should attend, and, in the case of the family, do this in collaboration with them, working to include both parents and any other primary caregivers such as grandparents.

2. Schedule the meeting at a mutually convenient time, even if this is somewhat inconvenient for you.

3. Prepare yourself to understand the family's cultural background particularly with regard to their likely reactions to the assessment information and recommendations, and learn how to address the adults in the family.

4. Provide adequate time to cover the materials and avoid feelings of pressure; about 1 to 1.5 hr should be adequate.

5. Arrange for an interpreter if this is necessary, and be sure to prepare the interpreter for the meeting.

6. At the start of the meeting, provide a brief overview of what will take place during the feedback session, encouraging the family or teachers to ask questions and request clarification as needed.

7. Begin with the referral questions; proceed to how these were addressed during the assessment; and conclude with the major findings and recommendations.

8. If there are concerns that are likely to be preoccupying the participants (e.g., questions of mental retardation or serious emotional disturbance), address these first so that these reactions can be relieved and the participants can focus on the rest of the information. If there is significant "bad news," you may suggest getting to the major issues right away so that the session can be spent dealing with reactions to this as well as recommendations, with attention to assessment details postponed or relegated to report reading.

9. Use graphs, descriptions of behaviors, and work samples when possible, and interpret standardized test results in terms of percentiles, which are usually more easily understood by nonpsychologists.

10. End with a summary and information regarding next steps; provide the family with information regarding names of program personnel, how to reach them, and any available printed materials describing suggested programs, procedures, and interventions.

11. Get in touch with the family or teacher a day or two after the conference to check their reactions and understanding of what occurred and to provide an opportunity for further questions or clarification.

12. Ask participants to complete a service-satisfaction form to provide feedback about the assessment and feedback process (see Form 10.2).

Forms such as this can be useful in several ways. First, they provide an opportunity for the consumers to evaluate the evaluator. This provides the consumer with some control and power. Second, consumer reactions are important for service providers so that services can be adjusted or modified appropriately. Third, this information makes it possible for assessors not only to receive positive feedback but also to head off any potentially festering negative reactions and prevent these from exploding into more major situations. Finally, such information is important for accountability purposes so that service providers can share these results with administrators and supervisors to document consumer reactions to service provision.

The feedback session should not be the first time the psychologist meets with the caregivers or program providers. This should have occurred at the very least at the start of the assessment. Even if collection of social history is delegated to others on the team such as social workers, it is important for the psychologist to meet with these important individuals to set the agenda for the assessment, develop a collaborative relationship, and fill in information that may be missing from other sources. Further meetings may occur throughout the assessment process. Caregivers may be present during the course of the assessment, and assessors will want to converse with teachers to solicit their experience and observations, as well as their ideas regarding intervention and service options. When the time arrives for the team meetings, the caregivers should not be walking into a room filled with strangers but should enter feeling that they are joining their consultant-collaborators to engage in fruitful planning for the future of their child (Jensen & Potter, 1990). Such early attention to relationship building will go far to prevent the antagonistic encounters that at times occur between caregivers and team members. The importance of turning we/they into we cannot be overemphasized.

Assessors need to keep in mind that although they are comfortable with dealing with children with special needs and do not react negatively to the idea of disability or handicap, this is

Service Satisfaction Form

Return Address:
Date:

Dear _____ ,

I very much enjoyed the opportunity to work with you and your child during my recent assessment. I hope you have found the information from this process helpful. I would very much appreciate hearing from you to help me provide as worthwhile a service as possible. Please complete the brief form below and return it right away in the enclosed envelope. Feel free to get in touch if you have any questions or desire any further clarification (phone number: _____). You do not need to sign this form if you prefer anonymity.

Sincerely,

School Psychologist

Please rate the following according to this scale:

4	3	2	1
Very Positive	Positive	Weak	Poor

1. How well do you feel your concerns were addressed?   4 3 2 1
2. How useful did you find the information from the assessment?   4 3 2 1
3. How useful did you find the recommendations?   4 3 2 1
4. How easy did you find the report to read?   4 3 2 1
5. How did you feel about the feedback session?   4 3 2 1

Is there anything you recommend to improve this service?

Please add comments:

Thank you!

Form 10.2

not likely to be a familiar or comfortable experience for the parent whose child is about to be labeled or classified. This experience may be the parents' first encounter with the special services bureaucracy, and it may also be parents' first encounter with the fact that they have a child with special needs. How this is handled can affect their relationship not only with the messengers but with their child as well (Murphy, 1990). They may have felt all along that there was something of concern about their child, but until the assessment their child was still just "Johnny." After the conference, the child may become Johnny with developmental delays, mental retardation, emotional disturbance, or, most frequently, speech-language disorder. This will inevitably affect their feelings about and perceptions of their child, and it will influence how they talk about their child to others, particularly within their family. The assessor can be helpful in addressing these concerns, as well as in providing a useful way to view and talk about their child. In order to do this, the assessor needs to explore how disabilities are viewed within the family's culture and how people in the community are likely to react to a family who has a child with special needs. Having a staff member who can serve as a cultural liaison can be very important here, and inclusion of this staff person in the meeting or in a follow-up session is highly recommended. Rather than providing explicit suggestions, the assessor could ask the caregivers what this information means to them and how they will explain their child's needs and receipt of services to others. This will help the caregivers process their reactions and begin some rehearsal of how they will cope with the information.

I have learned never to assume how caregivers will react to assessment feedback. It is important to be as tactfully honest and direct as possible, and, if the child needs to be labeled with terms such as mental retardation in order to receive services, it is important to use these terms with them. If they hear the terms from someone else in the future, they will feel greatly betrayed by the assessor who did not inform them (Murphy, 1990). It is also important not to make specific long-term predictions (Kamphaus, 1993). We simply do not know enough to do this, and there are so many things that can affect the course of a child's development. If a child is severely impaired, it is of course reasonable to suggest that the child is likely to require services for a considerable period of time. For other levels of difficulty, the assessor needs to assure the caregivers that the child's progress will be monitored and reassessed and that the caregivers will be consulted on an ongoing basis to determine the next steps along the way.

When reviewing test results with caregivers or teachers, it is helpful to use graphs to illustrate standardized testing information and to interpret these as percentiles rather than standard scores, although the graphs will show the standard scores. When providing information to teachers, Kamphaus (1993, p. 226) first of all warned, "Never starve a teacher!" This is sound advice because conferences often occur during lunch periods, and there is nothing more likely to breed resentment than interfering with someone's desire to eat! Kamphaus also reminds us that teachers are interested in issues of instruction, and assessors should be sure to address implications of the results for schooling and the classroom. As indicated earlier, suggestions are more likely to be followed if the individuals who are expected to implement them share ownership and feel that there is minimal intrusion into their program routines. Most of all, they need to understand the importance of the suggestions and feel capable of implementation; follow-up training and support may need to be offered. It is also very important to discuss perceived barriers to implementation with parents and teachers to promote both satisfaction with the assessment process and implementation of the recommendations (Human & Teglasi, 1993; Shapiro, 1987).

EVALUATING THE EFFECTIVENESS OF INTERVENTIONS

If school psychologists can be criticized for weak linkage between assessment and intervention, we assessors are even more vulnerable to criticisms for failing to follow up our cases and for working with teachers and other team members to design procedures to monitor and evaluate the effectiveness of the interventions we prescribe. However, we are not alone. The entire team—in fact, the entire special education process—can be taken to task for these omissions. When the question is limited to how many individuals you saw and not how well they did, there is no surprise about how professional time will be spent. The hopeful news is that this is an area of potentially unique contribution by the school psychologist on the team, and a role we need to promote, advocate, and develop. Determination of the effectiveness of interventions is not just a good idea; it is now mandated as a follow-up for functional behavior assessments, that is, for children with serious behavioral disturbances. No one has had the time to do this before. Now we must demand the time. In addition, when money is short and the need for accountability is long, documentation of effectiveness of service is both ethically and economically justifiable.

In my days of administering an interdisciplinary team that provided services for the children with special needs in Head Start, I engaged in some tiny baby steps to document the progress of the children in our care. I was not aware of many others who did what we did. Of course, we did our share of person counting: how many children we saw, with what special needs, how many hours of speech, occupational therapy, physical therapy, psychological services, parent conferences, training sessions, and so on. However, during the summer, when I was granted time by the agency (United Cerebral Palsy Association of Philadelphia and Vicinity gets credit for this), I wrote a very extensive and detailed report of our services during the prior year; this included reviewing each child's file to calculate percentage of Individual Education Plan objectives accomplished, compilations of ratings by participants in our staff and parent training sessions, feedback forms from parents and teachers following completion of assessments, and review of how many children were terminated from our services, as well as those who showed continuing need. This was a very beginning attempt to determine the response to intervention and satisfaction with services. Meanwhile, the whole agency adopted the Goal Attainment Scaling (discussed later in this chapter) approach for all of its departments, and we participated in this, setting goals for ourselves to which we could aspire for the following year. I regret not knowing and doing more at that time. We also engaged in a self-evaluation by dedicating our last team meeting to review and consideration of our procedures and struggles over the year and seeking ways to modify and improve our functioning; we also invited the people with whom we worked during the year—the special needs coordinators from the various agencies—to meet with us and reflect on the past year's service provision, brainstorming and anticipating service needs for the next year. These activities are difficult to support without adequate funding, but they are critical for good programming. We all need time to reflect about what we are doing and what impact we are having, without fear of attack if we find disappointing results. If we are going to engage in evaluation, including self-evaluation, we need a supportive and safe environment. How much easier it is not to seek, lest we find.

So how do we do this? How do we determine the effectiveness of the interventions we recommend and the satisfactions of our consumers with our services? Development of this methodology is still in process, but there are ways, and these differ with the nature of the behaviors and domains involved. None of these is perfect, as we are not able to control many of the variables. All of this involves engagement in what we would call an applied research role. We must begin with the questions of, What is expected to change? In what way? How is this best assessed? How can we attribute the change to the intervention? How can we do this in an efficient, effective, and least intrusive way?

Bricker and Gumerlock (1988) advocated for an array of evaluations that were daily-weekly, quarterly, and annually. Each of these would rely on different types of data sources. Daily-weekly monitoring is most appropriately accomplished through the use of curriculum-based measurement (CBM) probes such as those described by Deno (1986) and his colleagues at the University of Minnesota. Although these CBM approaches have been developed primarily in relation to basic levels of achievement in the domains of reading, math, and writing, it is not too far a stretch to apply the technique to some aspects of preschool functioning, such as language samples or early literacy and numeracy skills. The idea is to ask the child to engage in selected aspects of the task for a standard length of time, with both speed and accuracy monitored as indicators of task mastery. For example, it would be possible to ask the child to listen to and retell a short story, counting the number of elements, or to ask the child to count blocks or name colors. Other approaches to direct observation could also be used for frequent monitoring, such as behavior observation samples during peer play or circle time. Another source of this data would be work samples, particularly for prewriting and drawing skills. Quarterly assessments could be accomplished through readministration of a curriculum-based assessment, such as those discussed in Chapter 5, utilizing the same measure that was included in the initial assessment battery. Because these measures are often not sufficiently sensitive to detect small changes, the staff working with the child may wish to develop intermediate steps toward task accomplishment that are tailored to the specific individual. Other approaches are usually inappropriate for this purpose because the measures need to be repeatable (Deno, 1986).

Annual progress assessment can be accomplished through readministration of ratings scales used during the initial assessment. Although it is not possible to derive firm conclusions about the cause of changes that are indicated by such pre-post testing (Bailey & Simeonsson, 1988; Deno, 1986), it is at least possible to document whether there has been a change. Attribution of the source of this change to the interventions would require considerably more experimental control than is usually available in most programs. In optimal circumstances, failure to respond to treatment should have been detected much earlier than annually, through utilization of the more frequent sources of data, which should have led to adjustments in programming. This frequent monitoring that informs practice on an ongoing basis is called *formative evaluation*, whereas the posttesting that takes place, usually at the end of treatment, is called *summative evaluation*.

One of the most promising approaches for summative evaluation is Goal Attainment Scaling (GAS; Bailey & Simeonsson, 1988; Carr, 1979; Shuster, Fitzgerald, Shelton, Barber, & Desch, 1984; Simeonsson, Huntington, & Short, 1982). GAS provides a method of quantifying very child-specific goals and objectives, with input by those working with the child to achieve these objectives, including the caregivers. This method involves specifying the individual's goals in clearly behavioral terms, for example placing four goals at the head of each column going across the page (see Table 10.3 for an example). Under each goal there are levels that describe the expected level of accomplishment and two levels above and below to describe hierarchies of better and worse expectations regarding goal accomplishment. Expected level is assigned the number zero (0), and each level above and below is assigned the numbers +1, +2, −1, −2. The parents and teachers work together to determine the goals and reasonable expectations and to assign weights regarding the degree of importance of each goal; these weights need to add up to a total of 100. An example of a goal attainment scale appears in Table 10.2. This figure represents four goals and weights as follows.

There is a large ✓ to indicate the child's level of functioning prior to onset of intervention. The score for the child at this point would be the goal level times the weight, added together to obtain a total. In the case of the example, the total score would be –150. The levels are reevaluated at the appointed time, with the total recalculated. This yields a change score. Such scores can be calculated for all children in the classroom to indicate the progress of the class as a group. Lack of progress suggests the need to reevaluate the intervention approach, as well as the degree of compliance of the participants.

Table 10.3 appeared in my mailbox many years ago without a clue regarding source. I thought it was too cute not to share, and I offer it here as yet another model for GAS, this time applied to career evaluation. Table 10.3 is available to document how we all far exceed our job requirements.

Referring to GAS as time consuming and subjective, Wolery (1983) proposed the use of the proportional change index. The formula for this is:

$$\frac{\text{Developmental Gain}}{\text{Time in Intervention}} \div \frac{\text{Pretest Developmental Age}}{\text{Pretest Chronological Age}}$$

Developmental gain is the posttest developmental age minus the pretest developmental age. If we assume that the child has been in intervention for 9 months, shows a developmental gain (in the language domain) of 6 months, and has a pretest developmental age of 36 months and

Table 10.2 SAMPLE GOAL ATTAINMENT SCALE

	Goal 1 (Wt: 50) Sits with group/circle time	Goal 2 (Wt. 25) Sustains peer play	Goal 3 (Wt. 15) Imaginative play themes	Goal 4 (Wt. 10) Sentence length
Much Above Expected Level (+2)	Sits with class during circle time for 20+ min	Sustains peer play 20+ min	Complex/linked themes/independent play	average MLU* 6 words
Somewhat Above Expected Level (+1)	Sits with class during circle time for 15 min	Sustains peer play 15 min	Two sequences independent play	average MLU 5 words
Expected Level (0)	Sits with class during circle time for 10 min	Sustains peer play 10 min	One theme/ independent play	average MLU 3–4 words
Somewhat Below Expected Level (–1)	Sits with class during circle time for 5 min	Sustains peer play 5 min ✓	Functional play ✓	average MLU 2 words ✓
Much Below Expected Level (–2)	Sits with class during circle time < 5 min ✓	Sustains peer play < 5 min	Exploratory play	average MLU 1 word

* mean length of utterance.

Table 10.3   GOAL ATTAINMENT SCALE: CAREER EVALUATION

	Far Exceeds Job Requirements	Exceeds Job Requirements	Meets Job Requirements	Needs Some Improvement	Does Not Meet Requirement
Performance Factor					
Quality	Leaps tall buildings with a singe bound	Must take running start to leap over tall buildings	Can only leap over a short building or medium with no spires	Crashes into buildings when attempting to jump	Cannot recognize buildings at all
Timelines	Is faster than a speeding bullet	Is as fast as a speeding bullet	Not quite as fast as a speeding bullet	Would you believe a slow bullet	Wounds self with bullets
Effort	Is stronger than a locomotive	Is stronger than a bull elephant	Is stronger than a bull	Shoots the bull	Smells like a bull
Adaptability	Walks on water consistently	Walks on water in emergencies	Washes with water	Drinks water	Passes water
Communication	Talks with God	Talks with angels	Talks to her/himself	Argues with her/himself	Loses those arguments

pretest chronological age of 48 months, this child's proportional change index (PCI) is .89. This approach compares the assumed pretest rate of development with the intervention rate of development; when these are equal, the index is 1. This approach can be criticized for reliance on tests that may or may not be comparable from program to program and that may have psychometric problems. Most of these procedures are vulnerable to criticism for reliance on gain scores, which are noted to be unreliable.

Norm-based tests are often used for summative evaluations, but using standardized, normed tests for this purpose can be considered an oxymoron. There is general consensus that these tests are too insensitive to detect change because they are designed to reflect stability, not change (attributed to error of measurement, which test designers seek to minimize; Bricker & Gumerlock, 1988; Bricker & Littman, 1982; Garwood, 1982a; Keogh & Sheehan, 1981; Mott et al., 1986). Items that are not stable are removed; high marks are granted for strong test-retest stability. By definition, intervention is an attempt to refute this stability, to ignore predictions about the individual's progress, and to provide programming for all children, regardless of initial test results. Therefore, using these tests to determine intervention or program success is placing a significant obstacle in the path of this evidence. Furthermore, neither norm-based nor criterion-referenced tests were designed to reflect program goals, unless the program is in fact guided by the test content, as is sometimes done with procedures such as the Learning Accomplishment Profile.

As has been evident throughout this text, all assessment procedures have strengths and weaknesses, and there is no perfect approach—certainly not an ideal approach to evaluating response to intervention. As has also been evident throughout this text, the most valid and reasonable approach to assessment is to utilize multiple procedures so that the combination yields an integrated and comprehensive picture, rather than relying on one that is vulnerable to distortion and negative criticism. It is much more fruitful and relevant to be specific about what is expected to change, to determine in what way it is expected to change, and to devise direct measures of this when possible. When not possible, use of rating scales and other low-inference, judgment-based approaches can be employed. However, what is no longer acceptable is to state "teacher judgment" alone as an assessment measure. This would need to be more specific in terms of the criteria that will be employed by the teacher or by whoever will be the judge.

FINAL THOUGHTS

After considering all the stops and some detours we have made on this journey through the complex course of early childhood assessment, it should come as no surprise that some of us consider this an area requiring special preparation. It was not so long ago that there were no courses in early childhood assessment. Individuals such as myself had to train ourselves. My preparation in graduate school for assessing young children was to administer a Stanford-Binet Intelligence Scale (Form L-M at that!). When I was faced with a large number of young children to assess and scrambled for information to guide my way, I quickly discovered how little there was available. We have come a long way. We need to move further along, but, happily, there are now some guides and mentors to ease the way. It is up to you to use them and to use them well. Bon voyage!

SUMMARY

This chapter concludes the journey along the long and complex road of early childhood assessment. The chapter discusses report writing that involves linking the assessment information with recommendations for intervention with examples of reports provided to illustrate style and format. The chapter also addresses communication of results to caregivers and teachers. The issue of evaluation of interventions and programs is also discussed, with specific recommendations of how this can be done. Details of GAS are suggested for application to program evaluation.

SUGGESTED ACTIVITIES

1. Apply a full range and battery of procedures selected from each chapter of this text to one preschool-age child and generate a report based on these data. Make up a referral issue and referral questions even if these are semifabricated (because this is not a referred child) to help focus your assessment.
2. Design a plan for evaluating the child's response to the interventions you suggest in your assessment.

Appendix A

————— ◆ —————

National Association of School Psychologists Position Statement on Early Childhood Assessment

————— ◆ —————

The National Association of School Psychologists believes that early identification of developmental and learning problems in preschool and primary grade children is essential because of children's broad and rapid development. Intervention services for these children's psychological and developmental difficulties are essential, beneficial, and cost-effective. Because the accurate and fair identification of the developmental needs of young children is critical to the design, implementation, and success of appropriate interventions school psychologists must play a key role. Evidence from research and practice in early childhood assessment indicates that issues of technical adequacy are more difficult to address with young children who have short attention spans and go through periods of variable, rapid development. Therefore, standardized assessment procedures should be used with great caution in educational decision-making because such tools are inherently less accurate and less predictive when used with young children.

Multidisciplinary team assessments must include multiple sources of information, multiple approaches to assessment, and multiple settings in order to yield a comprehensive understanding of children's skills and needs. Therefore, assessments should center on the child in the family system and home environment, both substantial influences on the development of young children. Similarly, families' self-identified needs should drive the decision-making process concerning the identification of child and family services.

Because categorical identification of infants, toddlers, and young children is ineffective in meeting the special needs of young children, assessment of infants and young children requires specialized training and skills beyond those required for the assessment of older children. Longitudinal and functional assessment of behavior and development of infants, young children, and families in a variety of settings is needed to evaluate and document progress and response to intervention over time, and *must* guide early intervention strategies in meaningful ways.

Therefore, the National Association of School Psychologists will promote early childhood assessment practices that are:

Source: © 1999 National Association of School Psychologists, 4340 East West Highway, Suite 402, Bethesda MD 20814—301-657-0270. Used with permission.

- developmentally appropriate, ecological, comprehensive, skills-based, and family-focused;
- conducted by a multi-disciplinary team;
- linked to intervention strategies designed for young children, rather than to categorical classification;
- based upon comprehensive, educational and/or behavioral concerns, rather than isolated deficits identified by individual assessments;
- nondiscriminatory in terms of gender, ethnicity, native language, family composition, and/or socio-economic status; and
- technically adequate and validated for the purpose(s) for which they are used, including the provision of norms for minority children and children with physical disabilities.

ROLE OF THE SCHOOL PSYCHOLOGIST

NASP encourages the adoption of the philosophy of "parents as partners" and families as the focus to promote assessments and interventions for young children that include full integration of parents and families into the assessment and intervention components of early childhood services. This mandates methods of naturalistic and systematic observation and information gathering, including work sampling procedures and the involvement of the family, home environment, daycare/preschool, and the community ecology as part of the comprehensive assessment to gather information and input from parents and caregivers. School psychologists should provide leadership to the multidisciplinary team in ensuring that all information gathered through the assessment is clearly understood by parents so that they can make fully-informed decisions about interventions for their children.

NASP also advocates for pre-service and in-service education for school psychologists and other professionals to address the following issues: 1) normal as well as atypical developmental patterns of infants and young children; 2) practices, procedures, and instrumentation appropriate for screening and assessment of young children, their families, and their environments; 3) the selection of assessment techniques and utilization of findings from such assessments for the design, implementation, and efficacy evaluation of interventions; 4) and standards for early childhood psychological and educational assessment, including legal, ethical, and professional issues—all in the context of noncategorical service delivery for young children and their families.

SUMMARY

NASP supports early childhood assessment practices that allow for accurate and fair identification of the developmental needs of infants, preschoolers, and young children and facilitate interventions that involve parents and other caregivers. Sound early childhood assessment should involve a multi-disciplinary team, including school psychologists with specialized training in the assessment of the young child, and who view behavior and development from a longitudinal perspective.

Original version adopted by NASP Delegate Assembly, March 24, 1991
Revision adopted by NASP Delegate Assembly, July 24, 1999

ANNOTATED BIBLIOGRAPHY

Gridley, Betty. (1995). Preschool Screening. In A. Thomas & J. Grimes (Eds.), *Best Practices in School Psychology–III*, (pp 213–226). Washington, DC: National Association of School Psychologists.

This chapter discusses the purposes of screening, the importance of parental input to appropriate screening practices, commonly used screening instruments, and practical activities for parents to do to facilitate development and learning in their child.

Gullo, Domnic, F. (1994). *Understanding assessment and evaluation in early childhood education.* Teachers College Press: New York, NY.

This book will help early childhood practitioners develop the essential understanding required for appropriate use of informal and formal assessment and evaluation information. Appendices contain a glossary of assessment instruments in early childhood education and a case study of an alternative assessment program.

Harrington, Robert, H., & Tongier, Jane. (1993). The compatibility between state eligibility criteria for developmental delays and available early childhood assessment instrumentation. *Diagnostique 18*(33), 199–217.

This paper discusses the results of a survey of 50 state consultants in early childhood special education in the United States to evaluate whether they perceive available developmental assessment instrumentation to be satisfactory for the identification of children with developmental delays in the 3 through 5 year old range. Results showed a need for instruments that facilitate parent involvement and a need for special norms for minority children and children with physical disabilities.

Katz, L. (1997). *A developmental approach to assessment of young children.* Champaign, IL: ERIC Clearinghouse on Elementary and Early Childhood Education.

This paper describes the concept of developmental appropriateness as it applies to the assessment of young children. The various purposes of assessing individual children are discussed. A match between plans, strategies, and assessment instruments and specific assessment purpose is mandated.

McClean, M.E. (1993). Practices for Young Children with and without disabilities: A comparison of DEC and NAEYC Identified Practices. *Topics in Early Childhood Special Education, 13*(3), 274–292.

This article summarizes practices that represent consensus of professionals and consumers in the field of early childhood education and early intervention relative to useful practice. Practices identified through the work of the Division for Early Childhood (DEC) Task Force on Recommended Practice are compared with practices identified through the work of the National Association of the Education of Young Children (NAEYC). Similarities and differing emphases in the areas of inclusion, family involvement, assessment, program planning, curriculum and intervention strategies, service delivery models, and transition are discussed.

Neisworth, John. (1993). Assessment: DEC recommended practices. In *DEC recommended practices: Indicators of quality in programs for infants and young children.* (EC 301 933).

This paper lists practices recommended by the Division for Early Childhood for assessment in early intervention and early childhood special education programs for infant and young children with special needs and their families. Introductory text examines the role of assessment, materi-

als, and procedures used, and assessment principles, including: assessment must clearly identify developmental or behavioral objectives for change; assessment should help to select and guide treatment activities; assessment should contribute to evaluating intervention or program efficacy, assessment should identify goals and objectives that are judged as worthwhile and important; assessment methods and materials themselves should be judged as acceptable; assessment decisions must be based on a wide base of information; assessment batteries should contain several types of scales and include observation and interviews; assessment should include data and reports from parents and other significant individual; and assessment must be done on multiple occasions.

Preator, Karleen, K., & McAllister, J.R. (1995). Assessing infants and toddlers. In A. Thomas & J. Grimes (Eds.), *Best Practices in School Psychology–III,* (pp. 775–788). Washington, DC: National Association of School Psychologists.
This chapter discusses basic considerations when assessing infants and toddlers, particularly under the requirements of federal legislation. The role of the school psychologist in working with the medical community and working with families as team members, as well as how to formulate assessment strategies with this population are also included.

SERVE: Southeastern Regional Vision for Education. (1991). *Assessment in Early Childhood Education: Status of the Issue.* Office of Educational Research and Improvement: Washington DC (ED 368 507).
This research brief argues that standardized testing has been over-used and misinterpreted, particularly when tests do not have established reliability and validity, when readiness tests are substituted for screening tests, and when tests are used for purposes they were not designed for. The National Association for the Education of the Young Child recommends that the most important consideration in evaluating and using standardized tests with young children is utility. Staff must be trained to recognize what specific tests can and cannot measure. Assessment systems that can be used cooperatively by parents and teachers is recommended. Ongoing evaluation should consist of criterion-referenced checklists, portfolio collection of the child's work, and summative teacher report forms.

Schweinhart, Lawrence. (July, 1993). Observing young children in action: The key to early childhood assessment. *Young Children 48*(5), 29–33.
This article discusses practices such as performance-based assessment that are consistent with early childhood profession's process goals. Appropriate assessment practices are described including the use observational methods that use anecdotal notes to complement assessments with developmental scales of established reliability and validity.

Shephard, L., Kagan, S., & Wurtz, E. (1998) *Principles and recommendations for early childhood assessments.* Washington DC: National Education Goals Panel. http://www.negp.gov
This booklet discusses best practices for assessment of young children considering their unique development, recent abuses of testing, and legitimate demands for clear and useful information. General principles of assessment included address benefits, reliability and validity, age level appropriateness and language, and parent role in assessment.

Appendix B

◆

New York Association of School Psychologists (NYASP) Guidelines for Preschool Psychological Assessment in New York State

Nancy Evangelista and Lacy Rezek

◆

The New York Association of School Psychologists (NYASP) defines part of its mission as improving standards for practice and training in school psychology. Following changes in legislation mandating preschool special education and early childhood services (IDEA 1990), many school psychologists in New York State are now increasingly involved with assessment, educational planning, and interventions for preschool children. The public school district's contact with preschoolers with disabilities may also increase with the enactment of New York State's Universal Prekindergarten Program (1997), which has program goals for integrating preschool children with disabilities into prekindergarten settings.

School psychologists are broadly trained in child development, learning and cognition, educational foundations, mental health, and family functioning, which lead to their professional activities of assessment, intervention, consultation, and collaboration. However, many school psychologists have not had the opportunity to apply these skills with children under the age of five (Kaplinski, Lidz, & Rosenfield, 1992; Miranda & Andrews, 1994). In addition, there are differences between systems of service delivery and regulations for assessment of preschoolers and school age children. Therefore the purposes of this paper are to: (a) reiterate the New York State regulations regarding preschool assessment; (b) provide guidelines to answering questions regarding appropriate assessment for preschoolers and; (c) provide guidelines for ensuring ethical conduct and best professional practice.

WHO IS CONSIDERED A PRESCHOOL CHILD?

Special education services in New York State are organized into three age groups. Children from birth to approximately three years old may receive Early Intervention (EI) services provided through New York State Department of Health. Preschool services, provided through the Committee on Preschool Special Education (CPSE), address the needs of children from

Source: http://www.nyasp.org/preschool.htm. Used with permission.

ages three to approximately five, or until they are first eligible to attend Kindergarten. Preschool services may be provided to children at age two and a half who have been in the Early Intervention program. Services for school-aged children begin when they are first eligible for Kindergarten and extend through age 21. These services are provided through the Committee on Special Education (CSE).

NEW YORK STATE PART 200 REGULATIONS OF THE COMMISSIONER DEFINING ASSESSMENT

According to the Part 200 regulations, a preschool child referred to the Committee on Preschool Special Education (CPSE) due to suspected disability in one or more areas must receive an individual evaluation. The components of an individual evaluation are specified below:

200.4 (b)(1) An individual evaluation of the referred student shall be initiated by a committee on special education and shall include, at no cost to the parent, at least:

(i) a physical examination in accordance with the provisions of sections 903, 904, and 905 of the Education Law;

(ii) an individual psychological evaluation, except where a school psychologist determines after an assessment of a school-age student, pursuant to paragraph (2) of this subdivision, that further evaluation is unnecessary;

(iii) a social history; and

(iv) other appropriate assessments or evaluations as necessary to ascertain the physical, mental, and emotional factors which contribute to the suspected disabilities.

According to this regulation, a school psychologist may assess a child of *school age* and determine that further psychological evaluation is unnecessary. For a preschool child there is no such exception given; **a preschool child must receive an individual psychological evaluation.** The Part 200 definition of an individual psychological evaluation follows:

200.1 (w) Individual psychological evaluation means a process by which a New York State certified school psychologist or licensed psychologist uses, to the extent deemed necessary for purposes of educational planning, a variety of psychological and educational techniques and examinations in the student's dominant language, to study and describe a student's developmental, learning, behavioral, and other personality characteristics.

WHAT IS AN APPROPRIATE PRESCHOOL PSYCHOLOGICAL EVALUATION?

A New York State Education Department Memorandum published in May 1993 (Neveldine, 1993) provided direction for planning individual evaluations of preschool children.

The individual evaluation of a preschool child who is suspected of having a disability must include information pertaining to functional areas related to cognitive, language and communicative, adaptive, social-emotional or motor development in order to determine the child's individual needs as expressed on the individualized education program (IEP). Information must be obtained from a physical examination, an individual psychological evaluation, a social history, a parent interview, a structured observation of the child's performance and behavior and other assessment procedures as necessary to ascertain specific factors contributing to the suspected disability.

These procedures may include, but are not limited to, norm-referenced tests, criterion-referenced instruments, developmental checklists, teacher reports and other test results of the child. The amended regulations require that such evaluation must be individually administered, provided in the child's dominant language, not be dependent on a single procedure, administered by a multidisciplinary team, and be consistent with all other requirements found in Section 200.4(b)(1–4) of the Regulations of the Commissioner. All available information about the child must be reviewed and considered in comparison to accepted milestones of child development.

The psychological evaluation is one part of the multidiscipliunary evaluation, which must address all functional areas (cognitive, language and communication, adaptive, social-emotional and motor development). The regulations allow wide latitude in planning for an appropriate preschool evaluation, including allowing the evaluation team to decide which members will assess which functional areas. The psychological evaluation should thus be tailored to the individual needs and assessment questions presented by the child; in essence a flexible approach to assessment should be adopted. No one assessment method, and certainly no one test or set battery of tests, is appropriate for all children. Because most evaluations which are conducted in response to a CPSE referral are concerned with qualification for services, these evaluations will not be as fine-grained as those used for designing specific intervention programs and gauging progress (Batsche & Knoff, 1995). Nonetheless, using tools and procedures which can link to intervention planning is encouraged (Bagnato, Neisworth, & Munson, 1989). An extensive discussion of the various preschool assessment tools is beyond the scope of this paper, but can be found in Alfonso and Flanagan (1999), McLean, Bailey, and Wolery (1996), and Bracken (1991).

WHAT COMPETENCIES ARE NEEDED FOR APPROPRIATE PRESCHOOL ASSESSMENT?

Psychologists conducting evaluations for preschool children should understand early development, family functioning, and team functioning within the educational context. Certified school psychologists have training in essential assessment skills such as knowledge of psychometric methods and their limitations, skills in working with parents, observational skills, understanding of typical and atypical development, and linking assessment to intervention (Preator & McAllister, 1995). However, further training and experience with young children is highly recommended for preschool practice. In a jointly authored position paper, the School Psychology Educator's Council of New York State & New York Association of School Psychologists (Lidz et al., 1999) suggest that psychologists draw from competencies in the following areas in designing an evaluation of a young child:

developmental assessment	standardized cognitive	dynamic assessment
family-systems assessment	assessment	ratings scales
play-based assessment	curriculum-based	naturalistic and systematic
interview instruments/	assessment	observations
techniques	ecological assessment	archival assessment

WHO CAN CONDUCT A PRESCHOOL PSYCHOLOGICAL EVALUATION?

New York's model for preschool assessment utilizes evaluation providers who are approved by the New York State Education Department. Often community agencies (e.g., Association for Retarded Children, BOCES) are approved preschool evaluation providers.

Public schools are not automatically preschool evaluators, unless they apply for, and are granted approval. The Article 89 regulation pertaining to approved preschool evaluators is cited below.

Art. 89, Sect. 4410, subdivision 9

(a) A school district or a group of appropriately licensed and/or certified professionals associated with a public or private agency may apply to the commissioner for approval as an evaluator . . . Such application shall include, but not be limited to, a description of the multi-disciplinary evaluation services proposed to be provided and a demonstration that all agency employees and staff who provide such evaluation services shall have appropriate licensure and/or certification and that the individual who shall have direct supervision responsibilities over such staff shall have appropriate level of experience in providing evaluation or services to preschool or kindergarten-aged children with handicapping conditions.

As previously cited in Part 200.1(w), the appropriate professional providing the psychological evaluation must be either a licensed psychologist or certified school psychologist. Article 153 of New York State Education law regulates the profession of psychology and limits non-licensed psychologists (such as certified school psychologists) to practice only as *salaried* employees in exempt settings, which are defined as chartered elementary or secondary schools, or federal, state, county, or municipal agencies. Therefore a certified school psychologist, who is not also a licensed psychologist, is prohibited from independent contracting with agencies which may be approved preschool evaluators, and may perform such services only as a salaried employee in an exempt setting. School psychology interns may assist certified school psychologists in conducting preschool evaluations in exempt settings, but the supervising school psychologist carries ultimate responsibility for the details of the individual evaluation, and must observe and interact with the child for a sufficient amount of time to allow the supervisor to reach an independent conclusion regarding the child's performance (Freeborne, 1984).

Once a child has been referred to the Committee on Preschool Special Education (CPSE), parents select an approved evaluation provider from a list maintained by their school district. The evaluation results are reviewed at a formal meeting by the CPSE. If a preschool student is determined to be eligible for special education programs and services, this meeting is the basis for IEP development. In contrast to the Committee on Special Education (CSE) for school-age children, the school psychologist is not a mandated member of the CPSE. Certified school psychologists in some school districts are involved in chairing the CPSE or as the school district representative who is responsible for interpreting instructional implications of the evaluation results.

The model of utilizing approved evaluators outside the local school district results in an increased need to coordinate efforts with approved evaluators and agencies providing preschool services. Generally, service delivery is enhanced if local district evaluators and staff are involved with evaluating the needs and planning for interventions for preschool students.

WHAT IS CONSIDERED A DISABILITY FOR A PRESCHOOL CHILD?

New York State regulations (Part 200, May 1998 revision) specify the following criteria for determining whether a child meets the definition of a preschool student with a disability:

200.1 (ee) Commencing July 1, 1993 to be identified as having a disability a preschool student shall either:

(i) exhibit a significant delay or disorder in one or more functional areas related to cognitive, language and communicative, adaptive, socio-emotional or motor development which adversely affects the student's ability to learn. Such delay or disorder shall be documented by the results of the individual evaluation which includes but is not limited to information in all functional areas obtained from a structured observation of a student's performance and behavior, a parental interview and other individually administered assessment procedures, and, when reviewed in combination and compared to accepted milestones for child development, indicate:

(a) a 12 month delay in one or more functional areas; **or**

(b) a 33 percent delay in one functional area, or a 25 percent delay in each of two functional areas; **or**

(c) if appropriate standardized instruments are individually administered in the evaluation process, a score of 2.0 standard deviations below the mean in one functional area, or a score of 1.5 standard deviations below the mean in each of two functional areas; **or**

(ii) meet the criteria of autistic, deaf, deaf-blind, hard of hearing, orthopedically impaired, other health-impaired, traumatic brain-injured, or visually impaired as described in Section 200.1 (mm) of the Regulations.

This definition is designed to promote a noncategorical model for qualifying young children for special services, in contrast to the establishment of specific disabilities, as was required prior to 1993. Note that the disability categories of emotionally disturbed, learning disabled, mentally retarded, multiply disabled, and speech impaired are not utilized at the preschool level. The eligibility criteria are designed to prevent premature identification of young children as having disabilities which may be difficult to establish at the preschool level.

In establishing the presence of delays, either standard scores (expressed in standard deviations below the mean) or age equivalent scores are allowable. While age equivalent scores convey a readily understood comparison to accepted milestones for child development, they must be interpreted with caution. Psychometric problems such as ordinal scaling, use of interpolation and extrapolation in constructing age equivalents, and variations in development at different ages and across skills limit the interpretability of age equivalents (Salvia & Ysseldyke, 1998). Therefore if norm-referenced tests have been used, then standard scores are a more appropriate method of interpretation.

HOW OFTEN MUST A PRESCHOOL CHILD BE EVALUATED?

Annual reviews of preschool students with disabilities are required, just as they are for school age children. At the annual review information about the child's educational needs, individualized education program, services, and progress are evaluated and recommended for continuation or modification as needed. A psychological re-evaluation could be requested to assist the CPSE in determining the student's individual needs, educational progress and achievement, and the student's continued eligibility for special education.

The NYS regulations do not specify frequency for preschool psychological assessments, and the triennial evaluations could satisfy re-evaluation requirement. Yet it is prudent and appropriate practice to re-evaluate young children frequently. Young children demonstrate a great deal of variability in their rates of maturation and acquisition of skills, and especially in their attention and motivation during testing (Neisworth & Bagnato, 1992). Since the resulting predictive validity of preschool tests is quite weak, frequent reassessment is needed to provide a current picture of the young child's functioning. In addition, if a young child has been receiving intervention services, the developmental picture may be changing rapidly.

A preschooler's transition to school-age programming requires not only reassessment of needs, but planning for services and programs within a new service system. A psychological re-evaluation may be needed by the CSE to determine the appropriate handicapping condition for the child who is entering the school-age special education service system, and has previously been identified with the noncategorical CPSE designation of a preschooler with a disability. **As a member of the CSE, the district school psychologist should be encouraged to take an active role in the transition process, and may determine that a current psychological evaluation of a child entering the district from the CPSE is appropriate and necessary.**

WHAT SHOULD I DO IF I ENCOUNTER POSSIBLE INAPPROPRIATE OR UNETHICAL PRACTICE?

The majority of approved evaluating agencies are following the regulations regarding appropriate preschool assessment performed by properly trained and salaried psychologists. However, there may be instances where state regulations and best practices have been overlooked or misinterpreted. When questions about professional practice and ethical conduct arise, the National Association of School Psychologists (NASP) and the New York Association of School Psychologists (NYASP) will be invaluable resources.

The NASP Principles for Ethical Practice (1997) and NYASP Ethics and Professional Standards Manual (1996) give clear steps to take when faced with possible inappropriate, uninformed, or unethical practice. The first step is to attempt to resolve the situation informally. A collaborative approach aimed at sharing information and clarifying appropriate practice is likely to be welcomed. For example, a misunderstanding of regulations or procedures could be resolved by an informal conversation with a practitioner. Next, consulting with colleagues and seeking information and advice from relevant professional organizations, such as NASP or NYASP, will help to clarify the nature of perceived violations and to determine a course of action. Utilization of the committee review process for eligibility decisions can also help promote appropriate practice. For example, the Committee on Preschool Special Education has authority to accept or to reject evaluations. When an evaluation does not conform with regulations or appropriate practice, the CPSE may decide to ask for another, or a more complete, evaluation. These steps should be taken prior to consideration of filing a formal complaint with the State Education Department, or with the appropriate credentialing body or professional organization.

REFERENCES

Alfonso, V. C. & Flanagan, D. P. (1999). Assessment of cognitive functioning in preschoolers. In E. V. Nutall, I. Romero, & J. Kalesnik (Eds.), *Assessing and screening preschoolers* (2nd ed., pp. 186–217). New York: Allyn & Bacon.

Bagnato, S. J., Neisworth, J. T. & Munson, S. M. (1989). *Linking developmental assessment and early intervention: Curriculum-based prescriptions.* Rockville, MD: Aspen Publications.

Batsche, G. M. & Knoff, H. M. (1995). Linking assessment to intervention. In A. Thomas & J. Grimes (Eds.) *Best practices in school psychology–III* (pp. 569–586). Washington, DC: National Association of School Psychologists.

Bracken, B. (1991). *The psychoeducational assessment of preschool children* (2nd ed.). Boston: Allyn & Bacon.

Freeborne, G. F. (1984, September). *The role of the school psychologist intern in the examination of children with handicapping conditions.* Albany, NY: New York State Education Department.

Kaplinski, K.P., Lidz, C. S., & Rosenfield, S. (1992). Preschool assessment practices: A national survey of preschool psychologists. *Early Childhood Interests, 8,* 1–4.

Lidz, C. S., Alfonso, V., Mowder, B., Ross, R., Rubenstein, F. & Thies, L. (1999, Winter). School psychology services in early childhood settings. *The school psychologist, 53,* 12–15.

McLean, M., Bailey, D. B. & Wolery, M. (1996). *Assessing infants and preschoolers with special needs* (2nd ed.) Englewood Cliffs, NJ: Prentice-Hall.

Miranda, A. H. & Andrews, T J. (1994). Preservice preparation of school psychologists for providing related services in early childhood intervention: A university-preschool partnership. *Topics in Early Childhood Special Education, 14,* 521–538.

National Association of School Psychologists (1997). *Principles for professional ethics.* Bethesda, MD: Author.

Neisworth, J. T. & Bagnato, S. J. (1992). The case against intelligence testing in early intervention. *Topics in Early Childhood Special Education, 12,* 1–20.

Neveldine, T. B. (1993, May). *The definition of a preschool student with a disability.* Albany, NY: The New York State Education Department.

New York Association of School Psychologists (1996). *Ethics and professional standards manual.*

New York State Department of Education (May 1998). *Updated Part 200 Regulations of the Commissioner of Education.* Albany, NY.

New York State Department of Education (July 1996). *Use of certified school psychologists as independent contractors.* Albany, NY.

Preator, K. K. & McAllister, J. R. (1995). Best practices in assessing infants and toddler. In A. Thomas & J. Grimes (Eds.). *Best practices in school psychology–III* (pp. 775–788). Washington, DC: National Association of School Psychologists.

Salvia, J. & Ysseldyke, J. (1998). *Assessment* (7th Ed.) Boston: Houghton Mifflin.

Appendix C

◆

Division for Early Childhood of the Council for Exceptional Children Position Paper on Developmental Delay as an Eligibility Category

Adopted: December, 2000

◆

DEC believes in the uniqueness of the young child and that services and interventions must be responsive to these unique needs and patterns of development. We believe that the disability categories used for older school-aged children are often inappropriate for young children birth through 8 years and that the category *developmental delay* can be a more appropriate designation of disability for special education eligibility. We believe that the assessment of disabilities in young children requires consideration of the whole child through the use of multiple sources, informants, settings, and measures.

As defined by DEC in 1991, developmental delay is:

a condition which represents a significant delay in the process of development. It does not refer to a condition in which a child is slightly or momentarily lagging in development. The presence of developmental delay is an indication that the process of development is significantly affected and that without special intervention, it is likely that educational performance at school age will be affected (DEC, 1991, p.1).

Parent and professional members of DEC believe that a developmental delay category of eligibility should be available for all children from birth through age 8. Though DEC recommends that the category of developmental delay be available for birth through age 8, we do not disagree with the provision in IDEA 1997 permitting its use for birth through age 9. We believe that the requirement to identify children by traditional disability categories in the early years might result in a premature categorization or miscategorization of children and consequently inappropriate services. Furthermore, the use of the developmental delay category allows for the identification of children with disabilities at younger ages who otherwise might go unserved because of the difficulties in applying traditional disability categories to young children.

The recommendation to use the developmental delay category birth through age 8 is supported by a number of considerations. First, the period of development typically characterized as early childhood is birth through age 8, a period of development considered to be unique by

Source: http://www.dec-sped.org/positions/devdelayposition.html

252

both the National Association for the Education of Young Children (NAEYC) and DEC. Young children's development is characterized by a broad range of behaviors across developmental domains and is better described by developmental metrics than by those with a more educational or academic focus. Second, the use of standardized and norm-referenced assessments for the identification of diagnostic categories for young children continues to be problematic resulting in unnecessary miscategorization. Psychometric integrity for instruments typically used to classify students for categorical services is only slightly greater in reliability for children ages 6, 7, and 8 than for their younger peers. Third, for many children these early grades are a pivotal foundation for acculturation within the school community. Many children are transient or enter school at kindergarten or beyond. For these children, opportunities to understand and practice school behaviors are limited. Categorical classification during these years would be premature and potentially inaccurate. Fourth, informed team decisions utilizing professional judgments and family input should contribute to eligibility decisions. Finally, the special education services children receive have historically been determined by their disability category. The use of the developmental delay category during the full span of the early childhood years facilitates a broader, whole child perspective for intervention. This perspective would provide an overriding focus on the child's needs and the identification of services to meet those needs in developmentally appropriate ways.

DEC is aware of the state and local discretion available regarding the use of developmental delay as an eligibility category for children ages 3 through 9. DEC strongly recommends that state and local agencies develop and implement the consistent use of a developmental delay category to insure appropriate services and smooth transitions for children with disabilities and their families during the early childhood period of development.

Appendix D

◆

Responding to Linguistic and Cultural Diversity: Recommendations for Effective Early Childhood Education

National Association for the Education of Young Children Position Paper

◆

Linguistically and culturally diverse is an educational term used by the U.S. Department of Education to define children enrolled in educational programs who are either non-English-proficient (NEP) or limited-English-proficient (LEP). Educators use this phrase, linguistically and culturally diverse, *to identify children from homes and communities where English is not the primary language of communication (Garciá 1991). For the purposes of this statement, the phrase will be used in a similar manner.*

This document primarily describes linguistically and culturally diverse children who speak languages other than English. However, the recommendations of this position statement can also apply to children who, although they speak only English, are also linguistically and culturally diverse.

INTRODUCTION

The children and families served in early childhood programs reflect the ethnic, cultural, and linguistic diversity of the nation. The nation's children all deserve an early childhood education that is responsive to their families, communities, and racial, ethnic, and cultural backgrounds. For young children to develop and learn optimally, the early childhood professional must be prepared to meet their diverse developmental, cultural, linguistic, and educational needs. Early childhood educators face the challenge of how best to respond to these needs.

The acquisition of language is essential to children's cognitive and social development. Regardless of what language children speak, they still develop and learn. Educators recognize that linguistically and culturally diverse children come to early childhood programs with previously acquired knowledge and learning based upon the language used in their home. For young children, the language of the home is the language they have used since birth, the language they use to make and establish meaningful communicative relationships, and the language they use to begin to construct their knowledge and test their learning. The home language is tied to children's culture, and culture and language communicate traditions, values, and attitudes (Chang 1993). Parents should be encouraged to use and develop children's home language; early childhood educators should respect children's linguistic and cultural backgrounds and their diverse learning styles. In so doing, adults will enhance children's learning and development.

Just as children learn and develop at different rates, individual differences exist in how children whose home language is not English acquire English. For example, some children may experience a silent period (of six or more months) while they acquire English; other children may practice their knowledge by mixing or combining languages (for example, "Mi mamá me put on mi coat"); still other children may seem to have acquired English-language skills (appropriate accent, use of vernacular, vocabulary, and grammatical rules) but are not truly proficient; yet some children will quickly acquire English-language proficiency. Each child's way of learning a new language should be viewed as acceptable, logical, and part of the ongoing development and learning of any new language.

DEFINING THE PROBLEM

At younger and younger ages, children are negotiating difficult transitions between their home and educational settings, requiring an adaptation to two or more diverse sets of rules, values, expectations, and behaviors. Educational programs and families must *respect* and *reinforce* each other as they work together to achieve the greatest benefit for all children. For some young children, entering any new environment—including early childhood programs—can be intimidating. The lives of many young children today are further complicated by having to communicate and learn in a language that may be unfamiliar. In the past, children entering U.S. schools from families whose home language is not English were expected to immerse themselves in the mainstream of schools, primarily through the use of English (Soto 1991; Wong Fillmore 1991). Sometimes the negative attitudes conveyed or expressed toward certain languages lead children to "give up" their home language. Early childhood professionals must recognize the feeling of loneliness, fear, and abandonment children may feel when they are thrust into settings that isolate them from their home community and language. The loss of children's home language may result in the disruption of family communication patterns, which may lead to the loss of intergenerational wisdom; damage to individual and community esteem; and children's potential nonmastery of their home language or English.

NAEYC'S POSITION

NAEYC's goal is to build support for equal access to high-quality educational programs that recognize and promote all aspects of children's development and learning, enabling all children to become competent, successful, and socially responsible adults. Children's educational experiences should afford them the opportunity to learn and to become effective, functioning members of society. Language development is essential for learning, and the development of children's home language does not interfere with their ability to learn English. Because knowing more than one lan-

guage is a cognitive asset (Hakuta & Garciá 1989), early education programs should encourage the development of children's home language while fostering the acquisition of English.

For the optimal development and learning of all children, educators must **accept** the legitimacy of children's home language, **respect** (hold in high regard) and **value** (esteem, appreciate) the home culture, and **promote** and **encourage** the active involvement and support of all families, including extended and nontraditional family units.

When early childhood educators acknowledge and respect children's home language and culture, ties between the family and programs are strengthened. This atmosphere provides increased opportunity for learning because young children feel supported, nurtured, and connected not only to their home communities and families but also to teachers and the educational setting.

THE CHALLENGES

The United States is a nation of great cultural diversity, and our diversity creates opportunities to learn and share both similar and different experiences. There are opportunities to learn about people from different backgrounds; the opportunity to foster a bilingual citizenry with skills necessary to succeed in a global economy; and opportunities to share one's own cherished heritage and traditions with others.

Historically, our nation has tended to regard differences, especially language differences, as cultural handicaps rather than cultural resources (Meier & Cazden 1982). "Although most Americans are reluctant to say it publicly, many are anxious about the changing racial and ethnic composition of the country" (Sharry 1994). As the early childhood profession transforms its thinking,

The challenge for early childhood educators is to become more knowledgeable about how to relate to children and families whose linguistic or cultural background is different from their own.

Between 1979 and 1989 the number of children in the United States from culturally and linguistically diverse backgrounds increased considerably (NCES 1993), and, according to a report released by the Center for the Study of Social Policy (1992), that diversity is even more pronounced among children younger than age 6. Contrary to popular belief, many of these children are neither foreign born nor immigrants but were born in the United States (Waggoner 1993). Approximately 9.9 million of the estimated 45 million school-age children, more than one in five, live in households in which languages other than English are spoken (Waggoner 1994). In some communities, however, the number of children living in a family in which a language other than English is spoken is likely to be much larger. Head Start reports that the largest number of linguistically and culturally diverse children served through Head Start are Spanish speakers, with other language groups representing smaller but growing percentages (Head Start Bureau 1995).

The challenge for teachers is to provide high-quality care and education for the increasing number of children who are likely to be linguistically and culturally diverse.

Families and communities are faced with increasingly complex responsibilities. Children used to be cared for by parents and family members who typically spoke the home language of their family, be it English or another language. With the increasing need of family members to work, even while children are very young, more and more children are placed in care and educational settings with adults who may not speak the child's home language or share their cultural background. Even so, children will spend an ever-increasing amount of their waking lives with these teachers. What happens in care will have a tremendous impact on the child's social, emotional, and cognitive development. These interactions will influence the child's values, view of the world, perspectives on family, and connections to community. This places a tremendous responsibility in the hands of the early childhood community.

Responding to linguistic and cultural diversity can be challenging. At times the challenges can be complicated further by the specific needs or issues of the child, the family, or the educational program. Solutions may not be evident. Individual circumstances can affect each situation differently. There are no easy answers, and often myths and misinformation may flourish. The challenges may even seem to be too numerous for any one teacher or provider to manage. Nonetheless, despite the complexity, it is the responsibility of all educators to assume the tasks and meet the challenges. Once a situation occurs, the early childhood educator should enter into a dialogue with colleagues, parents, and others in an effort to arrive at a negotiated agreement that will meet the best interest of the child. For example,

- A mother, father, and primary caregiver each have different cultural and linguistic backgrounds and do not speak English. Should the language of one of these persons be affirmed or respected above the others? How can the teacher affirm and respect the backgrounds of each of these individuals?
- The principal is concerned that all children learn English and, therefore, does not want any language other than English spoken in the early childhood setting. In the interest of the child, how should the educator respond?
- An educator questions whether a child will ever learn English if the home language is used as the primary language in the early childhood setting. How is this concern best addressed?

Solutions exist for each of these linguistic and cultural challenges, just as they do for the many other issues that early childhood educators confront within the early childhood setting. These challenges must be viewed as opportunities for the early childhood educator to reflect, question, and effectively respond to the needs of linguistically and culturally diverse children. Although appropriate responses to every linguistically and culturally diverse situation cannot be addressed through this document, early childhood educators should consider the following recommendations.

RECOMMENDATIONS FOR A RESPONSIVE LEARNING ENVIRONMENT

Early childhood educators should stop and reflect on the best ways to ensure appropriate educational and developmental experiences for all young children. The unique qualities and characteristics of each individual child must be acknowledged. Just as each child is different, methods and strategies to work with young children must vary.

The issue of home language and its importance to young children is also relevant for children who speak English but come from different cultural backgrounds, for example, speakers of English who have dialects, such as people from Appalachia or other regions having distinct patterns of speech, speakers of Black English, or second-and third generation speakers of English who maintain the dominant accent of their heritage language. While this position statement basically responds to children who are from homes in which English is not the dominant language, the recommendations provided may be helpful when working with children who come from diverse cultural backgrounds, even when they only speak English. The overall goal for early childhood professionals, however, is to provide every child, including children who are linguistically and culturally diverse, with a responsive learning environment. The following recommendations help achieve this goal.

A. RECOMMENDATIONS FOR WORKING WITH CHILDREN

Recognize that all children are cognitively, linguistically, and emotionally connected to the language and culture of their home.

When program settings acknowledge and support children's home language and culture, ties between the family and school are strengthened. In a supportive atmosphere young children's home language is less likely to atrophy (Chang 1993), a situation that could threaten the children's important ties to family and community.

Acknowledge that children can demonstrate their knowledge and capabilities in many ways.

In response to linguistic and cultural diversity, the goal for early childhood educators should be to make the most of children's potential, strengthening and building upon the skills they bring when they enter programs. Education, as Cummins states, implies "drawing out children's potential and making them more than they were" (1989, vii). Educational programs and practices must recognize the strengths that children possess. Whatever language children speak, they should be able to demonstrate their capabilities and also feel the success of being appreciated and valued. Teachers must build upon children's diversity of gifts and skills and provide young children opportunities to exhibit these skills in early childhood programs.

The learning environment must focus on the learner and allow opportunities for children to express themselves across the curriculum, including art, music, dramatization, and even block building. By using a nondeficit approach (tapping and recognizing children's strengths rather than focusing the child's home environment on skills yet unlearned) in their teaching, teachers should take the time to observe and engage children in a variety of learning activities. Children's strengths should be celebrated, and they should be given numerous ways to express their interests and talents. In doing this, teachers will provide children an opportunity to display their intellect and knowledge that may far exceed the boundaries of language.

Understand that without comprehensible input, second-language learning can be difficult.

It takes time to become linguistically proficient and competent in any language. Linguistically and culturally diverse children may be able to master basic communication skills; however, mastery of the more cognitively complex language skills needed for academic learning (Cummins 1989) is more dependent on the learning environment. Academic learning relies on significant amounts of information presented in decontextualized learning situations. Success in school becomes more and more difficult as children are required to learn, to be tested and evaluated based on ever-increasing amounts of information, consistently presented in a decontextualized manner. Children learn best when they are given a context in which to learn, and the knowledge that children acquire in "their first language can make second-language input much more comprehensible" (Krashen 1992, 37). Young children can gain knowledge more easily when they obtain quality instruction through their first language. Children can acquire the necessary language and cognitive skills required to succeed in school when given an appropriate learning environment, one that is tailored to meet their needs (NAEYC & NAECS/SDE 1991; Bredekamp & Rosegrant 1992).

Although verbal proficiency in a second language can be accomplished within two to three years, the skills necessary to achieve the higher level educational skills of understanding academic content through reading and writing may require four or more years (Cummins 1981; Collier 1989). Young children may seem to be fluent and at ease with English but may not be capable of understanding or expressing themselves as competently as their English-speaking peers. Although children seem to be speaking a second language with ease, *speaking* a language does not equate to being *proficient* in that language. Full proficiency in the first language, including complex uses of the language, contributes to the development of the second language. Children who do not become proficient in their second language after two or three years of regular use probably are not proficient in their first language either.

Young children may seem to be fluent and at ease speaking a second language, but they may not be fully capable of understanding or expressing themselves in the more complex aspects of language and may demonstrate weaknesses in language-learning skills, including vocabulary skills, auditory memory and discrimination skills, simple problem-solving tasks, and the ability to follow sequenced directions. Language difficulties such as these often can result in the linguistically and culturally diverse child being over referred to special education, classified as learning disabled, or perceived as developmentally delayed.

B. RECOMMENDATIONS FOR WORKING WITH FAMILIES

Actively involve parents and families in the early learning program and setting.

Parents and families should be actively involved in the learning and development of their children. Teachers should actively seek parental involvement and pursue establishing a partnership with children's families. When possible, teachers should visit the child's community (for example, shops, churches, and playgrounds); read and learn about the community through the use of books, pictures, observations, and conversations with community members; and visit the home and meet with other family members.

Parents and families should be invited to share, participate, and engage in activities with their children. Parent involvement can be accomplished in a number of ways, including asking parents to share stories, songs, drawings, and experiences of their linguistic and cultural background and asking parents to serve as monitors or field trip organizers. Families and parents should be invited to share activities that are developmentally appropriate and meaningful within their culture. These opportunities demonstrate to the parent what their child is learning; increase the knowledge, information, and understanding of all children regarding people of different cultures and linguistic backgrounds; and establish a meaningful relationship with the parent. The early childhood educator should ensure that parents are informed and engaged with their child in meaningful activities that promote linkages between the home and the early care setting.

Encourage and assist all parents in becoming knowledgeable about the cognitive value for children of knowing more than one language, and provide them with strategies to support, maintain, and preserve home-language learning.

In an early childhood setting and atmosphere in which home language is preserved, acknowledged, and respected, all parents can learn the value of home-language development and the strength it provides children as they add to their existing knowledge and understanding. Parents and teachers can learn how to become advocates regarding the long-term benefits that result from bilingualism.

Parents and teachers recognize the acquisition of English as an intellectual accomplishment, an opportunity for economic growth and development, and a means for achieving academic success. There are even times when parents may wish for the ability, or have been mistakenly encouraged, to speak to their children only in English, a language of which the parents themselves may not have command. The educator should understand the effects that speaking only in English can have upon the child, the family, and the child's learning. The teacher must be able to explain that speaking to the child only in English can often result in communications being significantly hindered and verbal interactions being limited and unnatural between the parent and the child. In using limited English, parents may communicate to children using simple phrases and commands (for example, "Sit down" or "Stop"); modeling grammatically incorrect phrases (for example, "We no go store"); or demonstrating other incorrect usages of language that are common when persons acquire a second language. From these limited and incorrect verbal interactions, the amount of language the child is hearing is reduced, and the child's vocabulary growth is restricted, contributing to an overall decrease in verbal expression. When parents do not master the second language yet use the second language to communicate with their child, there is an increased likelihood that the child will not hear complex ideas or abstract thoughts—important skills needed for cognitive and language development. The teacher must explain that language is developed through natural language interactions. These natural interactions occur within the day-to-day setting, through radio and television, when using public transportation, and in play with children whose dominant language is English. The parent and the teacher must work collaboratively to achieve the goal of children's learning English.

Through the home language and culture, families transmit to their children a sense of identity, an understanding of how to relate to other people, and a sense of belonging. When parents and children cannot communicate with one another, family and community destabilization can occur. Children who are proficient in their home language are able to maintain a connectedness to their histories, their stories, and the day-to-day events shared by parents, grandparents, and other family members who may speak only the home language. Without the ability to communicate, parents are not able to socialize their children, share beliefs and value systems, and directly influence, coach, and model with their children.

Recognize that parents and families must rely on caregivers and educators to honor and support their children in the cultural values and norms of the home.

Parents depend on high-quality early childhood programs to assist them with their children's development and learning. Early childhood programs should make provisions to communicate with families in their home language and to provide parent–teacher encounters that both welcome and accommodate families. Partnerships between the home and the early childhood setting must be developed to ensure that practices of the home and expectations of the program are complementary. Linguistic and cultural continuity between the home and the early childhood program supports children's social and emotional development. By working together, parents and teachers have the opportunity to influence the understanding of language and culture and to encourage multicultural learning and acceptance in a positive way.

C. RECOMMENDATIONS FOR PROFESSIONAL PREPARATION

Provide early childhood educators with professional preparation and development in the areas of culture, language, and diversity.

Efforts to understand the languages and cultural backgrounds of young children are essential in helping children to learn. Uncertainty can exist when educators are unsure of how to relate to children and families of linguistic and cultural backgrounds different from their own. Early childhood educators need to understand and appreciate their own cultural and linguistic backgrounds. Adults' cultural background affects how they interact with and/or teach young children. The educator's background influences how children are taught, reinforced, and disciplined. The child's background influences how the child constructs knowledge, responds to discipline and praise, and interacts in the early childhood setting.

Preservice and inservice training opportunities in early childhood education programs assist educators in overcoming some of the linguistic and cultural challenges they may face in working with young children. Training institutions and programs can consider providing specific courses in the following topic areas or include these issues in current courses: language acquisition; second-language learning; use of translators; working with diverse families; sociolinguistics; cross-cultural communication; issues pertaining to the politics of race, language, and culture; and community involvement.

Recruit and support early childhood educators who are trained in languages other than English.

Within the field of early childhood education, there is a need for knowledgeable, trained, competent, and sensitive multilingual/multicultural early childhood educators. Early childhood educators who speak more than one language and are culturally knowledgeable are an invaluable resource in the early childhood setting. In some instances the educator may speak multiple languages or may be able to communicate using various linguistic regionalisms or dialects spoken by the child or the family. The educator may have an understanding of sociocultural and economic issues relevant within the local linguistically and culturally diverse community and can help support the family in the use and development of the child's home language and in the acquisition of English. The early childhood teacher who is trained in linguistic and cultural diversity can be a much-needed resource for information about the community and can assist in the inservice cultural orientation and awareness training for the early childhood program. The bilingual educator also can be a strong advocate for family and community members.

Too often, however, bilingual early childhood professionals are called upon to provide numerous other services, some of which they may not be equipped to provide. For example, the bilingual professional, although a fluent speaker, may not have the vocabulary needed to effectively communicate with other adults or, in some instances, may be able to read and write only in English, not in the second language. In addition, bilingual teachers should not be expected to meet the needs of *all* linguistically and culturally diverse children and families in the program, especially those whose language they do not speak. Bilingual providers should not be asked to translate forms, particularly at a moment's notice, nor should they be required to stop their work in order to serve as interpreters. Bilingual teachers should not serve in roles, such as advising or counseling, in which they may lack professional training. These assignments may seem simple but often can be burdensome and must be viewed as added duties placed upon the bilingual teacher.

Preservice and inservice training programs are needed to support bilingual early childhood educators in furthering educators' knowledge and mastery of the language(s) other than English that they speak, and training should also credit content-based courses offered in languages other than English. Professional preparation instructors must urge all teachers to support multilingual/multicultural professionals in their role as advocates for linguistically and culturally diverse children. Early childhood professionals should be trained to work collaboratively with the bilingual early childhood teacher and should be informed of the vital role of the bilingual educator. Additionally, there is a need for continued research in the area of linguistic and cultural diversity of young children.

D. RECOMMENDATIONS FOR PROGRAMS AND PRACTICE

Recognize that children can and will acquire the use of English even when their home language is used and respected.

Children should build upon their current skills as they acquire new skills. While children maintain and build upon their home language skills and culture, children can organize and develop proficiency and knowledge in English. Bilingualism has been associated with higher levels of cognitive attainment (Hakuta & Garciá 1989) and does not interfere with either language proficiency or cognitive development. Consistent learning opportunities to read, be read to, and see print messages should be given to linguistically and culturally diverse children. Literacy developed in the home language will transfer to the second language (Krashen 1992). Bilingualism should be viewed as an asset and an educational achievement.

Support and preserve home language usage.

If the early childhood teacher *speaks* the child's home language, then the teacher can comfortably use this language around the child, thereby providing the child with opportunities to hear and use the home language within the early childhood setting. Use of the language should be clearly evident throughout the learning environment (e.g., in meeting charts, tape recordings, the library corner). Educators should develop a parent information board, using a language and reading level appropriate for the parents. Teachers should involve parents and community members in the early childhood program. Parents and community members can assist children in hearing the home language from many different adults, in addition to the teacher who speaks the home language. Parents and community members can assist other parents who may be unable to read, or they can assist the teacher in communicating with families whose home language may not have a written form.

If the early childhood educator *does not speak* the language, he or she should make efforts to provide visible signs of the home language throughout the learning environment through books and other relevant reading material in the child's language and with a parent bulletin board (get a bilingual colleague to help review for accuracy of written messages). The teacher can learn a few selected words in the child's language, thus demonstrating a willingness to take risks similar to the risks asked of children as they learn a second language. This effort by the teacher also helps to validate and affirm the child's language and culture, further demonstrating the teacher's esteem and respect for the child's linguistic and cultural background. The teacher should model appropriate use of English and provide the child with opportunities to use newly acquired vocabulary and language. The teacher also must actively involve the parent and the community in the program.

If the teacher is *faced with many different languages* in the program or classroom, the suggestions listed above are still relevant. Often teachers feel overwhelmed if more than one language is spoken in the program; however, they should remember that the goal is for children to learn, and that learning is made easier when children can build on knowledge in their home language. The teacher should consider grouping together at specific times during the day children who speak the same or similar languages so that the children can construct knowledge with others who speak their home language. The early childhood educator should ensure that these children do not become socially isolated as efforts are made to optimize their learning. Care should be taken to continually create an environment that provides for high learning expectations.

Develop and provide alternative and creative strategies for young children's learning.

Early childhood educators are encouraged to rely on their creative skills in working with children to infuse cultural and linguistic diversity in their programs. They should provide children with multiple opportunities to learn and ways for them to demonstrate their learning, participate in program activities, and work interactively with other children.

To learn more about working with linguistically and culturally diverse children, early childhood educators should collaborate with each other and with colleagues from other professions. To guide the implementation of a developmentally, linguistically, and culturally appropriate program, collaborative parent and teacher workgroups should be developed. These committees should discuss activities and strategies that would be effective for use with linguistically and culturally diverse children. Such committees promote good practices for children and shared learning between teachers and parents.

SUMMARY

Early childhood educators can best help linguistic and culturally diverse children and their families by acknowledging and responding to the importance of the child's home language and culture. Administrative support for bilingualism as a goal is necessary within the educational setting. Educational practices should focus on educating children toward the "school culture" while preserving and respecting the diversity of the home language and culture that each child brings to the early learning setting. Early childhood professionals and families must work together to achieve high quality care and education for *all* children.

REFERENCES

Bredekamp, S., & T. Rosegrant, eds. 1992. *Reaching potentials: Appropriate curriculum and assessment for young children.* Vol. 1. Washington, DC: NAEYC.

Center for the Study of Social Policy. 1992. *The challenge of change: What the 1990 census tells us about children.* Washington, DC: Author.

Chang, H.N.-L. 1993. *Affirming children's roots: Cultural and linguistic diversity in early care and education.* San Francisco: California Tomorrow.

Collier, V. 1989. How long: A synthesis of research on academic achievement in second language. *TESOL Quarterly* 23: 509–31.

Cummins, J. 1981. The role of primary language development in promoting educational success for language minority students. In *Schooling and language minority students: A theoretical framework,* eds. M. Ortiz, D. Parker, & F. Tempes. Office of Bilingual Bicultural Education, California State Department of Education. Los Angeles: Evaluation, Dissemination, and Assessment Center, California State University.

Cummins, J. 1989. *Empowering minority students.* Sacramento: California Association for Bilingual Education.

Garciá, E. 1991. *The education of linguistically and culturally diverse students: Effective instructional practices.* Santa Cruz: National Center for Research on Cultural Diversity and Second Language Learning, University of California.

Hakuta, K., & E. Garciá. 1989. Bilingualism and education. *American Psychologist* 44 (2): 374–79.

Head Start Bureau, Administration on Children, Youth, and Families, Department of Health and Human Services. 1995. *Program information report.* Washington, DC: Author.

Krashen, S. 1992. *Fundamentals of language education.* Torrance, CA: Laredo Publishing.

Meier, T.R., & C.B. Cazden. 1982. A focus on oral language and writing from a multicultural perspective. *Language Arts* 59: 504–12.

National Association for the Education of Young Children (NAEYC) and National Association of Early Childhood Specialists in State Departments of Education (NAECS/SDE). 1991. Guidelines for appropriate curriculum content and assessment in programs serving children ages 3 through 8. *Young Children* 46 (3): 21–38.

National Center for Education Statistics (NCES). 1993. *Language characteristics and schooling in the United States, a changing picture: 1979 and 1989.* NCES 93-699. Washington, DC: U.S. Department of Education, Office of Educational Research and Improvement.

Sharry, F. 1994. *The rise of nativism in the United States and how to respond to it.* Washington, DC: National Education Forum.

Soto, L.D. 1991. Understanding bilingual/bicultural children. *Young Children* 46 (2): 30–36.

Waggoner, D., ed. 1993. *Numbers and needs: Ethnic and linguistic minorities in the United States* 3 (6).

Waggoner, D. 1994. Language minority school age population now totals 9.9 million. *NABE News* 18 (1): 1, 24–26.

Wong Fillmore, L. 1991. When learning a second language means losing the first. *Early Childhood Research Quarterly* 6: 323–46.

RESOURCES

Banks, J. 1993. Multicultural education for young children: Racial and ethnic attitudes and their modification. In *Handbook of research on the education of young children,* ed. B. Spodek, 236–51. New York: Macmillan.

Collier, V. 1989. How long: A synthesis of research on academic achievement in second language. *TESOL Quarterly* 23: 509–31.

Collier, V., & C. Twyford. 1988. The effect of age on acquisition of a second language for school. *National Clearinghouse for Bilingual Education* 2 (Winter): 1–12.

Derman-Sparks, L., & the A.B.C. Task Force. 1989. *Anti-bias curriculum: Tools for empowering young children.* Washington, DC: NAEYC.

McLaughlin, B. 1992. *Myths and misconceptions about second language learning: What every teacher needs to unlearn.* Santa Cruz: National Center for Research on Cultural Diversity and Second Language Learning, University of California.

Neugebauer, B., ed. 1992. *Alike and different: Exploring our humanity with young children.* Redmond, WA: Exchange Press, 1987. Reprint, Washington, DC: NAEYC.

Ogbu, J.U. 1978. *Minority education and caste: The American system in cross cultural perspective.* New York: Academic.

Phillips, C.B. 1988. Nurturing diversity for today's children and tomorrow's leaders. *Young Children* 43 (2): 42–47.

Tharp, R.G. 1989. Psychocultural variables and constants: Effects on teaching and learning in schools. *American Psychologist* 44: 349–59.

References

Abidin, R. R. (1995). *Parenting Stress Index* (3rd ed.). Odessa, FL: Psychological Assessment Resources.

Ahmad, S. A., & Warriner, E. M. (2001). Review of the NEPSY: A developmental neuropsychological assessment. *Clinical Neuropsychologist, 15*(2), 240–249.

Alfonso, V. C., & Flanagan, D. P. (1999). Assessment of cognitive functioning in preschoolers. In E. V. Nuttall, I. Romero, & J. Kalesnik (Eds.), *Assessing and screening preschoolers: Psychological and educational dimensions* (pp. 186–217). Boston: Allyn and Bacon.

Alfonso, V. C., Oakland, T. D., LaRocca, R., Spanakos, A. (2000). The course on individual cognitive assessment. *School Psychology Review, 29*(1), 52–64.

Allesi, G. J., & Kaye, J. H. (1983). *Behavior assessment for school psychologists.* Washington, DC: National Association of School Psychologists.

American Guidance Associated. *AGS Age Calculator.* Circle Pines, MN: Author.

American Psychological Association (Board of Ethnic Minority Affairs, Task Force on the Delivery of Services to Minority Populations). (1993). Guidelines for providers of psychological services to ethnic, linguistic, and culturally diverse populations. *American Psychologist, 48*(1), 45–48.

Ames, L. B., Gillespie, C., Haines, J., & Ilg, F. (1980). *The Gesell Institute's child from one to six: Evaluating the behavior of the preschool child.* New York: Harper and Row.

Aranov, Z. (1999). *Validity and reliability of the ACFS Behavior Observation Rating Scale.* Unpublished master's thesis, Touro College, New York.

Ascher, C. (1990). Assessing bilingual students for placement and instruction. *Education Digest on Urban Education, No.65, EDO-UD-90-5, ISSN 0889 8049* [Retrieved November 14, 2001, from http://eric-web.tc.columbia.edu/digests/dig65.html].

Asher, S. R., & Parker, J. G. (1989). Significance of peer relationship problems in childhood. In B. H. Schneider, G. Attili, J. Nadel, & R. P. Weissberg (Eds.), *Social competence in developmental perspective* (PP5-23). Norwell, MA: Kluwer Academic Publishers.

Athanasiou, M. S. (2000). Play-based approaches to preschool assessment. In B. A. Bracken (Ed.), *The psychoeducational assessment of preschool children* (3rd ed.). Boston: Allyn and Bacon.

Atkinson, J. (1985). Assessment of vision in infants and young children. In S. Harel & N. J. Anastasiow (Eds.), *The at-risk infant: Psychol socio-/medical aspects* (pp. 341–352). Baltimore: Brookes.

Aylward, G. P. (1988). Infant and early childhood assessment. In M. G. Tramontana & S. R. Hooper (Eds.), *Assessment issues in child neuropsychology* (pp. 225–248). New York: Plenum.

Aylward, G. P. (1997). *Infant and early childhood neuropsychology.* New York: Plenum.

Babiker, G., & Herbert, M. (1998). Critical issues in the assessment of child sexual abuse. *Clinical Child and Family Psychology Review, 1*(4), 231–252.

Baek, S.-G. (1994). Implications of cognitive psychology for educational testing. *Educational Psychology Review, 6*(4), 373–389.

Bagnato, S. J. (1981a). Developmental diagnostic reports: Reliable and effective alternatives to guide individualized intervention. *Journal of Special Education, 15*(1), 65–76.

Bagnato, S. J. (1981b). Developmental scales and developmental curricula: Forging a linkage for early intervention. *Topics in Early Childhood Special Education, 1*(2), 1–8.

Bagnato, S. J., & Neisworth, J. T. (1994). A national study of the social and treatment "invalidity" of intelligence testing for early intervention. *School Psychology Quarterly, 9*(2), 81–102.

Bagnato, S. J., Neisworth, J. T., & Capone, A. (1986). Curriculum-based assessment for the young exceptional child: Rationale and review. *Topics of Early Childhood Special Education, 6*(2), 97–110.

Bagnato, S. J., Neisworth, J. T., & Munson, S. M. (1997). *LINKing assessment and early intervention: An authentic curriculum-based approach.* Baltimore: Brookes.

Bailey, D. B., Jr., & Simeonsson, R. J. (1985). A functional model of social competence. *Topics in Early Childhood Special Education, 4*(4), 20–31.

Bailey, D. B., Jr., & Simeonsson, R. J. (1988). *Family assessment in early intervention.* Columbus, OH: Merrill.

Bailey, D. B., Jr., & Wolery, M. (1989). *Assessing infants and preschoolers with handicaps.* Columbus, OH: Merrill.

Barnett, D. W., Bell, S. H., & Carey, K. T. (1999). *Designing preschool interventions: A practitioner's guide.* New York: Guilford Press.

Barnett, D. W., Bell, S. H., Gilkey, C. M., Lentz, F. E., Jr., Graden, J. L., Stone, C. M., & Smith, J. J. (1999). The promise of meaningful eligibility determination: Functional intervention-based multifactored preschool evaluation. *Journal of Special Education, 33*(2), 112–124.

Barnett, D. W., Carey, K. T., & Hall, J. D. (1993). Naturalistic intervention design for young children: Foundations, rationales, and strategies. *Topics in Early Childhood Special Education, 13*(4), 430–444.

Barnett, D. W., & Hall, J. D. (1990). Best practices in designing preschool interventions. In A. Thomas & J. Grimes (Eds.), *Best practices in school psychology–II* (pp. 309–321). Washington, DC: National Association of School Psychologists.

Barnett, D., Macmann, G. M., & Carey, K. T. (1992). Early intervention and the assessment of developmental skills: Challenges and directions. *Topics in Early Childhood Special Education, 12*(1), 21–43.

Barton, E. J., & Ascione, F. R. (1984). Direct observation. In T. H. Ollendick & M. Husen (Eds.), *Child behavioral assessment: Principles and procedures.* Elmsford, NY: Pergamon.

Batsche, G. M., & Knoff, H. M. (1995). Best practices in linking assessment to intervention. In A. Thomas & J. Grimes (Eds.), *Best practices in schoolpsychology–III* (pp. 569–585). Washington, DC: National Association of School Psychologists.

Bayley, N. (1993). *Bayley Scales of Infant Development: Second edition. Manual.* San Antonio, TX: Psychological Corporation.

Becher, R. M., & Wolfgang, C. H. (1977). An exploration of the relationship between symbolic representation in dramatic play and art and the cognitive and reading readiness levels of kindergarten children. *Psychology in the Schools, 14*(3), 377–381.

Beckman, P. J., & Lieber, J. (1992). Parent-child social relationships and peer social competence of preschool children with disabilities. In S. L. Odom, S. R. McConnell, & M. A. McEnvoy (Eds.), *Social competence of young children with disabilities* (pp. 65–92). Baltimore: Brookes.

Bellinger, D. C., & Needleman, H. L. (1985). Prenatal and early postnatal exposure to lead: Developmental effects, correlates, and implications. *International Journal of Mental Health, 14*(3), 78–111.

Belsky, J., & Most, R. K. (1981). From exploration to play: A cross-sectional study of infant free play behavior. *Developmental Psychology, 17*(5), 630–639.

Bergman, M. (1985). Auditory development and assessment. In S. Harel & N. J. Anastasiow (Eds.), *The at-risk infant: Psycho-socio-/medical aspects* (pp. 309–315). Baltimore: Brookes.

Bersoff, D. N., & Ericson, C. R. (1972). A precise and valid measure of behavior and behavior change in the classroom. *Journal of School Psychology, 10*(4), 361–366.

Bersoff, D. N., & Grieger, R. M., II. (1971). An interview model for the psychosituational assessment of children's behavior. *American Journal of Orthopsychiatry, 41*(3), 483–493.

Bhavnagri, N. P., & Samuels, B. G. (1996). Children's literature and activities promoting social cognition of peer relationships in preschoolers. *Early Childhood Research Quarterly, 11*, 307–331.

Bigler, E. D. (1988). The role of neuropsychological assessment in relation to other types of assessment with children. In M. G. Tramontana & S. R. Hooper (Eds.), *Assessment issues in child neuropsychology* (pp. 67–91). New York: Plenum.

Boehm, A. E. (2001). *Boehm-3: Preschool. Boehm Test of Basic Concepts* (3rd ed.). San Antonio, TX: Psychological Corporation.

Boehm, A. E. & Sandberg, B. (1982). Assessment of the preschool child. In C. R. Reynolds & T. B. Gutkin (Eds.), *The handbook of school psychology* (pp. 82–120). New York: Wiley.

Boehm, A. E., & Weinberg, R. A. (1997). *The classroom observer: Developing observation skills in early childhood settings* (3rd ed.). New York: Teachers College Press.

Bond, L. A., Creasey, G. L., & Abrams, C. L. (1990). Play assessment: Reflecting and promoting cognitive competence. In E. D. Gibbs & D. M. Teti (Eds.), *Interdiscipinary assessment of infants: A guide for early intervention professionals* (pp. 113–128). Baltimore: Brookes.

Bondurant-Utz, J., & Luciano, L. B. (1994). *A practical guide to infant and preschool assessment in special education.* Boston: Allyn and Bacon.

Bornstein, M. H., & Haynes, O. M. (1998). Vocabulary competence in early childhood: Measurement, latent construct, and predictive validity. *Child Development, 69*(3), 654–671.

Bornstein, M. H., Haynes, O. M., Pascual, L., Painter, K. M., & Galperin, C. (1999). Play in two societies: Pervasiveness of process, specificity of structure. *Child Development, 70*(2), 317–331.

Bracken, B. A. (1998). *Bracken Basic Concept–Revised.* San Antonio, TX: Psychological Corporation.

Bracken, B. A. (Ed.). (2000a). *The psychoeducational assessment of preschool children* (3rd ed.). Boston: Allyn and Bacon.

Bracken, B. A. (2000b). Maximizing construct relevant assessment: The optimal preschool testing situation. In B. A. Bracken (Ed.), *The psychoeducational assessment of preschool children* (3rd ed., pp. 33–44). Boston: Allyn and Bacon.

Bradley, R. H. (1986). Play materials and intellectual development. In A. W. Gottfried & C. C. Brown (Eds.), *Play interactions: The contribution of play materials and parental involvement to children's development. Proceedings of the eleventh Johnson & Johnson Pediatric Round Table* (pp. 227–252). Lexington, MA: Lexington Books.

Bradley-Johnson, S. (1994). *Psychoeducational assessment of students who are visually impaired or blind: Infancy through high school* (2nd ed.). Austin, TX: Pro-Ed.

Bradley-Johnson, S., & Evans, L. D. (1991). *Psychoeducational assessment of hearing-impaired students infancy through high school.* Austin, TX: Pro-Ed.

Bradley-Johnson, S., & Johnson, C. M. (2001). *Cognitive Abilities Scale–Second edition. Examiner's manual.* Austin, TX: Pro-Ed.

Bredekamp, S., & Rosegrant, T. (Eds.). (1995). *Reaching potentials: Vol. 2. Transforming early childhood curriculum and assessment.* Washington, DC: National Association for the Education of Young Children.

Bricker, D., & Gumerlock, S. (1988). Application of a three-level evaluation plan for monitoring child progress and program effects. *Journal of Special Education, 22*(1), 66–81.

Bricker, D., & Littman, D. (1982). Intervention and evaluation: The inseparable mix. *Topics in Early Childhood Special Education, 1*(4), 23–33.

Bricker, D., & Squires, J. (1999). *Ages and Stages Questionnaires (ASQ): A Parent-Completed Child Monitoring System–Second edition.* Baltimore: Brookes.

Brigance, A. H. (1978). *Brigance Diagnostic Inventory of Early Development.* North Billerica, MA: Curriculum Associates.

Bronfenbrenner, U. (1976a). The experimental ecology of education. *Teachers College Record, 78*(2), 157–204.

Bronfenbrenner, U. (1976b). *Reality and research in the ecology of human development. Master lectures on developmental psychology.* Washington, DC: American Psychological Association.

Bronfenbrenner, U. (1979). *Ecology of human development.* Cambridge, MA: Harvard University Press.

Bronfenbrenner, U. (1989a). Ecological systems theory. *Annals of Child Development, 6,* 187–249.

Bronfenbrenner, U. (1989b). *The ecology of human development.* Cambridge, MA: Harvard University Press.

Bronson, M. B. (2000). *Self-regulation in early childhood: Nature and nurture.* New York: Guilford Press.

Brooks-Gunn, J., & Lewis, M. (1981). Assessing young handicapped children: Issues and solutions. *Journal of the Division for Early Childhood, 2,* 84–95.

Brooks-Gunn, J., & Lewis, M. (1982). Development of play behavior in handicapped and normal infants. *Topics in Early Childhood Special Education, 2*(3), 14–28.

Bruininks, R. H., Woodcock, R. W., Weatherman, R. F., & Hill, B. K. (1996). *Scales of Independent Behavior-Revised [SIB-R]. Comprehensive manual.* Itasca, IL: Riverside.

Burns, M. S. (1991). Comparison of two types of dynamic testing and static testing with young children. *The International Journal of Dynamic Testing and Instruction, 2,* 29–42.

Byrnes, J. P. (2001). *Minds, brains, and learning.* New York: Guilford Press.

Byrnes, J. P., & Fox, N. A. (1998). The educational relevance of research in cognitive neuroscience. *Educational Psychology Review, 10*(3), 297–373.

Caldwell, B., & Bradley, R. A. (1978). *Home Observation for Measurement of the Environment (HOME).* Little Rock: University of Arkansas.

Campbell, T. F., Needleman, H. L., Riess, J. A., & Tobin, M. J. (2001). Bone lead levels and language processing performance. *Developmental Neuropsychology, 18*(2), 171–186.

Campos, J. J., Campos, R. G., & Barrett, K. C. (1989). Emergent themes in the study of emotional development and emotion regulation. *Developmental Psychology, 1989, 25*(3), 394–402.

Carr, R. A. (1979). Goal attainment scaling as a useful tool for evaluating progress in special education. *Exceptional Children, 46,* 88–95.

Caspi, A., Henry, B., McGee, R. O., Moffitt, T. E., & Silva. P. A. (1995). Temperamental origins of child and adolescent behavior problems: From age three to age fifteen. *Child Development, 66,* 55–68.

Cassidy, J. (1994). Emotion regulation: Influences of attachment relationships. In N. A. Fox (Ed.), *The development of emotion regulation: Biological and behavioral considerations. Monographs of the Society for Research in Child Development (Serial No. 240), 39*(2–3), 228–249.

Chamberlin, R. W. (1981). The relationship of preschool behavior and learning patterns to later school functioning. *Advances in Behavioral Pediatrics, 2,* 111–127.

Chan, S.-Y., & Mpofu, E. (2001). Children's peer status in school settings: Current and prospective assessment procedures. *School Psychology International, 22*(1), 43–52.

Cheng, L. L. (1991). *Assessment Asian language*

performance: Guidelines for evaluating limited-English proficient students. Oceanside, CA: Academic Communication Associates.

Christie, J. F., & Johnsen, E. P. (1983). The role of play in social-intellectual development. *Review of Educational Research, 53*(1), 93–115.

Christophersen, E. R., & Mortweet, S. L. (2001). *Treatments that work with children: Empirically supported strategies for managing childhood problems.* Washington, DC: American Psychological Association.

Clarke, A. D. B., & Clarke, A. M. (1984). Constancy and change in the growth of human characteristics. *Journal of Child Psychology and Psychiatry, 25*(2), 191–210.

Cohen, J. A. (1960). A coefficient of agreement for nominal scales. *Educational and Psychological Measurement, 20,* 37–46.

Cole, D., & LaVoie, J. C. (1985). Fantasy play and related cognitive development in 2- to 6-year olds. *Developmental Psychology, 21*(2), 233–240.

Cole, K. N., Mills, P. E., & Kelley, D. (1994). Agreement of assessment profiles used in cognitive referencing. *Language, Speech, and Hearing Services in the Schools, 25,* 25–31.

Committee on Professional Practice and Standards (APA Board of Professional Affairs). (1999). Guidelines for psychological evaluations in child protection matters. *American Psychologist, 54*(8), 586–593.

Conners, C. K. (1990). *Conners' Rating Scales.* North Tonawanda, NY: Multi-Health Systems.

Connor, P. D., Sampson, P. D., Bookstein, F. L., Barr, H. M., & Streissguth, A. P. (2001). Direct and indirect effects of prenatal alcohol damage on executive function. *Developmental Neuropsychology, 18*(3), 331–354.

Coolahan, K., Fantuzzo, J., Mendez, J., & McDermott, P. (2000). Preschool peer interactions and readiness to learn: Relationships between classroom peer play and learning behaviors and conduct. *Journal of Educational Psychology 92*(3), 458–465.

Coons, C. E., Gay, E. C., Fandal, A. W., Ker, C., & Frankenburg, W. K. (1981). *The Home Screening Questionnaire.* Denver: John F. Kennedy Child Development Center School of Medicine, University of Colorado Health Sciences Center.

Coulter, W. A., & Morrow, H. W. (1978). *Adaptive behavior: Concepts and measurements.* New York: Grune & Stratton.

Creasey, G. L., Jarvis, P. A., & Berk, L. E. (1998). Play and social competence. In O. N. Saracho & B. Spodek (Eds.), *Multiple perspectives on play in early childhood education* (pp. 116–143). Albany, NY: State University of New York Press.

Cronbach, L. J., & Furby, L. (1970). How should we measure "change": Or should we? *Psychological Bulletin, 74*(1), 68–80.

Culbertson, J. L., & Willis, D. J. (Eds.). (1993). *Testing young children: A reference guide for developmental, psychoeducational, and psychosocial assessments.* Austin, TX: Pro-Ed.

Danielson, E. B., Lynch, E. C., Moyano, A., Johnson, B., & Bettenburg, A. (1989). *Assessing young children.* Washington, DC: National Association of School Psychologists.

Davidson, R. J. (1994). Temperament, affective style, and frontal lobe asymmetry. In G. Dawson & K. W. Fischer (Eds.), *Human behavior and the developing brain* (pp. 518–536). New York: Guilford Press.

Davis, H., Stroud, A., & Green, L. (1988). A comparison of the maternal linguistic environment of children with various types of mental handicap. In K. Marfo (Ed.), *Parent-child interaction and developmental disabilities: Theory, research, and intervention* (pp. 181–199). New York: Praeger.

Dawson, G., Meltzoff, A. N., Osterling, J., & Rinaldi, J. (1998). Neuropsychological correlates of early symptoms of autism. *Child Development, 69*(5), 1276–1285.

De Barona, M., & Barona, A. (1991). The assessment of culturally and linguistically different preschoolers. *Early Childhood Research Quarterly, 6,* 363–376.

Demaray, M. K., Ruffalo, J. C., Busse, R. T., Olson, A. E., McManus, S. M., & Leventhal, A. (1995). Social skills assessment: A comparative evaluation of six published rating scales. *School Psychology Review, 24*(4), 648–671.

Denham, S. A. (1998). *Emotional development in children.* New York: Guilford Press.

Denham, S. A., & McKinley, M. (1993). Sociometric nominations of preschoolers: A psychometric analysis. *Early Education and Development, 4*(2), 109–122.

Dennis, M. (1988). Language and the young damaged brain. In T. Boll & B. K. Bryant (Eds.), *Clinical neuropsychology and brain function: Research, measurement, and practice* (pp. 89–123). Washington, DC: American Psychological Association.

Deno, S. L. (1986). Formative evaluation of individual student programs: A new role for school psychologists. *School Psychology Review, 15*(3), 358–374.

Deno, S. L. (1989). Curriculum-based measurement and special education services: A fundamental and direct relationship. In M. R. Shinn (Ed.), *Curriculum-based measurement: Assessing special children* (pp. 1–17). New York: Guilford Press.

Deysach, R. E. (1986). The role of neuropsychological assessment in the comprehensive evaluation of preschool-age children. *School Psychology Review, 15*(2), 233–244.

Dichtelmiller, M. L., Jablon, J. R., Dorfman, A. B., Marsden, D. B., & Meisels, S. J. (1994). *The Work Sampling System: Teacher's manual.* Ann Arbor, MI: Rebus Planning Associates.

Dickinson, D. J. (1978). Direct assessment of behavioral and emotional problems. *Psychology in the Schools, 15*(4), 472–477.

Dinnebeil, L. A., & Rule, S. (1994). Congruency between parents' and professionals' judgments about the development of young children with disabilities: A review of the literature. *Topics in Early Childhood Special Education, 14*(1), 1–25.

Division for Early Childhood of the Council for Exceptional Children. (2000). *Developmental delay as an eligibility category: A position statement of the Division for Early Childhood of the Council for Exceptional Children.* Reston, VA: Author.

Doll, B., & Lyon, M. A. (1998). Risk and resilience: Implications for the delivery of educational and mental health services in the schools. *School Psychology Review, 27*(3), 348–363.

Dragsow, E., & Yell, M. L. (2001). Functional Behavioral Assessments: Legal requirements and challenges. *School Psychology Review, 30*(2), 239–251.

Dunst, C. J. (1993). Implications of risk and opportunity factors for assessment and intervention practices. *Topics in Early Childhood Special Education, 13*(2), 143–153.

Dunst, C. J., & Rheingrover, R. M. (1981). Discontinuity and instability in early development: Implications for assessment. *Topics in Early Childhood Special Education, 1*(2), 49–60.

DuPaul, G. J., & Echert, T. L. (1994). The effects of social skills curricula: Now you see them, now you don't. *School Psychology Quarterly, 9*(2), 113–132.

Eisenberg, N., & Harris, J. D. (1984). Social competence: A developmental perspective. *School Psychology Review, 13*(3), 267–277.

Eisert, D., & Lamorey, S. (1996). Play as a window on child development: The relationship between play and other developmental domains. *Early Education and Development, 7*(3), 221–234.

Elias, C. L., & Berk, L. E. (2002). Self-regulation in young children: Is there a role for sociodramatic play? *Early Childhood Research Quarterly, 17*(2).

Ellett, C. D., & Bersoff, D. N. (1976). An integrated approach to the psychosituational assessment of behavior. *Professional Psychology, November,* 485–494.

Elliott, C. D. (1990). *Differential Ability Scales.* San Antonio, TX: Psychological Corporation.

Elliott, S. N., & Ershler, J. (1990). Best practices in preschool social skills training. In A. Thomas & J. Grimes (Eds.), *Best practices in school psychology–II* (pp. 591–606). Washington, DC: National Association of School Psychologists.

Embretson, S. E. (1987). Toward development of a psychometric approach. In C. S. Lidz (Ed.), *Dynamic assessment: An interactional approach to evaluating learning potential* (pp. 141–170). New York: Guilford Press.

Epstein, H. T. (1978). Growth spurts during brain

development: Implications for educational policy and practice. In J. S. Chall & A. F. Mirsky (Eds.), *Education and the brain. The seventy-seventh yearbook of the National Society for the Study of Education* (pp. 343–370). Chicago: National Society for the Study of Education.

ERIC Clearinghouse on Disabilities and Gifted Education. (1991). *Communicating with culturally diverse parents of exceptional children.* Reston, VA: Author.

Ernhart, C. B., Graham, F. K., Eichman, P. L., Marshall, J. M., & Thurston, D. (1963). Brain injury in the preschool child: Some developmental considerations. *Psychological Monographs: General and Applied, 77.*

Ervin, R. A., Ehrhardt, K. E., & Poling, A. (2001). Functional assessment: Old wine in new bottles. *School Psychology Review, 30*(2), 173–179.

Ervin, R. A., Radford, P. M., Bertsch, K., Piper, A. L., Ehrhardt, K. E., & Poling, A. (2001). A descriptive analysis and critique of the empirical literature on school-based functional assessment. *School Psychology Review, 30*(2), 193–210.

Evangelista, N., & Rezek, L., (1999). *Guidelines for preschool psychological assessment in New York State.* Position statement of the New York Association of School Psychologists.

Fagan, A. J., & Fantuzzo, J. W. (1999). Multirater congruence on the Social Skills Rating System: Mother, father, and teacher assessments of urban Head Start children's social competencies. *Early Childhood Research Quarterly, 14*(2), 229–242.

Fantuzzo, J. W., Coolahan, K., Mendez, J., McDermott, P., & Sutton-Smith, B. (1998). Contextually-relevant validation of peer play constructs with African American Head Start children: Penn Interactive Peer Play Scale. *Early Childhood Research Quarterly, 13*(3), 411–431.

Fantuzzo, J. W., & Hampton, V. R. (2000). Penn Interactive Peer Play Scale: A parent and teacher rating system for young children. In K. Gitlin-Weiner, A. Sandgrund, & C. Schaefer (Eds.), *Play diagnosis and assessment* (2nd ed., pp. 599–620). New York: Wiley.

Fantuzzo, J. W., Mendez, J., & Tighe, E. (1998). Parental assessment of peer play: Development and validation of the parent version of the Penn Interactive Peer Play Scale. *Early Childhood Research Quarterly, 13*(4), 659–676.

Farran, D. C., Clark, K. A., & Ray, A. R. (1990). Measures of parent-child interaction. In E. D. Gibbs & D. M. Teti (Eds.), *Interdisciplinary assessment of infants: A guide for early intervention professionals* (pp. 227–247). Baltimore: Brookes.

Fein, G. G. (1981). Pretend play in childhood: An integrative review. *Child Development, 52,* 1095–1118.

Feuerstein, R., Rand, Y., & Hoffman, M. B. (1979). *The dynamic assessment of retarded performers: The Learning Potential Assessment Device: Theory, instruments and techniques.* Baltimore: University Park Press.

Feuerstein, R., Rand, Y., Hoffman, M. B., & Miller, R. (1980). *Instrumental enrichment: An intervention program for cognitive enrichment.* Baltimore: University Park Press.

Fewell, R. R. (1984). Assessment of preschool handicapped children. *Educational Psychologist, 19*(3), 172–179.

Fewell, R. R. (2000). Assessment of visual functioning. In B. A. Bracken (Ed.), *The psychoeducational assessment of preschool children* (3rd ed., pp. 234–248). Boston: Allyn and Bacon.

Fewell, R. R., & Glick, M. P. (1993). Observing play: An appropriate process for learning and assessment. *Infants and Young Children, 5*(4), 35–43.

Fewell, R. R., & Kaminski, R. (1988). Play skills developmental and instruction for young children with handicaps. In S. L. Odom & M. B. Karnes (Eds.), *Early intervention for infants and children with handicaps: An empirical base* (pp. 145–158). Baltimore: Brookes.

Fewell, R. R., Notari-Syverson, A., & Wheeden, C. A. (1997). The relationship between play and communication skills in young children with Down Syndrome. *Topics in Early Childhood Special Education, 17*(1), 103–118.

Fewell, R. R., Ogura, T., Notari-Syverson, A. N., & Wheeden, A. (1997). The relationship between play and communication skills in young children with Down Syndrome. *Topics in Early Childhood Special Education, 17*(1), 103–118.

Fewell, R. R., & Rich, J. S. (1987). Play assessment as a procedure for examining cognitive, communication, and social skills in multihandicapped children. *Journal of Psychoeducational Assessment, 2*, 107–118.

Fischer, K. W., & Rose, S. P. (1994). Dynamic development of coordination of components in brain and behavior: A framework for theory and research. In G. Dawson & K. W. Fischer (Eds.), *Human behavior and the developing brain* (pp. 3–66). New York: Guilford Press.

Fischer, M. A. (1988). The relationship between child initiations and maternal responses in preschool-age children with Down Syndrome. In K. Marfo (Ed.), *Parent-child interaction and developmental disabilities: Theory, research, and intervention* (pp. 126–144). New York: Praeger.

Fischetti, B. A. (2000). Psychological evaluation time and components: Connecticut suburban practices. *Communiqué (National Association of School Psychologists), 29*, 12–13.

Fowler, W. (1995). Language interaction techniques for stimulating the development of at risk children in infant and preschool day care. *Early Child Development and Care, 111*, 35–48.

Frankenburg, W. K. (1985). The concept of *n* revisited. In W. K. Frankenburg, R. N. Emde, & J. W. Sullivan (Eds.), *Early identification of children at risk: An international perspective* (pp. 3–17). New York: Plenum.

Frankenburg, W. K., Dodds, J., Archer, P., Shapiro, H., & Bresnick, B. (1992). The Denver II: A major revision and restandardization of the Denver Developmental Screening Test. *Pediatrics, 89*(1), 91–97.

Frick, T., & Semmel, M. I. (1978). Observer agreement and reliabilities of classroom observational measures. *Review of Educational Research, 48*(1), 157–184.

Fuchs, L. S., & Fuchs, D. (1997). Use of curriculum-based measurement in identifying students with disabilities. *Focus on Exceptional Children, 30*(3), 1–16.

Garber, H., & Slater, M. (1983). Assessment of the culturally different preschooler. In K. D. Paget & B. A. Bracken (Eds.), *The psychoeducational assessment of preschool children* (pp. 443–471). New York: Grune & Stratton.

Garvey, C. (1977). *Play.* Cambridge, MA: Harvard University Press.

Garwood, S. G. (1982a). (Mis)use of developmental scales in program evaluation. *Topics in Early Childhood Special Education, 1*(4), 61–69.

Garwood, S. G. (1982b). Piaget and play: Translating theory into practice. *Topics in Early Childhood Special Education, 2*(3), 1–13.

Gickling, E. E., & Rosenfield, S. (1995). Best practices in curriculum-based assessment. In A. Thomas & J. Grimes (Eds.), *Best practices in school psychology–II* (pp. 587–595). Washington, DC: National Association of School Psychologists.

Gitlin-Weiner, K., Sandgrund, A., & Schaefer, C. (Eds.). (2000). *Play diagnosis and assessment* (2nd ed.). New York: Wiley.

Glascoe, F. P. (1991). Developmental screening: Rationale, methods, and application. *Infants and Young Children, 4*(1), 1–10.

Glaser, D. (2000). Child abuse and neglect and the brain: A review. *Journal of Child Psychology and Psychiatry, 43*(1), 97–116.

Glazier, B. A. (1986). *A profile of mediated learning in low SES pre-school mother-child dyads.* Unpublished masters thesis, Bryn Mawr College, Bryn Mawr, PA.

Glazier-Robinson, B. A. (1990). *Improving the ability of low SES mothers to provide Mediated Learning Experiences for their four year old children.* Unpublished doctoral dissertation, Bryn Mawr College, Bryn Mawr, PA.

Gonzalez, V., Brusca-Vega, R., & Yawkey, T. (1997). *Assessment and instruction of culturally and linguistically diverse students with or at-risk of learning problems: From research to practice.* Boston: Allyn and Bacon.

Good, T. L., & Brophy, J. E. (1991). *Looking in classrooms* (5th ed.). New York: HarperCollins.

Goodman, J. F. (1990). Infant intelligence: Do we,

can we, should we assess it? In C. Reynolds & R. Kamphaus (Eds.), *Handbook of psychological and educational measurement of children* (pp. 183–208). New York: Guilford Press.

Goodman J. F., & Field, M. (1991). Assessing attention problems in preschoolers with the Goodman Lock Box. In C. E. Schaefer, K. Gitlin, & A. Sandgrund (Eds.), *Play diagnosis and assessment* (pp. 219–247). New York: Wiley.

Goodwin, W. L., & Driscoll, L. A. (1980). *Handbook for measurement and evaluation in early childhood education.* San Francisco: Jossey-Bass.

Gradel, K., Thompson, M. S., & Sheehan, R. (1981). Parental and professional agreement in early childhood assessment. *Topics in Early Childhood Special Education, 1*(2), 31–39.

Gredler, G. P. (1997). Issues in early childhood screening and assessment. *Psychology in the Schools, 34*(2), 99–106.

Greenspan, S. I. (1992). *Infancy and early childhood: The practice of clinical assessment and intervention with emotional and developmental challenges.* Madison, CT: International Universities Press.

Greenspan, S. I., & Meisels, S. (1994). Toward a new vision for the developmental assessment of infants and young children. *Zero to Three (National Center for Clinical Infant Programs), 14*(6), pp. 1–4.

Greenwood, C. R., Schulte, D., Kohler, F. W., Dinwiddie, G. E., & Carta, J. J. (1986). Assessment and analysis of ecobehavioral interaction in school settings. In R. J. Prinz (Ed.), *Advances in behavioral assessment of children and families* (Vol. 2, pp. 69–98). Greenwich, CT: JAI Press.

Gresham, F. M. (1981). Assessment of children's social skills. *Journal of School Psychology, 19*(2), 120–133.

Gresham, F. M. (1984). Social skills assessment and training. In J. E. Ysseldyke (Ed.), *School psychology: The state of the art* (pp. 57–80). Minneapolis, MN: School Psychology Inservice Training Network (University of Minnesota).

Gresham, F. M., & Elliott, S. N. (1990). *Social Skills Questionnaire (Ages 3–5)* [parent form

and teacher form]. Circle Pines, MN: American Guidance Service.

Gresham, F. M., Watson, T. S., & Skinner, C. H. (2001). Functional Behavioral Assessment: Principles, procedures, and future directions. *School Psychology Review, 30*(2), 156–172.

Gridley, B. E., Mucha, L., & Hatfield, B. B. (1995). Best practices in preschool screening. In A. Thomas & J. Grimes (Eds.), *Best practices in school psychology–III* (pp. 213–225). Washington, DC: National Association of School Psychology.

Grief, E. B. (1977). Peer interactions in preschool children. In R. S. Webb (Ed.), *Social development in childhood: Day care programs and research* (pp. 141–161). Baltimore: John Hopkins University Press.

Grotevant, H. D., & Carlson, C. I. (1989). *Family assessment: A guide to methods and measures.* New York: Guilford Press.

Guilford Press. (1997). School readiness assessment: A problematic concept. *Child Assessment News, 6*(4), 1, 4–5, 8–9.

Guralnick, M. J. (1980). Social interactions among preschool children. *Exceptional Children, 46*(4), 248–253.

Guralnick, M. J. (1992). A hierarchical model for understanding children's peer-related social competence. In S. L. Odom, S. R. McConnell, & M. A. McEnvoy (Eds.), *Social competence of young children with disabilities* (pp. 37–64). Baltimore: Brookes.

Guralnick, M. J. (1993). Developmentally appropriate practice in the assessment and intervention of children's peer relations. *Topics in Early Childhood Special Education, 13*(3), 344–371.

Guralnick, M. J., & Groom, J. M. (1987a). Dyadic peer interactions of mildly delayed and nonhandicapped preschool children. *American Journal of Mental Deficiency, 92*(2), 178–193.

Guralnick, M. J., & Groom, J. M (1987b). The peer relations of mildly delayed and nonhandicapped preschool children in mainstreamed playgroups. *Child Development, 58,* 1556–1572.

Guthke, J. (1982). The learning test concept: An alternative to the traditional static intelligence test. *German Journal of Psychology, 6,* 306–324.

Guthke, J., & Beckmann, J. F. (2000). The learning test concept and its application in practice. In C. Lidz & J. G. Elliott (Eds.), *Dynamic assessment: Prevailing models and applications* (pp. 17–69). Amsterdam: JAI/Elsevier Science.

Guthke, J., & Wingenfeld, S. (1992). The learning test concept: Origins, state of the art and trends. In H. C. Haywood & D. Tzuriel (Eds.), *Interactive assessment* (pp. 64–93). New York: Springer-Verlag.

Gutierrez-Clellen, V. F., & Quinn, R. (1993). Assessing narratives of children from diverse cultural/linguistic groups. *Language-Speech-Hearing Services in Schools, 24,* 2–9.

Hale, J. E. (1982). *Black children: Their roots, culture and learning styles.* Baltimore: Johns Hopkins University Press.

Hamers, J. H. M., Sijtsma, K., & Ruijssenaars, A. J. J. M. (Eds.). (1993). *Learning potential assessment: Theoretical, methodological and practical issues.* Berwyn, PA: Swets & Zeitlinger.

Hargis, C. H. (1987). *Curriculum-based assessment: A primer.* Springfield, IL: Thomas.

Harms, T., Clifford, R. M., & Cryer, D. (1998). *Early Childhood Environment Scale, Revised edition.* New York: Teachers College Press.

Harrington, R. G. (1984). Preschool screening: The school psychologist's perspective. *School Psychology Review, 13*(3), 363–374.

Harrison, H., & Kielhofner, G. (1986). Examining reliability and validity of the Preschool Play Scale with handicapped children. *American Journal of Occupational Therapy, 40*(3), 167–173.

Harrison, P. L. (1985). *Vineland Adaptive Behavior Scales, Classroom Edition. Manual.* Circle Pines, MN: American Guidance Service.

Harrison, P. L. (1990). *AGS Early Screening Profiles, manual.* Circle Pines, MN: American Guidance Service.

Harrison, P. L., & Boan, C. H. (2000). Assessment of adaptive behavior. In B. A. Bracken (Ed.), *The psychoeducational assessment of preschool children* (3rd ed., pp. 124–144). Boston: Allyn and Bacon.

Harrison, P. L., & Oakland, T. (2000). *Adaptive Behavior Assessment System.* San Antonio, TX: Psychological Corporation.

Harrison, P. L., & Robinson, B. (1995). Best practices in the assessment of adaptive behavior. In A. Thomas & J. Grimes (Eds.), *Best practices in school psychology–III* (pp. 753–762). Washington, DC: National Association of School Psychologists.

Hartman, A. (1978). Diagramming assessment of family relationships. *Social Casework, 59,* 465–476.

Hartup, W. W. (1979). Peer interaction and the processes of socialization. In M. J. Guralnick (Ed.), *Early intervention and the integration of handicapped and nonhandicapped children.* Baltimore: University Park Press.

Hartup, W. W. (1989). Social relationships and their developmental significance. *American Psychologist, 44*(2), 120–126.

Hartup, W. W., & Moore, S. G. (1990). Early peer relations: Developmental significance and prognostic implications. *Early Childhood Research Quarterly, 5,* 1–17.

Hauser-Cram, P., Warfield, M. E., Shonkoff, J. P., & Krauss, M. W. (2001). Children with disabilities: A longitudinal study of child development and parent well-being. *Monographs of the Society for Research in Child Development, Serial No. 266, 66*(3).

Haywood, H. C., Brooks, P., & Burns, S. (1992). *Bright start cognitive curriculum for young children.* Watertown, MA: Charlesbridge.

Haywood, H. C., & Tzuriel, D. (1992). The status and future of interactive assessment. In H. C. Haywood & D. Tzuriel (Eds.), *Interactive assessment* (pp. 504–507). New York: Springer-Verlag.

Haywood, H. C., Tzuriel, D., & Vaught, S. (1992). Psychoeducational assessment from a transactional perspective. In H. C. Haywood & D. Tzuriel (Eds.), *Interactive assessment* (pp. 38–63). New York: Springer-Verlag.

Hertzig, M. E., & Snow, M. E. (1988). The assessment of temperament. In C. J. Kestenbaum & D. T. Williams (Eds.), *Handbook of clinical assessment of children and adolescents* (Vol. 1, pp. 133–153). New York: New York University Press.

High/Scope Educational Research Foundation. (1992). *Child Observation Record.* Ypsilanti, MI: Author.

Hilliard, A. G. (1989). Back to Binet: The case against the use of IQ tests in the schools. *Diagnostique, 14,* 125–135.

Hintze, J. M., & Shapiro, E. S. (1995). Best practices in the systematic observation of classroom behavior. In A. Thomas & J. Grimes (Eds.), *Best practices in school psychology–III.* Washington, DC: National Association of School Psychologists.

Hodapp, R. M. (1988). The role of maternal emotions and perceptions in interactions with young handicapped children. In K. Marfo (Ed.), *Parent-child interaction and developmental disabilities: Theory, research, and intervention* (pp. 32–46). New York: Praeger.

Hodapp, R. M., & Mueller, R. (1982). Early social development. In B. Wolman (Ed.), *Handbook of developmental psychology.* Englewood Cliffs, NJ: Prentice-Hall.

Hooper, S. R. (1988). The prediction of learning disabilities in the preschool child: A neuropsychological perspective. In M. G. Tramontana & S. R. Hooper (Eds.), *Assessment issues in child neuropsychology* (pp. 313–335). New York: Plenum.

Hooper, S. R., Burchinal, M. R., Roberts, J. E., Zeisel, S., & Neebe, E. C. (1998). Social and family risk factors for infant development at one year: An application of the cumulative risk model. *Journal of Applied Developmental Psychology, 19*(1),85–96.

Howes, C. (1988). Peer interaction of young children. *Monographs of the Society for Research in Child Development, Serial No. 217, 53*(1).

Howes, C., & Matheson, C. C. (1992). Sequences in the development of competent play with peers: Social and social pretend play. *Developmental Psychology, 28*(5), 961–974.

Hresko, W. P., Miguel, S. A., Sherbenou, R. J., & Burton, S. D. (1994). *Developmental Observation Checklist System: A systems approach to assessing very young children: Examiner's manual.* Austin, TX: Pro-Ed.

Hubert, N. C., & Wallander, J. L. (1988). Instrument selection. In T. D. Wachs & R. Sheehan (Eds.), *Assessment of young developmentally disabled children* (pp. 43–60). New York: Plenum.

Hughes, F. P. (1998). Play in special populations. In O. N. Saracho & B. Spodek (Eds.), *Multiple perspectives on play in early childhood education* (pp. 171–193). Albany: State University of New York Press.

Hulburt, J. G. (1995). *A comparison of the usefulness of dynamic assessment reports, standard psychological reports and curriculum-based assessment reports to pre-school teachers in designing instruction for young children with disabilities.* Unpublished doctoral dissertation, Cleveland State University, Cleveland, OH.

Human, M. T., & Teglasi, H. (1993). Parents' satisfaction and compliance with recommendations following psychoeducational assessment of children. *Journal of School Psychology, 31,* 449–467.

Huttenlocher, P. R., Levine, S. C., Huttenlocher, J., & Gates, J. (1990). Discrimination of normal and at-risk preschool children on the basis of neurological tests. *Developmental Medicine and Child Neurology, 32,* 394–402.

Hynd, G. W., & Willis, W. G. (1988). *Pediatric neuropsychology.* Orlando, FL: Grune & Stratton.

Ilg, F. L., & Ames, L. B. (1965). *School readiness: Behavior tests used at the Gesell Institute.* New York: Harper and Row.

Ironsmith, M., & Poteat, G. M. (1990). *Journal of Clinical Child Psychology, 19*(1), 17–25.

Jensen, B. F., & Potter, M. L. (1990). Best practices in communicating with parents. In A. Thomas & J. Grimes (Eds.), *Best practices in school psychology–II* (pp. 183–193). Washington, DC: National Association of School Psychologists.

Jewsuwan, R., Luster, T., & Kostelnik, M. (1993). The relation between parents' perceptions of temperament and children's adjustment to preschool. *Early Childhood Research Quarterly, 8,* 33–51.

Johnson, B. H., McGonigel, M. J., & Kaufmann, R. K. (1989). *Guidelines and recommended practices for the Individualized Family Service Plan.* Washington, DC: National Early Childhood Technical Assistance System (NEC*TAS), Office of Special Education Programs, Office of Special Education and Rehabilitative Services, U.S. Department of Education.

Johnson, D. L., & McGowan, R. J. (1984). Comparison of three intelligence tests as predictors of academic achievement and classroom behaviors of Mexican-American children. *Journal of Psychoeducational Assessment, 2,* 345–352.

Johnson-Martin, N. M., Attermeier, S. M., & Hacker, B. (1990). *The Carolina Curriculum for Preschoolers with Special Needs.* Baltimore: Brookes.

Kagan, J. (1989). Temperamental contributions to social behavior. *American Psychologist, 44*(4), 668–674.

Kagan, J., & Snidman, N. (1991). Temperamental factors in human development. *American Psychologist, 46*(8), 856–862.

Kagan, S. L., & Shepard, L. (1998). *Principles and recommendations for early childhood assessments.* Washington, DC: National Education Goals Panel, Goal 1 Early Childhood Assessments Resource Group.

Kahn, R. J. (2000). Dynamic assessment of infants and toddlers. In C. S. Lidz & J. G. Elliott (Eds.), *Dynamic assessment: Prevailing models and applications* (pp. 325–373). Amsterdam: JAI/Elsevier Science.

Kalverboer, A. F. (1976). Neurobehavioral relationships in young children: Some remarks on concepts and methods. In R. M. Knights & D. J. Bakker (Eds.), *The neuropsychology of learning disorders* (pp. 173–183). Baltimore: University Park Press.

Kamphaus, R. W. (1993). *Clinical assessment of children's intelligence.* Boston: Allyn and Bacon.

Kamphaus, R. W., Dresden, J., & Kaufman, A. S. (1993). Clinical and psychometric considerations in the cognitive assessment of preschool children. In J. L. Culbertson & D. J. Willis (Eds.), *Testing young children: A reference guide for developmental, psychoeducational, and psychosocial assessments* (pp. 55–72). Austin, TX: Pro-Ed.

Karnes, M. B., Johnson, L. J., Cohen, T., &

Beauchamp, K. D. (1986). Metacognitive strategies with preschoolers. *Teaching Exceptional Children,* (18), 54–56.

Kaufman, A. S., & Kaufman, N. (1983). *Kaufman Assessment Battery for Children (K-ABC).* Circle Pines, MN: American Guidance Service.

Keith, L. K., & Campbell, J. M. (2000). Assessment of social and emotional development in preschool children. In B. A. Bracken (Ed.), *The psychoeducational assessment of preschool children* (3rd ed., pp. 364–398). Boston: Allyn and Bacon.

Kellaghan, T., Sloane, K., Alvarez, B., & Bloom, B. S. (1993). *The home environment and school learning: Promoting parental involvement in the education of children.* San Francisco: Jossey-Bass.

Keller, H. R. (1980). Issues in the use of observational assessment. *School Psychology Review, 9*(1), 21–30.

Kelley, M. F., & Surbeck, E. (2000). History of preschool assessment. In B. A. Bracken (Ed.), *The psychoeducational assessment of preschool children* (3rd ed., pp. 1–18). Boston: Allyn and Bacon.

Kelly, S. J., Day, N., & Streissguth, A. P. (2000). Effects of prenatal alcohol exposure on social behavior in humans and other species. *Neurotoxicology and Teratology, 22*(2), 143–149.

Kemp, S. L., Kirk, U., & Korkman, M. (2001). *Essentials of NEPSY assessment.* New York: Wiley.

Kemple, K. M. (1991). Preschool children's peer acceptance and social interaction. *Young Children, 46*(5), 47–54.

Kenny, T. J., & Culbertson, J. L. (1993). Developmental screening for preschoolers. In J. L. Culbertson & D. J. Willis (Eds.), *Testing young children: A reference guide for developmental, psychoeducational, and psychosocial assessments* (pp. 73–100). Austin, TX: Pro-Ed.

Keogh, B. K., & Burstein, N. D. (1988). Relationship of temperament to preschoolers' interactions with peers and teachers. *Exceptional Children, 54*(5), 456–461.

Keogh, B. K., & Sheehan, R. (1981). The use of developmental test data for documenting handicapped children's progress: Problems and recommendations. *Journal of the Division for Early Childhood, 3,* 42–47.

Kester, E. S., Peña, E. D., & Gillam, R. B. (2001). Outcomes of dynamic assessment with culturally and linguistically diverse students: A comparison of three teaching methods within a test-teach-retest framework. *Journal of Cognitive Education and Psychology* [online], *2,* 42–59.

Klauer, K. J. (1993). Learning potential testing: The effect of retesting. In J. H. M. Hamers, K. Sijtsma, & A. J. J. M. Ruijssenaars (Eds.), *Learning potential assessment: Theoretical, methodological and practical issues* (pp. 135–152). Berwyn, PA: Swets & Zeitlinger.

Knoblock, H., & Pasamanick, B. (1980). *Gesell Developmental Schedules.* New York: Harper and Row.

Knoff, H. M., Stollar, S. A., Johnson, J. J., & Chenneville, T. A. (1999). Assessment of social-emotional functioning and adaptive behavior. In E. V. Nuttall, I. Romero, & J. Kalesnik (Eds.), *Assessing and screening preschoolers: Psychological and educational dimensions* (pp. 126–160). Boston: Allyn and Bacon.

Kontos, S., & Wilcox-Herzog, A. (1997). Teachers' interactions with children: Why are they so important? *Young Children, 52*(2), 4–12.

Kopp, C. B. (1989). Regulation of distress and negative emotions: A developmental view. *Developmental Psychology, 25*(3), 343–354.

Korkman, M. (1999). Applying Luria's diagnostic principles in the neuropsychological assessment of children. *Neuropsychology Review, 9*(2), 89–105.

Korkman, M., Kirk, U., & Kemp, S. L. (1998). *NEPSY: A developmental neuropsychological assessment.* San Antonio, TX: Psychological Corporation.

Kramer, S. J., & Williams, D. R. (1993). The hearing-impaired infant and toddler: Identification, assessment, and intervention. *Infants and Young Children, 6*(1), 35–49.

Krechevsky, M. (1998). *Project Spectrum: Preschool assessment handbook. Project Zero framework for Early Childhood Education* (Vol. 3). New York: Teachers College Press.

Kuebli, J. (1994). Young children's understanding of everyday emotions. *Young Children, 49,* 36–47.

LaFreniere, P. J., & Dumas, J. E. (1995). *Social Competence and Behavior Evaluation: Preschool edition (SCBE).* Los Angeles: Western Psychological Services.

LaFreniere, P. J., & Sroufe, L. A. (1985). Profiles of peer competence in the preschool: Interrelations between measures, influence of social ecology, and relation to attachment history. *Developmental Psychology, 21*(1), 56–69.

Laosa, L. M. (1977). Nonbiased assessment of children's abilities: Historical antecedents and current issues. In T. Oakland (Ed.), *Psychological and educational assessment of minority children* (pp. 1–20). New York: Brunner/Mazel.

Largo, R. H., & Howard, J. A. (1979). Developmental progression in play behavior of children between nine and thirty months: I. Spontaneous play and imitation. *Developmental Medicine and Child Neurology, 21,* 299–310.

LaVoy, S. K., Pedersen, W. C., Reitz, J. M., Brauch, A. A., Luxenberg, T. M., & Nofsinger, C. C. (2001). Children's drawings: A cross-cultural analysis from Japan and the United States. *School Psychology International, 22*(1), 53–63.

LeBuffe, P. A., & Naglieri, J. A. (1999). *The Devereux Early Childhood Assessment (DECA): Technical manual.* Lewisville, NC: Kaplan Press.

Lehr, C. A., Ysseldyke, J. E., & Thurlow, M. L. (1987). Assessment practices in model early childhood special education programs. *Psychology in the Schools, 24,* 390–399.

Leland, H. (1983). Assessment of adaptive behavior. In K. D. Paget & B. A. Bracken (Eds.), *The psychoeducational assessment of preschool children* (pp. 191–205). New York: Grune and Stratton.

Lemerise, E. A., & Arsenio, W. F. (2000). An integrated model of emotion processes and cognition in social information processing. *Child Development, 71,* 107–118.

Lentz, F. E., & Wehmann, B. A. (1995). Best practices in interviewing. In A. Thomas & J. Grimes (Eds.), *Best practices in school psychology–III* (pp. 637–649). Washington, DC: National Association of School Psychologists.

Lesiak, W. J., & Lesiak, J. L. (1994). *Developmental Tasks for Kindergarten Readiness-II (DTKR II).* Brandon, VT: Clinical Psychology Publishing Company.

Levy-Shiff, R., & Hoffman, M. A. (1989). Social behavior as a predictor of adjustment among three-year-olds. *Journal of Clinical Child Psychology, 18*(1), 65–71.

Lewis, M., & Michalson, L. (1983). *Children's emotions and moods: Developmental theory and measurement.* New York: Plenum.

Lichtenstein, R., & Ireton, H. (1984). *Preschool screening: Identifying young children with developmental and educational problems.* New York: Grune & Stratton.

Lidz, C. S. (1979). Criterion-referenced assessment: The new bandwagon? *Exceptional Children,* 131–132.

Lidz, C. S. (1981). *Improving assessment of schoolchildren.* San Francisco: Jossey-Bass.

Lidz, C. S. (1983). Emotional disturbance in preschool children. *Exceptional Children, 15*(3), 164–167.

Lidz, C. S. (1986). Preschool assessment: Where have we been and where are we going? *Special Services in the Schools, 2*(2/3), 141–159.

Lidz, C. S. (Ed.). (1987). *Dynamic assessment: An interactional approach to evaluating learning potential.* New York: Guilford Press.

Lidz, C. S. (1990). Overview of an optimal approach to early childhood assessment. *Preschool Interests (National Association of School Psychologists Preschool Special Interest Group), 6*(1), 1, 3–6.

Lidz, C. S. (1991a). Issues in the assessment of preschool children. In B. A. Bracken (Ed.), *The psychoeducational assessment of preschool children* (2nd ed., pp. 18–31). Boston: Allyn and Bacon.

Lidz, C. S. (1991b). *Practitioner's guide to dynamic assessment.* New York: Guilford Press.

Lidz, C. S. (1995). Dynamic assessment and the legacy of L. S. Vygotsky. *School Psychology International, 16,* 143–153.

Lidz, C. S. (1996). Dynamic assessment approaches. In D. P., Flanagan, J. L. Genshaft, & P. L. Harrison (Eds.), *Contemporary intellectual assessment: Theories, tests, and issues* (pp. 281–296). New York: Guilford Press.

Lidz, C. S. (1997). Dynamic assessment: Psychoeducational assessment with cultural sensitivity. *Journal of Social Distress and the Homeless, 26,* 95–112.

Lidz, C. S. (1999). Reconceptualizing school readiness: What do children need to know in order to become competent thinkers and metacognitive learners? *Communiqué (National Association of School Psychologists), 28,* 24–26.

Lidz, C. S. (2000). The Application of Cognitive Functions Scale (ACFS): An example of curriculum-based dynamic assessment. In C. S. Lidz & J. G. Elliott (Eds.), *Dynamic assessment: Prevailing models and applications* (pp. 407–439). Amsterdam: JAI/Elsevier Science.

Lidz, C., & Ballester, L. (1986). Diagnostic implications of McCarthy Scale General Cognitive Index-Binet IQ discrepancies for low-socioeconomic-status preschool children. *Journal of School Psychology, 24,* 381–383.

Lidz, C. S., Bond, L., & Dissinger, L. (1990). Consistency of mother-child interaction using the Mediated Learning Experience (MLE) Scale. *Special Services in the Schools, 6,* 145–165.

Lidz, C. S., Eisenstat, G., Evangelista, N., Rubinson, F., Stokes, J., Thies, L., & Trachtman, G. (2000). *Flexible assessment.* Position paper of the School Psychology Educators Council of New York State and the New York Association of School Psychologists.

Lidz, C. S., & Elliott, J. G. (Eds.). (2000a). *Dynamic assessment: Prevailing models and applications.* Amsterdam: JAI/Elsevier Science.

Lidz, C. S., & Elliott, J. G. (2000b). Introduction. In C. S. Lidz & J. G. Elliott (Eds.), *Dynamic assessment: Prevailing models and applications* (pp. 3–13). Amsterdam: JAI/Elsevier Science.

Lidz, C. S., & Jepsen, R. H. (2000). *The Application of Cognitive Functions Scale (ACFS).*

Unpublished manuscript; Author; contact zdilsc@aol.com.

Lidz, C. S., Jepsen, R. H., & Miller, M. B. (1997). Relationships between cognitive processes and academic achievement: Application of a group dynamic assessment procedure with multiply handicapped adolescents. *Education and Child Psychology, 14,* 56–67.

Lidz, C. S., & Macrine, S. (2001). Identification of minority and immigrant students for gifted education: The contribution of dynamic assessment. *School Psychology International, 22*(1), 74–96.

Lidz, C. S., & Peña, E. D. (1996). Dynamic assessment: The model, its relevance as a nonbiased approach, and its application to Latino American preschool children. *Language, Speech, and Hearing Services in Schools, 27,* 367–372.

Lidz, C. S., & Thomas, C. (1987). The preschool learning potential assessment device. In C. S. Lidz (Ed.), *Dynamic assessment: An interactional approach to evaluating learning potential* (pp. 511–532). New York: Guilford Press.

Lieberman, A. F. (1977). Preschoolers' competence with a peer: Relations with attachment and peer experience. *Child Development, 48,* 1277–1287.

Lindahl, E., Michelsson, K., & Donner, M. (1988). Prediction of early school-age problems by a preschool neurodevelopmental examination of children at risk neonatally. *Developmental Medicine and Child Neurology, 30,* 723–734.

Linder, T. W. (1993a). *Transdisciplinary play-based assessment: A functional approach to working with young children* (Rev. ed.). Baltimore: Brookes.

Linder, T. W. (1993b). *Transdisciplinary play-based intervention: Guidelines for developing a meaningful curriculum for young children.* Baltimore: Brookes.

Linder, T. W. (2000). Transdisciplinary play-based assessment. In K. Gitlin-Weiner, A. Sandgrund, & C. Schaefer (Eds.), *Play diagnosis and assessment* (2nd ed.). New York: Wiley.

Linder, T. W., Holm, C. B., & Walsh, K. A. (1999). Transdisciplinary play-based assessment. In E. V. Nuttall, I. Romero, & J. Kalesnik (Eds.), *Assessing and screening preschoolers: Psychological and educational dimensions* (pp. 161–185). Boston: Allyn and Bacon.

Lipinski, D., & Nelson, R. (1974). Problems in the use of naturalistic observation as a means of behavioral assessment. *Behavior Therapy, 5,* 341–351.

Lopez, E. C. (1995). Best practices in working with bilingual children. In A. Thomas & J. Grimes (Eds.), *Best practices in school psychology–III* (pp. 1111–1120). Washington, DC: National Association of School Psychologists.

Losardo, A., & Notari-Syverson, A. (2001). *Alternative approaches to assessing young children.* Baltimore: Brookes.

Luria, A. R. (1973). *The working brain: An introduction to neuropsychology* (B. Haigh, Trans.). New York: Basic Books.

Lynch, E. W. (1998). From culture shock to cultural learning. In E. W. Lynch & M. J. Hanson (Eds.), *Developing cross-cultural competence: A guide for working with children and their families* (2nd ed., pp. 23–45). Baltimore: Brookes.

Lynch, W. W. (1977). Guidelines to the use of classroom observation instruments by school psychologists. *School Psychology Monograph, 3*(1), 1–22.

Lyon, G. R., Moats, L., & Flynn, J. M. (1988). From assessment to treatment: Linkage to interventions with children. In M. G. Tramontana & S. R. Hooper (Eds.), *Assessment issues in child neuropsychology* (pp. 113–142). New York: Plenum.

Lytton, H., Watts, D., & Dunn, B. E. (1986). Stability and predictability of cognitive and social characteristics from age 2 to age 9. *Genetic Psychology Monographs, 112.*

Madell, J. R. (1988). Identification and treatment of very young children with hearing loss. *Infants and Young Children, 1*(2), 20–30.

Mahoney, G., & Mahoney, F. (1996). *Developmental rainbow: Early childhood development profile.* Tallmadge, OH: Family Learning Center.

Mahoney, G., Porto, P. P., Rosenshein, M., & Woolley, J. (1995). *Assistive technology for preschoolers with disabilities: Collected resources.*

Akron, OH: Preschool Technology Training Team Project, Family Child Learning Center, Children's Hospital Medical Center of Akron and the Cuyahoga Special Education Service Center (Maple Heights, OH).

Mahoney, G., Spiker, D., & Boyce, G. (1996). Clinical assessments of parent-child interaction: Are professionals ready to implement this practice? *Topics in Early Childhood Special Education, 16*(1), 26–50.

Malone, D. M., Stoneman, Z., & Langone, J. (1994). Contextual variation of correspondences among measures of play and developmental level of preschool children. *Journal of Early Intervention, 18*(2), 199–215.

Mardell-Czudnowski, C., & Goldenberg, D. S. (1998). *Developmental Indicators for the Assessment of Learning-Third edition (DIAL-3).* Circle Pines, MN: American Guidance Service.

Marfo, K., & Kysela, G. M. (1988). Frequency and sequential patterns in mothers' interactions with mentally handicapped and nonhandicapped children. In K. Marfo (Ed.), *Parent-child interaction and developmental disabilities: Theory, research, and intervention* (pp. 64–89). New York: Praeger.

Mariner, C. L., Zaslow, M. J., & Sugland, B. (1998). *Factor structure and predictive validity of the HOME-Short Form for three racial/ethnic groups in the National Longitudinal Survey of Youth-Child Supplement* (202-362-5533; Methods Working Paper No. 98.2). Washington, DC: Child Trends.

Marston, D. B. (1989). A curriculum-based measurement approach to assessing academic performance: What it is and why do it. In M. R. Shinn (Ed.), *Curriculum-based measurement: Assessing special children* (pp. 18–78). New York: Guilford Press.

Martin, J. C., Barr, H. M., Martin, D. C., & Streissguth, A. P. (1996). Neonatal neurobehavioral outcome following prenatal exposure to cocaine. *Neurotoxicology and Teratology, 18*(6), 617–625.

Martin, R. P. (1983). Temperament: A review of research with implications for the school psychologist. *School Psychology Review, 12*(3), 266–273.

Martin, R. P. (1986). Assessment of the social and emotional functioning of preschool children. *School Psychology Review, 15*(2), 216–232.

Martin, R. P. (1988a). *Assessment of personality and behavior problems: Infancy through adolescence.* New York: Guilford Press.

Martin, R. P. (1988b). *The Temperament Assessment Battery for Children.* Brandon, VT: Clinical Psychology Publishing.

Martin, R. P. (1991). Assessment of social and emotional behavior. In B. A. Bracken (Ed.), *The psychoeducational assessment of preschool children* (2nd ed., pp. 450–464). Boston: Allyn and Bacon.

Martin, R. P., Drew, K. D., Gaddis, L. R., & Moseley, M. (1988). Prediction of elementary school achievement from preschool temperament: Three studies. *School Psychology Review, 17*(1), 125–137.

McCabe, J. R., Jenkins, J. R., Mills, P. E., Dale, P. S., & Cole, K. N. (1999). Effects of group composition, materials, and developmental level on play in preschool children with disabilities. *Journal of Early Intervention, 22*(2), 164–178.

McCarthy, D. (1972). *Manual for the McCarthy Scales of Children's Abilities.* San Antonio, TX: Psychological Corporation.

McClowry, S. G. (1998). The science and art of using temperament as the basis for intervention. *School Psychology Review, 27*(4), 551–563.

McConnell, S. R. (2000). Assessment in early intervention and early childhood special education: Building on the past to project into our future. *Topics in Early Childhood Special Education, 20*(1), 43–48.

McConnell, S. R., & Odom, S. L. (1999). A multimeasure performance-based assessment of social competence in young children with disabilities. *Topics in Early Childhood Special Education, 19*(2), 67–74.

McCune, L. (1986). Symbolic development in normal and atypical infants. In G. Fein & M. Rivkin (Eds.), *The young child at play: Reviews of re-*

search (Vol. 4, pp. 45–61). Washington, DC: National Association for the Education of Young Children.

McCune-Nicolich, L., & Fenson, L. (1984). Methodological issues in studying early pretend play. In T. Yawkey & A. Pellegrini (Eds.), *Child's play: Developmental and applied* (pp. 81–104). Hillsdale, NJ: Erlbaum.

McDevitt, S. C. (1988). Assessment of temperament in developmentally disabled infants and preschoolers. In T. D. Wachs & R. Sheehan (Eds.), *Assessment of young developmentally disabled children* (pp. 255–265). New York: Plenum.

McEvoy, M., & Barnett, D. W. (1988). Nonbiased assessment of the preschool child. In R. L. Jones (Ed.), *Psychoeducational assessment of minority group children: A casebook* (pp. 317–343). Berkeley, CA: Cobb & Henry.

McGrew, K. S., Wookcock, R. W., & Mather, N. (2000). *Woodcock-Johnson, Third edition (WJ III).* Itasca, IL: Riverside.

McLoyd, V. C. (1988). Are toys (just) toys? Exploring their effects on pretend play of low-income preschoolers. In M. B. Spencer, G. K., Brookins, & W. R. Allen (Eds.), *Beginnings: The social and affective development of black children* (pp. 81–100). Hillsdale, NJ: Erlbaum.

McWilliam, R. A. (1999). Controversial practices: The need for a reacculturation of early intervention fields. *Topics in Early Childhood Special Education, 19*(3), 177–188.

Meisels, S. J. (1985). *Developmental screening in early childhood: A guide* (Rev. ed.). Washington, DC: National Association for the Education of Young Children.

Meisels, S. J. (1987). Uses and abuses of developmental screening and school readiness testing. *Young Children, 42*(2), 4–9.

Meisels, S. J. (1993). Remaking classroom assessment with the Work Sampling System. *Young Children, 48,* 34–40.

Meisels, S. J. (1995). Performance assessment in early childhood education: The Work Sampling System. *ERIC Digest,* No. 073; ED382407.

Meisels, S. J. (1997). Performance assessment in early childhood education: The Work Sampling System. ED382407.

Meisels, S. J., & Anastasiow, N. J. (1982). The risks of prediction: Relationships between etiology, handicapping conditions, and developmental outcomes. In S. G. Moore & C. R. Cooper (Eds.), *The young child: Reviews of research* (Vol. 3, pp. 259–280). Washington, DC: National Association for the Education of Young Children.

Meisels, S. J., Liaw, F., Dorfman, A., & Nelson, R. F. (1995). The Work Sampling System: Reliability and validity of a performance assessment for young children. *Early Childhood Research Quarterly, 10,* 277–296.

Meisels, S. J., Marsden, D. B., Wiske, M. S., & Henderson, L. W. (1997). *Early Screening Inventory–Revised.* Ann Arbor, MI: Rebus.

Meisels, S. J., & Provence, S. (1989). *Screening and assessment: Guidelines for identifying young disabled and developmentally vulnerable children and their families.* Washington, DC: National Center for Clinical Infant Programs.

Meller, P. J., Ohr, P. S., & Marcus, R. A. (2001). Family-oriented, culturally sensitive (FOCUS) assessment of young children. In L. A. Suzuki, J. G. Ponterotto, & P. J. Meller (Eds.), *Handbook of multicultural assessment: Clinical, psychological, and educational applications* (2nd ed., pp. 461–496). San Francisco: Jossey-Bass.

Meltzer, L. J., Levine, M. D., Hanson, M. A., Wasserman, R., Schneider, D., & Sullivan, M. (1983). Developmental attainment in preschool children: Analysis of concordance between parents and professionals. *Journal of Special Education, 17*(2), 203–213.

Merrell, K. W. (1994). *Preschool and Kindergarten Behavior Scales: Test manual.* Brandon, VT: Clinical Psychology Publishing.

Merrell, K. W. (1996). Social-emotional problems in early childhood: New directions in conceptualization, assessment, and treatment. *Education and Treatment of Children, 19*(4), 458–473.

Miller, J., Tansy, M., & Hughes, T. L. (1998). Functional Behavioral Assessment: The link between problem behavior and effective intervention in schools. *Current Issues in Education, 1*(5). Retrieved from http://cie.ed.asu.edu/volume1/number5/

Miller, L., Gillam, R. B., & Peña, E. D. (2001). *Dynamic Assessment and Intervention: Improving children's narrative abilities.* Austin, TX: Pro-Ed.

Miller, L. J. (1993). *FirstStep: Screening Test for Evaluating Preschoolers.* San Antonio, TX: Psychological Corporation.

Mindes, G. (1982). Social and cognitive aspects of play in young handicapped children. *Topics in Early Childhood Special Education, 2*(3), 39–52.

Mosley-Howard, G. S. (1995). Best practices in considering the role of culture. In A. Thomas & J. Grimes (Eds.), *Best practices in school psychology–III* (pp. 337–345). Washington, DC: National Association of School Psychologists.

Mott, S. E., Fewell, R. R., Lewis, M., Meisels, S. J., Shonkoff, J. P., & Simeonsson, R. J. (1986). Methods for assessing child and family outcomes in early childhood special education programs: Some views from the field. *Topics in Early Childhood Special Education, 6*(2), 1–15.

Mowder, B. A. (1994). Consultation with families of young, at-risk, and handicapped children. *Journal of Educational and Psychological Consultation, 5*(4), 309–320.

Mullen, E. M. (1995). *Mullen Scales of Early Learning: Manual.* Circle Pines, MN: American Guidance Service.

Munson, L. J., & Odom, S. L. (1996). Review of rating scales that measure parent-infant interaction. *Topics in Early Childhood Special Education, 16*(1), 1–25.

Murphy, A. (1990). Communicating assessment findings to parents: Toward more effective informing. In E. D. Gibbs & D. M. Teti (Eds.), *Interdisciplinary assessment of infants: A guide for early intervention professionals* (pp. 299–307). Baltimore: Brookes.

Myers, C. L., McBride, S. L., & Peterson, C. A. (1996). Transdisciplinary, play-based assessment in early childhood special education: An examination of social validity. *Topics in Early Childhood Special Education, 16*(1), 102–126.

Nagle, R. J. (2000). Issues in preschool assessment. In B. A. Bracken (Ed.), *The psychoeducational assessment of preschool children* (3rd ed., pp. 19–32). Boston: Allyn and Bacon.

National Association for the Education of Young Children. (1995). *NAEYC position statement on school readiness.* Washington, DC: Author.

National Association for the Education of Young Children. (no date). *Responding to linguistic and cultural diversity: Recommendations for effective early childhood education: An NAEYC position statement.* Washington, DC: Author.

National Association for the Education of Young Children. (no date). *Testing of young children: Concerns and cautions (pamphlet).* Washington, DC: Author.

National Association for the Education of Young Children and the National Association of Early Childhood Specialists in State Departments of Education. (1990). *Guidelines for appropriate curriculum content and assessment in programs serving children ages 3 through 8: A position statement.* Washington, DC: Author.

National Association of School Psychologists. (1999). *Position statement on early childhood assessment.* Bethesda, MD: Author.

Needleman, H. L. (1982). The neurobehavioral consequences of low lead exposure in childhood. *Neurobehavioral Toxicology and Teratology, 4*(6), 729–732.

Needleman, H. L. (1985). The neurobehavioral effects of low-level exposure to lead in childhood. *International Journal of Mental Health, 14*(3), 64–77.

Needleman, H. L., Riess, J. A., Tobin, M. J., Biesecker, G. E., & Greenhouse, J. B. (1996). Bone lead levels and delinquent behavior. *Journal of the American Medical Association, 275*(5), 363–369.

Needleman, H. L., Shell, A., Bellinger, D., Leviton, A., & Allred, E. N. (1990). The long-term effects of exposure to low doses of lead in childhood: An 11-year follow-up report. *New England Journal of Medicine, 322*(2), 83–88.

Neisworth, J. T., & Bagnato, S. J. (1986). Curriculum-based developmental testing: Congruence of testing and teaching. *School Psychology Review, 15*(7), 180–199.

Neisworth, J. T., & Bagnato, S. J. (1992). The case against intelligence testing in early intervention. *Topics in Early Childhood Special Education, 12*(1), 1–20.

Neisworth, J. T., Bagnato, S. J., Salvia, J., & Hunt, F. M. (1999). *Manual for the Temperament and Atypical Behavior Scale: Early childhood indicators of developmental dysfunction.* Baltimore: Brookes.

Nelson, C. A. (1999). Change and continuity in neurobehavioral development: Lessons from the study of neurobiology and neural plasticity. *Infant Behavior and Development, 22,* 415–429.

Newborg, J., Stock, J., Wnek, L., Guidubaldi, J., & Svinicki, J. S. (1984). *Battelle Developmental Inventory.* Allen, TX: DLM/Teaching Resources.

Nichols, P. (2000). Role of cognition and affect in a Functional Behavioral Analysis. *Exceptional Children, 66*(3), 393–402.

Nihira, K . (1999). Adaptive behavior: A historical review. In R. L. Schalock (Ed.), *Adaptive behavior and its measurement: Implications for the field of mental retardation* (pp. 7–14). Washington, DC: American Association on Mental Retardation.

Nissen, S., Blader, J., Fleiss, K., Kurtz, S. M. S., & Courtney, M. (2000). *Staff development for school based support teams. Functional Behavioral Assessments and intervention plans.* New York: New York University Child Study Center (NYU School of Medicine).

Nuttall, E. V., Romero, I., & Kalesnik, J. (Eds.). (1999). *Assessing and screening preschoolers: Psychological and educational dimensions.* Boston: Allyn and Bacon.

O'Brien, M., & Huston, A. C. (1985). Development of sex-typed play behavior in toddlers. *Developmental Psychology, 21*(5), 866–871.

Odom, S. L., & McConnell, S. R. (1985). A performance-based conceptualization of social competence of handicapped preschool children: Implications for assessment. *Topics in Early Childhood Special Education, 4*(4), 1–19.

Odom, S. L., & McConnell, S. R. (1989). Assessing social interaction skills. In D. B. Bailey Jr. & M. Wolery (Eds.), *Assessing infants and preschoolers with handicaps* (pp. 390–427). Columbus, OH: Merrill.

Odom, S. L, McConnell, S. R., McEvoy, M. A., Peterson, C., Ostrosky, M., Chandler, L. K., Spicuzza, R. J., Skellenger, A., Creighton, M., & Favazza, P. C. (1999). Relative effects of interventions supporting the social competence of young children with disabilities. *Topics in Early Childhood Special Education, 19*(2), 75–91.

Ogbu, J. U. (1988). Cultural diversity and human development. In D. T. Slaughter (Ed.), *Black children and poverty: A developmental perspective. New Directions for Child Development, No. 42.* San Francisco: Jossey-Bass.

Okagaki, L., & Diamond, K. E. (2000). Responding to cultural and linguistic differences in the beliefs and practices of families with young children. *Young Children, 55*(3), 74–80.

Olson, S. L., & Lifgren, K. (1988). Concurrent and longitudinal correlates of preschool peer sociometrics: Comparing rating scale and nomination measures. *Journal of Applied Developmental Psychology, 9,* 409–420.

Olswang, L. B., Bain. B. A., & Johnson, G. A. (1992). Using dynamic assessment with children with language disorders. In S. F. Warren & J. Reichle (Eds.), *Communication and language intervention series: Vol. 1. Causes and effects in communication and language intervention* (pp. 187–215). Baltimore: Brookes.

Ortiz, S. O. (2001). Assessment of cognitive abilities in Hispanic children. *Seminars in Speech and Language, 22*(1), 17–37.

Paasche, C. L., Gorrill, L., & Strom, B. (1990). *Children with special needs in early childhood settings: Identification, intervention, mainstreaming.* Menlo Park, CA: Addison-Wesley.

Padilla, A. M. (2001). Issues in culturally appropriate assessment. In L. A. Suzuki, J. G. Ponterotto, & P. J. Meller (Eds.), *Handbook of multicultural assessment: Clinical, psychological, and educational applications* (2nd ed., pp. 5–27). San Francisco: Jossey-Bass.

Paget, K. D. (1989). Assessment of cognitive skills in the preschool-aged child. In D. B. Bailey Jr. & M. Wolery (Eds.), *Assessing infants and preschoolers with handicaps* (pp. 275–300). Columbus, OH: Merrill.

Paget, K. D., & Nagle, R. J. (1986). A conceptual model of preschool assessment. *School Psychology Review, 15*(2), 154–165.

Parker, J. G., & Asher, S. R. (1987). Peer relations and later personal adjustment: Are low-accepted children at risk? *Psychological Bulletin,102*(3), 357–389.

Parmelee, A. H., Sigman, M., Garbanati, J., Cohen, S., Beckwith, L., & Asarnow, R. (1994). Neonatal electroencephalographic organization and attention in early adolescence. In G. Dawson & K. W. Fischer (Eds.), *Human behavior and the developing brain* (pp. 537–554). New York: Guilford Press.

Parten, M. B. (1932). Social participation among pre-school children. *Journal of Abnormal and Social Psychology, 27,* 213–269.

Peisner-Feinberg, E. S., Burchinal, M. R., Clifford, K. M., Culkin, M. L., Howes, C., Kagan, S. L., & Yazejian, N. (2001). The relation of preschool child care quality to children's cognitive and social developmental trajectories through second grade. *Child Development, 72*(5), 1534–1553.

Pelligrini, A. D. (1996). *Observing children in their natural worlds: A methodological primer.* Mahwah, NJ: Erlbaum.

Pelligrini, A. D. (1998). Play and the assessment of young children. In O. N. Saracho & B. Spodek (Eds.), *Multiple perspectives on play in early childhood education* (pp. 220–239). Albany, NY: State University of New York Press.

Peña, E. D., Iglesias, A., & Lidz, C. S. (2001). Reducing test bias through dynamic assessment of children's word learning ability. *American Journal of Speech-Language Pathology, 10,* 138–154.

Piaget, J. (1962). *Play, dreams and imitation in childhood* (C. Gattegno & F. M. Hodgson, Trans.). New York: Norton.

Pianta, R. C. (1997). Adult-child relationship processes and early schooling. *Early Education and Development, 8*(1), 11–26.

Pianta, R. C., & McCoy, S. J. (1997). The first day of school: The predictive validity of early screening. *Journal of Applied Developmental Psychology, 18,* 1–22.

Poteat, G. M., Ironsmith, M., & Bullock, J. (1986). The classification of preschool children's sociometric status. *Early Childhood Research Quarterly, 1,* 349–360.

Powell, D. R. (1989). *Families and early childhood programs.* Washington, DC: National Association for the Education of Young Children.

Powless, D. L., & Elliott, S. N. (1993). Assessment of social skills of Native American preschoolers: Teachers' and parents' ratings. *Journal of School Psychology, 31,* 293–307.

Presley, R., & Martin, R. P. (1994). Toward a structure of preschool temperament: Factor structure of the Temperament Assessment Battery for Children. *Journal of Personality, 62*(3), 415–448.

Raver, C. C., & Zigler, E. F. (1997). Social competence: An untapped dimension in evaluating Head Start's success. *Early Childhood Research Quarterly, 12,* 363–385.

Reid, G. H., & Miller, L. J., (1997). *Leiter International Performance Scale–Revised.* Wood Dale, IL: Stoelting.

Reschly, D. J. (1982). Assessment mild mental retardation: The influence of adaptive behavior, sociocultural status, and prospects for nonbiased assessment. In C. R. Reynolds & T. B. Gutkin (Eds.), *The handbook of school psychology* (pp. 209–242). New York: Wiley.

Reschly, D. J., & Gresham, F. M. (1988). Adaptive behavior and the mildly handicapped. In T. R. Kratochwill (Ed.), *Advances in school psychology* (Vol. 4, pp. 249–282). Hillsdale, NJ: Erlbaum.

Rescorla, L. (2000). Do late-talking toddlers turn out to have reading difficulties a decade later? *Annals of Dyslexia, 50,* 87–102.

Reynolds, C. R., & Kamphaus, R. W. (1998). *Behavior Assessment System for Children (BASC).* Circle Pines, MN: American Guidance Service.

Reynolds, C. R., & Mayfield, J. W. (1999). Neuropsychological assessment in genetically linked neurodevelopmental disorders. In S. Goldstein & C. R. Reynolds (Eds.), *Handbook of neurodevelopmental and genetic disorders in children* (pp. 9–37). New York: Guilford Press.

Rickel, A. U., Eshelman, A. K., & Loigman, G. A. (1983). Social problem solving training: A follow-up study of cognitive and behavioral effects. *Journal of Abnormal Child Psychology, 11*(1), 15–28.

Risser, A. H., & Edgell, D. (1988). Neuropsychology of the developing brain: Implications for neuropsychological assessment. In M. G. Tramontana & S. R. Hooper (Eds.), *Assessment issues in child neuropsychology* (pp. 41–65). New York: Plenum.

Robbins, L. C. (1963). The accuracy of parental recall of aspects of child development and of child rearing practices. *Journal of Abnormal and Social Psychology, 66*(3), 261–270.

Robinson, C. C., Rosenberg, S. A., & Beckman, P. J. (1988). Parent involvement in early childhood special education. In J. B. Jordan, J. J. Gallagher, P. L. Hutinger, & M. B. Karnes (Eds.), *Early childhood special education: Birth to three* (pp. 111–127). Reston, VA: Council for Exceptional Children.

Rogers, S. J. (1982a). Assessment of cognitive development in the preschool years. In G. Ulrey & S. J. Rogers (Eds.), *Psychosocial assessment of handicapped infants and young children* (pp. 45–58). New York: Thieme-Stratton.

Rogers, S. J. (1982b). Developmental characteristics of young children's play. In G. Ulrey & S. J. Rogers (Eds.), *Psychosocial assessment of handicapped infants and young children* (pp. 65–83). New York: Thieme-Stratton.

Rogers, S. J. (1988). Cognitive characteristics of handicapped children's play: A review. *Journal of the Division for Early Childhood, 12*(2), 161–168.

Roid, G. H. (2002, February 26). The new Stanford-Binet Intelligence Scales–Fifth edition: Author perspective. Symposium paper presented at the NASP Annual Convention, Chicago.

Roid, G. H. (in press). *Stanford-Binet Intelligence Scales–Fifth edition.* Itasca, IL: Riverside.

Roopnarine, J. L., & Carter, D. B. (1992). The cultural context of socialization: A much ignored issue! In J. L. Roopnarine & D. B. Carter (Eds.) & I. E. Sigel (Series Ed.), *Parent-child socialization in diverse cultures. Annual advances in applied developmental psychology* (Vol. 5, pp. 245–252). Norwood, NJ: Ablex.

Rosenfield, S., & Nelson, D. (1995). The school psychologist's role in school assessment. Retrieved on June 21, 2000 from http://www.uncg.edu/ericcass/assessment/diga28.html

Ross-Reynolds, G. (1990). Test practices in report writing. In A. Thomas & J. Grimes (Eds.), *Best practices in school psychology–II* (pp. 621–633). Washington, DC: National Association of School Psychologists.

Rothbart, M. K., & Jones, L. B. (1998). Temperament, self-regulation, and education. *School Psychology Review, 27*(4), 479–491.

Rourke, B. P., Bakker, D. J., Fisk, J. L., & Strang, J. D. (1983). *Child neuropsychology: An introduction to theory, research, and clinical practice.* New York: Guilford Press.

Rubin, K. H. (1986). Play, peer interaction, and social development. In A. W. Gottfried & C. C. Brown (Eds.), *Play interactions: The contribution of play materials and parental involvement to children's development. Proceedings of the eleventh Johnson & Johnson Pediatric Round Table* (pp. 163–174). Lexington, MA: Lexington Books.

Rubin, K. H., Watson, K. S., & Jambor, T. W. (1978). Free-play behaviors in preschool and kindergarten children. *Child Development, 49,* 534–536.

Ruff, H. A., & Saltarelli, L. M. (1993). Exploratory play with objects: Basic cognitive processes and individual differences. In M. H. Bornstein & A. W. O'Reilly (Eds.), *The role of play in the development of thought: New directions in child development, no. 59* (pp. 5–16). San Francisco: Jossey-Bass.

Saltz, R., & Saltz, E. (1986). Pretend play training and its outcomes. In G. Fein & M. Rivkin (Eds.), *The young child at play: Reviews of research* (Vol. 4, pp. 155–173). Washington, DC: National Association for the Education of Young Children.

Salvia, J., & Hughes, C. (1990). *Curriculum-based assessment: Testing what is taught.* New York: Macmillan.

Sameroff, A. J., & Chandler, M. J. (1975). Reproductive risk and the continuum of caretaking casualty. In F. D. Horowitz (Ed.), *Review of child development research* (Vol. 4, pp. 187–244). Chicago: University of Chicago Press.

Sameroff, A. J., & Fiese, B. H. (2000). Models of development and developmental risk. In C. H. Zeanah Jr. (Ed.), *Handbook of infant mental health* (2nd ed., pp. 3–19). New York: Guilford Press.

Sanford, A., & Zelman, J. G. (1981). *Learning Accomplishment Profile.* Winston-Salem, NC: Kaplan School Supply.

Sarason, S. B. (1976). The unfortunate fate of Alfred Binet and school psychology. *Teachers College Record, 77*(4), 579–592.

Sattler, J. M. (2002). *Assessment of children: Behavioral and clinical applications* (4th ed.). San Diego, CA: Author.

Satz, P., & Fletcher, J. M. (1988). Early identification of learning disabled children: An old problem revisited. *Journal of Consulting and Clinical Psychology, 56*(6), 824–829.

Saunders, S. A., & Green, V. (1993). Evaluating the social competence of young children: A review of the literature. *Early Child Development and Care, 87,* 39–46.

Schaefer, C. E., Gitlin, K., & Sandgrund, A. (Eds.). (1991). *Play diagnosis and assessment.* New York: Wiley.

Schalock, R. L. (1999). Adaptive behavior and its measurement: Setting the future agenda. In R. L. Schalock (Ed.), *Adaptive behavior and its measurement: Implications for the field of mental retardation* (pp. 209–222). Washington, DC: American Association on Mental Retardation.

Schiefelbusch, R. L. (1981). Development of social competence and incompetence. In M. J. Begab, H. C. Haywood, & H. L. Garber (Eds.), *Psychosocial influences in retarded performance* (Vol. 1, pp. 179–196). Baltimore: University Park Press.

Schopler, E., Reichler, R. J., & Renner, B. R. (1986). *The Childhood Autism Rating Scale (CARS).* Los Angeles: Western Psychological Services.

Schottke, H., Bartram, M., & Wiedl, K. H. (1993). Psychometric implications of learning potential assessment: A typological approach. In J. H. M. Hamers, K. Sijtsma, & A. J. J. M. Ruijssenaars (Eds.), *Learning potential assessment: Theoretical, methodological and practical issues* (pp. 153–173). Berwyn, PA: Swets & Zeitlinger.

Segalowitz, S. J. (1994). Developmental psychology and brain development: A historical perspective. In G. Dawson & K. W. Fischer (Eds.), *Human behavior and the developing brain* (pp. 67–92). New York: Guilford Press.

Seligman, L. (1998). *Selecting effective treatments: A comprehensive, systematic guide to treating mental disorders* (Rev. ed.). San Francisco: Jossey-Bass.

Seligman, M., & Darling, R. B. (1989). *Ordinary families, special children: A systems approach to childhood disability.* New York: Guilford Press.

Sexton, D., Miller, J. H., & Rotatori, A. F. (1985). Determinants of professional-parental agreement for the developmental status of young handicapped children. *Journal of Psychoeducational Assessment, 4,* 377–390.

Shah, C. P., & Bliss, B. J. (2000). Assessment of auditory functioning. In B. A. Bracken (Ed.), *The psychoeducational assessment of preschool children* (3rd ed., pp. 249–281). Boston: Allyn and Bacon.

Shantz, C. U. (1975). *The development of social cognition.* Chicago: University of Chicago Press.

Shapiro, E. S. (1987). Intervention research methodology in school psychology. *School Psychology Review, 16*(3), 290–305.

Shapiro, E. S., & Derr, T. F. (1990). Curriculum-based assessment. In T. B. Gutkin & C. R. Reynolds (Eds.), *The handbook of school psychology* (2nd ed.). New York: Wiley.

Shapiro, E. S., & Skinner, C. H. (1990). Best practices in observation and ecological assessment. In A. Thomas & J. Grimes (Eds.), *Best practices in school psychology-II.* Washington, DC: National Association of School Psychologists.

Shinn, M. R., Nolet, V., & Knutson, N. (1990). Best practices in curriculum-based measurement. In A. Thomas & J. Grimes (Eds.), *Best practices in school psychology–II* (pp. 287–307). Washington, DC: National Association of School Psychologists.

Shonkoff, J. P., & Phillips, D. A. (Eds.). (2000). *From neurons to neighborhoods: The science of early childhood development.* Washington, DC: National Academy Press.

Shriver, M. D., Anderson, C. M., & Proctor, B. (2001). Evaluating the validity of Functional Behavior Assessment. *School Psychology Review, 30*(2), 180–192.

Shure, M. B., & Spivak, G. (1979). Interpersonal cognitive problem solving and primary prevention: Programming for preschool and kindergarten children. *Journal of Clinical Child Psychology, 8*(2), 89–94.

Shuster, S. K., Fitzgerald, N., Shelton, G., Barber, P., & Desch, S. (1984). Goal Attainment Scaling with moderately and severely handicapped preschool children. *Journal of the Division for Early Childhood, 8*(1), 26–37.

Siegler, R. S. (1996). *Emerging minds: The process of change in children's thinking.* New York: Oxford University Press.

Sigel, I., Stinson, E., & Flaugher, J. (1991). Socialization of representational competence in the family: The distancing paradigm. In L. Okagaki & R. J. Sternberg (Eds.), *Directors of development: Influences on the development of children's thinking* (pp. 121–144). Hillsdale, NJ: Erlbaum.

Sigman, M., & Sena, R. (1993). Pretend play in high-risk and developmentally delayed children. In M. H. Bornstein & A. W. O'Reilly (Eds.), *The role of play in the development of thought: New directions in child development, No. 59* (pp. 29–42). San Francisco: Jossey-Bass.

Simeonsson, R. J., & Bailey, D. B., Jr. (1988). Essential elements of the assessment process. In T. D. Wachs & R. Sheehan (Eds.), *Assessment of young developmentally disabled children* (pp. 25–41). New York: Plenum.

Simeonsson, R. J., Huntington, G. S., & Short, R. (1982). Individual differences and goals: An approach to the evaluation of child progress. *Topics in Early Childhood Special Education, 1*(4), 71–80.

Simeonsson, R. J., & Rosenthal, S. L. (Eds). (2001). *Psychological and developmental assessment: Children with disabilities and chronic conditions.* New York: Guilford Press.

Simons, C. J., Ritchie, S. K., Mullett, M. D., & Liechty, E. A. (1986). Parental recall of infant medical complications and its relationship to delivery method and educational level. *Journal of Developmental and Behavioral Pediatrics, 7*(6), 355–360.

Sitko, M. C., Fink, A. H., & Gillespie, P. H. (1977). Utilizing systematic observation for decision making in school psychology. *School Psychology Monograph, 3*(1), 23–44.

Smith, P. K., Takhvar, M., Gore, N. & Vollstedt, R. (1985). Play in young children: Problems of definition, categorization and measurement. *Early Childhood Development and Care, 19,* 25–41.

Smolucha, L., & Smolucha, F. (1998). The social origins of mind: Post-Piagetian perspectives on pretend play. In O. N. Saracho & B. Spodek (Eds.), *Multiple perspectives on play in early childhood education* (pp. 34–58). Albany, NY: State University of New York Press.

Sparrow, S. S., Balla, D. A., & Cicchetti, D. V. (1984a). *Vineland Adaptive Behavior Scales, Expanded Form.* Circle Pines, MN: American Guidance Service.

Sparrow, S. S., Balla, D. A., & Cicchetti, D. V. (1984b). *Vineland Adaptive Behavior Scales, Survey Form.* Circle Pines, MN: American Guidance Service.

Spector, J. (1992). Predicting progress in beginning reading: Dynamic assessment of phonemic awareness. *Journal of Educational Psychology, 84*(3), 353–363.

Sponseller, D. (1982). Play and early education. In B. Spodek (Ed.), *Handbook of research in early childhood education* (pp. 215–241). New York: The Free Press.

Squires, J., Bricker, D., Heo, K., & Twombly, E. (2001). Identification of social-emotional problems in young children using a parent-completed screening measure. *Early Childhood Research Quarterly, 16,* 405–419.

Squires, J., Bricker, D., & Twombly, E. (2002). *Ages and States Questionnaires: Social Emotional (ASQ:SE).* Baltimore: Brookes.

Sroufe, L. A. (1989). Relationships and relationship disturbances. In A. J. Sameroff & R. N. Emde (Eds.), *Relationship disturbances in early childhood: A developmental approach* (pp. 97–124). New York: Basic Books.

Stagg, V. (1988). Clinical considerations in the assessment of young handicapped children. In T. D. Wachs & R. Sheehan (Eds.), *Assessment of young developmentally disabled children* (pp. 61–73). New York: Plenum.

Steele, C. (1981). Play variables as related to cognitive constructs in three- to six-year-olds. *Journal of Research and Development in Education, 14*(3), 58–73.

Sternberg, R. J., & Grigorenko, E. L. (2001). Ability testing across cultures. In L. A. Suzuki, J. G. Ponterotto, & P. J. Meller (Eds.), *Handbook of multicultural assessment: Clinical, psychological, and educational applications* (2nd ed., pp. 335–358). San Francisco: Jossey-Bass.

Stone, B. J. (1995). Best practices in the use of standardized assessments. In A. Thomas & J. Grimes (Eds.), *Best practices in school psychology–III.* Washington, DC: National Association of School Psychologists.

Strain, P. S. (1986). Peer-mediated instruction for young children's social skill deficits. *PRISE Reporter, 17,* pp. 1–4.

Strain, P. S., & Shores, R. E. (1977). Social reciprocity: A review of research and educational implications. *Exceptional Children, 43,* 526–530.

Streissguth, A. P., Barr, H. M., Bookstein, F. L., Sampson, P. D., & Olson, H. C. (1999). The long-term neurocognitive consequences of prenatal alcohol exposure: A 14-year study. *Psychological Science, 10*(3), 186–190.

Streissguth, A. P., Martin, D. C., Barr, H. M., Sandman, B. M., Kirchnen, G. L., & Darby, B. L. (1984). Intrauterine alcohol and nicotine exposure: Attention and reaction time in 4-year-old children. *Developmental Psychology, 20*(4), 533–541.

Sugai, G., Horner, R. H., Dunlap, G., Hieneman, M., Lewis, T. J., Nelson, C. M., Scott, T., Liaupsin, C., Sailor, W., Turnbull, A. P., Turnbull, H. R., III, Wickham, D., Ruef, M., & Wilcox, B. (1999). *Applying positive behavioral support and Functional Behavioral Assessment in schools.* Washington, DC: OSEP Center on Positive Behavioral Interventions and Support (Office of Special Education Programs).

Sulzbacher, S., Thomson, J., Farwell, J. R., Temkin, N. R., & Holubkov, A. L. (1994). Crossed dominance and its relationship to intelligence and academic achievement. *Developmental Neuropsychology, 10*(4), 473–479.

Surber, J. M. (1995). Best practices in a problem-solving approach to psychological report writing. In A. Thomas & J. Grimes (Eds.), *Best practices in school psychology–III* (pp. 161–169). Washington, DC: National Association of School Psychologists.

Sutton-Smith, B. (1980). Children's play: Some sources of play theorizing. In K. H. Rubin (Ed.), *Children's play: New directions for child development* (pp. 1–16). San Francisco: Jossey-Bass.

Swanson, M. W., Streissguth, A. P., Sampson, P. D., & Olson, H. C. (1999). Prenatal cocaine and neuromotor outcome at four months: Effect of duration of exposure. *Journal of Developmental and Behavioral Pediatrics, 20*(5), 325–334.

Switzky, H. N., Ludwig, L., & Haywood, H. C. (1979). Exploration and play in retarded and nonretarded preschool children: Effects of object complexity and age. *American Journal of Mental Deficiency, 83*(6), 637–644.

Tamis-LeMonda, C. S., & Bornstein, M. H. (1993). Play and its relations to other mental functions of the child. In M. H. Bornstein & A. W. O'Reilly (Eds.), *The role of play in the development of thought: New directions in child development, No. 59* (pp. 17–28). San Francisco: Jossey-Bass.

Tassé, M. J., & Craig, E. M. (1999). Critical issues in the cross-cultural assessment of adaptive behavior. In R. L. Schalock (Ed.), *Adaptive behavior and its measurement: Implications for the field of mental retardation* (pp. 161–183). Washington, DC: American Association on Mental Retardation.

Taylor, O. L., & Lee, D. L. (1990). Standardized tests and African-American children: Communication and language issues. In A. G. Hilliard III (Ed.), *Testing African American students: Special re-issue of the Negro Educational Review* (pp. 67–80). Morristown, NJ: Aaron Press.

Teglasi, H. (1998). Temperament constructs and measures. *School Psychology Review, 27*(4), 564–585.

Telzrow, C. F., Fox, E. J., Sanders, K. E., Barnett, D. W., & Cryan, R. J. (1989). *The early childhood identification process: A manual for screening and Assessment.* Columbus, OH: Ohio Department of Education, Division of Educational Services, Early Childhood Section (also distributed through the National Association of School Psychologists).

Tharinger, D. J., & Lambert, N. M. (1989). The application of developmental psychology to school psychology practice: Information assessment, intervention, and prevention efforts. In C. R. Reynolds & T. B. Gutkin (Eds.), *The handbook of school psychology* (3rd ed., pp. 137–166). New York: Wiley.

Thomas, A., & Chess, S. (1977). *Temperament and development.* New York: Brunner/Mazel.

Thomas, A., Chess, S., & Birch, H. G. (1968). *Temperament and behavior disorders in children.* New York: New York University Press.

Thomas, A., Chess, S., Birch, H. G., Hertzig, M. E., & Korn, S. (1963). *Behavioral individuality in early childhood.* New York: New York University Press.

Thomas, J. M., & Tidmarsh, L. (1997). Hyperactive and disruptive behaviors in very young children: Diagnosis and intervention. *Infants and Young Children, 9*(3), 46–55.

Thompson, R. A. (1993). Socioemotional development: Enduring issues and new challenges. *Developmental Review, 13,* 372–402.

Thompson, R. A., & Nelson, C. A. (2001). Developmental science and the media: Early brain development. *American Psychologist, 56,* 5–15.

Tindal, G. (1988). Curriculum-based measurement. In T. L. Graden, J. E. Zins, & M. J. Curtis (Eds.), *Alternative educational delivery systems: Enhancing instructional options for all students* (pp. 111–136). Washington, DC: National Association of School Psychologists.

Touwen, B. C. L., & Prechtl, H. F. R. (1970). *The neurological examination of the child with minor nervous dysfunction.* Philadelphia: Lippincott.

Tramontana, M. G. (1988). Problems and prospects in child neuropsychological assessment. In M. G. Tramontana & S. R. Hooper (Eds.), *Assessment issues in child neuropsychology* (pp. 369–376). New York: Plenum.

Treharne, D. A. (1992) Parental recall of children's early development. *European Journal of Disorders of Communication, 27*(3), 221–230.

Trivette, C. M., Dunst, C. J., Deal, A. G., Hamer, A. W., & Propst, S. (1990). Assessing family strengths and family functioning style. *Topics in Early Childhood Special Education, 10*(1), 16–35.

Tzuriel, D. (2001). *Dynamic assessment of young children.* New York: Kluwer Academic/Plenum.

Tzuriel, D., & Haywood, H. C. (1992). The development of interactive-dynamic approaches to assessment of learning potential. In H. C. Haywood & D. Tzuriel (Eds.), *Interactive assessment* (pp. 3–37). New York: Springer-Verlag.

Vandenberg, B. (1978). Play and development from an ethological perspective. *American Psychologist, 78,* 724–738.

Vandenberg, B. (1984). Developmental features of exploration. *Developmental Psychology, 20*(1), 3–8.

Van der Aalsvoort, G. M., & Lidz, C. S. (2002). Reciprocity in dynamic assessment in classrooms: Taking contextual influences on individual learning into account. In G. M. van der Aalsvoort, W. C. M. Resing, & A. J. J. M. Ruijssenaars (Eds.), *Learning potential assessment and cognitive training: Actual research and perspectives in theory building and methodology* (pp. 111–144). Amsterdam: Elsevier/JAI Press.

Van der Aalsvoort, G. M., Resing, W. C. M., & Ruijssenaars, A. J. J. M. (2002). (Eds.). *Learning potential assessment and cognitive training: Actual research and perspectives in theory building and methodology.* Amsterdam: Elsevier/JAI Press.

Vaughn, B. E., Colvin, T. E., Azria, M. R., Caya, L., & Krzysik, L. (2001). Dyadic analyses of friendship in a sample of preschool-age children attending Head Start: Correspondence between measures and implications for social competence. *Child Development, 72(3)*, 862–878.

Vig, S. (1997–1998). Young children's object play: A window on development. *EITI Newsletter,* (winter), 1–3.

Vollmer, T. R., & Northup, J. (1996). Some implications of functional analysis for school psychology. *School Psychology Quarterly, 11*(1), 76–92.

Vondra, J., & Belsky, J. (1991). Infant play as a window on competence and motivation. In C. Schaeffer, K. Gitlin, & A. Sandgrund (Eds.), *Play diagnosis and assessment* (pp. 13–38). New York: Wiley.

VORT. (1995). *HELP for Preschoolers (3-6)*. Palo Alto, CA: Author.

Vygotsky, L. S. (1966). Play and its role in the mental development of the child. *Soviet Psychology, 5*(3), 6–18.

Vygotsky, L. S. (1978). *Mind in society: The development of higher psychological processes.* [M. Cole V. John-Steiner, S. Scribner, & E. Souberman, Eds.]. Cambridge, MA: Harvard University Press.

Wachs, T. D., & Sheehan, R. (Eds.). (1988a). *Assessment of young developmentally disabled children.* New York: Plenum.

Wachs, T. D., & Sheehan, R. (1988b). Issues in the linkage of assessment to intervention. In T. D. Wachs & R. Sheehan (Eds.), *Assessment of young developmentally disabled children* (pp. 397–406). New York: Plenum.

Walker, H. M., Severson, H. H., & Feil, E. G. (1995). *The Early Screening Project.* Longmont, CO: Sopris West.

Walton, J. R., & Nuttall, E. V. (1999). Preschool evaluation of culturally different children. In E. V. Nuttall, I. Romero, & J. Kalesnik (Eds.), *Assessment and screening preschoolers: Psychological and educational dimensions* (pp. 281–299). Boston: Allyn and Bacon.

Wechsler, D. (2002). *Wechsler Preschool and Primary Scale of Intelligence–Third Edition.* San Antonio, TX: Psychological Corporation.

Weinberger, L. A., & Starkey, P. (1994). Pretend play by African American children in Head Start. *Early Childhood Research Quarterly, 9,* 327–343.

Weinblatt, A. S. (1993). *Maternal style and mediational practices under varying mother-child interactive conditions.* Unpublished doctoral dissertation, Yeshiva University, New York.

Wenar, C., & Coulter, J. B. (1962). A reliability study of developmental histories. *Child Development, 33,* 453–462.

Westby, C. F. (1980). Assessment of cognitive and language abilities through play. *Language, Speech, and Hearing Services in Schools, 11,* 154–168.

White, B. L. (1973, January 25). *Play activities and the development of competence during the first years of life.* Paper presented at the Georgia Symposium on Play and Exploratory Behavior, Georgia State University, Atlanta, GA.

White, B. L. (1975). Critical influences in the origins of competence. *Merrill-Palmer Quarterly, 21*(4), 243–266.

White, B. L., Kaban, B., Shapiro, B., & Attanucci, J. (1977). Competence and experience. In C. Uzgiris & F. Weizmann (Eds.), *The structuring of experience* (pp. 115–152). New York: Plenum.

Widerstrom, A. H., & Mowder, B. A. (1989). The school psychologist's role in the early childhood special education program. *Journal of Early Intervention, 13*(3), 239–248.

Wieder, S. (1996). Climbing the "symbolic ladder": Assessing young children's symbolic and representational capacities through observation of free play interaction. In S. J. Meisels & E. Fenichel (Eds.), *New visions for the developmental assessment of infants and young children* (pp. 267–288). Washington, DC: Zero to Three, National Center for Infants, Toddlers, and Families.

Wiederholt, W. C. (2000). *Neurology for non-neurologists* (4th ed.). Philadelphia: Saunders.

Wiener, J. (1985). Teachers' comprehension of psychological reports. *Psychology in the Schools, 22,* 60–64.

Wilson, C. C. (1986). Family assessment in preschool evaluation. *School Psychology Review, 15*(2), 166–179.

Wise, P. S. (1986). *Better parent conferences: A manual for school psychologists.* Washington, DC: National Association of School Psychologists.

Witt, J. C., & Martens, B. K. (1984). Adaptive behavior: Tests and assessment issues. *School Psychology Review, 13*(4), 478–484.

Wittmer, D., Doll, B., & Strain, P. (1996). Social and emotional development in early childhood: The identification of competence and disabilities. *Journal of Early Intervention, 20*(4), 299–318.

Wolery, M. (1983). Proportional change index: An alternative for comparing child change data. *Exceptional Children, 50*(2), 167–170.

Wolery, M. (1989). Assessing play skills. In D. B. Bailey Jr. & M. Wolery (Eds.), *Assessing infants and preschoolers with handicaps* (pp. 428–446). Columbus, OH: Merrill.

Yarrow, L. J. (1960). Interviewing children. In P. Mussen (Ed.), *Handbook of research methods in child development* (pp. 561–602). New York: Wiley.

Yarrow, L. J. (1979). Emotional development. *American Psychologist, 34*(10), 951–957.

Yawkey, T. D. (1982). Effect of parents' play routines on imaginative play in their developmentally delayed preschoolers. *Topics in Early Childhood Special Education, 2*(3), 66–75.

Ysseldyke, J. E., & Christenson, S. L. (1988). Linking assessment to intervention. In J. E. Graden, J. E. Zins, & M. J. Curtis (Eds.), *Alternative educational delivery systems: Enhancing instructional options for all students* (pp. 91–109). Washington, DC: National Association of School Psychologists.

Zambrana-Ortiz, N. J., & Lidz, C. S. (1995). The relationship between Puerto Rican mothers' and fathers' mediated learning experiences and the competence of their preschool children. *Journal of Cognitive Education, 4,* 17–32.

Zeitlin, S. (1985). *Coping Inventory: A measure of adaptive behavior.* Bensenville, IL: Scholastic Testing Service.

Zeitlin, S., & Williamson, G. G. (1994). *Coping in young children: Early intervention practices to enhance adaptive behavior and resilience.* Baltimore: Brookes.

Zill, N., & West, J. (2001). *Entering kindergarten: Findings from the Condition of Education 2000.* Washington, DC: U.S. Department of Education.

Zimmerman, M. A., & Arunkumar, R. (1994). Resiliency research: Implications for schools and policy. *Social Policy Report/Society for Research in Child Development, 8*(4), 1–17.

◆ Author Index

◆ Subject Index

Carol Lidz has worked in a number of roles as a school psychologist for over 35 years. She received her BA in psychology from the University of Michigan, her MA in school psychology from the University of Tennessee, and her PsyD in school psychology from Rutgers University. She has worked in a wide variety of settings, including public schools, a mental health clinic, a rehabilitation hospital, and academia. Her intensive work in early childhood began at Moss Rehabilitation Hospital and continued when she became the director of an interdisciplinary team that provided services to Head Start centers throughout Philadelphia; this was under the auspices of the United Cerebral Palsy Association of Philadelphia and Vicinity. She then served as coordinator of the early childhood specialization for school psychologists at Temple University. Dr. Lidz then became the creator and director of the School Psychology Program at Touro College for eight years. She is now in private practice with Freidman Associates in Bala Cynwyd, Pennsylvania.

Dr. Lidz is the author of a number of books, chapters, and articles. Most of these concern assessment of preschool children, parent-child interaction, and dynamic assessment. She is codeveloper (with Lisa Childers) of a parent education program titled "Let's Think about It!" (adapted for use with deaf children in collaboration with Janice Berchin-Weiss), and (with Ruthanne Jepsen) of a dynamic assessment procedure for preschool children titled the "Application of Cognitive Functions Scale." Her dynamic assessment procedures (including curriculum-based dynamic assessment, as described in this text), as well as her parent education program, are currently being used and researched in the Southwark region of London, England, under the direction of Joan Figg, and her work on responsiveness of children to mediation during dynamic assessment has been researched by Diny van der Aalsvoort at Leiden University in The Netherlands.